The Renaissance and Reformation Movements

Revised Edition

Lewis W. Spitz

Stanford University

The Renaissance and Reformation Movements

Revised Edition

Volume I

The Renaissance

CONCORDIA PUBLISHING HOUSE · SAINT LOUIS

Library of Congress Cataloging in Publication Data

Spitz, Lewis William, 1922—
    The Renaissance.

    (His The Renaissance and Reformation movements; v. 1)
    1. Renaissance. I. Title.
CB359.S653 1980 vol. 1   [CB361]   940.2s   [940.2'1]
ISBN 0-570-03818-9   80-14460

15 16 17 18 19   09 08 07 06 05

TO
David M. Potter

Preface

Contemporary man is suffering from amnesia. He is drifting along in a state of mind that Sören Kierkegaard once referred to as "a kind of world historical forgetfulness." The French savant André Malraux intones somberly: "Western civilization has begun to doubt its own credentials." This condition is part of the price paid for modern man's pathetic attempt to live entirely in the "specious present," seeking relevance only in those fleeting moments that glide so quickly into the past. The loss of history means the loss of identity. The knowledge of history gives man "divine perspective." "Who I am," says the existential philosopher Karl Jaspers, "and where I belong, I first learned to know from the mirror of history."

The Renaissance and the Reformation were clearly high points of Western history. The Renaissance was an age of supreme cultural achievement and the Reformation was a time of most profound spiritual revolution. We have fallen heir to a golden age, but as St. Bernard once observed in his *De diligendo Deo,* "To possess what one knows nothing about, what glory can there be in that?" Certain implicit assumptions of this history merit explicit expression. This study emphasizes the thought, literature, art, morals, faith, and spirit of man, the culture and religion of the age, without neglecting its socioeconomic developments or political events. Highly personal ideas are as effective springboards for action as impersonal historical forces. It is not popular to cite Thomas Carlyle these days, but occasionally his observations still apply with epigrammatic force, as when he wrote in his *Essays:* "What is all knowledge, too, but recorded experience, and a product of history; of which, therefore, reasoning and belief, no less than action and passion, are essential materials?"

The age of the Renaissance and Reformation was not a static unified period within which time and history stood still. It was above all an age of movement, a time of accelerated transition. From Dante and Petrarch to Erasmus and Rabelais, from Giotto and Fra Angelico to Michelangelo and Pontormo, from Savonarola to Loyola, from Philip the Fair to Henry IV, from the Hundred Years' War to the Thirty Years' War, Europe was in motion. This critical period of history as a movement was felt in all aspects of life. In *The Future of Man*, Teilhard de Chardin accurately assigns to history its role in human knowledge:

> It is clear in the first place that the world in its present state is the outcome of move-ment. Whether we consider the rocky layers enveloping the earth, the arrangement of the forms of life that inhabit it, the variety of civilizations to which it has given birth, or the structure of languages spoken upon it, we are forced to the same con-clusion: that everything is the sum of the past and that nothing is comprehensible except through its history.[1]

One problem with many textbooks is that no one lives longer than a few lines. It is much like dividing up the beautiful Pacific coast and assigning several yards of it to each citizen of California. A better understanding of the past can be gained by focusing most of our attention on the major protagonists, allowing the leading actors in the drama of history to speak their pieces. Nor should the men of that day, any more than those of our own, escape all moral judgment. The great Catholic historian Lord Acton criticized Bishop Creighton, author of *A History of the Papacy from the Great Schism to the Sack of Rome,* for going "through scenes of raging controversy and passion with a serene curiosity, a suspended judgment, a divided jury, and a pair of white gloves." The real tragedy would be for the author to get in the way of the story itself or to trivialize the universality of the human experience in those exciting centuries. "There is only one way to make love," quipped Dorothy Sayers, "but there are a thousand ways to commit a murder." If this book kills the subject or deadens its impact, it would have been better left unwritten.

For a single historian to give an account of three centuries (1300–1600) of European history requires greater temerity than anyone should possess. Perhaps only a fool would make such a bold attempt. And yet in his *Praise of Folly* Erasmus observed: "There are two main obstacles to the knowledge of things, modesty that casts a mist before the understanding, and fear that, having fancied a danger, dis-suades us from the attempt." A general work such as this, after all, rests upon the research of hundreds and even thousands of specialists in the field. This book might well say with Tennyson's *Ulysses,* "I am a part of all that I have met." I am indebted to the work of many more scholars of various nations than could possibly be ac-knowledged in the notes. But I owe a special debt to certain colleagues, students, and friends.

For my general approach to Renaissance and Reformation history I am in-debted to my loyal friend and genial graduate school mentor, Dr. Myron P. Gil-

---

[1] Pierre Teilhard de Chardin, *The Future of Man* (New York, 1964), p. 12.

more, who now serves as director of the Villa I Tatti in Florence. Dr. Gene Brucker, chairman of the history department of the University of California at Berkeley, a noted authority on Florentine social history, read the portion on the Renaissance and gave me the benefit of a detailed critique, for which I am most grateful. My able colleague Dr. Paul Seaver read and improved upon the chapters concerned with English history. My energetic assistant Mr. Mark Edwards chose the illustrations and selected the maps for this volume. My heartfelt thanks to them and to my editor, Mrs. Barbara H. Salazar, who has refined the manuscript and prepared the index with skill, grace, and literary talent. I wish to express my appreciation also to Mrs. Wilbert Rosin and to Mrs. Linda Edwards, who did the typescript. My wife, Dr. Edna Spitz, aided in many ways and at all times during the years this book was under way.

I owe an equally genuine if less immediately obvious debt to my students. The undergraduates, with their ingenuous, intelligent, critical candor, have ways uniquely their own of keeping a professor reasonably honest and humble. The graduate students have contributed not only historical knowledge but human insights and new methodology of the greatest value. Among these young scholars, many already holding important teaching and research positions across the land, I wish to mention especially the following: of the women, Ruth Arnon, Cissie Bonini, Patricia Covey, Virginia DeMarce, Sue Diamondstone, Lynn Hunt, Sharon Kettering, Margaret King, Arlene Miller, Anne J. Schutte, Kay Solon, Linda Taber, and Sister Marian Leona Tobriner; of the men, Darrel Ashcraft, Michael Baylor, John Biddle, Jules Bouret, Noel Brann, John Bray, James Bullard, David Bycina, Michael Carter, Theodore Casteel, Abraham Friesen, James Hinz, Larkin Kirkman, James Kittelson, William Klaustermeyer, Robert Lear, David McNeil, Steven Ozment, William Painter, Louis Reith, Charles Stinger, and Hugh West. "The young, too," said Luther, "must soon stand up and speak out after us."

I dedicate this book to my distinguished colleague David M. Potter, who has this year been honored by the entire profession, becoming at the same time the president of the Organization of American Historians and of the American Historical Association. His tremendous learning is equaled by his great strength of character and his capacity for true friendship.

Lewis W. Spitz

October 1970
Stanford University

Preface to the 1987 Edition

THIS PREFACE is an expression of gratitude to all of the professors, students, and general readers who have made a new edition possible. In writing history one can only agree with the Roman historian Sallust that *in primiis arduum videtur res gestas scribere!* In writing history that includes theology one must also agree with Luther, *wenn es zur Theologie kommt, gehört eine gewisse Bescheidenheit dazu!* Yes, the writing of history is one of the most difficult things a person can do, and when it includes theology, a great deal of modesty is called for. What else can the author of a book say than heartfelt thanks to the many good and learned people who have helped him make another edition better and more reliable than those that preceded it? A proper correction, a detailed critique, new ideas, and better interpretations offered by one's learned friends constitute a *Donum Bonum,* a good gift from the *periti.* I wish to give my special thanks to all those scholars who have corrected, suggested, and admonished, and to whose asseverations both positive and negative I have tried to respond in this current edition of my account of the Renaissance and Reformation movements. I single out for special thanks, though merely in alphabetical order, John Biddle, J. Wayne Culver, Natalie Z. Davis, Leslie S. Domonkos, Mark U. Edwards, Kenneth Gouwens, Lowell C. Green, Marilyn J. Harran, Hans J. Hillerbrand, Ruth Ann Johnson, Robert Kingdon, James Kittelson, David Lazar, Jose C. Nieto, Steven Ozment, Peter Pierson, Richard Pollard, the late George Potter, Robert Rosin, Paul Seaver, the late Hermann Schüssler, Gerald Strauss, Barbara Sher Tinsley, and Morimichi Watanabe. In our imperfect striving for historical truth, we must ever bear in mind the words of John Milton: "Who knows not that truth is strong next to the Almighty!" At least to try to write history with an honest respect for the past is worth the effort!

L. W. S.

January 1987
Stanford University

Preface to The Renaissance

LEARNING TO KNOW and to appreciate European society and culture in the age of the Renaissance constitutes an essential part of every man's liberal education, Plato's royal science. Such knowledge enriches the basic humanity of all who can attain it and should not be the special preserve of the social or intellectual elite. "Knowledge," wrote Aeneas Silvius, "which causes the learned to stand out above the unlearned makes the former like unto God ... even those of the most humble origin it lifts to the level of the greatest." In the Renaissance the student encounters some of the most daring adventurers, exquisite intellectuals, and supreme artists ever to grace our human kind. They did not, however, act, think, and create in a vacuum or draw their sustenance from the atmosphere as the Polynesian airplant.

This volume undertakes, therefore, to describe ecclesiastical, political, social, and economic developments in such a way as to place the dramatic achievements of the age within their real life context. "Hamlet," Isaiah Berlin observed, "could not have been written at the court of Ghengis Khan." The Renaissance was, in a special sense, the gift of Italy, but other lands played a part, and when she faltered the torch was taken up by other hands. I cannot send this new printing of *The Renaissance and Reformation Movements* out into the world without expressing my appreciation to the many readers, professors and students, who have accorded the work such a warm reception.

L. W. S.

June 1972
Stanford University

Contents

ILLUSTRATIONS

MAPS

The maps entitled "European Civilization During the Renaissance," "The Operations of the Medicis and Fuggers," and "The Age of Discovery" are from *Atlas of World History,* ed. R. R. Palmer (Chicago: Rand McNally & Company, 1965). The others are from Bryce Lyon, Herbert H. Rowen, and Theodore S. Hamerow, *A History of the Western World,* cartography by Willis R. Heath (Chicago: Rand McNally, 1969).

CHAPTER 1

The Age
of the
Renaissance

When the great Swiss historian Jacob Burckhardt enrolled at the University of Berlin to study history in 1839, he was astonished by the first lectures he heard from Leopold von Ranke, Gustav Droysen, and August Boeckh, for he realized that the same thing was happening to him that had happened to Don Quixote. He had loved historical science when it was only hearsay to him, and suddenly here it was appearing before him in such splendid proportions that he had to lower his eyes. The student of history who first approaches the Renaissance is apt to feel a bit overwhelmed, for even the skeptical Voltaire described it as one of the four golden ages in European culture (together with the age of Pericles in Athens, the age of Augustus in Rome, and Voltaire's own age in Bourbon France). It was a time of outsized men, a culture studded with geniuses: Leonardo da Vinci, Alberti, Michelangelo. Italy emerged as a major intellectual and artistic force and assumed its proper place among the peoples of Europe. There was movement, excitement, joy and sorrow, vibrant life and sudden death. It was as though centuries of compressed action had been released in a few decades.

Even in the interest of scholarly blandness it would be wrong to minimize the achievements of these Renaissance men or to trivialize the universality of their life experience. Although our bourgeois mentality may prefer gradualism and feel uncomfortable in the presence of outstanding creativity and singular greatness, we must recognize the special dynamism of the Renaissance and its unparalleled accomplishments in many areas of social life and higher culture. Of course, in any exploration of the historical landscape, one cannot merely leap from peak to peak, but must descend into valleys, mount foothills, and then scale new heights. But by any criteria upon which most men of cultural experience can agree, the Renaissance towers above most other regions in history's topography. Just as some men achieve more than others, so some generations overshadow others. Such an exquisite moment in the millennia of man's past was the Italian Renaissance.

The Problem of the Renaissance

THE HISTORIAN necessarily defines periods of history as a conceptual framework upon which to construct his narrative. Whether his limits and divisions merely follow verbal conventions, whether they arbitrarily tear the "seamless web" of history, or whether they reflect history as past actuality are crucial questions. The Renaissance as an extremely complex sociopolitical and cultural phenomenon has defied easy categorization and remains a difficult and hotly debated concept. The standard division of all Western history into ancient, medieval, and modern came into being during the Renaissance itself, and entered historical literature toward the end of the seventeenth century when Christoph Cellarius (Keller) of Halle, a Lutheran who had enjoyed a classical education, introduced the term *medium aevum* to cover the period between ancient and modern times. Subsequently European historians who saw great unity from the fifteenth to the eighteenth centuries and saw the French Revolution as the decisive break with the past have referred to the years after 1789 as *histoire contemporaine*. To the communists, of course, the October Revolution of 1917 constituted the decisive breakthrough of a new era. Some contemporaries believe that the full impact of industrialization, mass population, and the electronic revolution in communications is only now being felt, and choose to speak of the present time as "postmodern."

The idea that the Renaissance and the Reformation constituted twin sources of modernity goes back to the humanists and reformers. Theodore Beza, Calvin's understudy and successor as the Protestant leader in Geneva, ascribed the revival of learning to the flight of the Greek scholars to the West after the fall of Constantinople in 1453. The date remained fixed in Western tradition as a most critical one, which conveniently divided medieval and modern times. The year is late, however, for after all Francesco Petrarch, who has been called the father of Renaissance humanism, lived and died in the fourteenth century (1304–1374). Boccaccio, Salutati, Poggio, Leonardo Bruni, and a host of lesser men had come and gone before 1453, and Greek scholars had traveled to the West seeking aid and imparting knowledge before the Turks captured their capital in the East. Absolute beginnings elude us, since in any era few events are not related in some way to some preceding event. Polyphony and polarity existed during the Renaissance, for innovative forces did not follow after the traditional ones, but rose up alongside them. The age had its share of the "already here" and the "lingering on." One cannot therefore paint a still life of any one moment in time. It is necessary rather to catch the trend and to see the direction in which the midpoint of contrary pressures is moving. If this is done intelligently, the modern element in the Renaissance will emerge as that which is no longer characteristically medieval, and the Renaissance itself will be seen not as a static epoch, but as movement.

Consciousness of Change

WHAT MEN BELIEVE to be true of themselves and of their times is often as great a force in moving history forward as are the more sober facts of the case. Fiction has a force of its own, and the "fortunate error" has been an important factor in history everywhere. Intellectuals during the Renaissance believed that their age had a natural coherence that set it off from the dark ages preceding it, that it marked a rebirth, a renewal, a restoration of classical antiquity, and the dawn of a new era.

The term Renaissance was itself not a novelty. Throughout the medieval period "renaissance" (in Latin, *renovatio*) was often used in the New Testament sense of a spiritual rebirth. (Jesus said to Nicodemus: "Verily, verily, I say unto thee, Except a man be born again, he cannot see the kingdom of God" [John 3:3].) The idea of Rome as the capital of the world and center of classical culture persisted throughout the Middle Ages. Roman law, which came into renewed prominence from the twelfth century on, used the term *restitutio*, or restoration. Moreover, the Italian Renaissance did not fall like a meteor from black skies. Although many humanists considered the Middle Ages as "a thousand years without a bath," in reality a series of educational and cultural flowerings had prepared the way for their own renaissance. Historians now speak of an Iro-Celtic renaissance by the monastic carriers of classical culture who preserved Latin and even some Greek learning after the barbarian invasions. Given the chaos that marked the demise of the Roman Empire and the primitive state of Germanic culture, one could argue with some plausibility that Europe never made such noticeable progress as between the fifth and eighth centuries. The appreciation of the classics at the court of Charlemagne and the achievements of Alcuin, Lupus of Ferrières, and other cultural heroes merit the name Carolingian renaissance. The Ottonian renaissance at the court of Otto the Great (crowned 962) was less impressive, but still a reality. Under Emperor Otto III (980–1002) there was talk of a "renewal of the empire" and a "renewal of the church." The twelfth-century renaissance was of quite a different order. Cathedral schools at Chartres and elsewhere broadened the educational base and produced men of impressive classical learning, such as John of Salisbury. But the twelfth-century renaissance was still very much a clerical phenomenon, sponsored by the church and cultivated in the shadow of Gothic cathedrals. At least one medievalist speaks of a series of renaissances between the twelfth-century renaissance and the Italian Renaissance.

While it is now possible to see the steps ascending toward the heights of the Renaissance, it seemed to Renaissance men themselves that their age had emerged suddenly from a great darkness. This view seemed legitimate to the humanists because there was an actual cultural lag between Italy and the higher culture of medieval France. Moreover, on an absolute scale, the achievements of the Italian Renaissance in letters, art, music, history, rhetoric, and classical learning, including Greek literature, far outstripped all preceding renaissances. Moreover, the Italian Renaissance was not limited to court circles or to the clergy. There was substantial lay participation. While it is useful to remember that the style and quality of life of the broad masses of the population were virtually untouched by the achievements of the Renaissance, it must also be acknowledged that Italian Renaissance culture affected a larger lay clientele of aristocrats and bourgeoisie than had any of the earlier cultural revivals.

As the Italian humanists conceived of the Renaissance, it involved two basic notions, the rebirth of culture in general and the rebirth of classical culture in particular. Petrarch set the style in viewing the centuries preceding as shrouded in the darkness of night. He distinguished the ancient times (*antiqua*) from modern times (*nova*), by which he meant the dark ages in which he still lived and from which culture had to be freed. Giovanni Boccaccio (1313–1375) asserted in his *Life of Dante* that the great poet was the first since the Romans to open the door to the Muses. The Florentine Giovanni Villani, who was inspired to write his chronicle by gazing on the ruins of Rome, made no division between the Middle Ages and the Renaissance. His Florentine chronicle ran from the creation of the world to 1348 and was continued by his brother Matteo. Matteo's son, Filippo Villani (1325–1405), added a final section. Writing around 1400, Filippo was already aware of a revival of culture. He saw the renewal of the plastic arts not so much as a reversion to antiquity as a reversion to nature, from which the artists "had strayed away in childish fashion through the ignorance of the painters."

For Leonardo da Vinci the mathematical precision and naturalism of his generation of artists constituted a reaffirmation of classical standards. Modern style (*maniera moderna*) equaled the good ancient style (*buona maniera antica*), in contrast to the old style (*maniera vecchia*) now being transcended. Palladio's Villa Rotonda (1552) was more like the Roman Pantheon than like the Gothic cathedrals of Milan or Orvieto. In his *Lives of the Most Eminent Painters, Sculptors, and Architects* (1550), the sixteenth-century painter, architect, and art historian Giorgio Vasari held up the period from Giotto (*c.* 1276–1337), who revived "the noble art of painting, which had fallen on evil days," to Michelangelo (1475–1564) as a new age. He used the word *rinascita* to describe the rebirth of art.

In letters too the period from Petrarch to Erasmus was held to mark a new day. Leonardo Bruni, the Florentine chancellor, held up Dante, Petrarch, and Boccaccio as three great moderns rivaling the ancients in stature. Paolo Giovio in his *Eulogies of Famous Men of Letters* applied the word *rinascita* to the rebirth of literature. In his famous description of Italy, *Italia illustrata* (1448–1453), Flavio Biondo praised Petrarch as the pioneer of the new style in literature. Few scholars would challenge the designation of the Renaissance as a new period in art and literature, one no longer medieval.

If the Italians sneered at Gothic as the German style (*maniera tedesca*), the Germans for their part paid the Italians the flattery of imitation. Albrecht Dürer, who more than any other artist introduced Italian Renaissance style to the north, referred to the Renaissance as a *Wiedererwachung,* or reawakening. The young German knight Ulrich von Hutten exclaimed: "What a century! What genius! It is sheer joy to be alive, even though not yet in tranquillity. Learning flourishes, men are spiritually quickened. O Barbarism, take a rope and prepare for extinction!" Guillaume Budé, the leading French humanist, exulted: "The best part I think we have in our hands saved from the deluge of more than a thousand years; for a deluge indeed, calamitous to life, had so drained and absorbed literature itself and the kindred arts worthy of the name, and kept them so dismantled and buried in barbarian mud, that it was a wonder they could still exist."[1] The sixteenth-century Frenchman Pierre Belon was among the first to use the French term *renaissance,* which has been more commonly used than the Italian *rinascimento*. The prince of the humanists, Desiderius Erasmus, wrote in a letter to Wolfgang Capito in 1517: "I anticipate the near approach of a golden age." There can be no doubt that the chief protagonists of Renaissance culture were convinced that they lived in a new age, an "age of light," as Rabelais called it.

Renaissance as an Operative Concept

THE SWISS HISTORIAN Jacob Burckhardt spoke of his book on *The Civilization of the Renaissance in Italy* (1860) as a "child of sorrow," which he had to write out

---

[1] Guillaume Budé, *De studio literatum* (1527); see Charles Sears Baldwin, *Renaissance Literary Theory and Practice* (New York, 1939), p. 4.

of "inner necessity." It was written, as Nietzsche said all books should be written, with blood. He was attracted so powerfully to the period because he believed that it was, like his own, an age of transition, in which the old was going and the new was not yet formed. Any bright young social scientist with insight into the problems of change and continuity in history can assert with aplomb that every period in history is an age of transition. But the Renaissance was not like every other period, for it was an age when transition was accelerated. The stream of history flows steadily toward the sea of infinity. It is always in motion, but it does not always flow at the same speed, any more than does the life of the individual. There are points along its course where various tributaries join to push it ahead through narrow channels and down angry cataracts. Action generates action, vital minds stimulate others, events crowd in on one another, history is made more speedily, things are set in motion. The Renaissance was such an age.

In all areas of life, aesthetic, moral, social, political, and religious, there was a renewed and very intense interest in man's achievements. Nor was the age secular in the sense of being irreligious. The Platonism that constituted a very important strand of Renaissance thought really tended to divinize the world itself. The formal piety of the elite and the great reservoir of popular religious fervor that fed the Savonarola incident and overflowed into the Catholic Reformation prove that Italy was anything but secular in a radical sense. It is possible, in fact, to speak of an increase of religious concern in northern Europe during the century and a half leading up to the Reformation. There was, however, a subtle shift toward interest in and anxiety about man in the here and now, as well as in the hereafter. The contemplative ideal gave ground to the active and studious life. One can with justice speak of greater intellectual freedom, fewer inhibitions, and a more pronounced individualism during the Renaissance than during the centuries preceding it. In his autobiography Albert Schweitzer used the term *Weltanschauung,* or world view, for the fundamental springboard of ideas propelling a man into action. The change in *Weltanschauung* during this period may be described as a move away from official other-worldliness to an interest in man in this world—sometimes a very religious interest, in fact. There was a change of course in man's mental evolution from the medieval to the modern world, for life was no longer merely a period of probation for the life beyond. One must be cautious, however, in assuming that this shift was experienced by all levels of society, for the articulate witnesses are drawn from the upper classes, not from among the mute masses. Nor were the new ideas expressed by the leading humanists and philosophers understood by lesser minds among the educated as their authors had intended them. What the nature of the accelerated transition in social and political life was, and what the actual content of the Renaissance mentality proved to be, can be learned only from a study of the age itself.

The Renaissance World

THE YOUNG German humanist Ulrich von Hutten (1488–1523) once wrote that all the world's a stage and all the men and women merely players, a thought he derived from the classics, well before Shakespeare. It will perhaps be useful to look briefly at the stage setting upon which the dramatic action of the Renaissance took place.

The historical savant Arnold J. Toynbee has observed that around the year 1300 all societies in the world were structurally very much alike. They were all agrarian, and in all of them the land was held by a relatively few men. The vast majority of the people lived as peasants, at or near subsistence level. One of the most astonishing developments in world history is the disintegration of Europe's agrarian economy and life style from the thirteenth through the nineteenth centuries, and the development of urbanization, capitalism, commerce, and industrialization. The age of the Renaissance saw the decline of the manorial economy and of feudal political institutions, both replaced with surprising speed by new economic and political forces.

The ethnographic map of Europe was practically the same in 1300 as it is today, except for the subsequent intrusion of the Turks into the Balkans and far up the Danube. The linguistic borders have shifted very little, a matter of a few kilometers here and there between the German and French areas of Switzerland, for example. The economic and political developments, however, tended to cover all of Europe, and were not exclusively the work of one or another ethnic or linguistic group.

MANORIAL AND FEUDAL DISINTEGRATION

At the beginning of the thirteenth century the economy of Europe still had a predominantly agrarian base. The manor was the smallest economic unit, and each manor strove for self-sufficiency in foodstuffs and clothing. The lord or seigneur who provided protection held the best portion of the land as his domain or demesne. The peasants worked his land and he was entitled to the manor's surplus products, if any. Concepts of ownership hardly applied; it was rather a matter of the right to the use of the land. Both free and unfree tenures existed, but always on the condition of some fees, payments, or rents owed to the lord. Agricultural methods were still primitive and productivity was low. In western and central Europe a somewhat heavier plow with an iron share was now in general use, made feasible by the earlier invention of the horse collar. But in eastern Europe, though the German colonists introduced the new plow east of the Elbe, the light hook plow was still in general use, with poor results.

Most manors in western and central Europe had by this time changed from a two-field system, which meant leaving half the land lie fallow each year, to a three-field system, which naturally increased production. Families of peasants by custom had the right to cultivate their strips in the two or three big fields adjoining the village, and each had a section of the vineyards or orchards. From the eleventh to the thirteenth centuries the agrarian economy expanded slowly but steadily, by internal colonization, the cutting back of forests, the clearing of swamps, and the cultivation of marginal land. The emigration east of the Elbe River relieved population pressure somewhat, but in the fourteenth and fifteenth centuries the agricultural economy and the rural population experienced a time of troubles.

With the stability achieved during the eleventh century, a century sometimes called the foundation of the Middle Ages, a general revival took place. The period from 1050 to 1250 was one of dramatic growth and creativity, notable for its political stability and demographic expansion. Greater localization and specialization of production developed together with increased exchange by trade and larger town markets. As a money economy evolved, the upper classes were under great pressure to keep up the appearances of their position by the conspicuous consumption of luxuries. The response of the nobles to their need for money took various forms. The lord could move to town and rent the land to tenants on a lease calling for payment in cash. Or he could convert the land to the production of a single crop, which would then be sold for a cash income. In England this development came early and continued beyond our period, with the conversion of land to enclosed pasture for the production of wool. The same trend was occurring in Castile. The lord could choose to stay on the land, but commute the dues of the peasants from payment in kind and in services to payment in cash. Some lords insisted upon the right of arbitrarily taxing their peasants. The enclosure system created a floating landless population by eviction, and a great many other peasants discovered that by emigrating to the colonial areas east of the Elbe or to newly cleared or drained lands they could improve their lot. Others found that by moving to town they could sometimes earn more as simple artisans plying a trade than they could accumulate by hard work on the land. Many towns served as safety valves for excess or expendable rural population, although some towns refused to allow the country folk to establish themselves within their walls.

As the political counterpart of the manorial socioeconomic system, feudalism evolved in tandem with it. Originally a system of military defense, it became less important for that function. During the fourteenth and fifteenth centuries, when the peasants suffered economically, the lesser nobility suffered with them. With the loss of real social utility the knights fell into increasingly desperate straits, and sometimes turned to highway robbery. They preyed upon the merchants moving from town to town, and some free cities kept their own militia to patrol the roads.

Noblemen who adapted to the new money economy cultivated a chivalric code that frequently was more a matter of posturing than of any social reality.

Despite the fact that the countryside of Europe suffered from many difficulties, particularly between 1350 and 1450 and especially where wheat was the main product, the manorial system survived as the foundation stone of its economy, though it underwent many changes. East of the Elbe it became entrenched, whereas west of the Elbe it lost strength and importance, for there towns and cities and a capitalistic economy made greater inroads. But the manorial system lingered on.

GROWTH OF TOWNS AND TRADE

In the agrarian society of the high Middle Ages the social classes corresponded basically to Plato's *oratores* (clergy), *bellatores* (nobility), and *laboratores* (serfs). With the growth of the towns a fourth class came into being, townsmen or burghers. Trade had never totally died out, not even during the Dark Ages, as numismatic evidences prove. But as the situation stabilized, trade increased and towns grew, especially in the twelfth century and after. Constantinople remained the only really large city in Europe, and the towns in the early fourteenth century had for the most part from two to three thousand residents. The Flemish cities of Ghent, Bruges, and Ypres had around 50,000 inhabitants, London about 25,000, Venice and Florence between 75,000 and 100,000. Town growth was more rapid in Italy, in the Netherlands, and along rivers such as the Rhine, Rhône, Thames, Seine, and Danube, which carried trade and supplied the hinterland. Roads were very poor, canals were nonexistent, and while the rivers were not controlled by regulated channels, they remained the most efficient means of transporting goods. The medieval towns grew for various reasons, including protection, but there can be no doubt that their importance as centers for trade was the main reason for their growth. The growth of towns and a money economy disturbed the traditional agrarian economy and gradually undermined feudal society.

The medieval city was both a juridical and an administrative entity, for by the twelfth century the city council wielded vast powers, which included tight control over commercial practices, so that it virtually regulated the city's whole economic life. As the protector of seller and buyer alike, it set what it considered just prices on commodities. The very heart of the medieval commune was the pledge of mutual assistance that was the idealistic basis of the laws and governmental administration. The merchants and craftsmen, who were gaining industrial skill in their specialized crafts, wielded power roughly commensurate with their wealth through a patriarchal guild system. But in the late fourteenth and in the fifteenth centuries, as individual capitalists amassed huge fortunes, as foreign trade over great distances increased, as monopolies and cartels grew powerful, the guild system broke down. Some of the more tradition-bound city trade centers, such as Bruges and Ghent, were outstripped by Antwerp and other new centers of trade, cities less hampered by the old regulations and traditional privileges for the few. Cartels even managed the financial policy of the state, when they could, in order to ensure the value of their holdings.

Maritime trade grew between west and east in northern Europe, and between Italy and the eastern Mediterranean ports. The more highly developed products, such as Flemish textiles, were exchanged for furs, amber, lumber, and other raw materials in Russia and the Baltic area. The Italian cities of Venice, Genoa, and to a lesser extent Pisa exploited the eastern Mediterranean virtually as an economic colony. Venice had played the role of villain in the devastation of Constantinople by the Latin army of the Fourth Crusade in 1204, and it benefited most from the difficulties of Byzantium, now under constantly recurring pressure from the Turks. Venice built trading posts and forts to protect them at strategic points throughout the East. Eventually it even eliminated Genoa, its only serious rival. The end of the imperial control exercised over the cities of northern Italy by the Hohenstaufens in 1250 allowed a new freedom for the communes. Prosperity and relative plenty were in evidence not only in Italy, but throughout the greater part of Europe. The period from the eleventh century to the end of the thirteenth saw the gradual improvement of economic conditions, but there followed then a century of disasters and economic setbacks of a most discouraging kind. Famine, the plague, war, and peasant revolts swept the continent like the four horsemen of the apocalypse.

A TRAUMATIC CENTURY: FAMINE, PESTILENCE, WAR, REVOLT

Famine.   Until very recently in man's history, hunger and famine stalked him like a beast of prey. In the medieval economic system there was a maldistribution of properties and income, and as a result people were tempted to consume and not to invest. Families could barely subsist on one, two, or three hectares of land. By the fourteenth century the exploitation of arable land had been pushed about as far as it could go. The marginal lands provided a less certain return, and formerly fertile lands were becoming eroded or impoverished for lack of fertilizers, by disregard of fallow periods, or because of inadequate rotation of crops. It was not possible to wrest new tillage from the forests, for those that remained were needed by the poor and were being exploited for metallurgical "factories" in industrial areas. There was as yet no scientific seed production or any radical technological breakthrough that would make for a higher yield on a limited acreage. It is possible also that a new climatic cycle began about this time, with colder winters and wetter summers inducing rust and rot in the wheat crop. Potatoes, with their high yield per square foot of land, were, of course, not yet known.

Moreover, just as in modern China and India, local famines were an inevitable result of poor transportation. Bad seasons increased after 1300, and starting in northern Europe terrible famines fell upon various countries from 1309 to 1315. A chronicler in Alsace reported that starving people cut corpses down from the gibbet and ate them. It is impossible to calculate how many victims hunger claimed in the remote rural areas. But in the big famine of 1315 to 1317 in the Lowlands, the leading Flemish textile and trading centers such as Ypres and Bruges lost from 5 to 10 percent of their populations, and the survivors were weakened by the ordeal. From the early fourteenth century until about 1450 there was a decline in the European population, which reached its lowest point shortly after 1400. This demographic retreat was not uniform, for some countries and places escaped it. But the evidence of deserted tenancies and villages, statistics showing the fall in city populations, reports on the hearth tax, and parish records all incontestably show a major decline in the population of Europe. Not until the sixteenth century did history usher in the era of population expansion which has lasted down to the present.

Pestilence. Death hovered over rich and poor alike. The food shortage that reduced so many people to the subsistence level weakened them and made them readily susceptible to disease. The crowded cities enclosed by heavy walls, with sewage poured into the streets and primitive conceptions of hygiene, were ripe for epidemics. The doctors were quick to flee when symptoms of contagion appeared, or worse yet, stayed and administered remedies that all too often further weakened the victims of disease. The year 1348 was the *annus horribilis* in which the Black Death struck Europe. The term Black Death refers specifically to bubonic plague, but pneumonic plague, a different though equally virulent form of the disease, seems to have been present at the same time. The plague germ (*Pasteurella pestis*) was carried by fleas on rats that were brought by ship from the Near East to Mediterranean ports in southern Europe. The plague spread from Italy, France, and Spain northward, scourging England and the Germanies the following year. It moved on then to Scotland and the Baltic area in 1350, spreading panic and terror, for it seemed to be like an invisible angel of death passing over the land, as during the slaying of the firstborn of Egypt during Israel's captivity.

The years that followed the Great Plague were perhaps the most gloomy in the history of Europe. At no other time in all the centuries of the Middle Ages was so much written about the miseries of human life. A profound pessimism and a renunciation of life pervaded the writings of the period and were reflected in its art. The dance of death became a common theme in etchings, woodcuts, and manuscript illuminations. No age was more acutely aware of the brevity of life and the certainty of death. In northern cathedrals there appeared sculptures of damsels that were beautiful to behold from the front, but which from the rear were seen to be hollowed by rot and decay, filled with lizards and tokens of vice and death. In Italy preachers such as Jacopo Passavanti drove home the lesson of the transiency of life to weeping crowds. In the predella below the madonna by Giovanni del Biondo in the Vatican there is a representation that has no precedent in Tuscan art. A bearded old hermit points in warning to a decaying corpse consumed by snakes and toads, while a man and his dog recoil in horror. "Remember that you must die!" is the message of mural and altarpiece. In the great fresco in the *campo santo* in Pisa, done around 1350, Francesco Tranini showed the sick and dying, the horror of rotting flesh, and the sudden, unpredictable coming of death.[2]

The plague often claimed as victims the very old, children, and adults with low resistance due to malnutrition, although it also struck down men in their prime. It caused fever, a swelling of the lymph nodes, and discoloration, and sometimes induced pneumonia. Modern historians agree with the chronicler Froissart that the Great Plague swept away a third of the population of Europe. During the summer months of 1348 more than half the inhabitants of Florence and Siena fell victim to the plague. In the *Decameron* Boccaccio wrote that Florence became a huge sepulcher, and described how the bodies were stacked up in trenches for burial like merchandise loaded in a ship. In little Givry in Burgundy the normal annual mortality ran from 14 to 43, but in the year of the Great Plague, deaths listed in the parish register leaped to 649. The weakened condition of the populace had the further result of reducing reproduction, and in some areas recorded births sank to a mere 60 percent of normal.

Italy suffered several major epidemics in the century and a half that followed the introduction of the Black Death. They declined in frequency and severity in the years following 1348, but recurred into the seventeenth century. It has been suggested that a species of brown rats killed off the black rats that carried the disease, that people built up immunities, or that the bacillus mutated into a less virulent form. But by then enormous damage had been done to mankind in body and spirit.

War.   The ravages of war were added to the losses of the plague as the English and French monarchs embarked upon a duel for England's continental possessions. The so-called Hundred Years' War dominated the history of England and France from 1337 to 1453, the closing act of a drama that began with the Norman conquest of England in 1066. From the time of William the Conqueror, the English kings had possessed large fiefs in France as the vassals of the French kings. Beginning with the reign of Louis VI, the French undertook the recovery of those territories, until early in the fourteenth century the English held only Gascony. But a series of incompetent French monarchs squandered their obvious military advantages, and in the fifteenth century the Burgundian rival to the east arose, so that the English were encouraged to attempt to regain their holdings on the continent.

---

[2] Millard Meiss, *Painting in Florence and Siena after the Black Death* (New York, 1964), p. 74.

Although the French suffered disaster in the early years of the war and occasionally thereafter, they had the advantage of being on the continent, while the English troops had to cross the channel. The English kings pressed on, and the armies of both sides, which were becoming increasingly made up of mercenary troops, wreaked havoc on the countryside. Even in the intervals between major campaigns, hostilities were continued by roving bands of freebooters. Mercenary troops led by professional guerrilla fighters made sweeping raids into the Lowlands and northern Italy, seeking spoil and plunder. English forces gutted the French countryside, and the French even applied a scorched-earth policy to their own land to starve out the English. Order broke down in the countryside as robber knights and highwaymen made the roads unsafe for commerce and travelers. The inefficiency and corruption revealed in the French and English governments alike further disillusioned the common people.

Revolt. There was an acute shortage of bullion in the fourteenth and early fifteenth centuries. Governments, burdened with war debts, indulged in monetary manipulation, devaluation of currency, and debasement of coinage. Taxes became increasingly more oppressive to finance the wars. The nobles proved unable to protect the peasants from marauders. The feudal system was discredited and the oppressive monarchs were hated. As is usually the case, the cost in blood and money eventually had to be borne by the lower classes.

Conflicting forces were at work on the peasantry. On the one hand, the decimation of the population by famine, plague, and war produced such a shortage of agricultural laborers that those who survived were in an advantageous position. Vast areas of land were going uncultivated and the free peasants purchased it at low prices. Bondsmen could either demand freedom as the price of staying with their lords or secure more favorable terms as tenants. On the other hand, the peasants were nevertheless restless, for much of the cost of the wars had fallen on them, and when the lords tried to retain their bondsmen by force or to impose seignorial obligations upon the free peasants, they rebelled. Liberty and serfdom do not make good bedfellows. Peasant revolts swept across Europe during the fourteenth, fifteenth, and early sixteenth centuries, yet another scourge for the embattled continent.

The peasant revolt in Flanders between 1323 and 1328 was the first major uprising and one of the bloodiest. The free Flemish peasants were furious at the subservience of the count and nobles to the French kings, resented seignorial taxation, refused to pay the tithe and other dues to the gentry, and resisted efforts to encroach upon the freedom and gains they had already won. In a reign of terror the Flemish peasants hacked and slaughtered the seigneurs, and even held the count of Flanders captive for a time. Encouraged and abetted by disgruntled members of the lesser guilds in the textile manufacturing and trading towns, the peasants had amazing durability. They resisted the gentry, defied a pacification attempt in 1326, and finally were defeated and crushed only when a French royal army joined the count of Flanders against them in the Battle of Cassel on August 23, 1328.

The revolt in Flanders poses a familiar question: Did the revolution come because of the peasants' desperation at the miserable conditions under which they lived or did it come after their position had been considerably improved? The census of those peasants who were killed at Cassel and whose property was confiscated provides fairly clear insight into the situation. In editing the lists, the great Belgian medievalist Henri Pirenne discovered that nearly all of those free peasants owned two or two and a half measures of land, a house, a barn, cattle, and other possessions. Only a few were without property. There is only one conclusion we can reach: that the peasants had in earlier decades improved their condition and that revolt followed only upon the attempts of the upper classes to reimpose old duties and former conditions of servitude.

In the area surrounding Paris a revolt known as the Jacquerie broke out in May 1358 in protest against the plundering of the countryside by troops quartered in and around the city. Artisans joined the peasants in their furious assault on the nobility, who had been unable and seemingly unwilling to protect the peasants from the soldiers. Castles were leveled and nobles killed. But the nobles quickly rallied, and by the end of June the rebellion was suppressed. It is estimated that twenty thousand peasants lost their lives in the fighting and by execution.

In England the peasants in the counties around London rose up in the Great Revolt of 1381, which began in Kent and spread to Essex. There was a profound feeling of unhappiness about legislation, specifically the Statute of Laborers, which attempted to freeze wages and prices, to keep the peasants tied to the land, and to impose new taxes, including a poll tax (1380) on everyone over fifteen. Wat Tyler led a march on London in June 1381. The rebels, joined by sympathizers in the city, administered their version of justice to certain officials and frightened the government into acceding to nearly all their demands. At the meeting Tyler was killed. Soon after the peasants had scattered, the government of Richard II canceled all its concessions. Just as in the Flemish revolt, certain egalitarian and agrarian communist sentiments were expressed by the revolutionaries. John Ball, who claimed clerical status, expressed anticlerical and egalitarian sentiments in a verse that became widely popular:

> When Adam delved and Eve span,
> Who was then the gentleman?

The revolts spread throughout Europe; there were others in central and eastern Europe, and there were at least a dozen smaller peasant revolts in the Germanies before the great conflagration of 1525. And Machiavelli in the early sixteenth century warned the state solemnly against putting arms into the hands of the unreliable peasantry.

When the whole situation is surveyed, several features stand out. The first is that the revolts tended to be associated with a rising level of expectation. The plagues, famines, and wars had reduced the manpower available and put the common peasants and laborers in a good bargaining position, which they used to gain privileges and to improve their lot. The revolutionary battles were fought by men who had made gains, not by the despairing and downtrodden. The peasants were impatient with the rate of improvement in their status and feared a forced return to their previous condition. The fact that the most important uprisings took place near urban centers suggests that the safety-valve aspect of city growth and the relative freedom of the artisans raised the hopes of the peasants in the surrounding countryside. The revolutionary ideology, with its admixture of anticlericalism fed by the heretical tenets of Lollard and sectarian preachers, was a straw in the wind indicating that the following centuries would see a proliferation of sects and heresies. In the sixteenth century "revolution" was a scientific term and not a political one.

Although these bloody revolts were shocking and dramatic, and their repression cruel and merciless, they had little effect on general economic trends. Serfdom was doomed by economic forces that ran deeper and were more inexorable than lords or peasants realized. The manorial system proved to be less productive than a freer system under which tenants paid rent and participated in the benefits of increased production, no longer living as serfs. The logic of this lesson was learned very slowly, and the emancipation of the serfs spread eastward so gradually that it took an act of state by Tsar Alexander II in 1861 to free the serfs in Russia.

THE QUATTROCENTO

As a whole, Europe made a gradual comeback in general stability and prosperity during the 1400s, especially during the second half of the century. Recovery may have begun sooner and progressed more rapidly in Italy than in the north, although some demographers believe that the statistics of population loss in Italian towns at the time of the plague do not allow for those who escaped to the country, and that therefore the recovery of normal populations in the cities may be attributed at least in part to the return of people who had been away only temporarily.

A *guerre de savants* is still being waged as to whether the fifteenth century in Italy reached the levels of prosperity attained at the close of the thirteenth century and the early decades of the fourteenth, when such families as the Bardis, Peruzzis, Frescobaldis, and Acciaiuolis accumulated enormous wealth in Florence. Some argue that the miracle of the Renaissance is that even in hard times people invested heavily in culture. There is some evidence, however (greater silk production, for example), of an increase in wealth over that of the depressed late fourteenth century. Then came foreign invasion (1494), wars for the control of Italy, and the denouement of the Renaissance.

CHURCH AND STATE

The two great medieval institutions, the Holy Roman Catholic Church and the Holy Roman Empire, lost universality and power during the late Middle Ages and the Renaissance. The proud boasts of preeminence in the *Unam sanctam* (1302) of Boniface VIII sounded quite hollow during the sequence of disasters that befell the papacy in the centuries that followed. The nearly seventy years of the church's "Babylonian Captivity," during which the French king dominated the papacy, were followed by the papal schism, which more than any single event weakened the authority of the pope and brought into question the line of succession and the validity of sacerdotal acts. Conciliarism, which sought constitutional change and made one final effort to reform and revitalize the church, succumbed at last to the monarchical episcopate of the papacy. In the second half of the fifteenth century and down into the Protestant Reformation itself the church degenerated under the disastrous rule of Renaissance popes who transported their princely privileges and proclivities into the Vatican.

The religious situation during the fifteenth century offered a seemingly contradictory spectacle. For just as the Italians could combine with a fear of death the enjoyment of a naïve vitality, so in some ways they displayed sloth and indifference to religious values and in others a will to reform and a great formal piety. The faithful, looking for miracles, could easily be caught up in saints' cults, witchcraft, and inquisitional persecutions. A bureaucratic, juridical, sophisticated hierarchy presided over people who were often zealous, emotional, even pagan in some folk superstitions. Together they built the beautiful temples of the Renaissance.

On the political scene, movement from the universal to the particular was the order of the day. The theoretical grand unity of the empire gave way to a plurality of states as the rising dynastic kingdoms asserted their independence from both the empire and the papacy above and from dependence on the feudal dukedoms below. Feudal monarchy, especially in France and England, made positive political advances, achieving a wider loyalty to the crown, especially among the burghers, adding to the royal domain, and developing a more effective bureaucracy and military organization. During the fifteenth century the Habsburg emperors lost control to an elite group of territorial princes in the diet. Burgundy virtually sheared off the Netherlands from the empire and the Swiss achieved de facto independence, although neither fact was formally acknowledged until the Peace of Westphalia in 1648.

Between the empire and France the duchies of Savoy, Burgundy, and Lorraine served as buffers, but also as prizes to be fought for. The Habsburg-Spanish alliance against France in 1495 set the stage for the Habsburg-Valois wars, which put Europe on the rack during the first half of the sixteenth century. An actual balance of power was achieved as the states consolidated and shifted into defensive formations.

Italy followed its own peculiar course. As the homeland of the papacy and with the Papal States stretching across the leg of the peninsula like a garter, Italy related to the church differently than did the other European states. The city-states thwarted the growth of a national state and the patriotism of the burghers was local, not attached to a monarch or emperor. The cities suppressed and absorbed the feudal nobility and bishops in the countryside surrounding them. The city-states combined against each other and carried on internecine warfare. The Mediterranean Sea served as a highway for Italy's merchants, but it also brought foreign raiders and hostile fleets.

The skills of international diplomacy developed by the Italian city-states during the course of the *Quattrocento* were imitated and widely adopted by the states outside of Italy. Even the Turkish sultan, successor to the Byzantine Palaeologi after 1453, respected and adopted certain Renaissance diplomatic usages. The revival of Roman law aided the princes in the consolidation of their territories and the establishment of more efficient rule over them.

The age of the Renaissance was an age of contrasts and contradictions. It was an age of powerful personalities, cruel military men, clever and ruthless statesmen, but also of exquisite artists, gentle poets, and dedicated scholars. There were men of enormous wealth, but multitudes who suffered abject poverty. It was a time when nights were consumed in debauchery, but also devoted to vigils and prayer. It was a time for display and pomp, but a time also for preachers of penitence, humility, and withdrawal to a solitary life. It was a day for progress coupled with retrogression. It boasted of the dignity of man but bewailed his misery. It could be humanistic and yet act totally inhumane. It coupled a pronounced interest in man with a weariness with life and a longing for a celestial home. The Renaissance was colored in many hues, changing sometimes subtly, sometimes sharply, often swiftly. Contrasts and contradictions are basic to human nature and present in nearly every man; what brings them so clearly into focus in the Renaissance is the fact that history was in rapid movement and Italy was in a state of accelerated transition.

Such, then, was the Renaissance world, the stage on which the action took place. But from the spectator's seat the stage is of little interest until the actors appear and, quite without previous rehearsal, bring their story to life. David Hume, a respectable philosopher and a historian not completely without merit, once exclaimed:

To see all [the] human race, from the beginning of time, pass, as it were, in review before us, appearing in their true colors, without any of those disguises which, during their lifetime, so much perplexed the judgment of the beholders—what spectacle can be imagined so magnificent, so various, so interesting?[3]

Bibliography

General histories, texts, and handbooks:
Aston, Margaret. *The Fifteenth Century: The Prospect of Europe.* New York, 1968.
Barbagallo, C. *L'Età della Rinascenza e della Riforma, 1454–1556.* Turin, 1936.
Burckhardt, Jacob. *The Civilization of the Renaissance in Italy.* London, 1892, and many other eds.; original German ed., Basel, 1860.
Chastel, André, and Robert Klein. *L'Europe de la Renaissance: L'âge de l'humanisme.* Paris, 1963.
Cheyney, E. P. *The Dawn of a New Era, 1250–1453.* New York, 1936.
Ergang, Robert. *The Renaissance.* Princeton, 1967.
Ferguson, Wallace K. *Europe in Transition, 1300–1520.* Boston, 1962.
Gilmore, Myron P. *The World of Humanism, 1453–1517.* New York, 1952.
Glass, D. V., and D. E. C. Eversley. *Population in History: Essays in History.* Chicago, 1965.
Goetz, Walter, et al. *Das Zeitalter der Gotik und Renaissance, 1250–1500.* Berlin, 1932.
Green, Vivian H. H. *Renaissance and Reformation: A Survey of European History Between 1450 and 1660,* 2nd ed. London, 1965.
Hassinger, Erich. *Das Werden des neuzeitlichen Europa, 1300–1600.* Brunswick, 1959.
Hauser, Henri, and Augustin Renaudet. *Les débuts de l'âge moderne,* 3rd ed. Paris, 1946.
Hay, Denys. *The Italian Renaissance in Its Historical Background.* Cambridge, 1961.
———. *Europe in the Fourteenth and Fifteenth Centuries.* New York, 1966.
Lucas, Henry S. *The Renaissance and the Reformation,* 2nd ed. New York, 1960.
Lucki, Emil. *History of the Renaissance, 1350–1550,* 5 vols. Salt Lake City, 1963–1965.
Nauert, Charles. *The Age of Renaissance and Reformation.* Hinsdale, IL, 1977.
Pirenne, Henri, et al. *La fin du moyen âge,* vol. 1, pp. 1285–1453; vol. 2, pp. 1453–92. Paris, 1931.
Plumb, John. H. *The Horizon Book of the Renaissance.* New York, 1961.
Potter, G. R. *The Renaissance, 1493–1520,* vol. 1 of *The New Cambridge Modern History,* ed. G. N. Clark et al. Cambridge, 1957.
Rice, Eugene Jr. *The Foundations of Early Modern Europe, 1460–1559.* New York, 1970.
Symonds, John Addington. *Renaissance in Italy,* 7 vols. London. 1875–1886.
Thomson, S. Harrison. *Europe in Renaissance and Reformation.* New York, 1963.
Trimborn, Hermann, et al. *Weltkulturen: Renaissance in Europa,* vol. 6 of *Propyläen-Weltgeschichte: Eine Universalgeschichte,* ed. Golo Mann and August Nitsche. Frankfurt and Berlin, 1964.
Twigg, Graham. *The Black Death: A Biological Reappraisal.* London, 1984; New York, 1985.

The concept of the Renaissance:
Chabod, Federico. "The Concept of the Renaissance," in *Machiavelli and the Renaissance,* pp. 149–200. New York, 1965.
Dannenfeldt, Karl H. *The Renaissance: Medieval or Modern?* Boston, 1959.
Durand, Dana B., and Hans Baron. "Tradition and Innovation in Fifteenth-Century Italy." *Journal of the History of Ideas,* 4 (1943): 1–49.
Ferguson, Wallace K. *The Renaissance in Historical Thought: Five Centuries of Interpretation.* Boston, 1948.
———. *Renaissance Studies.* London, Ont., 1963.
Hale, John, ed. *Europe in the Late Middle Ages.* Evanston, IL., 1965.

---

[3] David Hume, "Of the Study of History," in *Essays Moral, Political, and Literary,* vol. 2 (London, 1889), pp. 389–90.

————. *Renaissance Europe: The Individual and Society, 1480–1520.* Berkeley and Los Angeles, 1977; reprint of 1971 ed.

Hay, Denys; *Europe: The Emergence of an Idea.* Edinburgh, 1957.

————. *The Renaissance Debate.* New York, 1965.

Helton, Tinsley, ed. *The Renaissance: A Reconsideration of the Theories and Interpretations of the Age.* Madison, 1961.

Jacob, Ernest F., ed. *Italian Renaissance Studies.* London, 1960.

Lewis, Archibald, ed. *Aspects of the Renaissance.* Austin, 1967.

Panofsky, Erwin. "Renaissance and Renaissances." *Kenyon Review,* 6 (1944): 201–36.

"Il Rinascimento: Significato e limiti." *Atti del III convegno internazionale sul Rinascimento.* Florence, 1953.

Sellery, G. C. *The Renaissance: Its Nature and Origins.* Madison, 1950.

Werkmeister, William H., ed. *Facets of the Renaissance.* Los Angeles, 1959.

CHAPTER 2

The Church
in Crisis

When Catherine of Siena (1347–1380) was presented together
with her interpreter, Raimondo Capuano, O.P., to Pope Gregory XI, she bowed
low to the supreme pontiff. Then she slowly raised her head and said, "To the
honor of Almighty God I am not afraid to say that I smelled the stench of the
sins committed in the Roman See more strongly in my native town than do the
people in this very place who commit them here daily." The pope remained silent.

Catherine was a mystic and reformer whose ignorance of Latin did not keep
her from writing, perhaps through an amanuensis, to dukes, kings, and popes.
Her most urgent cause was bringing the papacy home to Rome, back from its
Babylonian Captivity in Avignon. The calls to reform in the late Middle Ages
were shrill, strident, desperate. The situation was deteriorating rapidly. Typical of
the criticism were the *Speculum aureum de titulis beneficiorum,* a "golden mirror"
revealing the abuses of the system of benefices, and the *Squalores curiae romanae,*
on the "filthiness" of the Roman curia.

One crisis after another racked the church: the exile of the papacy in Avignon
(1309–1377), the Great Schism (1378–1415), conciliarism, the more than half century of Renaissance popes, and then the Protestant Reformation. When the historian considers the frailty of the church, the force of the hostile waves beating
against her, and the tremendous assaults she has endured, he can only marvel at

her power of survival. The basic problem, as most medieval reformers saw it, was the involvement of the institutional church in the world. The role of the pope as ruler over the Papal States, originating in the supposed transfer of the keys of the city of Rome to the bishop of Rome when the emperor moved the capital to the east, involved the popes in all the political intrigues of the Italians. The estates of the church banded the Italian boot at mid-calf, where they were both strategically important and vulnerable. But there were deeper socioeconomic causes for the troubles of the church not readily apparent to the moralistic critics of the time. The church had become so involved in feudal society and the feudal economy that it had enormous difficulty in adjusting to the money economy and capitalist society. The papacy's administrative machinery and financial resources were not equal to the demands made upon them. With the best will in the world the most pious of pontiffs could hardly have coped with these tremendous difficulties, stemming from such deep underlying causes.

The Concept of Christendom

MEDIEVAL MEN thought of Christendom (*corpus christianum* or *respublica christiana*) as a religious-metaphysical entity encompassing the spiritual and secular authorities. As the spiritual head of the church, the pope held the power of the keys and wielded the spiritual sword. As Thomas More put it in the sixteenth century, the Roman Catholic Church is universal, visible, and organic (not just mystical). The emperor was the titular head of the Holy Roman Empire and the chief political authority. In the year 494 Pope Gelasius I had defined the independent powers of church and state as spiritual and secular swords. "There are," Gelasius wrote in a letter to the Byzantine emperor Anastasius I, "two powers by which this world is chiefly ruled: the sacred authority of the priesthood and the power of kings. Of these the importance of the priestly power is much greater, as even for kings of men it will have to give an account in the divine judgment." The spiritual sword, then, in having responsibility for the welfare of the secular ruler's soul, was held to have preeminence over the secular sword.

How much reality the concept of Christendom had in the minds of medieval men is difficult to determine. Dante in the fourteenth century and the Anglican theologian Thomas Hooker in the sixteenth century spoke of the *corpus christianum,* or the "common body of Christendom." It was a community of belief on a number of levels and a common structure of institutions with variations in local communities. While many men were doubtless not conscious of holding such a concept, others did articulate it. It is evident in late medieval maps, which show Christendom as distinct from other areas of the Roman world. During the Renaissance the humanists and imperial political theorists began using the term "Europa" instead of "Christendom." The name was derived from the Greek myth about a Phoenicean princess whom Zeus loved. Disguised as a white bull, he carried her off to Crete. As Christendom evolved into modern secular Europe, the church entered a period of crisis that many pessimists mistook for death throes, signs of the last times.

The Institutional Crisis

DURING THE FOURTH CENTURY the Christian church, intermittently and ineffectively persecuted by the state since the days of the apostles, not only was granted toleration by Emperor Galerius, but was even given official status by Emperor Theodosius I, who proscribed paganism. The popular identification of the Christian church with the Christian state was a development of momentous historical importance. It brought new prestige to the church, but at tremendous cost to its spiritual integrity.

The reversal of the historical situation inverted the prevailing theories of the relationship between church and state. St. Augustine had justified the state as a check on evildoers and as a promoter of relative justice in human society, with its authority rooted in natural law. The Augustinians of the Carolingian period, however, understood the term "justice" (*iustitia*) as righteousness in the theological or religious sense, rather than as the impartial administration of merited rewards and punishments, and came to the congenial conclusion that the state is duty-bound to support the cause of the church. During the Merovingian and Carolingian periods of Frankish history the rulers exercised virtually complete control over the church in their domains. On the local level, too, the processes of economic and political decentralization led to the feudalization of the church. There was general acceptance of the proprietary church as a legal construction under which the lord virtually dominated the church within his territory, controlling appointments to ecclesiastical offices and finances in the parish or diocese within his power.

From the time of Pope Gregory VII's struggle for "the right order of things in the world" in the eleventh century, the church became increasingly a clerical institution marked by ever greater centralization in the papacy. An unwholesome gap developed between clergy and laity, between the secular and the regular clergy, and between the upper clergy, drawn largely from noble families and on occasion from enterprising bourgeois families, and the lower clergy, drawn from the lower classes and given minimal education. Major historical movements tend to build up greater force than necessary to achieve limited and attainable objectives. Thus, to overcome the evils resulting from the control of the church on the local level by lay lords, under the proprietary arrangements typical of the early and high Middle

Ages, the papacy succeeded in establishing the claim, and some of the substance, of absolute rule over the church.

The theoretical basis of this claim was the assertion by some papal canonists that the pope possessed a "fullness of power," by which they meant power to rule not only over the church but at least indirectly over the entire world. Pope Innocent III took the title of "true emperor" seriously and accepted great kingdoms, including Naples and England, as vassalages subject to his feudal overlordship. In a letter to the archbishop of Ravenna, Innocent wrote: "Never is ecclesiastical liberty better provided for than when the Roman church possesses the plenitude of power in both temporal and spiritual things." When Innocent presided with hierocratic splendor over the great Fourth Lateran Council in 1215, pontifical preeminence reached its apex. But at that very council Pope Innocent charged the fathers with effecting reform within the church. During the thirteenth century, however, the church further centralized its administration, and although this was not at all a bad thing in itself, it did open the way for abuses. Innocent's pronouncement that "all churches and all things ecclesiastical are in the power of the pope" was given a practical application by Clement IV's famous decretal of 1265, which added the principle of provision (the right of the pope to name appointments to church posts not yet vacant) to the principle of general reservation (his right to fill vacant posts as he wished). Later popes could easily use this principle to reserve more and more patronage appointments for themselves.

Not quite a full century after Innocent III, Pope Boniface VIII gave the strongest expression to papal claims to preeminence in his bull *Unam sanctam* (1302), in which he asserted the effective possession by the church of both the spiritual and the secular swords, since the princes were to wield the secular sword on the instruction of the priestly power. He boldly declared that "it is altogether necessary to salvation for every human creature to be subject to the Roman pontiff." Boniface was a canon lawyer and may well not have intended the document to be so rigidly controlling as it sounded. At the most he claimed an indirect power of directing the secular powers to a "spiritual end," and not the day-by-day direction of affairs in the secular kingdoms. Egidius Romanus, a tutor of Philip the Fair of France, wrote a treatise entitled *On Ecclesiastical Power,* in which he developed the theory of papal dominion: All dominion must be held by those who are in proper communion with the church. Later other writers applied this argument to property, holding that Christians alone had the right to be property holders or that property holders should be Christians—a dangerous proposition should churchmen prove to be unworthy or unchristian! The reaction of the rising secular powers against papal pretension was signaled by the humiliation of Boniface VIII himself by Philip the Fair. Boniface's imprisonment by Philip's man Guillaume de Nogaret in 1303 marks the end of an era that began in 1077 with Emperor Henry IV standing barefoot in the snow at Canossa in repentance before Pope Gregory VII.

The Babylonian Captivity of the church, during the course of which the papal see was located in Avignon, where Pope Clement V, a Frenchman, moved it in 1309, was in itself detrimental to the prestige of the papacy and weakened the loyalty of the English, who were engaged in their century-long struggle with France. The period of the Avignonese papacy did great harm to the church. It was not merely the absence of the papacy from Rome that proved harmful, for popes had been away from Rome before this. Between 1100 and 1304, a period of 204 years, the popes had spent 122 years away from Rome, only 82 in Rome. They had a palace in Viterbo, where the climate was better, where the plague was less threatening, and where they could escape the disputes of the rival Orsini and Colonna factions. But certain developments during the pontifical residence in the grand palace above the bridge in Avignon brought the church ever nearer to the brink of disaster.

During this period the papacy further centralized the administration of the church. The extension of papal supervision and actual jurisdiction was justified on the grounds of the need to combat the evils still remaining in the proprietary churches. Establishing the "right order of authority" meant intervention from above to prevent local political control of the church by the appointment to church offices of the younger sons of the nobility. Bold hypothesizers have scored verbal triumphs with catchy formulas such as "No Innocent III, no Louis XIV!" The truth is that the monarchs of kingdoms such as France were in many respects ahead of the church in creating bureaucracies and professional armies. The Avignonese papacy, with worldwide obligations to administer justice in church courts, to manage its vast landholdings, to supervise benefices, and to exercise control over appointments, felt the same need for administrative expansion and evolved in the same way as the new dynastic states. If the monarch could tax his subjects, however, the pope had to tax his ingenuity to discover new sources of revenue to pay for his governmental structure. The *camera,* or office of finance, extended taxation and raised fees. Canon law became a concrete expression of the church's universal jurisdiction.

The distribution of benefices, church posts endowed with property or funds, provided one major source of income. By the thirteenth century there was canonical provision for direct papal disposition of benefices in certain cases. If an official died in Rome or Avignon—a cardinal, for example—then the papacy could dispose of his benefice. This papal privilege of reservation, the right to nominate to a vacant benefice, was extended during the fourteenth century, and churchmen even paid the equivalent of the first year's income, or annates, from a see in anticipation of appointment in case of the resignation or death of the incumbent. A charge that appears frequently in the literature of the period is that "everything is for sale in Avignon." The latest studies suggest, however, that the amount of annual income that the Avignonese papacy derived from taxation and various other financial devices has been wildly exaggerated. Europe experienced acute financial problems in the second half of the fourteenth century, exacerbated by plagues, wars, and famines. The returns to the papacy were very small compared with the income of the rising national states, or even of a city-state like Venice. Moreover, the Italian bankers who handled papal finances understood well how to use them to their own enrichment. The city of Rome was in constant turmoil, and half-independent *signori* took over control in almost every city in the Papal States. The loss of revenue from the Papal States forced the papacy to seek new sources of income from the church at large, which increased the general resentment against it.

The papacy was much weaker than outward appearances would suggest. During the late Middle Ages and especially during the decades of the Renaissance popes, the papacy was simply unable to assert effective control over the church outside of Italy. The popes could have done something by way of lofty precept or good example, but even if they had wanted to institute a thorough reform in all parts of the church, it is doubtful that they had the power to do so. The moralistic reformers in the late Middle Ages, however, looked at the outward show of pomp and the worldliness of the court and flayed the papacy. What people believe to be true is often historically a more powerful force than the actual facts, and people were beginning to think the worst of the papacy. They feared that the very dangers of ecclesiastical centralization, bureaucracy, and fiscalism, against which St. Bernard had warned in the twelfth century, were now coming to pass.

The way in which the fourteenth-century exile in Avignon ended, however, was more damaging than the absence from Rome itself. When the papal residence was returned from Avignon to Rome and a large group of dissident cardinals elected an antipope, they precipitated the Great Schism, destroyed the juridical unity of the church, and harmed its credibility and spirituality. A contemporary, Nicholas de Clémanges, wrote a treatise *On the Ruin of the Church*. The trouble started when Pope Gregory XI, who had returned to Rome in 1377, died soon after arriving. In 1378 the College of Cardinals met for the election of a new pope under tremendous pressure from the local populace, which rioted and screamed for the election of an Italian pontiff. The cardinals agreed on one candidate, pretended to be electing another, and finally voted for Pope Urban VI, who favored Rome. Urban VI very quickly managed to offend some of the cardinals, and a rump faction elected a French pope, who chose the name Clement VII.

The schism was not simply an expression of nationalistic opposition of French cardinals to the Italian pope. The basic cause for the rift was the development of the idea of a transfer to the College of Cardinals of some of the power centered in the papacy. Urban VI had been elected as a mediocre stopgap; Clement was chosen by the disaffected cardinals in part as an expression of their dissatisfaction with Urban's rule. Although the king of France was not responsible for the schism, he did help to perpetuate it. Generally France and to some extent Spain supported Avignon, while Germany and England supported the Roman line. In subsequent centuries the church officially concluded the question of the legitimacy of the succession in favor of the Roman line and against the two schismatic popes of Avignon, Clement VII (1378–1394) and Benedict XIII (1394–1424). The schism lasted nearly four decades, dividing the loyalties of all Europe, eroding the prestige of the papacy, and worst of all, rendering doubtful the validity of the sacraments by obscuring the authentic line of sacerdotal succession, a withering blight on piety and spirituality.

Critics and Conciliarists

FACED WITH this institutional crisis, concerned churchmen recognized that there were four ways of healing the schism: the relinquishment of the papacy by one pope or the other, a compromise between them, withdrawal of obedience to both of them, and a general council willing to take responsibility for breaking the impasse. During the early period of the schism, from 1381 on, they worked for the resignation of one pope or the other and for compromise, possibly by the resignation of both in favor of a third. But neither pope was willing to yield. Between 1398 and 1403 special efforts were made to secure the withdrawal of obedience to the popes by national synods and kingdoms, but by 1407 it was clear that this way was hopeless. The fourth and final way was a church council, as advocated by the conciliarists, on the theory that councils were higher in authority than the popes.

The strong desire for church unity was the main driving force behind the conciliar movement. Such a universal concern was sure to produce a host of programs for reform. Some of the proposals involved changes in the constitutional structure of the church itself. Some of the more radical conciliarists opposed the whole system of centralized papal authority, since the monarchical episcopate was so obviously vulnerable, as the schism itself was demonstrating. The church had to act as an effectively united organism even when it lacked a single head to maintain the powers of the entire church. A council representing the will of the church universal was to be the agency by which a single competent pope could be chosen; but this solution denied the unique competency of the pope through the very procedure by which it was to be reestablished. The conciliar theory stressed the corporate association of the members of the church as the true principle of ecclesiastical unity, which was to be exercised through the council when the single effective head failed to act or was rendered incapable of action because of a schism.

In a general move to broaden the base of the central authority, particularly the role of the College of Cardinals, churchmen in the papal curia took an active part in initiating the constitutional reform movement. In 1378, in fact, three Italian cardinals proposed the idea of calling a general council with this reform program in mind. But the university men were more articulate than the cardinals in expressing conciliar theory, and in the course of the councils assumed an increasingly important role in leadership.

There had been many demands for reform during the thirteenth and early fourteenth centuries, many of them associated with ideas for the constitutional reform of the church. One of the most radical of these writings was the *Defensor pacis* (1324), in which Marsiglio of Padua (*c.* 1275–1348) portrayed the church in a way scarcely related to the existing, visible, historical church. Thinking possibly of the model of the bourgeoisie in an Italian city-state such as Padua, Marsiglio spoke of the "company of citizens" as the sovereign body responsible for law and for the election of the ruler. By analogy he ascribed similar sovereign rights to the "totality of believers" in the church, represented by a general council consisting of clergy and laity. Marsiglio coupled this line of thought with an attack upon the scriptural and historical foundations of the papacy in a really radical assault upon the traditional structure of the church. The church should devote itself to spiritual functions and should be without wealth, provided for by the secular government. In view of Marsiglio's sharp attack on the hierarchical structure of the church, it is not at all surprising that Pope John XXII declared parts of his work to be heretical and excommunicated him.

William of Occam (*c.*1285–1350), who came under the influence of Marsiglio, joined the Franciscans and protested in favor of "evangelical poverty." He was a severe critic of the worldliness and wealth of Pope John XXII. Occam saw service—first to Christ, then to his followers—as a basic function of the church, with the power of law. The external church, whose societal structure involves it in the sphere of worldly power, must constantly be pressed to conform to the "true church" of service. He advocated principles that proved to be significant for conciliarism. The key to many of his writings was his attempt to define precisely and to delimit papal prerogatives. He was really more revolutionary than Marsiglio, though more difficult and less direct. Occam recognized the principle of representation: the emperor, he pointed out, was chosen by the electors, who in theory represented all the people in the empire and acted for their benefit. Similarly the acclamation *viva voce* of the pope and bishops in an earlier period was an example of election by the people. In appointing the prince, the people invested him with their own rights and yet retained as much liberty as considerations for the common good permitted. This conception of representation, while certainly not to be understood as democratic in the modern sense, was obviously important for the conciliar movement.

Another fourteenth-century radical, John Wycliffe (*c.* 1328–1384), studied at Balliol College, Oxford, where he earned his M.A. degree and a doctorate in theology. He considered himself a disciple of Marsiglio of Padua and William of Occam, and was very sympathetic to the Franciscan ideal of apostolic poverty.

He entered the service of the English crown, somewhat embittered by his failure to receive a lucrative position promised him by Pope Gregory XI. King Edward III presented him with the parish of Lutterworth, which supported him the rest of his life. He encountered papal financial manipulators when he was sent to Bruges to negotiate for England in a dispute about the tribute that England had owed to the papacy ever since King John became a feudal vassal of the pope. By the time Wycliffe entered public service in 1374 he had developed his concept of lordship, which logically justified the confiscation by the state of ecclesiastical property under certain conditions. In two treatises based on his Oxford lectures, *On Divine Lordship* (1375) and *On Civil Lordship* (1376), he developed his ideas more fully.

Wycliffe argued that "divine lordship is the basis of any lordship of the creature." Man has been given dominion over all things below him in creation. Divine lordship is not diminished when God extends some dominion to man, for man serves as a steward who holds his power in trust from God. Only so long as a man is in the state of grace can he be said to hold his possessions righteously. Therefore a pauper in the state of grace has a stronger moral right to dominion than an emperor or a pope who is in a state of mortal sin. Since only the righteous are justified in holding possessions, ecclesiastical lords are lords only when they are truly servants of others and not their masters. Therefore, when churchmen manifest by the wickedness of their lives that they are not in a state of grace, the secular authority should deprive them of their property. Wycliffe believed that wealth and temporal power were the ruination of the church. He urged the king to expropriate the property of the "Caesarean" clergy, disendow the "delinquent" church, and re-establish a priesthood of grace.

He had an Augustinian view of the church as the body of predestined believers and described the state of the church as the church militant here on earth, the church triumphant in heaven, and the sleeping church of those in purgatory. In a treatise *On the Power of the Pope* (1379) he flatly denied the divine origin of the papal office as it was constituted and argued that the bishop of Rome held only a spiritual office. He identified the pope as the Antichrist and his followers as the "twelve daughters of the diabolical leech." When he died he was busy training poor priests to preach the gospel in the language of the people. Wycliffe based his reform upon the supreme authority of the Scriptures, which he described as "the standard of faith" for every Christian and "of all human perfection." This emphasis on the Scriptures and the work of his poor preachers, nicknamed Lollards for their restrained style of preaching (their detractors, accustomed to priestly declamation, derided them for "lolling," or muttering), linked Wycliffe to the Reformation of the sixteenth century.

The papal schism itself served as the great catalyst for conciliar thinking. Two German professors at the University of Paris, Henry of Langenstein and Conrad of Gelnhausen, were early conciliar theorists. In his *Letter on Behalf of a Council of Peace,* Henry of Langenstein (d. 1397) wrote of the great corruption in the church and the responsibility of those who exercised royal authority to seek to bring about a reformation with the help of a council. He emphasized the representative nature and the responsibility of the council, but he was by no means clear as to precisely who should summon the council or how it was to be organized. He referred to the secular princes in a general way, but did not indicate how the initiative was to be exercised. Conrad of Gelnhausen, in a number of works, including his *Letter of Concord,* analyzed the constitution of the church theoretically, trying to skirt the need of the pope to summon a council. Christ is the head of the church, and when his vicar fails to act, others can act in his name. "It is impossible," he wrote, "for the general council to be held or celebrated without the authority of the pope." He defined the church as "the congregation of the faithful in the unity of the sacraments."

The great French theologian Pierre d'Ailly and his student Jean Gerson dominated the period of the councils of Pisa (1409) and Constance (1414–1418). D'Ailly reminded Christendom that the church was built upon Christ and not upon the papacy, and observed that even the pope may become guilty of heresy. Neither a pope nor a council is strictly infallible, but only the church universal. Since the council represented the church universal, all of the faithful, including the pope, had to submit to its decisions. D'Ailly formulated concrete suggestions as to the structure of the council, applying to the church constitutional doctrines that political philosophers applied to the state. While he supported the claim of an ecumenical council to superiority over the pope, he nevertheless respected the dignity of the papacy itself. D'Ailly was not a flaming radical either in his program of reform or in his doctrine of the church; he was really a staunch advocate of the established theology of his day. The canonist Francesco Zabarella supported his contention that, since schism produced heresy, the cardinals had the privilege of calling a council to deal with it.

Jean Gerson, who succeeded D'Ailly as chancellor of the University of Paris, in 1409 wrote the treatise *On Unity,* which virtually represented the program of the Council of Pisa. Gerson was not a radical attacking the papacy, but a devoted scholar and patriot. He was a member of the leading theological faculty and a churchman with a high regard for the see of St. Peter. He argued that equity must supersede legalism in order to reestablish the indispensable unity of the church. The pope was subject to the general council and might even be imprisoned, if it should come to that, for the good of the church. The cardinals should elect no pope who would not be assured of being universally acknowledged. Although a general council could not abolish the papacy, it did have control over the method of electing the pope. Since popes change while the office remains permanent, a council could remove an undeserving incumbent and replace him with another.

Two German churchmen, Dietrich of Niem and Nicholas Cusanus, represented respectively the most radical assaults on papal centralization and the most comprehensive statement of conciliar theories. Dietrich of Niem, who had served as an official in the papal court itself, argued in his treatise *On Ways of Uniting and Reforming the Church in Universal Council* that merely healing the schism would not cure the ills of the church, for the real cause of all the troubles would remain: the centralization of power in papal hands and the attendant corruption in the church. The usurped powers of the pope must be either limited or abolished, if private interests and greed were to be eliminated from the heart of the universal church.

Nicholas Cusanus (d. 1464), at first a conciliarist, then from 1437 on a member of the papal party, bishop of Brixen, and cardinal, wrote the finest and most comprehensive statement of the conciliar position in his work *On Catholic Harmony*. Cusanus enthusiastically supported the elective principle in the church as well as in the empire. He favored the naming of delegates by small homogeneous units, so that the whole church might be well represented. He sought to demonstrate that the church was a united and comprehensive body, willing to accept and comprehend those who differed, for in the totality of the church all differences were harmonized.

More could be said about the evolution of conciliar thought within the very tradition of canon law and its interpretation on the part of the decretists, decretalists, and the like prior to the Great Schism. But it is important now to get on with the story of the councils themselves. These were the conciliar theories, but the course of the conciliar movement in history is even more instructive.

The Councils

WHEN THE FIFTEENTH CENTURY opened, the church was still torn by schism, with a French and a Roman pope. The Avignonese pope, Benedict XIII, was a skilled canonist who had many good qualities and won the respect of his contemporaries. He was supported by the French king and the French national synod of 1398. His opponent was the Neapolitan Boniface IX (1389–1404), a clever diplomat and strong ruler, who restored the Castel Sant' Angelo and fortified the Vatican for defense. It was well that he did, for in January 1400 he had to fight off an attempted coup d'état by the powerful Colonna family. He also had to oppose the duke of Milan, Gian Galeazzo Visconti. After Gian Galeazzo's unexpected death, Boniface gained Bologna and Perugia for the Papal States. Not only did he do nothing to heal the schism, adamantly insisting that his rival resign, but he further scandalized the church by authorizing massive sales of indulgences. His successor, Innocent VII (1404–1406), was equally set against concessions.

Pressure against both popes was now building up, as concerned churchmen grew impatient with their callous obstinance. Innocent's successor, Gregory XII (1406–1415), was at the outset willing to compromise and even to resign in order to restore unity, but he was urged by various rulers, including the rulers of Hungary and Bohemia, Naples, and the Venetian Republic, not to make any concessions that would strengthen French influence. He thereupon did an about-face and forbade his cardinals to attend the negotiations with the Avignonese curia scheduled for May 1408. Most of them went anyway and made an appeal to a general council against their own pope. Meanwhile, Benedict XIII was losing the nearly solid backing he had enjoyed among the French. When the French king himself declared France's neutrality in the dispute, Benedict withdrew to Perpignan in his native Aragon, for he now enjoyed the support only of Spain and Scotland. Cardinals of both obediences joined in summoning a general council to Pisa on March 25, 1409.

The Council of Pisa was an impressive assembly, which for a time numbered over five hundred, including four patriarchs, twenty-four cardinals, eighty bishops, and a host of abbots, canon lawyers, and theologians. The day after the council opened, proceedings against the two popes were begun. Thirty-seven articles were read aloud, accusing them of heresy, of misgovernment, and even of practicing sorcery. It was necessary to charge heresy in order to facilitate the deposition. On June 5, 1409, both popes were condemned as heretics and *ipso facto* deposed. The French faction at the council was very strong, and the conclave elected the Venetian archbishop of Milan, born in Candia, Crete, pope as Alexander V (1409–1410). The council did little more about reform than to present a list of desiderata to the new pope. Since the proposed reforms encroached upon papal prerogatives, Alexander V dissolved the council on August 7, 1409. Because the other two popes did not acknowledge the legitimacy of the council and still had adherents, Christendom was now stuck with three heads instead of one.

Kindly Pope Alexander V was succeeded by a crafty Neapolitan, John XXIII (1410–1415), a worldly militarist and simoniac who had no conscience about reform. Now the emperor felt it necessary to intervene in behalf of the church. In the days of the ancient church Emperor Constantine had sanctioned the conciliar theory, and the great ecumenical councils, preeminently the Council of Nicea in 325, had enabled the church to achieve confessional unity and organizational strength. In this grave crisis a millennium later, the Holy Roman emperor as a Christian authority looked to a general council to save Christendom from schism. Emperor Sigismund (1410–1437), as protector of the church, had Pope John XXIII convoke a council to convene on November 1, 1414. It actually did meet in Constance on November 5 and lasted nearly four years. Sigismund invited Byzantine Emperor Manuel II Palaeologus (1391–1425) to Constance, for Byzantium was now hard-pressed by the Turks, and the need for East-West unity was increasingly urgent.

The need for restoring unity at any cost was so desperate that even conciliarists such as D'Ailly, cardinal bishop of Cambrai, who had been active at Pisa, recognized the need for a completely fresh start. John XXIII, who had come to Constance expecting to see his rivals deposed, sensed that he himself might be cut off. He escaped in disguise with the connivance of Duke Frederick of Austria, who kept him in his fortress of Schaffhausen. Sigismund declared war on the duke, and on May 29, 1415, the council deposed Pope John XXIII. The Roman pontiff, Gregory XII, saw the handwriting on the wall and resigned "voluntarily." Deposing the resourceful Benedict XIII proved to be a complicated matter, but finally on November 4, 1416, the council began proceedings against him and deposed him as a schismatic and notorious heretic. On November 11, 1417, the fifty-three conclavists assembled and elected Oddo Colonna as Pope Martin V (1417–1431). Martin proved to be a wily statesman who concluded a series of favorable concordats with various secular rulers in order to assure himself of continued continent-wide approval. The schism was ended and unity was restored.

The council passed two startling decrees, the *Haec sancta* (1415) and the *Frequens* (1417). The *Haec sancta* boldly asserted that a general council derived its authority directly from Christ, the true head of the church, and therefore the whole universal church was bound by its decisions. Pope Martin V and his successor accepted this decree, it is interesting to note. The *Frequens* called for regular council meetings, the first to take place after five years, the second after seven, and decennially thereafter. The specific reform measures were much disputed, and the council finally instructed the pope to negotiate the specifics of reform with each nation. On this weak note the council adjourned on April 22, 1418.

Eugenius IV succeeded Martin V in 1431, and after a bitter battle with the Colonna clan, which had come to take a proprietary view of the throne of St. Peter, was able to turn his attention to the problems of the church universal. He opened the Council of Basel on July 23, 1431. But a duel developed between the conciliarists of Basel, who proclaimed the superiority of the council over the pope, and Eugenius, who insisted on his own prerogatives. Finally, on September 18, 1437, the pope dissolved the council and set Ferrara as the location for future meetings.

Eugenius IV was much concerned about the welfare of the eastern "Roman Empire" and church, for the Turks were tightening their grip on Byzantium. He convened a papal council in Ferrara on January 8, 1438, to discuss reform and to explore the possibility of reunion with the Eastern church. A year later, because of the plague, the council was moved to Florence. Finally in June, after long debate, Eastern churchmen agreed with reservations to acknowledge the supremacy of the pope and to yield on other disputed points. On July 6, 1439, the bull *Laetentur coeli,* "Let the heavens rejoice," proclaimed the reunion of the Roman and Greek churches, separated for so many centuries. The *Te Deum* rose upward in the Florentine cathedral, where a golden plaque celebrating the reunion of

Christendom is still to be seen. Some Greek churchmen, such as Bessarion, remained in the West rather than face hostility to their concessions at home. Some enraged Greek Orthodox zealots even declared that they would prefer the Turks to the pope, and they very shortly got what they wanted with the fall of Constantinople in 1453.

Meanwhile, back in Basel, the antipapal conciliarists triumphed. The Basel decree *Sacrosancta* incorporated the *Haec Sancta* decree of Constance. Still holding to the premise that councils are superior to popes, they annulled the papal decree of dissolution and deposed Eugenius IV on June 25, 1439. They then elected as pope Duke Amadeo VIII of Savoy, who took the name of Felix V. He was acknowledged, however, only in Savoy, Switzerland, southeast Germany, and Denmark. The Holy Roman emperor Frederick III recognized Eugenius IV as the rightful pope. With the death of Felix V in 1449, Christendom saw the last of the rival popes. Eugenius IV had died two years earlier. His successor, Nicholas V, is usually called the first of the Renaissance popes.

Although we now rehearse the succession of popes and councils in a prosaic way, it would be a mistake to think that these events were of no special importance to the people of the period. The fervor and fears, faith and despair, hope and hate of millions were invested in the outcomes of these struggles. In 1460 Pope Pius II issued the bull *Execrabilis,* designed once and for all to end appeals to a council over the head of the pope. Pius declared an appeal to a council to be a detestable thing that made one automatically a schismatic and heretic. Yet he realized that terrible storms were brewing which would rock the ark of the church. "Dangerous times are before us," he warned. "Storms threaten everywhere. . . . The waves of Basel have not subsided. . . . We won through force, they say, and not by convincing arguments." A priest may also be a prophet.

The Hussite Revolt

PIUS II had once written a history of Bohemia, including accounts of the Hussite wars, and firsthand knowledge of that unhappy land may have contributed to his pessimistic outlook, for Bohemia was still filled with a fierce hostility to the Roman see. The Council of Constance declared the teaching of John Wycliffe to be heretical and had the poor man's bones exhumed and burned. Less fortunate were Jan Hus and Jerome of Prague, who were summoned to Constance and had safe-conducts issued by Emperor Sigismund, but were burned at the stake, Hus on July 6, 1415, and Jerome on May 30, 1416. They were victims of the casuistry that safe-conducts do not hold for heretics.

It was once held that Jan Hus (1374–1415) was little more than an echo of John Wycliffe. After Wycliffe's death, Lollardy continued to be popular in England, quietly tolerated by King Richard II (1377–1399). Despite their condemnation by ecclesiastical courts, the Lollards even dared in 1395 to petition the parliament for help in "reforming religion according to the precepts of Scripture." King Henry IV (1399–1413), however, needed the support of the hierarchy, and he put the secular sword into the service of the church. In 1401 the statute *De haeretico comburendo* was directed against the Lollards and serious efforts were made to destroy them. But the movement continued underground, and Lollardy was still a significant element in the sixteenth-century Reformation. There was a dynastic tie between England and Bohemia, for Richard II had married Anne, a daughter of King Wenceslas of Bohemia. The political connection increased traffic and facilitated the transfer of ideas between the two lands. This consideration, plus the affinity of several of the ideas of Hus and Wycliffe, very naturally led to the traditional assumption that Hus was merely a pale version of Wycliffe.

The fact is that there was an independent Czech reform movement before the public emergence of Hus, with Matthew of Janov as its leading protagonist. Hus became the spokesman for this native reform movement, particularly after 1402, when he was appointed preacher in Bethlehem Chapel, near the university in the heart of Prague. Jan Hus was born into a poor family, studied at the Charles University in Prague, and became a lecturer there in 1398. Deeply pious and concerned about the moral impact of his preaching, he quickly gained a reputation as a popular lecturer and powerful preacher. Jerome of Prague was actually the man who introduced Wycliffe's works into Bohemia. In 1403 there was a flurry of excitement over Wycliffism. Two older leaders of the reform movement were cited to Rome and subsequently experienced a change of heart.

At this juncture Hus moved to the fore as leader of reform. He debated with Johann Hübner on simony and obedience to the pope. Preaching in Czech, Hus rapidly became a national hero. Fearing his popularity and the implications of his teachings, the local clergy urged Archbishop Zbynek of Prague to proceed against him, and the curia condemned Hus's teachings. The controversy tore the university apart, and in 1409 the German students and masters, alienated by the fierce Czech nationalism, left Prague to found the University of Leipzig. When Hus was forbidden to preach in Bethlehem Chapel, he persisted, declaring that "in the things pertaining to salvation God is to be obeyed rather than man." In March 1411 the ban was again pronounced against Hus as a disobedient son of the church. Shortly thereafter the whole city was put under the interdict for harboring a heretic.

The situation now reached a new critical phase. In May 1412 a papal emissary arrived in Prague to proclaim papal bulls authorizing the sale of indulgences remitting the canonical penances and purgatorial punishment due for sins. The proceeds were to be used to finance a papal war against the excommunicated King Ladislas of Naples. Hus denounced the sale, declaring that an indulgence can never be sold without simony and should not be granted by the church except when the recipient is truly contrite and repentant.

It would be difficult to imagine a greater contrast than the rascally John XXIII and the pious Jan Hus. The bulls were paraded through the streets of Prague in a popular demonstration and burned. At this juncture King Wenceslas intervened in the interest of public order, and three young men were sentenced to death for declaring the indulgences unlawful after all had been enjoined to silence. At the insistence of the king, Hus withdrew to the estates of sympathetic Czech nobles outside of Prague. He used this period of a year and a half in relative seclusion to write expositions on the faith, the Decalogue, the Lord's Prayer, simony, and, most important of all, *On the Church*. He proposed a highly spiritual conception of a church of believers under the headship of Christ, which reflected several of Wycliffe's key ideas. "O Christ," Hus exclaimed, "it will take a long time before the proud priests will become so humble as to subject themselves to the church for sin, as thou, being innocent, hast subjected thyself!"

The Council of Constance now summoned Hus, for the problem of Bohemia was at the top of the agenda. Hus had a presentiment of death and put his private affairs in order before starting out for Constance on October 14, 1414. Emperor Sigismund provided a safe-conduct promising his safe return to Bohemia no matter what decision the council reached on his teachings. Hus was confined by the bishop of Constance and his case finally was heard on June 5, 1415. The charges against him were for the most part based upon his *On the Church*. When he tried to speak in his own defense he was shouted down, and finally he concluded quietly, "In such a council as this I had expected to find more propriety, piety, and order."

Pierre d'Ailly, the Parisian conciliarist, presented the final resolution of the council: (1) Hus should humbly confess that he had erred in all the articles cited against him; (2) he should under oath promise not to hold or ever teach them again; and (3) he should make a public recantation. Hus refused, and for four weeks withstood enormous pressure to change his position. He wrote to his supporters in Prague: "I write this in prison and in chains, expecting tomorrow to receive sentence of death, full of hope in God that I shall not swerve from the truth, nor abjure errors imputed to me by false witnesses."

On July 6 the council condemned him to death in the presence of Emperor Sigismund and committed his soul to the devil. Hus, a pale, thin wisp of a man, stood with uplifted eyes commending his soul to Christ. He was then delivered to the "secular arm," led to the place of execution, tied to a stake, and burned. When the faggots were piled around him he was called upon once again to recant, but he answered, "God is my witness that I have never taught or preached that which false witnesses have testified against me. He knows that the great object of all my preaching and writing was to convert men from sin. In the truth of that gospel which hitherto I have written, taught, and preached, I now joyfully die." As the flames licked at his body, huge blisters formed under his skin. Before the smoke choked out his voice he was heard to pray, *"Kyrie eleison"*—Lord, have mercy!

The Hussite movement in Bohemia took a revolutionary turn as soon as news of Hus's death reached Prague. The outrage felt at the execution of the Czech hero and at the emperor's treachery was enormous. Nobles favorable to reform sent to the council a *Protestatio bohemorum* angrily condemning the execution. Sigismund made matters worse by writing the Czechs that he would very soon "drown all Wycliffites and Hussites!" In some parishes the people drove out their Roman priests, and rebellion was under way.

The Hussites very soon divided into two major parties, the moderate Utraquists or Calixtines and the radical Taborites. The name Utraquist was derived from the Latin words *sub utraque specie,* "under both kinds," and refers to the bread and wine of the Eucharist. The Utraquists believed that communicants should receive both bread and wine, not merely the bread, as the church had decreed. The name Calixtine was derived from *calix,* cup, and also indicates a demand that communicants share in the drinking of Christ's blood. The Taborites took their name from the city of Tabor, which became the main center of their activities. They recognized only two of the traditional seven sacraments, baptism and communion, and were opposed to elaborate church ceremonies. Both parties of Hussites spread through the countryside and roused the people for war against Sigismund, who was urging King Wenceslas, his brother, to suppress them.

Great forces in history are often released by relatively trifling incidents. On July 30, 1419, when a priest led a Hussite procession through the streets of Prague, rocks were hurled at them from the windows of the city hall. The hot-tempered John Zizka (1376–1424) stormed the building and threw the mayor and several city councilmen out the window. They survived the fall but were murdered by the mob below. King Wenceslas had a seizure when he was told of the incident, and he died a few days later. Riots broke out all over Bohemia and a fierce battle between royal mercenaries and Hussites gutted Prague. Zizka and his followers withdrew from Prague to Pilsen and from there to Tabor, where they established the capital of their new democratic government. As one of four elected captains of the people, Zizka organized a formidable and well-disciplined army.

On March 17, 1420, Pope Martin V proclaimed a crusade against the "Wycliffites, Hussites, and all other heretics in Bohemia." Sigismund, various German princes, and a rabble of freebooters descended on Prague and laid siege to the city. Sigismund rejected the Articles of Prague, in which the Hussites laid down their basic tenets. He was fought to a standstill and had to withdraw. In August 1421 Sigismund launched another invasion, largely with German troops, but on January 6, 1422, Zizka won a decisive victory at Nemecky Brod.

Then a civil war developed between the Utraquists, with Prague as their capital, and the Taborites, led by Zizka, with Zizka once more victorious. A papal call for another crusade failed. In 1424 Zizka died, but the Hussites fought on, repelling foreign invasions in 1426 and 1427. In 1434 the Utraquists thoroughly defeated the Taborites in the Battle of Lipan. Since they now had control, they formulated a more moderate position, and the Council of Basel granted the Utraquists an official status within the church. They remained the established church of Bohemia until after the Battle of the White Mountain in 1620, at the outset of the Thirty Years' War. The Habsburg victory over Bohemia led to the proscription of all churches other than the Roman Catholic. The Bohemian Brethren, however, and some other groups later identified with Protestantism have managed to maintain themselves in Bohemia and Moravia to the present time. Jan Hus was truly prophetic when he declared: "You may burn this goose [*hus* in Czech], but the swan will come which you will not be able to burn." During the sixteenth-century Reformation, the evangelicals identified the swan of which Hus spoke with Luther.

Crisis in Spirit

A MEDIEVAL PREACHER would immediately have recognized these lines as coming from the book of Proverbs (18:14): "The spirit of a man will sustain his infirmity; but a wounded spirit who can bear?" The institutional crisis of the medieval church took an enormous toll in spirituality. If some of the very churchmen who should have served as models of deportment and provided inspiration were patently worldly and cynical, their influence on lesser churchmen and the laity was sure to be negative. Even the strong defender of papal power Álvarez Pelayos warned: "Those who rule in the church are wolves: they feed themselves with blood, every soul is burdened with blood." Pope Pius II could speak of the struggle for the golden fleece in this way: "It is not about the pasture of the sheep, but about their wool." The fact that the church survived the traumatic experiences of the fourteenth and fifteenth centuries prompts one to ask what resources of intellect and heart made survival and even an increase in religious fervor possible.

There was, of course, much health left in the body of the church, the "seven thousand in Israel, all the knees which have not bowed unto Baal, and every mouth which hath not kissed him." There were not only reformer types in the upper ranks, but thousands of parish priests and monks who were pious and faithful shepherds. And there were other spiritual forces stirring within the church. The most powerful of these was a spiritual phenomenon usually given the imprecise name of mysticism. There was, moreover, more life in late scholasticism than the humanists, reformers, and most modern scholars have been willing to concede. Christian humanism of the Renaissance, with its renewed stress on moral philosophy, patristic writings, and the Scriptures, contributed a religious dimension that offset somewhat the pagan influence of classical antiquity. Finally, popular religious impulses welled up from the depths and stirred the masses.

MYSTICISM

Because of its highly personal, protean, and evanescent quality, mysticism is difficult to define in a general way. It has to do with the intuitive and emotive appeal of spiritual reality. Goethe once referred to it as "the dialectic of feeling." Mysticism is based on the assumption that the ultimate nature of reality or the divine essence may be known by the mystic through immediate apprehension, insight, or intuition. The mode of perception differs from all ordinary sensation and ratiocination, for the mystic experiences union or intercourse with the divine being in vision, in trance, or by absorption. Since the experience is unattainable by the natural intellect, it cannot be communicated or analyzed by ordinary linguistic tools, and a sense of its nature can best be suggested by symbols. Within the Western Christian tradition all mystics agree that true beatitude consists of union with God and that this union is attained through ecstatic contemplation. The nature of this contemplation is love, and this love is made possible by a life of discipline and order regulated to that end.

Certain general concepts important for later mysticism developed during the early Middle Ages, especially among those thinkers who were under the influence of St. Augustine. The first of these was the body-soul dichotomy. This was not a metaphysical dualism, for the body was believed to be necessary to the nature of man. The mystics held that man should never be identified merely with his soul, for man is a composite substance. The second concept was perfectionism, for they considered anything short of perfection to be sin. The life of monastic renunciation in flight from the world was the most promising way to attain perfection. Many mystics belonged to the regular clergy. The third concept was that of love, seen as a ground of reference above reason. Since the religious experience transcends reason and ordinary vocabulary used in propositional statements, the need to resort to symbolism was early recognized. John Scotus Erigena in the ninth century offered a good explanation of the problem when he stated that a divine revelation that needs symbolic interpretation does not imply that the universe is irrational, but that there is much more to it than the rational. The use of symbol is the first step toward the realization of the complexity of the universe.

Certain fundamental ideas appear in various expressions of medieval mystical experience. One of these is that the mystical experience is achieved only as a result of a long, difficult, and even arduous effort. The word "ascent" is often used, and the motive force is overwhelming love of God. A second idea is that the mystic way requires an astringent ascetic preparation in order to drive out the baser elements, a *vita purgativa*. A third idea is that the course of mystical ascent draws one away from the senses and into meditation and contemplation. This contemplation is of varying modalities, some mystics stressing intellectual effort, others a willful gazing with the "inner eye of the soul."

In his "Essay on Immortality" the philosopher Alfred North Whitehead comments that every philosophy must find a basis in experience. For the mystic, his personal experience offered proof of the existence of God and the truth of Christian doctrine. Many of the most important high medieval mystics were influenced by St. Augustine: St. Bernard of Clairvaux in the twelfth century, the Victorine mystics Hugh, Richard, and Walter, and St. Bonaventure in the thirteenth century. Many Franciscans were in the mystical tradition, and many leading nominalists—scholastics who stressed the priority of the individual to the universal—were Franciscans. The mystics of the fourteenth and fifteenth centuries described their mystical experiences in increasingly concrete terms.

The thirteenth century saw the greatest triumph of scholastic philosophy in the incomparable summary of theology (*Summa theologica*) of St. Thomas Aquinas (*c*. 1225–1274). Thomas devoted his encyclopedic learning to reconciling Aristotelianism and Christian dogma, harmonizing reason and revelation, so far as this was possible. The fourteenth century witnessed a great resurgence of mysticism side by side with a continuance of scholasticism. A general revival of Augustinianism in theology and of Platonism in philosophy provided a broad setting for the new developments in mystic thought, but the mystical experience is a highly personal thing, so that only the individual mystic can speak with authority on this dimension of spiritual experience.

The unrivaled master of "cerebral mysticism" was the Dominican Johannes Eckhart (1260–1327). In view of what has been said about mysticism, the Franciscans, and the nominalists, it is fascinating to note how much the Dominicans too contributed to the flowering of fourteenth-century mysticism, along with their Thomistic theology. Their mystical piety, which was cultivated in the Dominican friaries along the Rhine, especially in Cologne and Strassburg, was spread by their writings and sermons to their sister convents and to lay groups in the cities. Mechthild of Magdeburg (d. 1277), a Cistercian nun in a convent near Eisleben, had already written mystical treatises in German, and several German theologians at the turn of the century had written speculative mystical treatises, but Meister Eckhart towers so far above them that they have been all but forgotten.

Of a noble family near Gotha, Meister Eckhart became a Dominican and received his master's degree at Paris in 1302. From 1303 to 1311 he served as provincial head of the order in Saxony. He returned to teach in Paris in 1311, spent some time in Strassburg, and rounded out his career as lecturer in Cologne. He wrote a large scholastic theological work, German tracts, and sermons he had preached in a Dominican convent, expressing his mystical theology in nontechnical language for the ladies, most of whom were of course considered too weak-minded to follow a technical discourse, and in any case had received little education. Because of his notion of the divine spark in man, which unites with the divinity in the mystical experience, he was accused of pantheistic tendencies. He died while his heresy trial

was under way, and when it was concluded two years later, the inquisitors condemned twenty-eight of his sentences.

Eckhart was influenced by Bernard of Clairvaux, the Arabic philosophers
Avicenna and Averroës, the Jewish Aristotelian Moses Maimonides, and most of all
St. Thomas. His work was largely concerned with traditional church dogma, and
the trend of his thought was toward a Neoplatonic interpretation of St. Thomas.
He believed God to be absolute being (*Esse est deus*). The central religious experience is the mysterious occurrence of the birth of God in the soul. Through this birth
the downward flood of the divine reaches its goal and proceeds in that same in-
stant to flow again toward its center in the heart of God. The mystical way begins
with negation, a mental purgative, an emptying of the soul of every created thing,
of all images. In this state of emptiness one is overwhelmed by a feeling of despair
—the dark night of the soul, as the Spanish mystic St. John of the Cross was later
to call it. At that moment, when one feels that one is farthest from God, there
occurs the birth of God in the soul. The divine spark (*scintilla*) in man leaps
across the chasm and experiences momentary union with God. The traditional
dogmas of sin, grace, the incarnation in Christ fade into the background in this
context, and pantheistic tendencies are truly in evidence.

Two passages from Eckhart's sermons will serve to illustrate not only his central theme, but also the way in which he endeavored to make his mystical theology
religiously effective.

> God is foolishly in love with us; it seems that He has forgotten heaven and
> earth and happiness and deity; His entire business seems to be with me alone, to
> give me everything to comfort me; He gives it to me suddenly, He gives it to me
> wholly, He gives it to me perfect, He gives it all the time, and He gives it to all
> creatures [Sermon XCI].

> Know then that God is bound to act, to pour Himself out [into thee] as soon
> as ever He shall find thee ready. . . . Finding thee ready, He is obliged to act, to
> overflow into thee. . . . God cannot leave anything void and unfilled. . . . It is one
> flash the being ready and the pouring in: the instant spirit is ready, God enters
> without hesitation or delay. Thou needest not seek Him here or there, He is no
> further off than the door of thy heart; there He stands lingering, awaiting whoever
> is ready to open and let him in. He waits more patiently than thou for thee to open
> to Him. He longs for thee a thousandfold more urgently than thou for Him: one
> point, the opening and the entering [Sermon IV].

Eckhart's influence upon later intellectual history was very great, one religious line
running through the Reformation to Pietism, another philosophical line running to
Nicholas Cusanus, Jakob Böhme, Immanuel Kant, and German idealism. But his
most immediately powerful influence was upon younger German mystics.

Johann Tauler (*c.* 1300–1361), a famous preacher in Strassburg in the best
Dominican tradition, was strongly under the influence of Eckhart. He stressed the
inwardness of religious experience, sought to avoid the pantheistic implications of

Eckhart's theology, and stressed the practical good to be derived from the mystical experience when the believer returns from union with God to perform works of love toward his neighbor. He had an important influence upon the fifteenth-century Rhenish mystic-reformer Wessel Gansfort, who died in Groningen in 1489. Tauler also made a great impression upon Luther in his formative years.

Henry Suso (1295–1366), a Dominican of a noble Swabian family, lived most of his life in Constance and Ulm. A delicate, poetic, gentle soul who lived a strenuously ascetic life, he wrote a sweet life of *The Blessed Henry Suso Himself,* which reveals his inward experiences. His *Book of Eternal Wisdom* was a beautiful expression of mystical experience.

The leading mystic in the Netherlands was Johannes van Ruysbroeck (1293–1381), a priest and later a canon near Brussels. Nicknamed the *doctor ecstaticus,* this Augustinian mystic stressed the simplicity of the Christian life and the participation of the laity in religious life.

Groups of devout folk joined together in loose associations during these years to share and encourage each other in their efforts toward mystical experience. The Friends of God, like other groups of the kind, included both lay members (Ruleman Merswin, a Strassburg merchant, was one) and religious (Henry Suso's spiritual friend Elsbeth Stagel, a nun in Winterthur, was another). It is difficult at times to distinguish associations of this kind from the heretical sects that sprang up in the Rhineland during these centuries of the waning Middle Ages.

Mysticism was not exclusively a German phenomenon by any means. England produced the *Book of the Nine Rocks.* Catherine of Siena was, of course, Italian. Two of the greatest mystics of all time, St. Teresa and St. John of the Cross, lived in Spain's golden age in the sixteenth century. A militant young girl who heard the voices of saints, Joan of Arc, was the heroine of the French. And the most influential movement of the time, the Brethren of the Common Life, was Dutch in origin and inspiration.

In Gerard Groote (1340–1384) the Netherlands produced a most remarkable man. Born in Deventer, he studied first in Aachen and then took up medicine, theology, and canon law at the Sorbonne in Paris, returning home when scarcely eighteen years old. He taught in the cathedral school in Deventer and at the University of Cologne, well supported by prebends. A former fellow student at the Sorbonne warned him so earnestly of the vanity of his life that Groote underwent a conversion experience and retired to an ascetic life of devotion. An encounter with the mystic Johannes van Ruysbroeck further deepened his mystical impulses, and he spent three years in repentance and prayer. He received a license to preach and attracted a devoted following. His best student, Florentius Radewyns, once put to him this question: "Master, why do we not pool our efforts and earnings, why do we not work and pray together under the guidance of our common Father?" And so the Brethren of the Common Life came into being, a free religious organization of clerics and laity living a life monastic in style but without an official vow. Groote dreamed of organizing the various communities at Zwolle, Deventer, and Windesheim into a brotherhood of canons regular, but he died of the plague while caring for the sick and further organization was left to Radewyns.

Groote was a successful practical mystic. Whereas for Eckhart and other cerebral mystics speculative reason played an important part in the preliminary stages of the mystical experience, the love of God so moved the "voluntaristic mystics" to love their neighbors that they were impelled to apply in everyday life the religious inspiration derived from the mystical experience. This practical emphasis explains the activist philosophy of the Brethren. It was possibly one more manifestation of the shift during the Renaissance away from the contemplative life as the highest good in itself to an appreciation of the active life as the expression of the inner spirit of man.

The Brethren of the Common Life, or *Devotio moderna,* attempted to live like the primitive Christian communities described in Acts 4. Laymen were in a majority, and each community was likely to select a layman as rector. Thomas à Kempis (*c.* 1380–1471) became the virtual embodiment of the Brethren's ideals of piety. His life spanned ninety-one years, and he lived through most of the vigorous first century of the association's growth. The son of a peasant, Thomas was educated at Deventer in mystical theology and practical benevolence. He was a withdrawn, scholarly man, and on the counseling of Florentius Radewyns he entered the Augustinian convent of Mount St. Agnes in Zwolle. The order of Augustinian or Austin canons had a certain affinity with the Brethren in theology and way of life, and contributed much to religious reform in the Netherlands and the Germanies. Thomas labored as a copyist, wrote biographies of Groote, Radewyns, and other Brethren, composed tracts on the monastic life, and was the author or compiler of one of the most influential books the world has ever seen, *The Imitation of Christ,* which exists in hundreds of editions and has been translated into more languages than any other book with the exception of the Bible itself. The *Imitation* taught a practical piety, offered useful admonitions, and recommended a devout way of life in imitation of the Master. There is nothing of a highly rationalized theology, but rather, as in the fourth book on the Sacrament, a communication of the religion of the heart filled with celestial love.

The brothers worked as artisans in shops, instructed the poor, taught in their own schools, supported homes for poor students near cathedral schools and in university towns, copied classical and Christian manuscripts, and operated printing presses for devotional and even some scholarly material. In the schools they used the texts of the "safe classics"—that is, the moral philosophy of Seneca and Cicero, the clean poets, and pedagogically sound rhetoricians. They have, in fact, been described with some truth as one source of the northern Renaissance. Their spiritualist emphasis and Stoic ethic inadvertently tended to minimize the importance of the sacerdotal apparatus for the salvation of the individual.

From Deventer, Zwolle, and Windesheim the Brethren spread through the

Netherlands, along the Rhine through Westphalia, Hesse, and Württemberg, as well as eastward along the North and Baltic Seas into Saxony and as far as Kulm. Many of the most famous men of the fifteenth and sixteenth centuries were educated or supported by the Brethren, including Cusanus, Agricola, Celtis, Mutian, Erasmus, and Luther. Only one of the Brethren's communities joined the Protestant Reformation as a group, for they represented essentially an efflorescence of late medieval piety. They declined rapidly in the second half of the sixteenth century, and by the middle of the seventeenth century all the houses had passed out of existence.

When we look back upon this great efflorescence of mysticism in these centuries, it is hard to resist speculating on why it occurred when and where it did. It was a time of turmoil and crisis, of course, and one could easily conclude that such times drive people to an internal migration. But other periods of crisis failed to produce such a movement, and the Spanish mystics emerged at a time when their land was flourishing. Perhaps with the desiccation of theology by the later scholastics, religious impulses found natural expression in mysticism. But the absolute contrast once made between scholasticism and mysticism seems no longer tenable, for some scholastics had a mystical component to their thought, and at least some mystics, such as Eckhart, were schooled in scholasticism. Nor can mysticism be considered a form of rebellion against institutional religion, for most of the mystics were obedient and devoted sons of the church. The implications of the mystics' direct encounter with God were nonsacerdotal and could be nonsacramental. But mysticism cannot be communicated to the masses, so it must be considered more a personal reaction than a general form of rebellion.

Another fascinating theory is that there is a pendular movement in intellectual history from the rational to the nonrational, or from rationalism to romanticism. The Augustinian Platonic period in the early Middle Ages was followed by the first stage in the development of scholastic theology in the eleventh century. There followed then the twelfth-century Renaissance of humanism and mysticism. The high period of scholastic thought in the thirteenth century and the first half of the fourteenth century was then superseded by humanism in Italy and mysticism in the North during the fourteenth and fifteenth centuries.

There is some small element of truth in each of these explanations. But the more immediate source of mysticism was the intensification of religious feeling in the fourteenth and fifteenth centuries, a direct product of the crisis in spirit that accompanied the medieval institutional breakdown and the accelerated pace of historical change.

SCHOLASTICISM

In the medieval vision of reality the whole universe belonged to an objective and cosmic system. Everything had its place in a static hierarchy of complexity and value. This order was ideal and could be grasped by the human mind. This general optimistic confidence in man's intellectual capacity was a necessary precondition for the philosophical and theological enterprise of the scholastic doctors, for they believed that theology as well as philosophy was well ordered and could be treated systematically, even by logical syllogisms.

A scholarly controversy still rages around the question of the decadence or vitality of scholasticism in its third and final phase at the end of the Middle Ages. The older view, still widely held, was that the thirteenth century saw the grand synthesis in the Dominican St. Thomas' *Summa theologica* and *Summa contra gentiles,* and that the fourteenth century was dominated by the Franciscan nominalists, who precipitated the disintegration of scholastic philosophy. Late scholasticism was a decadent form of school learning, not only lacking in creativity and originality, but given to an antirational voluntarism, semi-Pelagianism, and epistemological skepticism.

This view of late scholasticism as a school subject cultivated by Johnny-come-latelies derived from the very days of the Renaissance, when humanists and reformers poured scorn upon the scholastic doctors as pedants and bores. Erasmus wrote them off with phrases such as this: "A scab of a fellow, theology incarnate!" His friend Sir Thomas More sneered: "A man might as soon obtain bodily nourishment by milking a he-goat into a sieve as spiritual nourishment by reading the schoolmen." The futility of refined scholastic distinctions became a fixed idea in literature. The French playwright Molière has a famous satirical passage in which the scholastic student recites by rote the profundity that opium makes one sleep because it is possessed of a dormitive virtue. In referring to the famous scholastic argument from the purpose of created things, Francis Bacon made the wicked thrust: "Teleology is like a virgin consecrated to God, it is noble but produces no offspring." Given a press like that, it is little short of miraculous that late scholasticism should find apologists and a revisionist school to defend it.

The founder of the *via moderna* in scholastic thought was William of Occam, the critic of the church discussed previously, who wrote during the first half of the fourteenth century. An English Franciscan, Occam knew the works of the subtle doctor John Duns Scotus. He lived for some time in Paris. In 1328 he fled to the protection of Ludwig of Bavaria, who as secular ruler was defying the pope, and died in Munich. The modernists celebrated Occam as their "venerable teacher," and he was highly regarded in this theological tradition as late as the time of Luther, who spoke of "Occam, my dear master." Occam wrote no complete summa as such, and yet from the great bulk of his writings a fairly consistent point of view and unified system emerge.

The position he took on the question of universals is perhaps the most widely known feature of his thought, important for the problem of knowledge in philosophy as well as for its theological implications. On the question of whether universals exist prior to the particular (*universalia ante rem:* high realism), whether they exist in the particular (*universalia in rem:* moderate realism), or whether they are terms derived from the particular (*universalia post rem:* terminism), Occam most nearly approached the third position. This epistemological assumption that universals are terms (*termini*) or symbols, which have no reality outside the mind of man, came to be known from the fifteenth century on as nominalism, a term derived from *nomen,* name, since the universal was merely a convenient name for a collection of particulars. Occam was accused of fostering skepticism, and certain later nominalists were flatly accused of being skeptics, since it was readily seen that a consistent nominalism made certain theological concepts, such as the Trinity and transubstantiation in the Eucharist, very difficult to hold. The revisionist view on Occam, however, while granting his importance for symbolic logic, denies that he was an extreme empiricist or an extreme skeptic. For Occam the mind works actively on an object, and therefore a high degree of empirical knowledge is possible. Nor were his followers thorough skeptics either in philosophy or in theology.

On the question of faith and reason, Occam was said to hold that faith and knowledge are far from each other and that it is impossible to base faith upon reason. This position contributed to a double theory of truth, it has been asserted: that some things are true in philosophy that are not true in theology and vice versa. Occam argued that religious truth had to be accepted upon the authority of the church. Like Thomas Aquinas, Occam believed that some things are known by reason and some by revelation. He did lower the line between the two realms, putting a larger number of religious truths within the scope of revelation. Occam resorted to the Bible and to the authority of the church as the basis of religious truth. Two characteristic statements read:

> Therefore the Christian is not by the necessity of salvation bound to believe; nor is he to believe what is neither contained in the Bible, nor can be inferred by necessary and manifest consequence alone from the things contained in the Bible.
>
> This is my faith, since it is the Catholic faith; for whatever the Roman church believes, this alone and not anything else do I believe either explicitly or implicitly.

It is interesting to note that Occam was never officially condemned by the church for his teachings, any more than was St. Thomas when certain of his propositions were called into question.

A central question in theology was the doctrine of justification: how man, a sinner, is made righteous and acceptable to God. Occam stressed the omnipotence of God and the force of his will so strongly that the idea that God quite arbitrarily predestines some men to salvation and some to condemnation seemed to be a natural corollary. At the same time, Occam seemed to emphasize man's freedom of will and his ability to do good works, and thus to contribute to his own salvation. A closer study of Occam, however, shows that he stressed the difference between divine omnipotence as an absolute power (*potentia absoluta*), by which God can do anything he chooses to do, and a regulated power (*potentia ordinata*), by which God actually does only those things he has chosen to do. God has set limits to his own actions, so that they are not arbitrary, but regulated. The terms of salvation that he has laid down for man in revelation and in church teaching allow for a substantial contribution by man to his own salvation. Occam and his followers were consistently semi-Pelagian on the question of justification. The idea that man, while dependent for salvation upon God's forgiving grace, can and must, on his own initiative, take steps to accept or reject God's help in overcoming original sin harmonized nicely with church teachings and popular religious practices in those centuries.

Erasmus professed to be badly bewildered by the many schools of thought and the refined differences among the scholastics. "One might sooner," he sighed, "find one's way about a labyrinth than through the intellectual mazes of the Realists, Nominalists, Thomists, Albertists, Occamists, Scotists." Although Erasmus habitually put the worst construction on things, he was justified in professing confusion in this instance, for the picture of two fairly well-defined scholastic systems at war with each other is much oversimplified. The renowned "battle of the *viae*" in the universities, with the *via antiqua* of Thomas engaged in a struggle to the death with the *via moderna* of Occam, was really less a pitched battle between well-ordered forces than a running skirmish and confused guerrilla warfare. Many philosophers and theologians were trained in both *viae*, and the humanists, followed by the reformers, were variously educated in one or the other of them.

The mendicant orders were in decline during these last two centuries, with rival groups within both the Dominican and Franciscan orders. Moreover, the universities, which were still important centers of intellectual life in the fourteenth century, lost their preeminence in intellectual life to academies and court circles during the fifteenth century. The newer universities in the empire, founded for the most part by princes and city councils, showed greater vitality, but did not reach the level of eminence Oxford or Paris had held. Universities became a major force again in the sixteenth century with the founding of new Lutheran and Calvinist universities and the revitalization of some older Catholic centers.

The overall picture that emerges from the newer studies of late scholasticism is not one of complete decadence. Nominalism was not uniformly skeptical or subversive of theology. If many minor figures and pedantic teachers of logic killed the subject with nice but unimportant distinctions, there were other men, such as Marsilius of Inghen and Gabriel Biel, still capable of thinking through the problems posed by Thomas and Occam. Their writings reveal deep pastoral concern and cover a broad range of theological subjects. But if one asks whether the late scholastics were truly creative in the sense of innovation and insight beyond the achievements of the great schoolmen, the response must be in the negative. Perhaps their theology, to say nothing of their philosophy, had run its course. The humanists and reformers certainly overstated their case against the schoolmen and misled even modern scholars with their vilifications; but the alternatives they offered had more appeal to their contemporaries, and so history moved from medieval thought into the Renaissance and Reformation.

POPULAR RELIGION

The gap that always exists between the highly educated intellectual elite and the great mass of the people was an enormous chasm in the fourteenth and fifteenth centuries. An apt parallel could perhaps be drawn between the scholastic theologians and superstitious masses then and today's handful of high-energy physicists, who really understand what can be known of the secrets of the atom, and the great bulk of the population, which enjoys only some faint glimmer of what science has to teach. There were then far fewer educational and technological devices for the dissemination of learning than today, so that to find the masses given not only to a primitive piety but often to abject superstition is not at all surprising.

During the somber fourteenth century an apocalyptic mood settled over Europe and it lasted into the sixteenth century, with some relief in Renaissance Italy in the *Quattrocento*. The Great Plague in the middle of the fourteenth century and the continued recurrence of this pestilence brought home to everyone the transiency of life. The shadow of the crescent across Christendom, as the Turks made their seemingly irresistible advance up the Danube and repeatedly landed in Italy, contributed to the feeling of despair. At the end of the fifteenth century a new scourge in the form of syphilis, against which Europeans had virtually no immunity or resistance, swept across the continent. On all levels of society, rich and poor, powerful and powerless, men feared an early and miserable death. In the fourteenth-century tapestries in the Cathedral of Angers, the woodcuts of the depressed Albrecht Dürer, the paintings of the great flood to come by Leonardo da Vinci—everywhere brooded death and impending catastrophe.

The masses were swept up into feverish religious activity. Old religious practices were revived and embraced with new fervor. New forms of religious expression were devised with astonishing ingenuity. Prayers at the fourteen stations of the cross along the *via dolorosa* were introduced. The use of the rosary became common. Mary became the gentle intermediary between the sinner and Christ, the stern judge who will preside at the last day. As a corollary to the idea of the Immaculate Conception of Mary, a Scotist idea that the Franciscans championed against Dominican resistance, the cult of St. Anne, the mother of Mary, spread across Europe from Spain to Poland. New saints came into vogue: St. Christopher for travelers and St. Rochus, a special protector against the plague. New relics, massive sales of indulgences, and new shrines for pilgrims appeared everywhere. Tens of thousands of pilgrims clogged the roads to the shrine of Loreto near Ancona, to St. James of Compostela in Spain, to St. Michael's in Normandy, to

Jerusalem, and to the graves of the apostles in Rome. With the invention of printing, travel guides and city directories to local shrines were published. Artisans and merchants, men and women alike, joined in sodalities or brotherhoods, in order to combine their prayers, good works, and spiritual efforts to build up a treasury of merit for their mutual insurance.

This religious fervor affected all classes: kings, princes, burghers, countrymen. The mighty men of earthly kingdoms, and some wise humanists, donned monkish garb to die and were buried in monastic churches. In the age of the Renaissance people of wealth added an individualistic innovation: rather than involving themselves with the whole community in the construction of cathedrals, as in the Middle Ages, they built small but impressive private chapels. One thinks almost immediately of the Pazzi Chapel, begun in 1429, the Brancacci Chapel at the Church of the Carmine in Florence, the Medici Chapel, the Fugger Chapel in Augsburg, and the many new oratories. The city of Cologne, with nineteen parish churches, had at this time more than a hundred chapels, many of them privately built and endowed.

Inside the cathedrals the aristocratic and wealthy bourgeois families endowed their own altars, side-aisle chapels, stained-glass windows, liturgical ornaments and vestments. Anxious patrons subsidized altar paintings and murals. Enrico Scrovegni, eager to atone for the evil done by his father, a notorious usurer whom Dante relegated to the seventh circle of hell (*Inferno,* Canto 17, lines 64–66), endowed the fresco cycle in the Arena Chapel in Padua, Giotto's most wonderful surviving monument. The paintings of the time took up new religious themes, with a special predilection for the passive, as if to encourage the viewer to contemplate the sufferings of Christ and the saints. In the fourteenth century the theme of Mary weeping for her dead son lying across her lap was transposed from poetry to art and appeared in the sculptured *Pietà.* Christ, formerly seen as remote and passionless, was now frequently represented as a man of sorrow and acquainted with grief. A new technique was employed for achieving a central perspective in altar paintings. But despite all the innovations and additions, the high altar dominated all the rest as mother church remained for the time being intact.

It is a striking fact that when the printing press began the large-scale production of books, devotional tracts and prayerbooks by far outnumbered titles of any other kind. It is necessary to bear this religious fervor in mind, for one cannot otherwise understand the impact of Savonarola's preaching, the sweetness of Raphael's Madonnas, or the very existence of Ludovico il Moro's beautiful black vellum prayerbook.

In such a garden of religious flowers, the devil was sure to plant his seeds of superstition, deceit, black magic, and witchcraft. The ignorance and credulity of the age provided fertile soil for some of the most heinous outgrowths ever to afflict the earth. Popular religion consisted of a fascinating mixture of Christian and old pagan elements. The world was still full of demons and things that go bump in the night. The fear of the incubus and succubus, male and female evil spirits that lay in intercourse upon mortals, was a real terror to many simple folk. Incantations and magic formulas offered some sort of control over the mysterious forces of nature and the supernatural. The declining Middle Ages saw the greatest flourishing of the art of alchemy. With the spread of the Neoplatonic cosmology, with its light metaphysic and theory of the sympathetic bonds that held all parts of the universe together and related a man to the stars, belief in astrology actually increased during the star-crossed Renaissance. It appealed not only to the simple, but to men in high stations. Kings and scholars consulted their horoscopes.

Emotional religious groups of flagellants—the Beghards, Beguines, Humiliati, Brethren of the Free Spirit, and others—were not simply drawn from the urban proletariat or from the illiterate peasantry. Attractive though the theory may be that these were assemblies of the dispossessed, early victims of a heartless industrial society, the truth is that their membership was not drawn solely from the textile workers or uprooted peasants. Members included people of all walks of life, and their literature is replete with admonitions to put away luxuries, warnings the desperately poor hardly needed.

Even though the church had worked for centuries at rooting out pagan idolatries and superstitions, in these decades churchmen did unspeakable damage by lending credence and support to a most vicious form of demonology. In 1484 Pope Innocent VIII authorized two Dominicans, Heinrich Krämer and Jakob Sprenger, talented inquisitors, to root out witchcraft in the diocese of Constance. The papal bull *Summis desiderantes affectibus* graphically described the evil deeds of witches and even prescribed ecclesiastical punishment against anyone who protested against the prosecution of witches. The two experienced "hounds of the Lord" then published in 1487 a book entitled *Malleus maleficarum (The Hammer of Evildoers)*, which codified the many devices of witches and told how they could be recognized. This book had appeared in over thirty editions by the middle of the seventeenth century. The craze lasted well into the seventeenth century (there was an isolated case of the execution of a witch in Mexico as late as the nineteenth century) and claimed the lives of hundreds of thousands of poor wretches, many burned alive. Not until the twentieth century did man's inhumanity to man equal these horrors. Innocent VIII, it must be remembered, was not a prelate of the Dark Ages, but a famous Renaissance pope of good family.

The Renaissance Popes

A THOUSAND YEARS had passed into history since St. Ambrose wrote to St. Augustine, "If you are at Rome, live in the Roman style; if you are elsewhere; live as they live elsewhere." A good moralist could hardly recommend living in the Roman style to a saint in the *Quattrocento;* quite the opposite. An embittered realist, the historian-statesman Francesco Guicciardini, wrote, "So much evil cannot be said of the Roman curia that more does not deserve to be said of it, for it is an infamy, an example of all the shame and wickedness of the world." Bemoaning the ills of one's own age is a pastime not without value and certainly not without precedent. At the height of Roman civilization the poet Horace wailed, "We are the degenerate descendants of fathers who in their turn were degenerate from their forebears." But the decades of the Renaissance popes marked the nadir in the long history of the papacy.

It is ironic that just when Pius II marked the triumph of the monarchical episcopate over councils with his bull *Execrabilis* (1460) and the popes were in a position to reassert verbally their claims to fullness of power, they were reduced to the status of Italian princes. The papacy, largely because it possessed the Papal States, became the plaything of powerful Italian and Spanish families. Both Sixtus IV and Alexander VI seriously contemplated secularizing the papal territories into a family principality.

The tone of the whole curia was exceedingly worldly. The cardinals, analogous to the old Roman senate under the emperor, thought it their duty to live as princes of the church, with courts of their own. These lofty wearers of the red hat in conclave elected new popes, counseled the pontiff on financial, diplomatic, and legal questions, facilitated appointments to office, served as secretaries, legates, and nuncios, and acted in many other important capacities. The Renaissance popes were free with appointments and greatly enlarged the college. Pope Sixtus IV created thirty-four cardinals and Alexander VI and Leo X each created forty-three. From the close of the year 1471 to May 1527 there were 183 cardinals, about 90 percent of whom resided in Rome and served as part of the curia. Since many were elderly at the time of their appointment, an average of twenty-five or thirty were members of the curia at any given time.

Many came from princely families or rich bourgeois Italian banking families, and lived in Roman *palazzi* in the style to which they were accustomed. Cardinal Pietro Barbo's palace and the Riario palace rivaled the papal palace itself in size and grandeur. In 1509 the average cardinal's household had 154 servants, with many additional attendants. The cardinals served as official hosts to visiting royalty and high ecclesiasts, and so needed a high income. Erasmus wrote in 1535 that no one with an income of less than three thousand ducats a year could become a cardinal. In reality a few cardinals had incomes well over twelve thousand ducats a year. They drew their incomes from curial sources (fees for services and so on), revenues from benefices, pensions, and private fortunes; for some owned mines, and others, like the Farneses, had rich family estates.[1] These grandees, given to

---

[1] D. S. Chambers, "The Economic Predicament of Renaissance Cardinals," in *Studies in Medieval and Renaissance History,* ed. William M. Bowsky, 5 vols. (Lincoln, Nebr., 1963–1968), vol. 3, pp. 289–371. See also P. Partner, "The Budget of the Roman Church in the Renaissance Period," in *Italian Renaissance Studies,* ed. E. F. Jacob (London, 1960), pp. 256–78.

splendid living and enjoying great power, were not likely to be very reform-minded or to welcome a pontiff who would be a radical renovator.

The Renaissance pope, successor to St. Peter, the lowly fisherman, was in a difficult position. He was the head of a worldwide institution and prince of an Italian state, but at the same time he was the spiritual leader looked to for inspiration by all Christendom. Moreover, in such a brilliant age the lure of beauty was apt to cast a powerful spell. "The beautiful," a fifth-century Christian had declared, "wherever it may be, is the property of the truth." This thought may well have served as the motto, or the rationalization, for the popes of the Renaissance.

NICHOLAS V

The first of the Renaissance popes, Nicholas V, elected in 1447, still had the task of facing down Felix V, the Council of Basel's counterpope. He was taken with two big ideas, internal reform and external crusade. He envisioned a spiritual renewal in Christendom and encouraged John of Capistrano in his preaching mission in Italy, the empire, and Poland. He entrusted to Cardinal Nicholas Cusanus the reform of abuses among the secular and regular clergy of the empire (1450–1452), but Cusanus' ability to accomplish much in this direction also came into question by his failure as bishop of Brixen, where he had been besieged by the archduke of Austria and nearly killed. The pope entrusted to cardinal William d'Estouteville the reform of schools and colleges in France. He himself undertook the overhaul of government in Rome and the Papal States.

Nicholas V was a great patron of men of art and letters. The humanist Poggio Bracciolini served as one of his secretaries. He founded anew the Vatican library and developed grandiose schemes for rebuilding Rome. He repaired the walls of the city, refurbished its churches, began the rebuilding of St. Peter's, and offhandedly tore down the basilica of Constantine to make room for a new building in the Renaissance style. The famous Trevi Fountain was built during his pontificate. In 1450 he presided over a grand jubilee, which drew great throngs of people to Rome, but the plague struck with disastrous fury.

Shaken by the message that the Turks had taken Constantinople, he planned a crusade to free the city, a futile gesture. That very year a young nobleman was caught in a plot to assassinate him. So well intentioned and yet so often frustrated, Pope Nicholas died in March 1455, it is said of grief and sorrow.

CALIXTUS III

The election of the Spanish cardinal Alfonso Borgia as Pope Calixtus III was ominous, for it was a sign that Spain's shadow was lengthening over Italy. Notorious for nepotism, he brought to Rome his nephew Rodrigo Borgia, the future

Alexander VI. His love of his nephew was equaled only by his hatred for the Turks. He swore that he would shed his own blood to liberate Constantinople. He called the princes to a crusade and sold many of his own belongings to build a papal fleet. In the Magyar noble János Hunyadi he found his man. Mohammed II planned to take the rich plains of Hungary and needed to capture Belgrade as the key to the central Danube valley. Hunyadi fortified Belgrade and on July 14, 1456, his flotilla annihilated the Turkish fleet. A week later he captured the Turks' camps and forced the sultan to withdraw to Constantinople. Hunyadi died of the plague only three weeks after his great victory, and although Belgrade itself remained in the hands of the Hungarians, internal dissention in Hungary enabled the Turks to bring all the rest of Serbia under their control within three years. The Turks then turned their attention southward; and on the very day that Corinth fell, Pope Calixtus III died.

PIUS II

In his *Memoirs* the humanist Aeneas Silvius Piccolomini left to posterity a beautiful document providing exciting insights into his mind and view of life. He wrote descriptions of Bohemia and praised German culture, which flourished under the aegis of the Roman church. He was a member of the imperial chancery in the service of Frederick III in Vienna, 1442–1445. He wrote a novel, *Eurialus et Lucretia,* in which he portrayed the primitive passions of a love affair between a German knight and a Sienese lady. He also wrote a comedy entitled *Chrysis.* But once he was elected pope in 1458, Aeneas abandoned his secular literary pursuits and became a serious churchman. Taking the name Pius, he urged everyone to *"Aeneam reiicite, Pium recipite"* (reject Aeneas, accept Pius).

As pope he had to struggle against the exuberance of his times. His former fellow humanists were disappointed that he showed them fewer favors than they had hoped to receive. In a visit to Florence he was received like a Renaissance prince. The city staged a great spectacle by turning loose in the Piazza della Signoria a swarm of lions, dogs, deer, and other beasts for a general melee. But the lions lay down lazily and refused to attack, to the general disappointment of the crowd.

Pius II was most serious about a crusade against the Turks, who were now making punitive raids on Italy itself, and announced that he would personally lead a crusade against them. But other business detained him, and by the time the fleet of twelve galleys that he had summoned from Venice arrived at Ancona, on the Adriatic coast, on August 12, 1464, his other forces had dwindled away. Pius had been waiting for the ships at Ancona for some time. Though he knew a crusade was impossible now, he blessed the ships, and three days later he died—of a broken heart, it was said. "A good death," Pius declared, "atones for an evil life."

PAUL II

The conclave chose next a luxury-loving Venetian, Paul II, who reigned from 1464 to 1471. The new pope loved beauty, collected antiquities, and was a friend of learning. He was much maligned as illiterate by the humanists, because he suppressed as pagan the Roman Academy, headed by Pomponius Laetus. The academy drew many of its members from the College of Abbreviators in the papal chancery. They affected ancient Roman styles, celebrated Plato's birthday, and made a convincing show of reviving the pagan past. A man of courage, Paul II deposed George of Podiebrad, king of Bohemia, for his heretical "Hussite" beliefs.

SIXTUS IV

Paul's successor, Francesco della Rovere, the first of the three evil geniuses of the Renaissance papacy, had been general of the Franciscan order, and seemed determined by his lavish spending to reduce the whole church to the poverty of the mendicants. An unabashed nepotist, he sought to carve out of the Papal States a principality for his nephew Girolamo Riario. He almost certainly knew of Riario's involvement in the plot that resulted in the assassination of Giovanni de' Medici and the wounding of Lorenzo the Magnificent in the Florence Cathedral in 1478.

Although he lived a simple and fairly austere life himself, he was a veritable Maecenas, giving away papal money as long as he had any to give. He favored the mendicants, of course, and built a foundling hospital. He built the Sistine Chapel and patronized Domenico Ghirlandaio, the famous fresco painter, as well as the splendid artists Botticelli and Perugino.

INNOCENT VIII

The most notorious of the bad popes was quite literally *pappa*. The sire of sixteen children, he acknowledged his bastards openly and celebrated their nuptials in the Vatican. Cynicism and corruption corroded the moral fiber of the whole curia. The pope's vice-chamberlain was quoted as saying, "The Lord desireth not the death of a sinner, but that he live and pay." A ring of cardinals made a huge sum of money by forging bulls for sale. The pope had to pawn his triple tiara in 1484 for 100,000 ducats. It is not surprising, then, to see him accepting 40,000 ducats annually from the Turkish sultan Bayazid II to keep as his prisoner Djem, the sultan's brother and rival for the throne, who had fled for protection to the Knights of St. John. As though to choke off criticism by a show of force, the pope encouraged Torquemada and the Inquisition, issued a bull calling for the extermination of the Waldensians, an ascetic evangelical sect that had been persecuted for centuries, and sponsored a sale of indulgences to finance another drive against them.

ALEXANDER VI

Rodrigo Borgia, the nephew of Calixtus III, virtually bought the papacy. With most of Spain united by the marriage of Isabella of Castile and crafty Ferdinand of Aragon, Spanish fortunes were in the ascendancy. When Innocent VIII died in 1492, the same year that the reconquest of Spain from the Moors was completed, Rodrigo Borgia was in a splendid financial condition to bribe enough cardinals to assure himself of the two-thirds of the votes necessary to elect him to the papacy. As Alexander VI he was a good manager of papal finances, but his aim was subversive, for he sought to carve out of the Papal States a principality for his family.

His favorite son, Giovanni, was possibly murdered by another of his sons, Cesare, many believed, and his body dumped into the Tiber. His daughter Lucretia was in charge of the papal palace. Notoriously immoral as a young woman, she seems after her marriage and with added years to have become a respectable matron. But Cesare Borgia became legendary as an unscrupulous murderer and assassin, thanks largely to the attention that Machiavelli paid to his methods of statecraft. Until his repudiation of the offices in 1498, Cesare was archbishop of Valencia and a cardinal. He fought fierce and bloody battles against the Roman nobility and feudal lords. The death of Alexander VI in 1503, perhaps of malaria, and Cesare's near-fatal illness, presumably caused by poison intended for a cardinal, ruined the Borgias. Cesare fled to Spain, where he died in 1507 in the service of the king of Navarre. The ultimate degradation, Friedrich Nietzsche once sneered, would have been Cesare Borgia as pope.

Alexander VI played the role of an earthly potentate in international relations. The Turk Djem was his personal friend and companion. The pope even sided with the sultan against the most Christian king of France. He excommunicated and engineered the burning of the reformer Girolamo Savonarola in Florence. It was Alexander VI who issued the bulls dividing up the newly discovered Western Hemisphere between Spain and Portugal.

Alexander VI was also a distinguished patron of the arts. He renewed the section of the city around the Vatican called the Borgo. He rebuilt and enlarged the Borgian apartments in the Vatican. He had Pinturicchio ornament them with their famous frescoes, one of which shows Alexander kneeling devoutly as he views the miracle of the resurrection.

JULIUS II

After the very brief interlude of Pius III in 1503, Alexander VI was succeeded in the same year by the nephew of Sixtus IV, Giuliano della Rovere, who became pope as Julius II. His countenance is familiar to us from the portraits of Bramante and Michelangelo, but above all from Raphael's painting showing him in armor astride a steed—not the prince of peace, but the victorious leader of the church militant. Guicciardini said of Julius II:

> He would have been a pope worthy of the highest renown, if he had been a secular prince or if the care and diligence he showed in glorifying the church in the temporal sphere and through the art of war had been used to glorify it in the spiritual sphere through the arts of peace; yet he was worthier than any of his predecessors to be honored and held in illustrious remembrance.

Julius II continued the wars of Cesare Borgia in order to secure actual control over the Papal States. He wished to build up the estate of the church, not of his own family. Julius battling for Mirandola, laying siege in the cold winter, with frost glistening on his white beard, makes a curious picture. Observers spoke of his *terribilità,* his fierce and restless energy. He took Perugia and Bologna, and then, in alliance with the French, pressed on against Venice. Then he joined with Venice and Spain to organize the Holy League in order to drive out the king of France. He even called upon Henry VIII of England to occupy France. Louis XII of France reaffirmed the pragmatic sanction giving the Gallican church great independence, and in 1511 he summoned a council to Pisa to act against Julius II. But the Milanese and Swiss, friendly to Julius, sabotaged the council, and the French army had to withdraw north of the Alps. Thereupon Julius put the Council of Pisa under the interdict and convoked the Fifth Lateran Council as a counterthrust (1512–1517). In 1513 Pope Julius II enjoyed a triumphal entry into Rome worthy of a conquering caesar.

Julius spent lavishly not only on war, but on works of art, for he wished to make Rome a capital without equal. Already as a cardinal he had the architect Giuliano da San Gallo build for him a splendid *palazzo.* Now he had the renowned architect Bramante tear down the basilica of St. Peter and begin the construction of the greatest edifice in Christendom, St. Peter's Cathedral. Designed in the shape of a Greek cross and crowned by a mighty dome, it was to be the capitol of the Roman Catholic Church. Construction began on April 18, 1506. Bramante built additional structures north of the Vatican to extend this complex. Julius employed Perugino and Sodoma to redecorate with new frescoes the rooms above the Borgian apartments. From 1508 till his death in 1520, the incomparable Raphael executed the frescoes in the Julian apartments, which critics revere as perhaps the most beautiful of the entire Renaissance. With his taste for classical art, Julius had the Greek sculpture of Laocoön, unearthed in 1506 near the Baths of Titus, placed in the Belvedere Palace of the Vatican. No less an artistic giant than Michelangelo was commissioned to do a magnificent tomb for Julius, celebrating his military triumphs over the various principalities he had conquered. From 1508 to 1512 Michelangelo painted the frescoes on the ceiling of the Sistine Chapel, portraying the creation and the fall of man.

A peculiar combination of worldling and supernaturalist, Julius in 1507 sanctioned as a shrine the holy house of Loreto, which was commonly believed to have been the Lord's boyhood home, miraculously transported by angels from Nazareth. But even such gestures of piety or credulity were not enough to assuage the anger and disgust of religious men who believed that Christ's kingdom was truly not of this world. One of Julius' most devastating critics was the Christian humanist Erasmus. Erasmus had witnessed Julius II riding triumphantly into Bologna. Julius was, as a matter of fact, so proud of his victory that he commissioned Michelangelo to create a giant statue of himself, which he then placed over the entrance to the Church of San Petronio in Bologna. The Bolognese so hated Julius that at their first opportunity they tore it down and, since it was made of copper, melted it down and used it to make a cannon. Erasmus caught the grim irony and futility of the triumph of Pope Julius II, successor to St. Peter. In his *Praise of Folly* (1511) he wrote:

> Although in the Gospel the Apostle Peter says to his divine Master: We have left all and followed Thee, yet the popes call His patrimony lands, cities, tribute, principalities; for which, being enflamed with the love of Christ, they contend with fire and sword, and not without loss of much Christian blood, and boast that they have then most apostolically defended the Church, the spouse of Christ, when the enemy, as they call them, are valiantly routed. . . . Here you'll see decrepit old fellows acting the parts of young men, neither troubled at their enormous cost nor wearied with the labor involved . . . becoming, in short, the scourges of the human race.

Erasmus was so shocked that he could not let go of the subject. In his treatise *The Complaint of Peace* (1517) he still had Julius II in mind when he wrote, "What have the helmet and miter in common? What connection is there between the Holy Gospel and the buckler? How, O bishop standing in the room of the Apostles, dare you teach the people the things that pertain to war?"

Erasmus was so notorious as a scourge of Pope Julius that when an anonymous tract appeared in France attacking Julius, it was almost immediately attributed to Erasmus, although he just may have been truthful in disclaiming authorship. This dialogue, entitled *Julius exclusus*, has the pope appearing at last before the pearly gates:

> *Julius:* Open the door quick. If you had done your duty, you would have met me with the full ceremonies of heaven.
> *St. Peter:* You seem to like giving orders. Tell me who you are.
> *Julius:* You recognize me, of course.
> *St. Peter:* Do I? I've never seen you before, and at the moment I find the sight extraordinary.
> *Julius:* You must be blind. Surely you recognize this silver key. . . . Look at my triple crown and my jeweled pall.

St. Peter: I see a silver key. But it looks nothing like the keys which Christ, true
pastor of the Church, gave me. . . .[2]

Forbidden to enter, Julius threatens that when more of his troops arrive, he will
batter down the gates of heaven.

A tidal wave of moral indignation was sweeping across Europe on the very
eve of the Reformation.

LEO X

When Giovanni de' Medici, the unspiritual, art-loving, libertine son of Lorenzo
the Magnificent, entered the city of Rome as Pope Leo X in 1513, he came as
though celebrating a Roman triumph disguised as a Corpus Christi procession. The
cardinals and their families appeared in gorgeous attire. Then came the pope himself in ceremonial robes, riding under triumphal arches and flanked by columns
mounted with naked statues. One bold inscription read: "Once Venus ruled, then
Mars, but now Pallas Athena." The reference was obviously to Alexander VI,
Julius II, and Leo X.

Less warlike than Julius II, Leo X was an even more lavish spender. Already
in 1513 his debts amounted to more than 125,000 ducats. He loved luxury, pageantry, and entertainment, the more decadent the better. He loved to go hunting on
his estates, following the chase in a sedan chair carried by servants. He was entertained in the papal palace by three court jesters, two renegade monks, and a legless
cripple. Balthasar Castiglione, author of *The Courtier,* related in a letter to the
marquis of Mantua how Leo X had attended a revue at a carnival in 1521.
The pope particularly applauded the last tableau, which portrayed a group of
handsome young men, in the garb of monks, sleeping. Cupids entered and danced,
awakening the young men with their arrows. The monks stirred, joined in the
dance, and flung their frocks into the fire with joyful abandon.

King Manuel of Portugal understood the pope's mentality very well. He delighted Leo with the gift of a rhinoceros and an elephant. Leo rode through Rome
atop the elephant.

Leo X was no warrior, but a wily diplomat. He skillfully managed the Fifth
Lateran Council (1512–1517), which offered the last chance for conciliar reform before the great Protestant rebellion. In the opening address Aegidius (Giles) of
Viterbo had called for reform and offered a Christian humanist program for achieving it. But the council consisted mostly of reliable Italian churchmen, so that Leo X
had not too much to fear from them.

There was a general consensus at the council that the Turks were a terrible

---

[2] Owen Chadwick, *The Reformation* (Grand Rapids, 1965), p. 17.

threat, and on March 11, 1513, Leo X organized the Brotherhood of the Holy Crusade. The council decreed that heresy and schism should be suppressed; that the immortality of the soul must be held as the orthodox position against the Averroist denial; that the mobs must be restrained from looting the *palazzi* of cardinals when a pope died; and that unauthorized preachers must be forbidden to teach and the publication of bad books must be stopped. The council took a position against episcopalism, a condemnation that Leo X trumpeted in his bull *Pastor aeternus* (1516). And much to Leo's satisfaction, as a final act the council reaffirmed the claims of the bull *Unam sanctam* (1302), which had helped to bring such great misery down upon the church under Boniface VIII. It almost seemed as though the churchmen in the council assembled had indeed learned nothing and forgotten nothing, even after the passage of two disastrous centuries.

As a Medici, Leo X enjoyed all the advantages and suffered all the handicaps of coming of age in an urbane, sophisticated, and somewhat overrefined social situation. When as a mere boy he was made a member of the College of Cardinals, his worldly-wise father admonished him to be virtuous and added a warning: "I well know that as you are now to reside at Rome, that sink of all iniquity, the difficulty of conducting yourself by these admonitions will be increased. . . . You will probably meet with those who will particularly endeavor to corrupt and incite you to vice."[3] Leo X had a smooth and somewhat unctuous manner. He was affable rather than cordial, always controlled and poised, whether granting an official audience or peering at a masquerade through his jeweled opera glasses. He loved the company of men of letters such as Cardinal Pietro Bembo and Cardinal Jacopo Sadoleto. He was a patron of humanists and artists in the very best Medici tradition.

The years of Leo's pontificate are commonly referred to as the Leonine Age, for the special stamp that Leo impressed upon Renaissance art. A man of exquisite taste, he appreciated the genius of Raphael, and like his predecessor Julius II he commissioned Raphael to do many frescoes in the Vatican. One of the best known of these was in the room called Heliodorus, showing Leo I as the savior of Rome confronting Attila and the Huns. Raphael used the face of the tenth Leo to portray the first. Bramante had built a loggia on the Vatican's third story, and Raphael ornamented it with a fascinating combination of classical and Christian subjects. Bramante continued as chief architect for St. Peter's until he died in 1514, and then Leo appointed Raphael as his successor. Leo recognized the great genius of Michelangelo as well. He had him plan the façade for the Church of San Lorenzo in Florence, though nothing came of this, and commissioned him to do the massive tombs of the Medicis in the Church of San Lorenzo, a monument that will remain for all times a great triumph of Western art.

---

3 William Roscoe, *The Life of Lorenzo de' Medici,* 10th ed. (London, 1851), pp. 285–86.

Periodization in history is always open to discussion. Some scholars prefer to end the line of the Renaissance popes with Leo, for his death in 1521 coincided with the emergence of Luther upon the world scene at the Diet of Worms, ushering in the age of the Reformation. Others consider that the year 1527, when Rome was sacked by the troops of Charles V, more appropriately marks the close of the high Renaissance. Still others see the reign of earnest Adrian VI (1522–1523) as a mere interlude, and the pontificate of the second Medici pope, Clement VII (1523–1534), as still an integral part of the Renaissance. The somber Paul III (1534–1549) was the first pope of the Catholic Reformation. With Adrian, a Dutchman, and the pontificate of Clement, however, events in northern Europe became the critical determinants of the course of church history. Leo X was the last pope who in every way belonged to the age of the Italian Renaissance.

The Renaissance popes were really as much victims of their circumstances as they were the villains that historians have chosen to make them. They represented, even Alexander VI, a peculiar mixture of worldliness and formal personal piety, cynicism and credulity, evil design and good intentions. They managed to build up an enormous reservoir of distrust and hate and did the church untold harm; but the presence of unworthy men in ecclesiastical office did not in itself destroy the efficacy of the church. The judgment of Ludwig Pastor, the great nineteenth-century Catholic historian of the papacy, merits a sympathetic hearing:

> An imperfect setting does not affect the intrinsic worth of the jewel, nor does the golden coin lose its value when it passes through impure hands. In so far as the priest is a public officer of a holy Church, a blameless life is expected from him, both because he is by his office the model of virtue to whom the laity look up, and because his life, when virtuous, inspires in onlookers respect for the society of which he is an ornament. But the treasures of the Church, her Divine character, her holiness, Divine revelation, the grace of God, spiritual authority, it is well known, are not dependent on the moral character of the agents and officers of the Church. The foremost of her priests cannot diminish by an iota the intrinsic value of the spiritual treasures confided to him.[4]

Bibliography

Angeleri, Carlo. *Il Problema religioso del Rinascimento.* Florence, 1952.

Aubenas, R., and R. Ricard. *L'Église et la Renaissance, 1449–1517,* vol. 15 of *L'Histoire de l'Église,* ed. A. Fliche and V. Martin. Paris, 1951.

Barraclough, Geoffrey. *Papal Provisions.* Oxford, 1935.

Brooke, Z. N. *The English Church and the Papacy.* Cambridge, 1931.

Chambers, D. S. *Cardinal Bainbridge in the Court of Rome, 1509–1514.* London, 1965.

Clark, J. M. *The Great German Mystics: Eckhardt, Tauler, and Suso.* Oxford, 1949.

---

[4] Ludwig Pastor, *Geschichte der Päpste seit dem Ausgang des Mittelalters,* vol. 3 (Freiburg, 1895), p. 475, cited in "Alexander VI," in *The Catholic Encyclopedia* (New York, 1907), vol. 1, p. 293.

Creighton, M. *A History of the Papacy from the Great Schism to the Sack of Rome,* 6 vols. London, 1887–1894; new ed., London, 1903–05.

Dannenfeldt, Karl H. *The Church of the Renaissance and Reformation.* St. Louis, 1970.

Douglas, E. J. Dempsey. *Justification in Late Medieval Preaching: A Study of John Geiler of Keisersberg.* Leiden, 1966.

Ferguson, Wallace K. "The Church in a Changing World." *American Historical Review,* 59 (1953): 1–18.

Flick, A. C. *The Decline of the Medieval Church,* 2 vols. London, 1930.

Fromherz, Uta. *Johannes von Segovia als Geschichtsschreiber des Konzils von Basel.* Basel, 1960.

Fusero, Clemente. *The Borgias.* New York, 1972.

Gill, Joseph, S. J. *The Council of Florence.* New York, 1959.

———. *Eugenius IV: Pope of Christian Union.* Westminster, MD, 1961.

Guillemain, B. *La cour pontificale d'Avignon (1309–1376): Étude d'une société.* Paris, 1963.

Haller, Johannes. *Das Papsttum: Idee und Wirklichkeit,* 5 vols. Stuttgart, 1934–1950.

Heymann, Frederick G. *John Zizka and the Hussite Revolution.* Princeton, 1955.

Hughes, Philip. *A History of the Church,* vol. 3. London, 1947.

Jacob, Ernest F. *Essays in the Conciliar Epoch,* rev. ed. South Bend, IN, 1963.

Kaminsky, Howard. *A History of the Hussite Revolution.* Berkeley, 1967.

Knowles, Dom David. *The Religious Order in England,* vols. 1 and 2. New York, 1955.

Koch, Josef. *Nikolaus Cues und seine Umwelt.* Heidelberg, 1944/48.

Lerner, Robert E. *The Heresy of the Free Spirit in the Later Middle Ages.* Berkeley, 1972.

Lortz, Joseph. *Geschichte der Kirche in ideengeschichtlicher Betrachtung,* 2 vols., 23rd ed. Münster, 1962.

Lunt, W. E. *Papal Revenues in the Middle Ages,* 2 vols. New York, 1934.

McDonald, E. W. *The Beguines and Beghards in Medieval Culture.* New Brunswick, NJ, 1954.

Macek, Josef. *The Hussite Movement in Bohemia.* Prague, 1958.

Methuen, Erich. *Nikolaus von Kues 1401–1464: Skizze einer Biographie.* 2nd ed., Münster, 1967.

Mollat, G. *Les papes d'Avignon, 1305–1378,* 9th ed. Paris, 1949; London and New York, 1963.

Monticelli, G. *Chiesa e Italia durante il pontificato avignonese.* Milan, 1937.

Morrall, J. B. *Gerson and the Great Schism.* Manchester, 1960.

Oakley, Francis. *The Political Thought of Pierre d'Ailly: The Voluntarist Tradition.* New Haven, 1964.

———. *Council over Pope?* New York, 1969.

Oberman, Heiko A. *The Harvest of Medieval Theology: Gabriel Biel and Late Medieval Nominalism.* Cambridge, MA, 1963.

———. *Forerunners of the Reformation: The Shape of Late Medieval Thought.* New York, 1966.

———. *Werden und Wertung der Reformation: Vom Wegestreit zum Glaubenskampf.* Tübingen, 1977.

Odlozilik, O. *Wycliffe and Bohemia.* Prague, 1937.

O'Malley, John W. *Giles of Viterbo on Church and Reform.* Leiden, 1968.

———. *Praise and Blame in Renaissance Rome: Rhetoric, Doctrine, and Reform in the Sacred Orators of the Papal Court, c. 1450–1521.* Durham, NC, 1979.

Parker, G. H. W. *The Morning Star: Wycliffe and the Dawn of the Reformation.* Exeter, 1965.

Partner, Peter. *The Lands of St. Peter: The Papal State in the Middle Ages and the Early Renaissance.* Berkeley, 1972.

———. *The Papal State Under Martin V.* London, 1958.

Pastor, Ludwig von. *The History of the Popes,* 40 vols., 3rd ed., vols. 1–16. St. Louis, 1891–1953.

Post, R. R. *The Modern Devotion: Confrontation with Reformation and Humanism.* Leiden, 1968.

Ranke, Leopold von. *History of the Popes: Their Church and State,* 3 vols. New York, 1901.

Renouard, Y. *Les relations des papes d'Avignon et des compagnies commerciales et bancaires de 1316 à 1378.* Paris, 1941.

Seppelt, Franz X. *Das Papsttum im Spätmittelalter und in der Zeit der Renaissance.* Leipzig, 1941.

Southern, R. W. *Western Society and the Church in the Middle Ages.* Harmondsworth, 1970.

Spinka, Matthew. *John Hus and the Czech Reform*. Chicago, 1941.
——— . *John Hus' Concept of the Church*. Princeton, 1966.
——— , ed. *Advocates of Reform from Wyclif to Erasmus*. London, 1953.
Tierney, Brian. *Foundations of the Conciliar Theory*. New York, 1955.
Ullmann, Walter. *The Origins of the Great Schism*. London, 1948.
——— . *The Growth of Papal Government in the Middle Ages*. New York, 1955.

CHAPTER 3

The State in Transformation

"States are great engines moving slowly," Francis Bacon observed in his *Advancement of Learning.* The nation-states of modern Europe did evolve slowly through the centuries, but the rate of transformation seems to have quickened during the era of the Renaissance and Reformation movements. While the Holy Roman Empire was losing all semblance of universality and was being denied its claims to Italy and to Rome itself, the new monarchies in France, England, and Spain were developing the dynastic strength and political cohesion that enabled them to enter the modern world as well-defined nation-states. Those political developments were of critical importance for the rise of modern Europe.

Shakespeare's Richard II saw in history little more than "sad stories of the death of kings." But however sad their endings, the kings of Europe were transforming their feudal suzerainties into more centralized and effective monarchies at the expense of feudal lords, urban communes, and the church.

Political and economic developments were intimately related and mutually reinforcing. During the early and high Middle Ages economic life was largely agrarian and was very much restricted to the local scene. Where towns flourished, trade was for the most part limited to dealings with the people of the surrounding countryside. But as a money economy developed, trade expanded, and larger territories and political jurisdictions proved to be more favorable for its development than the local feudal institutions. The kings and territorial princes were able to exploit the new money economy in order to build up their governmental bureaucracies and military forces. The new capitalists and burghers, in turn, favored the central government over local feudal lords. The landholding nobles were involved in economic difficulties, for just as they were commuting payments in kind to money payments, currencies were often subjected to devaluation. Moreover, the price of most items they had to purchase rose. With the increasing use of mercenaries by kings and princes, the nobility was losing utility as a military factor. This situation and other troubles, such as the problem of the peasants, especially during the second half of the fourteenth century, worked great hardship on the feudal nobles and left them poorer and weaker than before. Monarchies and territorial states, kings and princes came out ahead.

These developments varied in different parts of Europe. In the Holy Roman Empire the emperor was prevented by unique political circumstances from capitalizing upon the social and economic tendencies favorable to the development of a strong central government. Since the position of emperor was elective, not hereditary, and the emperor actually ruled only in his own hereditary domain, the emperors were unable to build up a strong centralized government. The territorial princes pursued their own interests and exploited the economic trends to build up the virtual sovereignty of their principalities. In the Germanies and in Italy, where the small city-states failed to coalesce, national unification was not achieved until late in the nineteenth century.

In France, England, and Spain, however, the royal monarchs were able to build kingdoms stronger and more unified than those over which their medieval predecessors had reigned. France, which had been the most completely feudalized country of Europe, developed a strong centralized monarchy. The law of primogeniture (or succession by the eldest son), the unbroken line of Capetian kings, lasting nearly three and a half centuries, and the long reigns of some of its strongest kings enabled the monarchy to build up the royal domain until it embraced a large part of central France. The French kings built up the machinery of government, the sources of revenue, and the military establishment essential to a truly national monarchy. Dynastic monarchy prepared the way for eventual national unity.

England not only was smaller and more compact than France, but also had a much smaller population. The Norman conquest in 1066 and the subsequent imposition of a feudal organization from above gave to English society a somewhat different structure than that in France. The English king and his feudal barons had their landholdings distributed over the whole land and not just in one central royal domain or in more or less independent feudal duchies out in the provinces, as in France. This fact gave to the central government a distinct advantage, since its jurisdiction followed its holdings throughout most of the king-

dom. During the Lancastrian period the parliament and other representative institutions made progress. The trials of the century—long war with France and the
acute internal crisis of the baronial wars in the fifteenth century—did not prevent
the development of a national monarchy analogous to those of France and Spain.

Spain developed political unity much later than did France. The Iberian peninsula was inhabited by many races and a large part was occupied for a long time
by Moslem invaders. The kingdom of Aragon was itself made up of three major
constituent parts. It was oriented toward Mediterranean trade and culture. The
kingdom of Castile stretched from north to south across mountains and arid highlands. Its major rivers flowed parallel to each other to the west, providing no
natural center for the country. The kingdom of Portugal had not only an independent political history, but even a different language. In the south the kingdom
of Granada had absorbed much Islamic art and culture. None of these disparate
kingdoms were effectively joined together until 1479, when the crown of Aragon
was inherited by Prince Ferdinand, who ten years earlier had married Isabella,
daughter of the king of Castile. Isabella had meanwhile inherited the Castilian
crown; thus when Ferdinand became king of Aragon, their kingdoms were joined.
From then on there was steady and reasonably rapid progress toward centralization and consolidation, although Portugal was added only in the next century and
the road to unity was rocky.

Despite the general tendency toward greater cohesion and centralization in
western and, to a lesser extent, in central Europe, there was no inexorable natural
law in operation, drawing nations together under unifying monarchies. A case in
point is the situation in Scandinavia, where a promising coalition of states, which
might have led to national unity, disintegrated. The diets of Denmark and Norway
had in 1387 elected Margaret, daughter of King Waldemar IV, queen of both
countries. In 1388 the diet of Sweden followed suit, so that Margaret in her own
person embodied the union of Scandinavia. All three kingdoms sent representatives to Kalmar, a seaport town on the Baltic coast, where they signed a formal
document establishing the Union of Kalmar (1397). The three kingdoms were to
retain their individual identities, but were to have but a single ruler and were to
work for their mutual interest.

In view of their close ethnic relationship, common background, and many
mutual interests in war and peace, every prospect favored the continued organic
growth of a great Scandinavian nation. But Margaret made blunders that subverted the strength of the union. For one thing, she appointed a disproportionate
number of Danes to office. A rebellion broke out in 1434 against her successor, Eric,
and in 1439 he was deposed in Denmark and Sweden. After a protracted struggle
the Swedes established their marshal Karl Knutsson as King Charles VIII. The
rivalry of the Danes, Norwegians, and Swedes proved to be stronger than any
forces working toward unity. People, not impersonal laws, make history.

The Holy Roman Empire

LORD BRYCE, in his classic history of the Holy Roman Empire, comments that if someone had learned in August 1806 of the resignation of Emperor Francis II, he might have known that the oldest political institution in the world had come to an end. The miracle of the Holy Roman Empire is that it could remain on its feet so long after it had actually turned moribund. During the late medieval and Renaissance period the empire continued to lose significance as a political institution. The territorial principalities within its borders grew in strength and achieved virtual sovereignty. The national monarchies outside its borders increased in power, and France began to whittle away at the western territories.

The empire was undermined when, during the investiture controversy between the papacy and the empire in the eleventh and twelfth centuries, the princes were freed of their obligations of loyalty to the emperors. When Emperor Frederick II (d. 1250) transferred his headquarters to southern Italy in the thirteenth century and lost interest in the Germanies, the princes took advantage of the situation, and the pope made an all-out attack on the last of the Hohenstaufen family. There followed an interregnum from 1254 to 1273, during which a virtual state of anarchy ruined what remained of central government or imperial unity. The electors finally chose as emperor a minor Swabian prince, Rudolf of Habsburg, whom they considered strong enough to restore order but not so strong as to pose a threat to the princes themselves. The emperors were almost entirely dependent upon the goodwill of the princes, for they could not raise troops or levy taxes outside their own family territories. It is no wonder that most of the emperors concentrated on enlarging their hereditary estates through conquest or marriage rather than attempting to unify or strengthen the empire as such.

HENRY VII AND DANTE

The electors' calculated policy of building weakness into the imperial setup had the desired result. Since Rudolf of Habsburg, who was handsome, strong, and energetic, proved to be effective, they next chose Adolf of Nassau. He was deposed soon thereafter, and Albrecht, another Habsburg, was elected. A nephew and a band of hired assassins murdered him. The electors felt uneasy about the ability and aggressiveness of the Habsburgs, so they turned next to a small and seemingly innocuous prince, Henry of Luxemburg, whom they elected in 1308, initiating nearly a century of Luxemburg emperors. This Henry VII literally bought the election, and his own brother, as archbishop of Trier, was one of the electors. As Ovid once observed of ancient Rome, "Truly now is the golden age; the highest honor comes by means of gold!" Although Luxemburg was part of the empire, Henry's education had been French, and he was oriented more toward France and Italy than toward eastern Europe. He gave Bohemia to his son John, and in order to win French support he gave Burgundy as a fief to the son of King Philip the Fair. Then with a small army he went to Italy in the fall of 1301 to be crowned emperor.

The exiled Florentine poet Dante Alighieri (1265–1321) hailed Henry VII as the hero who would free Florence and Italy of Guelph oppression and raise the empire to its ancient glory. During the second half of the thirteenth century Florence had become predominantly Guelph (on the side of the papacy) and anti-Ghibelline (against the empire). Now the city was torn by Black and White Guelph factions. The Blacks favored Pope Boniface VIII and Charles of France, his ally. At the very close of the thirteenth century, before Henry VII's invasion, the Blacks suppressed the Whites. They exiled Dante and even condemned him to death by burning should he return. Dante bombarded Henry VII with letters and tracts urging him to come to Italy. When Henry came, Dante traveled to Milan to persuade him to attack Florence. He wrote a letter to Florence announcing that the time of judgment was at hand.

This political situation explains the thrust of Dante's treatise *De monarchia.* Dante argued that a universal monarchy is necessary for the peace and stability of human society. He believed that Christ's birth within the jurisdiction of the Roman Empire indicated divine sanction for it. He asserted that the emperor received the imperial monarchy directly from God and not merely indirectly, through the papacy. Dante did not argue for a single autocratic ruler governing all of Christendom. He favored rather a hierarchy: the individual, the city, the province, the kingdom, the empire. The first four levels were consistent with the scheme of Aristotle, and in the final chapter Dante drew on Aristotle to describe the natural end of man. But Dante went beyond this to argue that an overall empire is necessary because of man's sinful condition. Each member of this hierarchy is supreme within the limits of his sphere. The emperor is therefore not supreme or absolute, but rather the highest authority in rank. Dante's political theory was backward-looking, running counter to the tendencies of the times. Lord Bryce dubbed his *De monarchia* "an epitaph rather than a prophecy."

In hoping for an imperial victory in Italy, Dante was indulging in wishful thinking, for the cities of Lombardy and Tuscany joined the pope in opposing Henry VII. There was a symbolic confrontation between the old and the new, for Emperor Henry paid his troops with gold coins transported in a wagon while Florence paid its soldiers with letters of credit. When Henry VII made his way to Rome, it was more as a suppliant than as a conquering hero. On June 29, 1312, three cardinals crowned him emperor in the Church of St. John Lateran. Much of Italy rose up against him and the world witnessed the spectacle of the Holy Roman emperor, following the will-o'-the-wisp medieval concept of empire, entrapped in the quicksands of Italian politics. His death of disease in a convent near Siena in 1313 was perhaps the easiest way out of a hopeless situation.

LUXEMBURG AND HABSBURG REIGNS

There followed a brief interlude in which Ludwig the Bavarian charged head-long into a first-class imbroglio with Pope John XXII. Ludwig gained the support of Milan, Verona, Mantua, and Lucca, and moved into Rome in January 1328, forcing King Robert of Naples to withdraw. The pope put Rome under an inter-dict, but Ludwig retaliated by deposing the pope for *lèse majesté* and heresy. He called the pope a veritable Antichrist and had a counterpope elected in Rome. In August 1338 the diet in Frankfort declared that the power of the emperor was derived directly from God and not indirectly through the pope. Ludwig gave sanctuary to such antipapal writers as Marsiglio of Padua and William of Occam. In October 1347 Ludwig died unexpectedly while on a hunt.

With the election of Charles IV (1347–1378) the imperial crown returned to the house of Luxemburg. Charles proved to be in nearly every respect a remark-able ruler. He made of Prague a beautiful capital city, and in 1348 founded there the first university in German lands. He learned a great deal from the France of Philip the Fair, and introduced into Bohemia methods of centralized government, establishing more precise fiscal control, the use of Roman law, and a territorial law codified as the *Majestas carolina*. At the diets of Nuremberg, 1355, and of Metz, 1356, he gave the empire the beginnings of a written constitution.

The Golden Bull of 1356 regularized in law the imperial electoral college, which had grown up by custom and long usage. Three ecclesiastical princes (the archbishops of Mainz, Trier, and Cologne) and four secular princes (the king of Bohemia, the margrave of Brandenburg, the duke of Saxony, and the count pala-tine of the Rhine) were to serve as the seven electors. The territories of the electors were declared to be indivisible and the four secular principalities were to be in-herited by the law of primogeniture. Charles's aim had been to regularize election proceedings and thus to stabilize the political situation in the empire. The effect of the Golden Bull was to elevate the most powerful princes to a state of virtual sovereignty and to acknowledge legally their authority in the empire, to the dis-advantage of the emperor.

Under Wenceslas (1378–1410), the son of Charles IV, the empire quickly got out of hand, for Wenceslas was a playboy. The Rhenish electors deposed him, gave the crown to Rupert of the Palatinate, and finally turned to a younger son of Charles IV, Sigismund. Sigismund (1410–1437), the last of the Luxemburg em-perors, had been married to the daughter of King Louis of Hungary and Poland. When Louis died it seemed that Sigismund would rule over a mighty kingdom embracing Poland, Bohemia, and Hungary, but the Poles broke away and elected as their king Prince Jagiello of Lithuania. Sigismund took possession of Hungary, but that triumph brought him face to face with the terrible Turk. The Turks defeated the Serbs in 1389 and at Nicopolis in 1396 they slaughtered the Hungarians and came close to capturing Sigismund himself. Luckily for Sigismund, the Turks then turned their attention to Greece and Byzantium, giving the West a brief respite. The highlight of his career was the role he played as a "new Constantine," leading in the reform of the church at the Council of Constance. But the burning of Jan Hus precipitated the Hussite revolt in his own Bohemia. Sigismund died without a male heir.

With the election of Sigismund's son-in-law Albrecht II (1438–1439) the Habsburgs once again assumed the imperial title. During the long reign of his lethargic successor, Frederick III (1440–1493), the Habsburgs suffered tremendous losses. Not only did the emperor lose Bohemia and Hungary, but he even evacuated Vienna and ruled from Linz out of fear of King Matthew Corvinus of Hungary. The independent Swiss confederation encroached further on Habsburg holdings and various lands were disbursed among members of the Habsburg family. On the other hand, Frederick III lost none of the Habsburg talent for arranging profitable marriages for his family. He married his son Maximilian to Mary, daughter of Duke Charles the Bold of Burgundy, thereby bringing under Habsburg control France-Comté, Luxemburg, and various prosperous industrial provinces in the Netherlands.

On Frederick's death his son Maximilian (1493–1519) aroused high hopes for a restoration of vigorous imperial leadership. He was an athletic type, renowned as a bear hunter and mountain climber, gallant and chivalrous, every inch a knight. He was the darling of the nationalistic German humanists for his patronage of artists and authors and for the promise he offered of the restoration of German greatness. The imperial eagle would at last soar far above the Gallic cock and the Venetian lion! But in both domestic and foreign policy Maximilian proved to be impractical and ineffective. Yet once again Habsburg fortunes rose, for they gained before the altar what they failed to win by the sword.

Philip, the son of Maximilian and Mary, was married in 1496 to Joanna, daughter of King Ferdinand and Queen Isabella of Spain. When in October Philip arrived to claim his bride, he was eighteen and she sixteen. The two young people fell madly in love at first sight. Overwhelmed by passion, they could not wait for a formal church wedding. The court chaplain married them that evening and they slept together that very night. But alas, Philip's ardor soon cooled, and a chronicler relates that while Joanna "loved her husband with a great passion, he did not respond to her feelings in a like manner." Hell has no fury like a woman scorned, as a number of people have had occasion to remark, and Joanna attacked Philip with a pair of scissors. She was declared to be quite mad. But for all their personal difficulties, the laws of dynastic inheritance were still operative. Through Joanna

Philip came into possession of Castile. Furthermore, Joanna bore him a son, Prince Charles, who was to inherit an empire in Europe and in faraway lands discovered by an Italian adventurer whose voyages had been sponsored by his grandmother.

Charles, born in 1500, inherited from Philip the Burgundian lands and Castile when he was only six years old. In 1516, on the death of his grandfather, King Ferdinand, he fell heir also to Aragon, Sicily, Naples, Sardinia, and Hispanic America. When Maximilian died in 1519, Charles received in addition the Austrian lands from Tyrol to Styria. In that same year the electors chose him emperor of the Holy Roman Empire. Charles ruled over half of Europe as Charles I of Spain and Charles V of the empire. The clever turn of phrase applied in later centuries to the Austrian branch of the family was no less true of the early Habsburgs: "Others make war, but you, fortunate Austria, marry!"

TERRITORIAL PRINCIPALITIES

Within the empire the power of the princes steadily increased from the fourteenth to the sixteenth centuries. The emperors themselves were for the most part dependent upon the revenues and manpower of their family territories. In effect, they were princes who bore also the title of emperor. The electors and other princes of the empire, great and small, long persisted in treating their lands as feudal possessions, but they gradually learned to administer their territories as integral states. The territories developed diets (*Landtage*) analogous to the imperial diets. The princes employed learned chancellors, built up bureaucracies and standing armies, developed fiscal systems, and introduced Roman law, just like the national monarchs to the west. Württemberg, Bavaria, Hesse, Brandenburg, the Palatinate, and Saxony were already powerful states at the start of this period. They never ceased to aggrandize themselves further at the expense of the church, their smaller neighbors, the emperor, and the cities.

The cities were gradually losing their freedom and initiative. The Hanse cities in the north were in decline and the free cities in the west and south were tiny enclaves embedded in territorial principalities, hemmed in and unable to expand. Within the walls the city councils exercised great control over the hospitals, endowments, chapels, and churches.

The territorial princes assumed astonishing prerogatives in governing the church within their own domains. They were in many cases virtually lay bishops over the proprietary church, for they nominated clergy for appointments, controlled finances, cared for church buildings, and even, like sacramental kings, decided matters of a spiritual nature. The duke of Cleves, for example, declared himself to be "pope in his own land." Rudolf IV of Austria in the fourteenth century announced, "On my soil I intend to be pope, archbishop, bishop, archdeacon, and deacon." Even when one makes allowances for rhetoric, it is obvious that the princes were in the ascendancy. The empire as a political power was in decline and the church was experiencing increasing difficulties.

The New Monarchies

IN CONTRAST to the empire, the kingdoms of France, England, and Spain developed national monarchies and eventually became nation-states. Certain lawyers of the period, in order to explain the obvious discrepancy between the theoretical subordination of a king to the emperor and the actual independence of the monarchs in the west, coined the phrase "A king is emperor in his own kingdom."

FRANCE

France enjoyed a more advantageous geographic location than the empire, which had no natural frontiers. With the sea on three sides, France was almost inevitably impelled toward the Rhine, its natural boundary on the east. France was also fortunate in the amazing continuity of its royal lineage. From Hugh Capet in 987 to Louis Philippe in 1848, all its kings were princes of the Capetian line. Many of its rulers were strong and able, such as Philip II Augustus in the twelfth century, Philip IV (the Fair) at the end of the thirteenth century and the beginning of the fourteenth, and the dynamic Louis XI near the end of the fifteenth century.

The French monarchy succeeded in developing a centralized bureaucracy designed for the efficient mobilization of societal resources, in contrast to the feudal self-regulating society, which distributed social functions according to status groupings that were defined by custom and inheritance. During the second half of the thirteenth century the council of the king (*curia regis*) began differentiating its functions more clearly. There developed the *parlement* for justice, the *chambre de comptes* for finance, and the *grand conseil* to serve the king. During the fifteenth century this council divided into a large council and a smaller secret or privy council, which during the following century came to be known as the *conseil des affaires*. Royal authority was represented locally by agents called the *prévôts*, who served as judges and financial officers. The central government learned early to appoint deputies (called *baillis* in the north and *sénéchaux* in the south) to represent it in specific divisions of the royal domain, which by the end of the fifteenth century included most of the realm.

During the thirteenth and fourteenth centuries the French monarchs were still relatively weak and had to turn to the provincial estates for financial support, beyond the revenue drawn from their own domain. The estates general evolved as a "national institution," although for a long time the representatives of the north and of the south (Languedoc) met separately. The feudal duties of vassals to provide aid (*auxilium*) and advice (*consilium*) were reflected in the deliberation of the estates general, which could articulate grievances only after having first voted funds for the ruler. These taxes were significantly known as *aides*. As the French monarchs gained in strength, they found that they could manage well without convening the estates general, which became increasingly insignificant as the fourteenth and fifteenth centuries wore on, and in reality did not represent the whole realm.

The French monarchy developed a royal army that was not dependent upon the feudal obligations of vassals. The Great Ordinance of 1439 forbade powerful feudal lords to retain private troops and reserved to the king the power of appointing captains. The century-long war with England greatly accelerated the changes in the bureaucracy, the fiscal system, and the military organization as France underwent its metamorphosis from a feudal state to a more unified monarchy.

The Hundred Years' War. As France and England developed a stronger sense of national identity, they were drawn into conflict. For the English king held the duchy of Guienne, in southwestern France, as a fief under the French crown, and therefore was required to do homage to the French king as his vassal. The English crown enjoyed valuable revenue from the export-import duties on Bordeaux wine from Guienne, but resented holding it as a dependency and wished to assert a full sovereign claim to it. Another conflict of interest involved Flanders, an industrial area that was a rich fief highly coveted by the French, but which was also of great economic importance to the English. Four-fifths of England's raw-wool exports went to Flanders in exchange for finished textiles, and the English king profited from duties on the trade. The English therefore supported the counts of Flanders in their efforts to retain independence, and when Flanders was overrun by the French, the English encouraged the cities of Flanders to resist them.

The first serious clash came in 1294 in a trial of strength between the dynamic French king Philip the Fair (1285–1314) and one of England's greatest monarchs, Edward I (1272–1307). But both were distracted by other problems and made peace in 1303. In 1337 Edward III (1327–1377), grandson of Edward I, initiated a war with the French which was to drag on for over a century. The English were angry with the French for supporting their ancient foes the Scots. Moreover, the French king Philip VI (1328–1350) seemed to be unusually vulnerable, for he was a dreamer who cultivated a fanciful court life and schemed to acquire the imperial crown, to win new lands in Italy, and even to retake the Holy Land. Edward III managed his finances cleverly, licensing wool exports, forbidding wasteful tourneys, raising taxes against the hated French, and repudiating debts to Italian bankers. He had the English well organized militarily, with two musters a year, increased use of foot soldiers, who were less expensive than cavalry, and companies of longbowmen. His strategy was to raid at will, ravaging the countryside throughout western France and thus weakening his rival. In this long first phase of the war the English won three particularly important victories, one by sea and two on land. In the sea battle at Sluis, the port for Bruges, a combined English and Flemish fleet destroyed the French flotilla. In 1346 at Crécy, near the Somme River, the English won a pitched battle against the French army. From an elevated position above a valley, hundreds of English longbowmen rained death on the French below. The longbow could be shot much more rapidly than the crossbow, which needed to be rewound after each shot. Though the English were greatly outnumbered, their superior weapons and mobility proved devastating to the French in their cumbersome armor. The French king's own brother fell, and Philip VI himself had two horses killed under him. The English went on to attack Calais and took it after a siege lasting nearly a year. Calais was an important port and bridgehead for troop landings. The French were glad to accept an armistice in 1347. Both sides were so ravaged by the Black Death in the two or three years that followed that they felt no great urge to kill each other.

The reign of Philip VI's son and successor, John II (1350–1364), was disastrous for France. The English thought the time ripe to strike again. Edward III's heir, Edward the Black Prince, who was a brilliant field commander, landed troops at Bordeaux in 1355 and led them southward almost to the Mediterranean. The next year he won the second great land battle in the first phase of the war, the battle of Poitiers. The French had learned nothing from Crécy, fought ten years before, and sent succeeding waves of heavily armored knights straight into a hail of arrows. The English cavalry rode around behind the French and took King John II himself captive. The French gladly accepted the Treaty of Brétigny in 1360, which assured the English of sovereignty over Calais and their territory in the southwest.

With the king in a London prison, France nearly disintegrated. The estates general, led by a wealthy merchant, Étienne Marcel, turned on the dauphin, Charles, executed some of his courtiers, and forced him to accept some reforms. The peasants, enraged by taxes and the failure of the king and feudal lords to protect them from marauding bands of mercenaries, unleashed a terrifying revolt, called the Jacquerie (the gentry, who could hardly be expected to concern themselves with peasants' names, called them all Jacques). Marcel allied himself with the peasants, but in a street uprising in the city he was killed, and the dauphin reentered Paris. When King John II died in London, the dauphin ascended what was left of the throne as Charles V.

Charles V (1364–1380) earned the sobriquet "the Wise" by introducing a new style of government. He placed the fiscal system on a firmer basis by requiring regular and continuous taxation. He reorganized the royal army, and sent able captains such as the wily Bertrand du Guesclin into the field when he renewed the war in 1369. Constable Guesclin avoided pitched battles, but harassed the English until he wore them down. The French retook all the English territories except Calais, Bordeaux, Bayonne, and some minor fortified places. In 1375 Pope Gregory XI managed to arrange an armistice, just in time for a change in the cast of characters. The Black Prince died in 1376, Edward III died in 1377, and Charles V died in 1380. There followed about thirty-five years of relative quiet, for both countries were beset by internal difficulties. Under its next two kings France fell into nearly complete chaos.

Royal power reached its nadir under Charles VI (1380–1422), known in the chronicles as "the Mad." He was only twelve when fate lifted him to the throne. The Flemish burghers took advantage of his minority to revolt and the feudal lords seized the opportunity to regain their former independence. On an expedition in 1382 to Brittany, which the French had long sought to unite with their realm, the first unmistakable signs of the king's mental disorder appeared. The next year several people were burned to death at a ball, and at the sight of this horror the king went completely out of his mind.

Then civil war broke out, for the houses of Orléans and Burgundy saw an opportunity to move into the power vacuum. Duke Louis of Orléans, the king's brother, opposed the ascendancy of the house of Burgundy. In 1407 Duke John of Burgundy had the duke of Orléans assassinated in a Paris street. His son, Charles of Orléans, and his supporters, called the Armagnacs after his tough father-in-law, who came from Armagnac in southwestern France, took up arms against John of Burgundy. The butchers and artisans of Paris rose up, organized a commune, declared in favor of Burgundy, and seized the Bastille, while the mad king donned the white cap of the Parisians. But the Armagnacs triumphed, suppressed the revolt, made war on the duke of Burgundy, and kept the king under control.

To the English the moment seemed right to strike again. In 1415 they renewed the war, closing the second phase of relative quiescence and initiating the third and final phase, which began with victories for the English and ended with their defeat. The bellicose young King Henry V (1413–1422), urged on by the English nobility, saw a chance for glory. Henry V not only claimed the territories once taken by Edward III, but declared himself to be the rightful heir to the French throne and demanded the daughter of Charles VI for his queen. His claim was not wholly fanciful. Edward III, Henry's great-grandfather, had actually been more closely related to Charles IV of France than Philip VI, who inherited Charles's throne. Philip was the son of Charles's uncle; Edward was the son of Charles's sister, who had married Edward II of England. Philip claimed the throne of France under Salic law, which barred females from the line of succession, but the English had ever since claimed that the French throne should have gone to Edward, and after him to his heirs.

Henry V landed at Calais and in the legendary battle of Agincourt he inflicted a near total defeat upon the French. The French confronted him there with a feudal army, largely made up of the Armagnacs, and repeated the blunders of Poitiers and Crécy. The crossbowmen were placed in the rear, where they were ineffective. The knights dismounted and sloshed forward in heavy armor until, weary and mired down in inches of mud, they were virtually immobilized. Those who escaped the rain of arrows were cut down where they stood by English foot soldiers. The flower of French chivalry lay dead on the field at the close of the day, including Charles of Orléans and the duke of Bourbon.

Even with the hated English on its soil, France was torn apart by civil war. The Burgundians acknowledged Henry V as king of France, entered Paris, and slaughtered the Armagnacs. In 1419 the Armagnacs treacherously murdered Duke John the Fearless of Burgundy to avenge the assassination of the duke of Orléans twelve years before. The new duke of Burgundy, Philip the Good (1419–1467), joined England's Henry V, who had been systematically conquering Normandy, in an offensive against the dauphin, Charles. By the Treaty of Troyes, 1420, Henry V was made heir to the French throne. He married Catherine, the daughter of Charles VI, and entered Paris with Charles. The estates general accepted the treaty and the dauphin retreated south of the Loire. At this critical juncture Henry V died. Then occurred one of the strangest episodes in all of French history.

Henry VI (1422–1461) was a ten-month-old infant when he was proclaimed in Paris to be the king of England and France. During his minority his two uncles, the duke of Gloucester and the duke of Bedford, governed for him in England and France respectively. North of the Loire River only Orléans held out against the English, and in 1428 Bedford undertook to bring it to submission. The French claimant to the throne, Charles VII, was a weakling, dubbed the king of Bourges for his provisional capital, who had neither the will nor the ability to save Orléans. In this major crisis France was saved by a peasant girl and the will of an aroused people, who hated the foreigners on French soil.

At Domrémy in Champagne, Joan of Arc heard the voices of saints urging her to free France and to bring Charles VII to Rheims for his royal coronation. Born in 1412, Joan was the youngest child in a family of five. She could neither read nor write, but she was a pious, serious girl who learned to spin and sew like other peasant girls. When only thirteen Joan first became aware of voices speaking to her, sometimes accompanied by a blaze of light—the voices of St. Michael, St. Margaret, and St. Catherine, and the voices of angels. By May 1428 she was certain of her mission to save France, and a few weeks later she presented herself to the commander of Charles VII's troops in the nearby town of Vancouleurs. The commander told the cousin who had come with her to "take her home to her father and give her a sound thrashing."

The voices were insistent: "It is God who commands it." In January 1429 Joan appeared again before the skeptical officer and impressed him by announcing the

French defeat near Orléans days before the news arrived. On March 8 she was permitted to travel in male attire to Chinon to see Charles VII. He disguised himself among his attendants to test her, but she spotted him immediately and spoke to him of her mission. A commission of bishops and theologians found nothing heretical in her views. She then ordered the English to leave France and led an attack against them. On April 30 she entered Orléans. On May 7 she was wounded by an arrow in the breast, but the next day the last English stronghold outside the city fell.

The king's fearful counselors hesitated to follow up the victory with a quick campaign against the English, but they opened up the road to Rheims. There, with all the ancient pomp and ceremony, Charles VII was crowned on July 17, 1429. Joan stood by, bearing her standard, for, she said, "since it had shared in the labor, it was only fair that it should share also in the victory." An attempt to take Paris late in August failed, and Joan, wounded in the thigh by a bolt from a crossbow, was out of action for the winter.

On May 24, 1430, she led the French troops into Compiègne at sunrise to prevent its occupation by the Burgundians. Toward evening she was captured on a sortie outside the walls. The Burgundians sold Joan to the English for a handsome price. Charles VII, to his shame, did nothing to rescue her. Imprisoned in Rouen, at first in an iron cage with her neck, hands, and feet in chains, she was tried for heresy before the unscrupulous bishop of Beauvais, a tool of the Burgundians. On May 30, 1431, she was executed. Tied to the stake, she asked for a cross, and someone brought her one. As the flames and smoke rose up around her she gazed at the cross, called upon Jesus, and until the last "declared that her voices came from God and had not deceived her." Her ashes were scattered into the Seine.

Charles VII, tagged "the Well Served," had good counselors. He introduced regular and systematic tax levies not dependent on the approval of the estates general. He took advantage of a truce with the English to reorganize his troops into twenty "ordinance companies" under professional captains. Each company consisted of a hundred lances, each lance made up of six cavalrymen and accompanied by bowmen and artillery. In 1449 the French renewed the offensive, liberated Normandy, and seized Bordeaux and Bayonne. In 1453 the French repulsed a new invasion attempt at Castillon, and the long war was over. The English retained a toehold on the continent, however, by keeping Calais until 1558 and the channel islands to the present time.

The Emergence of Strong Monarchy. During the century that followed the end of the Hundred Years' War four French kings of unusual ability graced the throne. All of them were able to build upon the administrative, fiscal, and military reforms of Charles VII. The first of these was Charles VII's son Louis XI (1461–1483), who won a place in history as one of France's great monarchs. A man of feverish impatience, he worked with restless energy to make his centralized government more efficient. Philippe de Commynes, a famous historian, who went over to the king from Burgundy, analyzed his tactic of finding support with the burghers and common people against the feudal forces. He improved the economy by introducing new textile industries in the north, a silk industry in Lyon, and an improved system of government inspection and quality control. He was ostentatiously pious in order to hold the loyalty of the clergy.

He needed all the strength he could muster, for the forces of feudalism in alliance with the land of Burgundy now made one last effort to challenge the king and the consolidation of a national dynasty. Charles the Bold (1467–1477) of Burgundy had visions of building an independent state in the old Lotharingian territories by adding Alsace and Lorraine to Burgundy and Flanders. He even envisioned winning the French crown or the imperial crown. Luckily for Louis XI, Charles was killed outside the walls of Nancy in 1477 and the threat subsided. Louis XI succeeded in gaining only a small portion of Burgundy for France, however, for Mary, the heiress of Burgundy, married Maximilian of Austria in 1477. When she died in 1482, Maximilian and Louis XI concluded the Treaty of Arras, by which Maximilian yielded a sizable part of French-speaking Burgundy to Louis XI.

Charles VIII (1483–1498) was a boy of thirteen at the time of his father's death. He grew up to be a man of action like his father, but he lacked judiciousness. He foiled the Habsburgs' scheme to acquire Brittany by their usual method, marriage. They arranged for Princess Margaret of Austria to wed Charles VIII, while Maximilian was to marry Anne of Brittany. But in a sudden reversal, Charles VIII marched into Brittany and compelled Anne to marry him.

Although it might appear that Charles was showing concern for rounding out the natural frontier of France by securing the great peninsula reaching out into the sea, he proved very shortly that he was still thinking dynastically rather than nationally. For in 1494–1495 he embarked upon an ill-fated Italian expedition to assert French claims upon Naples. Only a fool or a madman would have done it, Commynes observed, for he risked much with but little to gain. But it was a spectacle that long excited the imagination of patriotic Frenchmen. When those foot soldiers of Charles VIII padded down into the plains of Lombardy, the nineteenth century French historian Jules Michelet later burbled, "The Alps were lowered forever!" Charles VIII withdrew within a year, for his troops were decimated by disease and he feared that his long communication line might be cut. But that unhappy adventure initiated a series of invasions and decades of dominance over Italy by the great states of the north and west.

Louis XII (1498–1515) of the house of Orléans married Charles VIII's widow, Anne of Brittany. He devoted himself to further strengthening the central government and to subduing feudal vassals. It was fortunate for France that he succeeded so well, for as a result of further adventures in northern Italy involving claims to Milan, he became embroiled in a struggle with the Habsburgs. His successor, Francis I (1515–1547) of the house of Angoulême, had to fight out four wars with Emperor Charles V, whose lands encircled France on nearly all sides. Under Francis I Renaissance culture flowered in France.

Even this necessarily abbreviated account of French history from the fourteenth to the sixteenth centuries makes quite clear how the vicissitudes of war, the accidents of life and death, the will of the people when the king lacked one, the most bizarre and unforeseeable events all made the formation of the French national monarchy and state anything but a foregone conclusion. The tendencies toward political centralization and the development of a capitalist economy were active as historical forces, but the will and ability of men aided or frustrated by seemingly chance events determined the actual course of French history.

BURGUNDY

Strange as such a judgment may seem against the somber account of the Hundred Years' War, the most serious threat to the French state may have been posed by Burgundy. The dukes of Burgundy came very close to establishing a rich and powerful "middle kingdom" that would have shut France off from eastward expansion and left it in a relatively weak position. The dukes of Burgundy, as a French line, succeeded in winning the loyalty of many French-speaking areas and were deeply involved in the struggle against the dukes of Orléans and the French kings themselves. Ironically, a French monarch quite inadvertently gave to Burgundy its opportunity for a century of greatness.

When the Burgundian ducal family died out after 330 years, King John II of France bestowed Burgundy upon his youngest son, Philip the Bold (1364–1404), as a feudal appanage, and Philip began the process of territorial aggrandizement that eventually made of Burgundy a major power. When he married Margaret, heiress of Flanders and Artois, he combined agricultural Burgundy with industrial Flanders, a potentially dynamic union. In subsequent decades the dukes of Burgundy added Picardy, Brabant, Hainault, Zeeland, Holland, Luxemburg, and Gelders. John the Fearless (1404–1419) contributed less to the rise of Burgundy, but Philip the Good (1419–1467) and Charles the Bold (1467–1477) worked toward a centralized administration for Burgundy, although the only tie with Flanders and their other territories remained dynastic and personal rather than constitutional and public.

The final confrontation of France and Burgundy came during the reigns of King Louis XI and Duke Charles the Bold. Charles the Bold was consumed with the ambition of building a kingdom between France and the empire which would correspond to ancient Lotharingia. His territory would run from Switzerland to the North Sea, and he would no longer be duke, but king, under the suzerainty of the Holy Roman emperor. During his last years Charles seemed increasingly to lose his grip on reality and to undertake rash and ill-advised adventures. At last, on January 5, 1477, while besieging Nancy, Charles the Bold was killed by the duke of Lorraine. Half his army betrayed him and the other half was slaughtered in flight. Charles's body was found two days later, surrounded by the bodies of Burgundian nobles. His head was split from the crown to the jaw and his face had been gnawed away by wolves.

Burgundy was an anomaly, for even while the duke was centralizing its administration and introducing ordinance companies into its military on the French pattern, court life and manners remained chivalric. In society and custom it was the classic example of the waning of the Middle Ages. In 1430 Philip the Good created the Order of the Golden Fleece, an exclusive fraternity of aristocrats limited at first to twenty-four and then to thirty gentlemen. Olivier de la Marche recounted how in 1454, after the fall of Constantinople, the court held a great banquet in order to rally the men of good blood for a crusade. The decorations included such elaborate ornaments as a cake with twenty-four musicians inside playing their instruments. At the climactic moment the noble knights arose, took a vow to go on a crusade to free the Christian East from the Turks, and then went home again. In the decadence of fifteenth-century Burgundy, the substitution of symbol for action seemed perfectly reasonable.

In retrospect it is easy to see some of the weaknesses inherent in the Burgundian position that made the dreams of Charles the Bold impossible. Unlike France, which had a geographical center and a nucleus in the royal domain on which to build, Burgundy stretched along the Rhine from Switzerland to the North Sea, with its nuclei of power strung out in a wavering line. Theoretically the economy was diversified and complementary: Burgundy was agricultural and Flanders was industrial, which should have made for cohesion and strength. But the trade lines were set in other directions—Flanders engaged in trade with England, for example—and rationalizing the economy on a major scale was beyond the conception of the dukes and surely beyond their ability. Moreover, the dukes were at a political disadvantage, for the French monarch enjoyed the aura of divinity that hedges round a king, while the duke of Burgundy never acquired the status of royalty. He was duke of Burgundy, duke of Brabant, but count of Flanders, with no single title for all his domains. In the seventeen provinces of the Netherlands he had to deal with the estates in terms of local law and custom. A century did not provide sufficient time for Burgundy to coalesce into a unified power.

ENGLAND

The fourteenth and fifteenth centuries were of critical importance for the development of the English state, for they witnessed the decline of medieval institutions and the transition to a new style of monarchy. The king had enjoyed nearly unrestrained powers in a relatively narrow sphere. Now the conception of a primarily tenurial relationship with lines running down through the feudal hierarchy gave way to a broader vision of the king as leader of all the people of the realm, concerned with the common welfare. People in turn were conceived of less in relation to their positions in the feudal hierarchy than as members of estates or orders within society. The king came to consult these estates, represented in parliament, rather than merely his feudal tenants in chief as part of his council. The estates gradually came to appreciate the fact that those who had the power to grant the requests of the king also had the power to refuse them, and thus the formal political instrument for restraining the king and his bureaucracy came into being. The bureaucracy itself established procedures, created precedents, and developed traditions that made the workings of government less personal and served as a restraint upon the will of the king. A feeling of identity as a people and of identification with the king, an incipient form of nationalism, developed as a corollary to the new relation of the monarchy to the people. The old schism between Norman overlords and Anglo-Saxon underlings gave way to a common feeling of Englishness that was to help sustain the realm against foes on the island and across the channel.

King and Parliament. The fourteenth century opened with one of England's greatest monarchs on the throne, Edward I (1272–1307) of the Plantagenet line. A tall and handsome man, he had a passion for military exercises and tournaments. The general effect of his reign, however, was to move England away from feudalism toward a new phase in political life. As a strong ruler he kept the barons under control. He broadened the sources of royal revenue to include property taxes and customs duties. He appointed councilors who served as efficient bureaucrats in carrying out the ordinary duties of government and in preparing legislation for parliament to act on. During the first two decades of his reign, which were relatively peaceful, a large body of legislation was enacted into law which codified as statutes the precedents of common law in both civil and criminal matters. Finding himself in great difficulty as a result of a rebellion in Wales, Scottish resistance, and trouble with France, he summoned the "Model Parliament" in 1295, representing all three estates, clergy, nobility, and commons. The magnates and representatives of the shires and towns approved the grants of money that the king needed for his governmental and military operations. In his summons to the parliament, Edward I expressed the idea that the parliament represented the nation: "What touches all should be approved of all, and it is also clear that common dangers should be met by measures agreed upon in common."

Parliament grew out of the Great Council of the king's ecclesiastical and lay vassals. From the outset Edward I summoned it frequently, and in 1295 he called together a parliament made up of the lords temporal and spiritual, two or more knights elected from each shire by the freeholders at the shire court, and two or more burgesses from every city, borough, and important town. He wished to gain the support of the propertied classes for his policies and to strengthen the ties between the central and local governments. Subsidies for the crown voted by the barons and the representatives of shires and towns assembled in parliament constituted a legal impost upon the whole realm. Voting taxes upon oneself was considered a dubious privilege. The clergy remained aloof and met in its own convocations in Canterbury and York to vote subsidies. Many representatives of the commons were reluctant to vote taxes, were shy about sitting with the great magnates, and were discouraged by their fellows from collecting their expense money of two shillings a day, and so they absented themselves whenever they could. Ironically, it was due to the fact that the king was strong enough to make them attend parliamentary sessions that parliament developed as the most important institution in English political life. It was not at first thought of as a check by the people upon the arbitrary use of royal power.

The fact that parliament was summoned always to a specific place, Westminster, instead of to various towns about the country, gave it a more permanent character than it would otherwise have had. Parliament developed important judicial functions as a high court to hear petitions and order the redress of grievances, handling cases not within the competence of the common law courts. A fixed place of meeting also encouraged the development of parliament as a court of appeal.

The reign of Edward II (1307–1327), a weak and ineffective king, was fairly disastrous at home and abroad. He was dominated by his queen, Isabelle of France, imprisoned, and finally murdered by his custodians. In his one great military adventure his army was soundly beaten at Bannockburn by Robert Bruce and the Scots in 1314. His very ineffectiveness, however, enabled parliament to insist upon the right to approve the king's councilors and to punish them for abuse of their authority. The parliament finally even deposed the king and declared the succession of his son.

The long reign of Edward III (1327–1377) was of tremendous importance for the political evolution of England, for the king's war with the Scots and his deep involvement in the Hundred Years' War meant that he had to make great concessions to parliament at home. The king's need for the goodwill and support of the populace led to constitutional developments important not only for England but for the whole Western democratic tradition. The question of whether officials were responsible to the king as his servants, as Edward III held, or to the entire realm represented in parliament was crucial. During Edward's preoccupation with the French war parliament pressed for the principle of impeachment, the Lords bringing officials to trial at the request of the Commons.

Parliament itself went through a critical development during this period as it assumed what was to be its permanent shape. Up to this time the lower clergy had deliberated separately, while the knights and burgesses, recognizing their common social and economic interests, began to sit together. By the mid-fourteenth century parliament had separated into two houses, Lords and Commons, with somewhat specialized functions. Edward III summoned to the Great Council, metamorphosing into the House of Lords, men whose fathers had belonged to the Great Council, thus developing a parliamentary peerage. The ecclesiastical component of the Lords was reduced, but remained numerically preponderant. But perhaps even more significant was the formalization of the House of Commons, made up of the knights of the shire and the representatives of the towns. The principle of representative government, which already had a long tradition in the local courts, was thus transferred to the national central institution. The House of Commons met separately in the chapter house of the abbot of Westminster. It still had an inferior position to the House of Lords, to which it presented petitions for action. If these were passed and accepted by the king they became official statutes. Gradually the Commons established the custom that all financial legislation had to be initiated by them. The purse strings thus came more and more into the hands of the Commons, and if the Commons could grant money, they soon learned also how to refuse it.

In the early fourteenth century statutes were not framed by the judges and entered on the statute rolls until parliament had been discharged from attendance. Significant discrepancies began to appear between the intent of parliament and the final form of statutes. It was not until early in the fifteenth century that legislation by bill and statute was regularized so that the will of parliament was no longer expressed merely by petitions subject to change by the king's ministers. Who could tell that the future belonged to parliament and the people, not to king or queen?

Royal Government. The development of the royal government was one of the most striking political facts of the fourteenth century. Members of the king's *curia regis,* officials who were part of his personal entourage, became more specialized in function as a court of exchequer, a court of common pleas, and, under Edward I, a court of king's bench, which evolved in response to the need for expertise in handling fiscal and legal matters. The House of Lords became well established as the supreme court of the land. Since the king was to administer justice, but was otherwise occupied, the chancellor assumed this duty, and from this developed a new court of the chancellor.

Further noteworthy developments took place in the judiciary as concomitants of the development of local government. The establishment of justices of the peace was a most portentous innovation, for the JPs became very important instruments for implementing the will of the royal government on the local level. The king appointed these justices, usually from among the landed gentry and lesser land-holders. They took over many of the duties once exercised by the sheriffs and took charge of police-court jurisdiction, licensing of alehouses, and setting of wages for laborers, when the central government undertook by statute to regulate prices and wages. The Statute of Laborers of 1351, for example, was designed to force laborers to accept job offers at the same pay scale as prevailed before the labor supply was reduced by the Great Plague of 1349, and the JPs were expected to enforce it locally. They were quite ineffective, however. In 1388 the quarterly sessions were estab-lished, requiring the JPs to meet four times annually to hear cases and to admin-ister certain legislation collectively. Thus, paradoxical as it may seem, the reign of a king whose preoccupation was so predominantly with foreign policy and war proved to be of tremendous importance for England's internal development. The war, in fact, forced Edward III to delegate authority in the interests of fiscal, bureaucratic, and military efficiency. By accentuating his dependence upon the propertied people with land or capital, it furthered the cause of parliamentary government.

During the last quarter of the fourteenth century England went through a severe governmental crisis. If there was something naively heroic about Edward III, the career of his successor, Richard II (1377–1399), evokes pity. He was a boy of ten when he inherited the crown, and a council ruled the kingdom during the first difficult years. Shortly after his accession an ill-considered poll tax and other prob-lems precipitated the great peasant revolt of 1381. As the king began to assert his personal control over the government, his weaknesses became apparent, for he was a spendthrift, had a bad temper, and catered to favorites. His idyllic marriage with Anne of Bohemia, daughter of Emperor Charles IV, ended in sorrow with her death in 1394. Richard struck down a traitor, Thomas of Gloucester, who opposed peace with France, and undertook to exercise absolute power, pronouncing laws from the throne and levying taxes arbitrarily. While the king was off in Ireland, Henry of Lancaster led a baronial revolt against him. The king surrendered and in the Tower of London was forced to abdicate. Parliament deposed Richard II and declared Henry of Lancaster king as Henry IV.

Crises and New Direction.   For England the fifteenth century was one long series of crises. During the first half of the century it scored a triumph in the Hundred Years' War with France and then went down to final defeat. During the second half of the century England was torn apart by baronial warfare until the triumph of the first Tudor king, Henry VII.

In Shakespeare's play *Henry IV* the king declaims, "Uneasy lies the head that wears a crown." Henry IV was beset with trouble on all sides: a revolt in Wales, Scottish resistance, French attacks on the coast, and a rebellion of the earl of Northumberland. Henry beheaded the archbishop of York, who had supported the earl. Executing a man of the church brought great odium upon him, and the populace ascribed Henry's lingering illness to the wrath of God.

His son Henry V (1413–1422) sought to establish peace in the realm by a kind of consensus politics. He gave Richard II an honorable reburial and recalled sworn enemies to court. He reestablished unity in the English church by adopting a hard line against the Lollards and effectively drove their movement underground. With peace and order achieved in church and state, Henry V was free to concentrate on foreign affairs. In that sphere he enjoyed brilliant success, triumphing on the battlefields of France and very nearly winning for himself and his heirs the crown of France. But he left behind an infant son, Henry VI (1422–1471), who was never too bright and at the age of thirty went out of his mind. His rule was chaotic and England suffered losses abroad and disorder at home.

It was in the final year of the Hundred Years' War that the king became mentally deranged. Richard, duke of York, became protector and ruled England until Queen Margaret drove him from power and out of England. Richard returned with an army and launched the first of a series of civil wars known as the Wars of the Roses. The red rose was the badge of Lancaster, the white rose the symbol of York. After a bloody struggle Edward of York emerged as King Edward IV (1461–1483). He devoted his last years to consolidating his power by reducing to impotence the feudal families that opposed him. When he died he left behind two young sons and several daughters. His brother, Richard of Gloucester, became protector of the realm and apparently began to prepare for the coronation of his nephew. But quite precipitously parliament pronounced the two sons of Edward IV to have been illegitimate. Duke Richard assumed the crown at Westminster as Richard III (1483–1485).

Richard III had the two princes imprisoned in the Tower of London and presumably had them killed and buried there. The rumors that the king had murdered his nephews were widely believed throughout England. The *Chronicles of London* relate that for this "cause Richard lost the hearts of the people." When the rumor spread that he was about to marry his niece, Elizabeth of York, popular feeling shifted even more strongly in favor of his rival, Henry Tudor of the house of Lancaster. Richard was not the monster that Tudor historians have made him out to be, but he clearly did not enjoy a good press or a very savory reputation even in his own day.

Henry introduced the great age of the Tudors, which witnessed the birth of English humanism, the Reformation, and the Elizabethan age, by winning with the help of French troops a sensational battle at Bosworth on August 22, 1485. Richard III died fighting fiercely, betrayed by many of his own men, and Henry Tudor became king as Henry VII. He wisely honored the promise he had made to his Yorkist supporters and married Elizabeth, the oldest daughter of Edward IV and the sister of the two princes who had died in the Tower. The white and the red roses were united and all occasion for further fighting was removed, although Henry VII did subsequently have to contend with some annoying Yorkist plots. The Wars of the Roses had been largely confined to the nobility, who fought with their bands of retainers (bastard feudalism) for mastery. They involved no great constitutional principle and no class conflict, and the great mass of the people were not directly concerned. Nevertheless, the unruly barons caused considerable damage, and the constant insecurity and lack of stability were so costly that the townsmen and the gentry alike were thoroughly sick of the whole thing. They were ready now to support a strong king who would check anarchy and establish peace and order. That man was Henry VII.

In spite of the historical legend derived in part from Francis Bacon's history of his reign, Henry VII was not in actual fact a great innovator. He did not inaugurate a "new monarchy," but actually did very little that had not already been begun by the Yorkist kings. In his nearly quarter of a century as king he summoned parliament only three times. His council acted as the court of the Star Chamber, named after the room in which it met, which helped to consolidate his power and restrain insurrection. He was very conservative in his expenditures and husbanded his resources so carefully that in his last years he acquired the reputation of a miser. The security he established encouraged trade and commerce. The people were very grateful and responded with a show of genuine patriotism. An aura of success and pride in the English nation prevailed.

In order to assure the continuity and greatness of his house, Henry VII arranged for the marriage of his oldest son, Arthur, to Catherine, the daughter of Ferdinand and Isabella of Spain. Catherine came to England and married Arthur in St. Paul's Cathedral in 1501. The young prince was only fifteen at the time and their cohabitation was delayed until he should further mature, but maturity never came to him: the following year he died. The king married his daughter Margaret to James IV of Scotland in a move designed to pacify that troublesome neighbor to the north. This marriage had important results in later times, when the Stuarts came to succeed the Tudors on the throne of England. Another daughter, Mary, became the wife of Louis XII of France. Henry VII's second son, Henry, was married to his brother Arthur's widow, Catherine of Aragon. In 1509 he succeeded to his father's throne as King Henry VIII.

SPAIN

A casual glance at the map would suggest that if any state in Europe has natural boundaries set by geography and should have achieved unity with relatively little struggle, that state is Spain. The Iberian peninsula is not only bounded on all sides by the seas, but is marked off by the Pyrenees along its land attachment to neighboring France. Moreover, the national consciousness of Catholic

Spain in subsequent centuries would seem to imply that there was something almost inevitable about the unification of Iberia under Spanish rule.

But in reality centrifugal forces were so powerful that, upon closer examination, the unification of Spain strikes one as having been almost fortuitous. The Iberian peninsula was populated with peoples of a variety of backgrounds and languages. The Basques were different in ethnic background and language from the Castilians. The Navarrese were oriented toward France. The Aragonese spoke a Castilian dialect, but the Catalonians and Valencians, as well as the inhabitants of the Balearic Islands, spoke Limosé, a southern French dialect. The Galicians spoke a language of their own, quite different from the Andalusians'. Moreover, the political history of the constituent parts varied greatly. Castile was plagued with a succession of minor and incompetent kings. Aragon was for centuries oriented toward a Mediterranean policy, and Portugal, which was not united with Spain until 1580, and then only temporarily, had a language, tradition, and foreign policy of its own. The national unification of Spain was anything but assured. In fact, Spain's two most prominent constituent states, Castile and Aragon, maintained separate political institutions and tariff barriers beyond the sixteenth century.

Like the territories of the Holy Roman Empire, both Castile and Aragon increased the centralization of their separate political institutions, but this very fact made their coalescence into a unified Spain more difficult. The king in each country had a great amount of power that could be used despotically. The cortes, or parliament, was not a national institution, for even though Castile and León had a common cortes after 1301, Aragon, Catalonia, and Valencia each had a cortes of its own, and these were never united. Moreover, the basis for representation in the cortes differed in each state. Although the townsmen gained representation as the third estate in every cortes, there was no systematic representational principle. In Castile and León some eighteen leading towns finally preempted the right of representation for the third estate. But no formal constitution defined the rights of the cortes, and the legislative power of the assembly was very limited. How much influence it exercised over the country depended entirely upon the strength or weakness of the monarch. Royal power vacillated wildly, especially in Castile.

The union of Castile and Aragon was achieved in the marriage bed. With the marriage in 1469 of Isabella of Castile (1474–1504) and Ferdinand of Aragon (1479–1516), the two kingdoms were united in the persons of their rulers. The two Catholic monarchs were proclaimed king and queen of Castile together, although Isabella never conceded any of her sovereign power to Ferdinand.

The Spanish Inquisition became an important instrument for the unification of Spain, for it was for a long time the one institution common to all parts of the kingdom. It was authorized by Pope Sixtus IV in 1478, and the three chief inquisitors functioned as a department of the government. Spain still glowed with crusading fervor from the long, hard drive against the Moors. The Inquisition now undertook to complete the Catholicization of the land, forcing the converted Jews (*Marranos*) and Moslems (*Moriscos*) to give up their former religious practices or suffer the consequences. In 1492 the Jews who resisted conversion were expelled from Spain. The cost to Spain in able tradesmen and intellectuals was enormous, as many of its most energetic and enterprising citizens fled to other parts of Europe.

Between 1481 and 1492 Ferdinand and Isabella completed the final subjugation of Granada, the last independent Moslem state on the Iberian peninsula. In a series of measures culminating in their final exile in 1502, the Moslems were driven out. With the homeland secure, Spain's monarchs were now free to promote the exploration of new routes to the Far East. Their support of Columbus' first voyage in 1492 proved to be one of the best investments ever made.

Ferdinand manipulated his foreign policy very cleverly. In exchange for a promise to remain neutral while the French king Charles VIII embarked upon his expedition to Naples in 1494, Ferdinand won the return of Roussillon to Spain. In 1497 Ferdinand intervened in Italy himself and began a duel with France for the domination of Italy that continued in the Habsburg-Valois wars in the sixteenth century. He managed his family marriages in such a way as to make maximum gains for his dynasty, principally directing them as diplomatic weapons against France. He married his daughter Catherine of Aragon, it will be recalled, to Prince Arthur, the oldest son of Henry VII of England, and then to Arthur's brother, Henry. Ferdinand's daughter Joanna married Philip, the son of Emperor Maximilian. By this alliance, however, Spain was drawn into the Habsburg political nexus and the affairs of central Europe, instead of remaining free to pursue its own rather obvious national interests of expansion into Portugal and North Africa. But on the surface it seemed like a brilliant match.

Ferdinand's domestic rule was for a decade ably administered by the brilliant Cardinal Ximénez, archbishop of Toledo. When, therefore, Ferdinand's grandson became King Charles I of Spain, he inherited a powerful kingdom that had made great strides toward world leadership. Small wonder that Machiavelli, who so prided himself on his political realism, held Ferdinand in great esteem as an admirable and successful prince.

IN RETROSPECT

The rise of the modern states of Europe was a long, slow process. But the engines of state were in motion, no matter how slow, uncertain, and unpredictable their movement. The general trend in the political development of western Europe was clearly toward centralization. The economic change in the direction of a capitalistic or money economy reinforced this political tendency by subverting the old feudal institutions and supporting monarchs and territorial princes. In turn the rising centralized states, with their more efficient bureaucracies, stronger fiscal policies, and more effective armies, provided an environment more congenial to the new economic forces. As it turned out, France and England developed the strongest national monarchies of all. The overall tendency in France was toward a strong, not to say absolutist, monarchy. The limitations imposed upon the English king by law and parliament contrasted significantly with the French monarchy by the end of the fifteenth century. The century-long war between France and England increased national patriotism in both countries. Unification and centralization came later to Spain, but eventually they came with force. What happened on a national scale in western Europe took place on the level of territorial principalities within the empire, sealing the doom of that venerable universal medieval institution through the triumph of particularism.

At the beginning of the fourteenth century Dante could call upon the Holy Roman emperor Henry VII to save Florence and restore the empire. But at the end of the fifteenth century Savonarola summoned a national monarch, Charles VIII of France, to save Florence and restore Italian liberty. Italy retained its system of small, independent city-states throughout the period. In the end it was overshadowed and overpowered by the great states to the north and west. It became, in fact, the battlefield where the giants fought, with Italy itself as the prize to be won.

Bibliography

General:
Bush, M. L. *Renaissance, Reformation and the Outer World, 1450–1660.* London, 1967.
Cohn, Henry J. *Government in Reformation Europe 1520–1560.* London, 1971.
Cowie, Leonard W. *Sixteenth Century Europe.* Edinburgh, 1977.
Fueter, Eduard. *Geschichte des Europäischen Staatensystems von 1492–1559.* Munich and Berlin, 1919; reprint, Osnabrück, 1972.
Hale, J. R.; J. R. L. Highfield; and B. Smalley, eds. *Europe in the Late Middle Ages.* London, 1965.
Kiernan, V. G. *State and Society in Europe 1550–1650.* New York, 1980.
Koenigsberger, H., *Estates and Revolutions: Essays in Early Modern European History.* Ithaca, NY, 1971.
Lee, Stephen J. *Aspects of European History 1494–1789.* London, 1978.
Mack, Phyllis and Margaret C. Jacob, eds. *Politics and Culture in Early Modern Europe: Essays in Honor of H. G. Koenigsberger.* Cambridge, 1987.
Strayer, Joseph R. *On the Medieval Origins of the Modern State.* Princeton, 1970.
———. *Medieval Statecraft and the Perspectives of History.* Princeton, 1974.
Ullmann, Walter. *Principles of Government and Politics in the Middle Ages.* London, 1961.
Waugh, W. T. *A History of Europe, 1378–1494,* 3rd ed. London, 1949.

Holy Roman Empire:
Andreas, Willi. *Deutschland vor der Reformation,* 5th ed. Stuttgart, 1948.

Bachmann, Adolf. *Deutsche Reichsgeschichte im Zeitalter Friedrich III und Maximilian I,* 2 vols. Leipzig, 1884–1894.
Barraclough, G. *The Origins of Modern Germany.* Oxford, 1946.
Below, Georg von. *Der deutsche Staat des Mittelalters,* 2nd ed. Leipzig, 1925.
Beneke, G., *Society and Politics in Germany 1500–1750.* London, 1974.
Cohn, Henry. *The Government of the Rhineland Palatinate in the Fifteenth Century.* London, 1965.
Hsia, R. Po-chia. *Society and Religion in Münster, 1553–1618.* New Haven, 1984.
Kraus, V. von, and K. Kaser. *Deutsche Geschichte am Ausgang des Mittelalters,* 2 vols. Stuttgart, 1905–1912.
Rodes, John E. *Germany: A History,* chaps. 4 and 5. New York, 1964.
Ulmann, Heinrich. *Kaiser Maximilian I,* 2 vols. Stuttgart, 1884–1891.
Waas, Glenn. *The Legendary Character of Kaiser Maximilian.* New York, 1941.
Wiesflecker, Hermann. *Kaiser Maximilian I,* 5 vols. Vienna, 1971 ff.

France:
Beaucourt, Gaston du Fresne. *Histoire de Charles VII.* Paris, 1881–1891.
Bridge, J. S. C. *A History of France from the Death of Louis XI.* 5 vols. Oxford, 1921–1936.
Cherrier, Claude de. *Histoire de Charles VIII, roi de France,* 2 vols., 2nd ed. Paris, 1870.
Dupont-Ferrier, Gustave. *La Formation de l'état français et l'unité française,* 2nd ed. Paris, 1934.
Gandilhon, R. *Politique économique de Louis XI.* Paris, 1941.
Grosjean, G. *Le sentiment national dans la Guerre des Cent Ans.* Paris, 1927.
Lavisse, Ernest. *Histoire de France, depuis les origines jusqu' à la révolution,* 9 vols., vols. 3–5. Paris, 1900–1911.
Major, J. Russell. *Representative Institutions in Renaissance France.* Madison, 1960.
Maulde, La Clavière, René de. *Histoire de Louis XII,* 6 vols. Paris, 1889–1893.
Perroy, É. *The Hundred Years' War.* New York, 1951.
Shennan, J. H. *Government and Society in France 1461–1661.* London, 1969.

Burgundy and the Low Countries:
Calmette, J. *The Golden Age of Burgundy.* London, 1962.
Cartellieri, O. *The Court of Burgundy.* London, 1929.
Dumont, Georges. *Histoire des Belges,* 3 vols. Brussels, 1954–1956.
Huizinga, Johan. *The Waning of the Middle Ages.* London, 1924.
Pirenne, Henri. *Histoire de Belgique,* 3rd ed., vol. 3;
4th ed., vol. 2. Brussels, 1923, 1947.
———. *Early Democracies in the Low Countries.* New York, 1963.
Vaughan, Richard. *Philip the Bold.* Cambridge, 1962.
———. *John the Fearless.* Cambridge, 1966.

England:
Chrimes, S. B. *English Constitutional Ideas in the Fifteenth Century.* Cambridge, 1936.
Gairdner, James. *Henry the Seventh.* London and New York, 1889.
Jacob, E. F. *The Fifteenth Century, 1399–1485.* Oxford, 1961.
Lapsley, G. T. *Crown, Community, and Parliament in the Later Middle Ages.* New York, 1951.
McIlwain, Charles H. *The High Court of Parliament and Its Supremacy.* New Haven, 1910.
McKisack, M. *The Fourteenth Century, 1307–1399.* Oxford, 1959.
Maitland, F. W. *The Constitutional History of England.* Cambridge, 1908.
Stubbs, William. *Constitutional History of England,* 3 vols. Oxford, 1874–1878.
Wilkinson, B. *Constitutional History of Medieval England,* 3 vols. London 1948–1958.

Spain:
Altamira y Crevea, Rafael. *La Historia de España y de la civilización española,* 4 vols., 3rd ed. Barcelona, 1900–1930.

Calmette, J. *La formation de l'unité espagnole*. Paris, 1946.

Chapman, Charles E. *A History of Spain*. New York, 1927. (A summary of Altamira, *Historia de España*.)

Elliott, John. *Imperial Spain*. London, 1963.

Mariejol, J. H. *The Spain of Ferdinand and Isabella*. New Brunswick, NJ, 1961.

Scandinavia:

Birch, J. S. H. *Denmark in History*. London, 1938.

Larsen, K. *A History of Norway*. Princeton, 1948.

Roberts, Michael. *The Early Vasas: A History of Sweden, 1523–1611*. New York, 1968.

Stromberg, A. A. *History of Sweden*. New York, 1931.

CHAPTER 4

Italy:
Home of the
Renaissance

"You may have the universe if I may have Italy," wrote Temistocles
Solera in his libretto for Verdi's opera *Attila*. He was reflecting the sentiment not
only of Huns, Germans, and Turks, but of the Holy Roman emperors themselves.
At the center of the Mediterranean world, home of the mother church and heir to
the grandeur that was Rome, Italy enjoyed an importance in the minds of Western
men not equaled by any other land.

A vague feeling of national identity was developing in Italy, though it was less
pronounced than in France, England, or Spain. Certainly an Italian consciousness
can be recognized not merely in enthusiastic poets such as Dante and Petrarch,
but in such a political realist as Machiavelli. In the famous Chapter 26 of *The Prince*
Machiavelli penned his exhortation to the Medici prince to liberate Italy from the
barbarians. Writing in 1513, Machiavelli urged Lorenzo de' Medici, grandson of
Lorenzo the Magnificent, to free Italy of all barbarian domination, now that his
house controlled both Florence and the papacy.

> This opportunity must not, therefore, be allowed to pass, so that Italy may at
> length find her liberator. I cannot express the love with which he would be received
> in all those provinces which have suffered under these foreign invasions, with what
> thirst for vengeance, with what steadfast faith, with what love, with what grateful
> tears. What doors would be closed against him? What people would refuse him
> obedience? What envy could oppose him? What Italians would withhold allegiance?

An Italian could be fiercely loyal to his own city-state, ready to die for it. The contemporaries of Machiavelli, subjected as they were to foreign invaders, were conscious of the difference between Italians and "barbarians." But few had a concept of Italy as a political entity or conceived of an alliance or confederation of city-states which would repel all invaders. The city-states proved to be too small and too selfish for such an ideal solution to the Italian problem. Moreover, geography and history worked against the unification of Italy and the rise of a national dynasty that would provide a standard to which loyal Italians could repair. Even though the Italian peninsula was clearly delineated on the map as a boot surrounded by the sea, the Apennine mountain range ran down the center like a spine, dividing the land and isolating many smaller states. Moreover, Italians learned early that the sea itself was a convenient highway for invaders, making Italy vulnerable to attack on all sides.

The south was overrun by Greeks and Moors. The Normans had set up their kingdom in Naples and Sicily, holding them as fiefs under the pope. The Hohenstaufens, as Holy Roman emperors, had moved to the two Sicilies and resided there virtually as local kings. Although the pope brought in the house of Anjou and destroyed the Swabian rule, the people arose in the revolt known as the Sicilian Vespers (1282) and massacred nearly all the French on the island. The house of Aragon was enthroned in Sicily by the Treaty of Caltabellotta (1302). The popes aspired to extend their temporal kingdom from Rome across the width of the Italian boot. Although the emperors from 1300 on had no real control over Italy, Henry VII, Ludwig the Bavarian, Charles IV, Frederick III, and the others did intervene in Italian affairs and had an unsettling effect upon them. In the north the Po valley was a rich land and a great prize for conquerors, contested first by Milan and Venice, then by the great powers of the north. In little Tuscany in the center, hemmed in by Rome to the south and Milan to the north, Florence had to be content with lesser ambitions—the possession of Pisa, the conquest of Lucca.

Thus history as well as geography worked against the unification of Italy during those centuries. It is ironic and one of history's notorious injustices that even though the greatest cultural and social achievements emerged from the city-states in the fourteenth and fifteenth centuries, wherever the cities were the strongest, whether in Flanders, the Hanse cities, the Rhineland, south Germany, or Italy, national unity with its obvious benefits came latest. In fact, it did not come until the nineteenth century. The city-states were very successful culturally, just as they had been in classical antiquity. Plato had favored politically small units for the full development of the individual within his closed society. Aristotle had ventured to say that ideally a state should be small enough so that a citizen could see across it from one side to the other. Some of the smaller Italian states, such as Urbino, with very active cultural life at their ducal courts, nearly fitted this ideal pattern, but most of them were considerably larger. Most of them also put greater stress upon the liberty of citizens (by which they meant the nobility and the successful men of commerce) than the classical city-states. Lord Acton was more right than wrong when he argued that in the classical form of the state "the passengers existed for the sake of the ship." Aristotle himself considered the worst government to be that which left men "free to live as they please." The catchwords of the Italian states, in contrast, were "peace" and "liberty." The people even accepted new despots only in the name of liberty.

In spite of their cultural glories, the city-states in the long run failed politically. No leagues of cities held up against outside pressures, and within the cities, except for Venice, regimes were constantly changing. The national states proved to be politically more successful because they managed to develop institutions representing the interests of a larger part of the population than did the oligarchic and despotic city-states, and because they had superior resources. The idea of the individual represented in a collective body as a "corporate person" was developed in Roman private law. With the revival of Roman law from the twelfth century on, this conception was once again consciously articulated. People came to look upon corporations as legal persons, entirely natural and real, not merely as fictitious persons. This concept of representation was transferred to representative bodies in the government, such as the parliament in England (1295), the estates general in France (1302), the cortes of Aragon and Castile, the estates of Naples, and the imperial diet (*Reichstag*) or territorial diets (*Landtage*) in the empire. The late thirteenth, fourteenth, and early fifteenth centuries have been called the "corporative period," following the feudal period of individual relationships and preceding the modern period, in which the state has come to be a collectivity of individuals.

In this corporative period the individual was not conceived of as an isolated atom in the body politic, but as a member of a corps, such as the church, nobility, guild, and the like. The corps then coalesced into orders, and each order or estate appeared as a unit in the representative assembly. Western Europe had its tradition of a strong monarch asserting his power from a territorial center. This period saw neither absolute monarchy nor exclusively representative government, but states operated on the basis of a functional dualism. The policy of kings was determined by their need for support and counsel (*auxilium et consilium*). The clergy, the nobility, and the third estate, which made its first appearance as a town association, could cooperate with the monarch or resist his designs, according to their own collective interest. Custom and precedent played important roles in legal thought in this period and served as guiding and restricting forces upon royalty. In Poland and the empire the estates were strong, while in the west the kings grew in power.

In the medieval commune four social elements were universally present: (1) the nobility or patricians; (2) the merchant capitalists, some of them newly enriched (*gente nuova*); (3) the petty bourgeois class, made up of members of the lesser guilds, craftsmen, and shopkeepers; and (4) the unorganized and property-less workers. The pattern of political dominance varied a great deal in the city-states and there was great flexibility during the fourteenth and fifteenth centuries. In a Hanse city such as Lübeck, the participation of nobility in government was very prominent. In Venice the merchant oligarchy ruled supreme. In Florence the patricians or magnates (*grandi*), a class formed by the intermarriage of rich merchant families and the nobility from the estates of Tuscany, dominated the commune in its formative years. But newly rich families pressed into prominence as the fourteenth century moved on. Political life was marked by the struggle of the greater and lesser guilds for power. It is fascinating to observe how the meanest guildsmen closed ranks with the upper classes in fighting off the unorganized wool workers during the Ciompi revolt of 1378. The peasants in the countryside were frequently a threat, for they were excluded from the political processes altogether; they suffered exploitation, had little hope for a better life, and thus had nothing to lose either by revolting or by joining an alien power.

The historian is bound to the concrete and must resist the temptation to construct an ideal type of Italian Renaissance city-state and to manipulate parts of the model. For whatever similarities existed, each state had its own historical background and its unique political experience. "The principal foundation of all states," Machiavelli pronounced, "is good laws and good arms." The conception of what constitutes good laws and the success of good arms varied so greatly from state to state and from decade to decade that each must be examined separately and concretely. Milan, Venice, and Florence had distinct kinds of government. But they experienced a parallel development from urban communes into very centralized territorial states. Naples differed in having a feudal monarch and in being so vulnerable to foreign domination. The situation in Rome was complicated by the presence of the papacy.

Rome

THE IDEA OF ROME as the capital of the empire and center of the Western world was very much alive throughout the Middle Ages. But as a reality the city fell far short of the grandeur that was ancient Rome's. By the fourteenth century the city had gained in population over its near pastoral state in the earlier medieval period. The people were clustered around various centers, such as the Capitoline Hill, the old Lateran Palace, and St. Peter's. The economy was sustained by the income of the ecclesiastical bureaucrats, administrative and judicial, and by the pilgrims who came to visit the sacred shrines. There was little trade and hence virtually no bourgeois class.

Power was held by the feudal magnates, families such as the Orsinis and Colonnas, with city palaces and landed estates outside Rome. The papacy contended with these families for local control, but as a result of the Babylonian Captivity in Avignon and the schism, papal authority declined enormously. The Roman mob not only intimidated the College of Cardinals during the election of a new pope, but even frightened away the pope himself, as in 1434 when they forced out Eugenius IV. Central control over the Papal States was extremely tenuous during the fourteenth century and the first half of the fifteenth. The popes had to accept the virtual autonomy of many cities nominally in their territory, such as Bologna and Ferrara, as well as lesser towns in Romagna and Emilia. Only with the Renaissance popes, from Nicholas V on, did the security of the popes in the city and their control of the communes and lesser dynasties become in any sense effective. Since the Papal States reached to the northeast well beyond the confines of Tuscany, many foreign forces that wished to avoid the Florentines found it convenient to pass through the Papal States instead. Being in the center of that strife-torn peninsula had certain advantages, but Rome was by the same token open to attack from the north and the south, as well as from the sea.

Rome's most fascinating political adventure during the Renaissance was its revival of the republic under Cola di Rienzo (1313–1354). Rienzo has captured the imagination of political as well as literary romantics. When Napoleon was taken captive after Waterloo, a life of Cola di Rienzo was found in his baggage. Lord Byron honored him with a poem and Bulwer-Lytton celebrated him with an epic. Wagner did an opera (1838–1840) on Rienzo, the "last Roman tribune." Some of his followers claimed that he was an illegitimate son of Emperor Henry VII, for he happened to have been born in 1313, when Henry had been in Italy. In reality he was the son of a laundress and a tavern keeper. Rienzo became a notary and developed an interest in Roman history and archeology. In the *Lex regia* he read how the Roman people had delegated their power to the emperors. Rienzo delivered a rhetorically powerful oration at the Forum, telling the people of Rome that they were the true source of political power and preparing them for a republican revolution.

In 1342 Rienzo became the head of a delegation to Avignon. There he first met Petrarch, the great humanist, and impressed the politically naïve poet. Petrarch addressed a series of letters to Rienzo and the Roman people encouraging them to restore Rome to its ancient glories. In 1347 Rienzo led a popular revolt and declared himself to be the tribune of the Roman people, and proved it by appearing in a tribune's garb. He claimed to rule the city and the empire "by the authority of our lord Jesus Christ." A powerful orator, he spoke of *Italia sacra* with patriotic fervor. "You will die in freedom," he declared, "so that posterity may be born in freedom." He wished a renovation, a renaissance, of the imperial rule and of the church. But Rienzo failed to win the support of the powerful Roman princely families, and the great revolt came to an ignominious end in 1349 when the Orsinis combined with the Colonnas to suppress it. Rienzo fled for refuge to the Franciscans.

Rienzo believed that he had relied too heavily upon the papacy and that the emperor might prove to be a more effective ally. In 1350 he went to Prague and was ushered into the presence of Emperor Charles IV. Charles thought him interesting but erratic, and finally imprisoned him. At the pope's request Charles IV delivered him to Avignon, where he was put on trial. Finally a new pope devised a plan to use Rienzo to pacify Italy and to prepare Rome for the return of the papacy. He appointed the papal legate Cardinal Albornoz as Rienzo's protector. Rienzo's true character was revealed in his moment of triumph, when he turned into a petty tyrant. In 1354 he entered Rome and had himself proclaimed a senator, with a banner bearing the ancient emblem SPQR (*Senatus populusque romanus*). At last the very lowest classes, on whose support he counted, turned against him. He attempted to escape wearing a disguise, but was caught and killed by a mob at the foot of the Capitoline Hill.

Rienzo foreshadowed Italian national patriotism and possessed a humanist's interest in ancient Rome. In a way, Rienzo was very much a man of the Renaissance. Exaggerated claims have been made for his role in introducing the Renaissance to the court of Charles IV and thus initiating the northern Renaissance. But at the same time he was not unlike medieval figures such as Arnold of Brescia, who centuries earlier had dreamed of restoring Rome to its ancient glory.

Naples and Sicily

THE ONLY KINGDOM in Italy with a well-established monarchy was Naples. Its history was complicated during the fourteenth and fifteenth centuries by its involvement with Sicily, its vulnerability to the conflicting claims of foreign dynasties, and the ambitions of its rulers to dominate other parts of Italy, preeminently Rome. The Angevins, who ruled during the fourteenth century, were involved in a constant struggle with the Aragonese in Sicily.

When King Robert succeeded to the throne in 1309, he was immediately involved in a war with Sicily, and sent a series of punitive expeditions into the island to lay it waste. He had more the appearance than the reality of royal power. An able man, scholarly, and a friend of Petrarch, he was unsuccessful in his attempts to control the rebellious barons at home, and before long lost his position as the leader of the Guelph party in Italy. When he died in 1343 his granddaughter Joanna, the wife of Andrew of Hungary, succeeded him. When a band of conspirators, perhaps with Joanna's connivance, murdered Andrew, Andrew's brother Louis, king of Hungary, came to Naples to avenge his death and to assert his claims to the throne. He drove out Joanna and her new husband, Louis of Taranto, but his excesses alienated all of Italy, and in 1352 the papal legate crowned Joanna and her husband in Naples. When the papal schism began in 1378, Joanna supported Clement VII, the antipope. Pope Urban VI thereupon declared the throne vacant and offered it to Charles of Durazzo. In this crisis Joanna appealed to Louis of Anjou for help, in return for which she made him her legal heir. Clement supported Louis, of course, but in 1382 Charles of Durazzo captured Naples, had Joanna put to death, and ruled in her stead as Charles III. When he died a few years later, civil war broke out between his son Ladislas, then seventeen, and Louis of Anjou. By 1400 Ladislas conquered the kingdom, occupied Rome, and even threatened Florence. He died at the right moment (1414) for Rome and Florence, but Naples sank into a state of virtual anarchy.

Joanna II, the sister of Ladislas, was involved in a maze of intrigues and assassinations that it is pointless to record here. She was eventually succeeded by her last lover, Alfonso of Aragon, whom she designated as her heir. Sicily and Naples were at last once again united under this Alfonso the Magnanimous, who proved to be a brilliant ruler and a great patron of arts and letters. When he died in 1458, his illegitimate son Ferrante succeeded him as King Ferrante I. He had the usual task of subduing the unruly barons (barons, it seems, are always unruly). In alliance with Pope Sixtus IV and Milan, he made war on Florence in 1479. It was then that Lorenzo de' Medici made his daring trip to confront Ferrante I in person and persuaded him to make peace. Ferrante died in 1494 as King Charles VIII of France was undertaking a wild invasion of Italy to assert Angevin claims to Naples. Charles VIII did take Naples and drove out Ferrante's grandson Ferrantino. When the French withdrew, Ferrantino moved back in, but he soon died and the kingdom was plunged into civil war and virtual anarchy. France and Spain fought for the spoils, and finally, at the end of the year 1502, the Spaniards seized and held the kingdom. Clearly the Neapolitan monarchy, with the many claims and counterclaims upon it and its inability to control the nobility, provided no more continuity and security than the rules of communes and *signori* were able to offer in the other states of Italy.

Milan

THE POLITICAL DEVELOPMENTS in the north were hardly more inspiring than those in the south. In Lombardy the medieval communes, with some assured civic liberties, evolved in a few decades into despotisms. By 1300 many towns were ruled by *signori* rather than by the councils of the communes. "The cities of Italy," Dante lamented, "are full of tyrants and every clown that comes to play the partisan becomes a Marcellus" (*Purgatorio,* Canto 6, lines 125–26). This development was almost everywhere the same. An able or particularly aggressive leader, whether the *podestà* (the chief executive) or the *condottiere* or *capitano del popolo* (the military commander), assumed the leadership of the state for a limited term. The term was then renewed or extended in time as the internal or external crisis persisted. His powers were enlarged and he undertook to entrench himself by manipulating opposing factions and currying popular favor. He then sought to make the succession in office hereditary. By successfully expanding the territory of the state at the expense of neighboring cities, the ruler achieved a double purpose, for he appealed to the pride and patriotism of the citizens and at the same time ensured the existence of hostile neighbors who would perpetuate the state of crisis and make a strong ruler a necessity. The people invariably accepted the new provincial despot in the name of liberty and peace. Milan provides the classic example, with the rise of the Viscontis to power and the Sforza takeover.

In the center of the rich Po valley, Milan was strategically located, and from Roman times played an important role in Italian history. During the thirteenth century the city freed itself from Hohenstaufen domination, but was torn internally by the struggle for power of the old nobility and the rising merchant class. In 1262 Otto Visconti became lord of Milan, and except for the years 1302–1310, when the rival della Torre family was in control, the Visconti family ruled from then until their line came to an end in 1447. Before his death in 1295 Archbishop Otto had his nephew Matteo elected *capitano del popolo*. Matteo secured the additional title of "imperial vicar," confirmed in 1299. Under Visconti leadership Milan expanded its territories along the Po valley to include Bologna, Parma, Lodi, Bobbio, Cremona, Brescia, Bergamo, Como, Novara, and other cities.

When Matteo's son Giovanni died, these territories were governed by three of his nephews, Matteo, Bernabò, and Galeazzo. A bit of loving family history came into play, for Matteo was murdered by his brothers in 1355. Bernabò reigned in Milan (1354–1385) and Galeazzo (1354–1378) in Pavia. Galeazzo was followed by his son Gian Galeazzo, who murdered Bernabò and ruled over the entire Milanese dominion after that. In 1395 he bought the title of duke from Emperor Wenceslas. He was an energetic, formidable ruler, who began the building of the great Gothic cathedral of Milan and the Certosa in Pavia. He also began the expansion of Milan into Tuscany, taking Vicenza, Verona, Pisa, and Siena, and threatening the encirclement and conquest of Florence itself. His death in 1402 saved Florence. Two sons succeeded him, Giovanni Maria (d. 1412) and Filippo Maria (d. 1447). The Viscontis lived the extravagant lives of petty potentates. They spent lavishly and taxed the people harshly. Filippo Maria kept a menagerie of leopards, English hounds, and falcons that cost three thousand gold pieces a month for care and upkeep. For all his grandeur, Filippo Maria died without a legitimate heir. At this juncture the Milanese, weary of their extravagant rulers, set up the Ambrosian Republic, named after St. Ambrose of Milan, and undertook to restore the old commune.

The Ambrosian Republic lasted only three years, for there was too little of the old communal spirit left to sustain it. Francesco Sforza, the military commander or *condottiere* (*condotta* was the contract for mercenary service), betrayed the republic. Venice was expanding up the valley against Milan, so the republic needed to employ mercenary forces, which were captained by Sforza. He had married Bianca, an illegitimate daughter of Filippo Visconti, and felt that he deserved special prerogatives in the city. When the council refused his demands, he went over to Venice and conquered Milan with its aid. His was a naked power grab and his success depended on the soldiery. He built the great red-brick castle that still looms formidably over Milan with its massive round towers. He declared that the 130 captains of castles throughout Milan's territories were the defense and backbone of the state.

Ludovico il Moro, who ruled from 1480 on, conducted the Milanese court with all the grandeur of a monarch. He was very anxious to ally his family by marriage with European royalty. As a political conniver he went too far. He was guilty of a fatal blunder in encouraging the French to intervene in Italian affairs, for they had claims on Milan itself. In 1499 the French king Louis XII drove Ludovico from power. Swiss mercenaries reinstated him for a short time, but in 1500 they turned him over to the French, who kept him imprisoned until his death in 1508. For a few years Massimiliano Sforza ruled as a protégé of the Habsburg emperor, for Emperor Maximilian's second wife was Ludovico's daughter Bianca. In 1515 the French king Francis I won a stunning victory at Marignano and dominated Milan until the imperial forces occupied the city in 1522. The Spanish crown controlled Milan from 1535 until 1714. Then Austria dominated the city until Napoleon placed upon his own head the iron crown of Lombardy.

Milan experienced two distinct styles of political domination during the Renaissance. The Viscontis gradually changed their magistracy into a hereditary position. They grasped power but retained the forms of legitimacy and legality, retaining in office the traditional magistrates and civic councils. The Sforzas had no real interest in conforming to legal forms. They made a straight power play and had so little regard for traditional government that the Council of Nine Hundred met very infrequently, and then merely to approve decisions already made or actions already taken. Machiavelli was fascinated by the success of the Sforzas and asked why they triumphed whereas Cesare Borgia failed.

In government Milan was typical of the city-states of northern Italy. The Scaligeri family in Verona, the Estes in Ferrara, the Carraras in Padua, the Gonzagas of Mantua, and the Malatestas of Rimini conformed to the Visconti pattern of political aggrandizement. But several of the Malatestas were sufficiently vicious and tyrannical to evoke the image of Ludovico il Moro.

Before leaving the north one must take note of an area that was to loom large in Italy's future. Savoy and Piedmont were organized into a unified state by Amadeo VI, Amadeo VII, and especially Duke Amadeo VIII (1391–1451). Its influence reached as far north as Geneva.

Genoa and Venice

IF MILAN AND VENICE engaged in a struggle on land in the fifteenth century, a far older rivalry existed on the sea between Genoa and Venice for the control of maritime routes and the lion's share of the Levant trade. At one time Pisa, too, had competed for trade in the Levant, but Pisa was being pressed by Milan and Florence and was torn by internal strife, and never recovered its former strength after being decisively defeated by Genoa in 1284. The two great rivals that remained provide a fascinating contrast in government, for Genoa represented an extreme of political instability, whereas Venice was a model of law and order. In the long run the orderly succession of governments in Venice meant that it could recover from losses and come back after reverses abroad. Venice triumphed and Genoa declined.

Located on the beautiful Ligurian coast, Genoa had ready access to the sea. Since Genoa controlled Corsica, Genoese ships could freely sail the western Mediterranean and Tyrrhenian Seas, and had ready access to rich markets also in the East. But it was torn by the struggle of rival aristocrats, the Spinolas, Dorias, and other families. Competing groups of merchants further disrupted civic life and fought in the overseas markets. The commoners were hostile to the upper classes, and the popular government during the fourteenth and fifteenth centuries was constantly in a state of uproar and rebellion. After domination by the German, Neapolitan, and Milanese rulers, Genoa finally achieved a greater measure of independence early in the fourteenth century. In 1339 it paid its rival Venice the flattery of imitation by appointing its first doge, giving him an appointment for life. This step did not in itself provide stability, however, for in one three-month period in 1393 five doges held office. The next century saw continued disturbances, especially from 1413 to 1421 and again in 1435.

The rivalry with Venice lasted from the thirteenth to the sixteenth centuries and was particularly acute during the fourteenth century, when trade suffered in general and the Ottoman Turks began to restrain trade by their military action in the Levant. The thirteenth century witnessed two major conflicts, from 1261 to 1270 and from 1294 to 1299. In one of these clashes, in 1298, Marco Polo was captured by the Genoese. It was during his imprisonment that he wrote his account of the Far East. Another great war was fought from 1351 to 1355. But the most deadly was the War of Chioggia, 1377–1381, which took its name from the bold attack made by Genoa's fleet upon the Venetian lagoon. The Venetians fought off the Genoese, but it was the closest they had come to defeat. The Genoese were in deep trouble at home, for unlike Venice, at the far end of the Adriatic, Genoa was exposed to attack by major powers. It fought Alfonso of Aragon, king of Naples, for the possession of Sardinia and lost. Then it was alternately overrun by the Milanese and the French. Finally in 1528 the great admiral Andrea Doria freed Genoa of French domination and reestablished home rule as a Habsburg satellite, a status that Genoa retained until the time of the French Revolution.

The most amazing example of political stability and governmental continuity in Italy was Venice, queen of the Adriatic. Not only did its strategic position off the mainland and its open communications on the sea keep it free from siege and conquest by enemies outside, but its unique political institutions kept it secure from rebellion and civil war at home. Venice was fortunate in not having a feudal countryside, and therefore having no need to tame or absorb a landholding nobility, as other Italian cities had to do. It was not entangled in the Guelph-Ghibelline rivalries. Basically a merchant oligarchy, the Venetian government was relatively stable, run by the patricians in the interest of their own social and economic interests. Cicero's sardonic definition of oligarchy applied perfectly to the Venetians: "When a group of men controls the commonwealth by virtue of their wealth, their birth, or any advantages they happen to possess, they form an oligarchy, but they call themselves leading citizens." From the "closing of the council" in Venice in 1297 to the fall of the republic in 1797, exactly half a millennium of history had gone by, a remarkable achievement for a city-state.

So far as the lesser nobility and the common people were concerned, liberty was virtually a myth. When Wordsworth lamented "The Extinction of the Venetian Republic" and celebrated Venice as "the eldest child of liberty, a maiden city bright and free," he was using poetic license. For the government remained firmly in the hands of the rich old families, and after 1297 no one was able to become a member of the Great Council who could not claim an ancestor who had been a council member. This meant that political authority was effectively in the hands of some two hundred or so wealthy families. Machiavelli could scoff at these hucksters who assumed the "style of nobility," but the relative prosperity of Venice is proof enough that on the whole they used their authority wisely. The constitution of Venice merits examination.

The Venetian government had a fascinating scheme for the allocation and use of power. There were three basic parts. The senate ostensibly represented all the people and served as the main legislative body. The Great Council elected the senate and eventually served the main function of assisting in the selection of the executive committees, executive officers, and lesser magistrates. The doge performed ceremonial functions and did the will of the Great Council and the senate. He was usually an older man who could be relied upon to remain ornamental and not to press his personal ambitions, although several doges in the early fifteenth century, such as Michele Steno, Tommaso Mocenigo, and Francesco Foscari, did attempt to increase their political power.

In order to prevent any one faction from securing the election of its candidate as doge, the Great Council developed an elaborate system of election by lot which went through many steps. The whole council selected by lot thirty members, from which number nine members then chose forty. Of the forty members, twelve were selected who chose forty-five. The forty-five were reduced to eleven, and the eleven chose the final group of forty-one, who elected the doge. This built-in safety device worked well and was essential precisely because the doge was elected for life. After 1335 an executive committee of ten, the *Dieci,* could assume emergency powers in times of crisis. They were chosen annually by an electoral group of twenty, ten of whom were selected by the council and ten by the doge and executive officials. The *Dieci* received anonymous charges of crime, conspiracy, or sedition, which could be slipped through a slot in the thick wall of their chamber, and they deliberated in secret. The Bridge of Sighs led from the doge's palace, where they met, to the prison on the other side of the canal.

The constitution of Venice gave every appearance of providing a system of checks and balances among the legislative, executive, and judicial branches of government. Enlightened political theorists in the eighteenth century considered Venice's stability to have been a result of this system of checks and balances. Actually, the complexly interlocking functions and the restraint of the *Dieci* in the exercise of authority are the most fascinating features of Venetian government. Any lesson on the separation of powers learned from the Venetian experience needs to be modified by consideration of Venice's history and the facts of life.

In the *Inferno* Dante has grafters in public office punished in a smoky, fiery place, sulfurous and smelling of pitch. It is a description of the arsenal near the mouth of the Grand Canal in Venice, where the great galleys were repaired and the tar boiled and bubbled for calking the ships back from battles with the enemy and storms at sea. The state galleys were the largest and were ordered by special officials. The senate supervised every detail of their construction, for on them depended the prosperity and safety of the state. Like the Florentine florin, the Venetian sequin provided one of the very few stable currencies for trade in all of Italy, which was very important for Venice's international merchants.

Near the doge's palace on the Piazzetta stand two slender columns bearing the lion of St. Mark, the patron saint of the city, whose body had been brought to the city from Egypt, and the crocodile of St. Theodore, another symbol of Venice's tie to the Near East. Following the fourth crusade in 1204, in which Venice played an ignoble part in the sack of Constantinople, Venice steadily expanded its Mediterranean possessions. Over the gate of its great seventeenth-century fortress on the hill overlooking Nauplia in Greece its great lion of St. Mark is still to be seen. Venice's policy was to set up fortresses and merchant colonies at the mouths of rivers and at ports in order to control trade, rather than occupy the territory and control political developments in the hinterland. That its fleet could take on the naval forces of mighty empires such as that of the Turks is a tribute both to the skill and to the courage of the Venetians. Venice had a responsible ministry at home and a well-trained civil service to sustain its commitments abroad.

Florence

WESTERN INTELLECTUALS have carried on a perpetual love affair with Florence, the queen city of the Renaissance. To Elizabeth Browning, Florence seemed to be "the most beautiful of the cities devised by man." Robert Browning described Giotto's campanile as "completing Florence as Florence Italy." When Jacob Burckhardt had at last made his way to the "lazy South" and come to Florence, he said, "The view from Brunelleschi's dome placed the crown on everything. This is the most beautiful thing I have seen in my life." In the fourteenth century a noted chronicler, Giovanni Villani, described the glories of Florence at the height of its prosperity in 1338. "Florence," he wrote, "the daughter and creature of Rome, was in the ascendancy and destined for great things."

In the twelfth and thirteenth centuries the social and political organization of Florence was communal. It was a natural outgrowth of the struggles of the late Middle Ages. The last of the Hohenstaufen emperors, Frederick II, had failed to maintain a hold on northern Italy, in spite of the brutalities of his *condottiere,* Ezzelino da Romano. In Florence a "republic" was established, *Il primo popolo,* from 1250 to 1260. Following bitter Guelph-Ghibelline struggles a second "republic" was established with the creation of a new executive authority in 1293, a committee of *priori,* and new "ordinances of justice." Then came the final fight of two powerful factions, the Blacks and the Whites, which ended with the exile in 1301 of the Whites, including Dante, the father of Petrarch, and other illustrious citizens.

With a population of about 90,000, Florence was the fifth largest city in Christendom. The Florentines had a mystical conception of their city, referring to the *polis* as the mystical body of Christ and to the treasury as *Christus fiscus.* During the first half of the fourteenth century Florence was ruled by the upper classes, the *popolo grasso* or "fat people." In the years 1328–1342, 71 percent of the magistrates of the republic came from three of the major guilds, wool, banking, and cloth. The seven most powerful associations or guilds, the *arti maggiori,* were the judges and notaries, the money changers or bankers, the wool cloth manufacturers, the cloth importers, the silk merchants, the physicians and apothecaries, and the furriers.

Two powerful guilds controlled the wool industry: the cloth manufacturers, the *Arte della Lana,* and the cloth finishers, the *Arte di Calimala,* who imported unfinished textiles from Flanders. The guilds were not made up of master artisans, as they were during the Middle Ages, but were really associations of merchant industrialists. They were organized in order to control the laborers, manipulate prices, maintain monopolies, and control government economic policies by the use of political pressure. A limited number of the most important members of each of these major guilds elected an executive committee for a half-year term.

The five guilds of the so-called middle crafts made up the *arti medie.* These five were the blacksmiths, the shoemakers, the carpenters and masons, the second-hand clothes dealers, and the butchers. In the course of the decades nine additional lesser guilds, the *arti minori,* came into existence to represent the lower bourgeois shopkeepers and artisans: innkeepers, bakers, armorers, and tradesmen who sold salt, oil, and cheese. The great mass of unorganized workers made up the *popolo minuto.* The "little people" were miserably paid and lived in squalid housing. It was communal policy to keep grain and meat prices low, but the guilds kept the prices of many other articles artificially high.

The board of *priori,* or *signoria,* was the keystone of the communal edifice. The six (later eight and nine) *priori* were chosen by lot, their names drawn from a purse by guild leaders. Candidates had to be Guelph citizens over thirty who were guild members and who were not noblemen or tax delinquents and had never been bankrupt. They were named for a term of two months and formed the most important governing body of the state. By 1361 over five hundred Florentines were eligible to serve on the *signoria.* Its nine members were responsible both for formulating policy and for the actual administration of the government. The very broad powers they exercised were stated in the statute of the *capitano del popolo* in these words: "The *priori* and *gonfaloniere* [standard-bearer of justice, an executive post] should work diligently for the safety, exaltation, conservation, and growth of the peaceful and tranquil state of the people and commune of Florence." They selected magistrates, initiated legislation, guided proposals through the councils, and directed foreign policy. To assure some distribution of responsibility, a *priore* could not serve again in the *signoria* until three years after the expiration of his previous term.

The years 1336–1338 saw the high point of Florentine prosperity. The great banking houses of the Bardis and Peruzzis, upon which the economic prosperity of Florence depended, were peaking, but in 1338 the first indications of their coming bankruptcy were beginning to shake the business community. The Bardis and Peruzzis had unwisely made immense political loans of around a million florins. In May 1339, King Edward III of England suspended payment on loans he had received from them. Since the Bardi bank had a highly centralized structure, it collapsed. Moreover, Florence was waging war against Lucca, which proved to be enormously costly. The chronicler Giovanni Villani estimated that the city had spent 600,000 florins on the war, that the public debt was 450,000 florins, and that the tax revenues for the next six years were committed to the reduction of the war debt. All this spelled economic disaster, and when it came, the Florentines turned to a strong man to save the state.

In September 1342 the Florentines chose the military captain Walter of Brienne, titular duke of Athens, as ruler for life. The factions within the city continued to feud and the duke proved to be totally unable to cope with the complicated economic and internal political situation. *Il popolo* screamed, "Death to the duke and his followers!" In July 1343 all classes combined to expel him. The Florentines seemed to have learned their lesson, for never again did they resort to one-man rule in a crisis, and when in the next century one man did emerge as the supreme leader, his power was at least circumscribed by the forms of republican government. During the two decades following the explusion of Brienne, Florence was in a state of perpetual crisis.

In 1348 the Black Death struck Florence. Although contemporary chroniclers estimated that three-fifths of the population died of the plague, more conservative contemporary estimates suggest losses of 30,000 to 45,000 out of a population of 80,000 to 90,000. Hardly a family escaped without a death. For the next thirty years the population seems to have fluctuated between 50,000 and 60,000. It took a century for the population to rise well above the level of 1348. One estimate is that by 1500 the population had climbed to nearly 130,000.

The disasters that befell Florence make a depressing story. The chronicler Matteo Villani (d. 1363) remarked that history is essentially a narration of the calamities and disasters that befall the human race. After the plague, famine struck the land in 1352–1353, 1369–1370, and 1373–1375. Another grave economic crisis developed in 1396. As though the buffeting of nature were not enough, Florence was involved in four costly wars: two with Milan (1351–1353 and 1369–1370), one with Pisa (1362–1364), and one with the papacy (1375–1378). Tuscany suffered from pillaging by armed bands of mercenaries. Factional strife within the city increased as pressure from the outside mounted. From 1350 on internal hostility crystallized around two rival families, the Albizzis and the Riccis. The patrician families tended to give way to the new families (*gente nuova*), who made their way into the upper echelons of the Florentine business class. "New men" (*novi cives*) who were impatient with the leisurely patrician world of the commune entered the government. They insisted upon a more rigorous rule of law, a more equitable administration of justice, and tighter fiscal control. The communal debt mounted even higher, for mercenaries were far more costly than militia. This debt grew so large that it could not be taken care of by simply borrowing from wealthy individuals or private groups. It had to be funded by the *monte communale*, which sold public shares and kept public books. The *monte communale* became a mainspring of civic life and helped to "democratize" public life. The Florentine commune developed into a territorial state, which the civic humanists then justified in their political treatises.

Perhaps the low point of Florentine fortunes was reached with the Ciompi revolt of 1378. In the winter and spring of 1377–1378 Florence suffered a severe internal crisis. Nearly a hundred Florentines fell victims to Guelph terror. On June 21 the masses rioted and burned the houses of the Albizzis and other wealthy oligarchs. In the fall the day laborers and especially the unorganized wool carders, known as Ciompi for the wooden shoes they wore, struck out against the whole oligarchy and guild system. They gathered outside the city and plotted to overthrow the *signoria* and set up a popular government. They fought for better pay and legal recognition. *"Viva il popolo!"* was the cry. But even the lowest artisan guilds with some stake in society opposed the unorganized laborers in this crisis and helped to crush them. After the Ciompi were suppressed, the innkeepers petitioned the *signoria* to proclaim the anniversary of the Ciompi downfall as a holiday.

During the brief time in which the Ciompi were masters of the city, they reformed the constitution, created three new guilds, and appointed a new board of *priori*. The new board was made up of three representatives of the major guilds, three of the lesser guilds, and three of the new guilds. Each of these classes was to have a turn at appointing the *gonfaloniere*, but the first one appointed was very naturally one of the Ciompi, Michele di Lando. By popular demand Piero degli Albizzi and other *grandi* were charged with conspiracy and executed, and many others were exiled. The Ciompi behaved badly, constantly interrupting the meetings of officials and breaking into frequent rioting, and reduced the city to near anarchy.

Their foolish excesses very naturally produced a decisive reaction. In 1382 the guilds regained power and introduced a revised constitution that provided that half of the *priori* should come from the major guilds and half from the lesser guilds. They eliminated the three new guilds set up to accommodate the lower classes. They executed or exiled the rabble-rousers and so firmly established their control over the state that they easily suppressed subsequent Ciompi strikes and riots for better pay. Florence regained internal stability just in time, for it was now threatened by a deadly enemy that was determined to subdue it and take away all of Tuscany.

By 1390 Gian Galeazzo Visconti had conquered a large part of northern Italy and was now expanding the domain of Milan southward. He had designs on Siena, Perugia, and Pisa, then the Tuscan lands around Florence, and finally Florence itself. Florence employed a mercenary captain named Hawkwood as *condottiere* with some seven thousand men to defend the city. He fought off the Milanese and a temporary peace was signed in 1392.

In 1393 a wealthy member of the powerful wool guild, the *Arte della Lana*, Maso degli Albizzi, became *gonfaloniere*. Although Maso held this office only two months, he used his position to suppress rival families, such as the Albertis, and drove many prominent citizens into exile. The Albizzis and their merchant oligarchy reigned supreme, despite minor disturbances and the intrigues of the exiles. In 1397 and 1398 Gian Galeazzo advanced once more into Tuscany and defeated the troops Florence had hired from Emperor Rupert. Florence stood alone and seemed doomed. But at that very moment fate intervened and Gian Galeazzo died in 1402.

Florence now pressed its advantage in order to gain possession of Pisa, whose location at the mouth of the Arno River made it highly desirable as an outlet to the sea for Florence's maritime trade. A Visconti still ruled in Pisa, and the Florentines failed to take the city in 1404. But they persisted, and in 1406 they besieged Pisa for six months until it fell. Florence had gained at last the port it had so long coveted.

From 1409 to 1414 the Florentines had to ward off King Ladislas of Naples, but fortunately he died before he could capture the city. The Viscontis threatened Florence once again in 1421, when Filippo Maria took Forli and moved against Tuscany. Florence declared war, even though a peace party, headed by one Giovanni de' Medici, favored negotiations. The Milanese beat them badly in several battles, and the pope in Rome was against them as well. Florence was saved when the Venetians joined the war on their side and forced the Viscontis to sign an unfavorable peace in 1427. Florence was sorely tempted by the plucky little city of Lucca nearby and made a number of attempts to capture it, but Lucca always successfully resisted. One of Florence's attacks on Lucca brought on another war with Milan in 1432–1433. The whole campaign was badly handled and brought Florence once again close to a military debacle.

The leader of the oligarchy, Rinaldo degli Albizzi, favored the war effort. The leader of the popular party, Cosimo de' Medici (1389–1464), Giovanni's son, favored peace. Although the Medicis belonged to the privileged classes, they had been associated with popular causes ever since one member of the family, Salvestro de' Medici, had been sympathetic to the commoners during the Ciompi revolt. Rinaldo drove Cosimo into exile and tightened his grip on the government. He plotted a coup d'état, but failed to gain the needed support.

Much to Rinaldo's consternation, in 1434 a *signoria* was chosen favorable to the Medicis. The *signoria* summoned Rinaldo to the Palazzo Vecchio to answer charges that he was scheming to overthrow the state. Rinaldo gathered an armed band of some eight hundred men and civil war threatened. Pope Eugenius IV, in the city at the time, intervened. The wheel of fortune turned, and Rinaldo degli Albizzi and his aristocratic supporters were sent into exile. On October 6, 1434, Cosimo entered Florence to popular acclaim. For the next three centuries the history of Florence was inseparably intertwined with the fortunes of the Medici family.

Cosimo de' Medici was a political realist of the first order. "States are not ruled by *paternosters*," he once growled. The way in which he controlled the city of Florence is well worth analyzing. The fundamental precept of government in republican Florence had been the formulation of policy through group consultation. Cosimo kept up the practice of consultation, retained all the forms of republican government, and only very cautiously took those steps necessary to establish and consolidate his power.

One source of Cosimo's tremendous power in the city was his enormous wealth. His father, Giovanni, had acquired a great fortune through his banking and trading operations. Cosimo maintained a keen personal interest in the business and based his personal power upon his financial strength. The tax records of 1457 reveal the Medicis to have been by far the wealthiest family in Florence. Cosimo was able to lend as much as 20,000 to 30,000 florins to the city in times of crisis. He could subsidize such *condottieri* as Francesco Sforza in defense of the city. He could lend money and thus place prominent citizens under obligation to him. Moreover, the three Medici textile factories, two manufacturing woolen cloth and one silk, made a great many workers dependent for their livelihood upon the success of the Medici enterprises. Cosimo was often personally present when wages were paid, so that the laborers were made aware of their benefactor. Cosimo served as an official on the board of the *monte communale*. He understood how to use the *catasto*, a form of graduated income tax introduced earlier, in order to secure tax breaks for himself and his supporters. The reform of the *catasto* in 1458 worked to the disadvantage of the older families and in favor of the party that supported Cosimo.

When Cosimo returned in 1434 he forced into exile some seventy-three of his enemies during the first two months. This was not a large number, but they were key people of great importance. Cosimo preferred indirect control and seldom held public office himself. In 1435 he became the *gonfaloniere*, but he was very moderate, dismissed the guard that the *signoria* had set up to protect the Palazzo Vecchio, and moved about the city freely and with complete confidence. Cosimo could act decisively and with a show of force when he was pressed. In 1458 there was a minor disturbance over the arrest of Girolamo Machiavelli, a prominent member of the opposition. The *signoria*, mindful of Cosimo's interests, had several citizens arrested, tortured, and exiled. They put a hundred and fifty citizens under house arrest and forbade them to appear in public until given permission. But Cosimo and the *signoria* found few occasions that required force. The longer Cosimo retained his leadership, the more families came over to his side, until those who resisted him were too few to form an effective opposition.

The key to Cosimo's control over the government of Florence was the influence he exercised over the electoral system. The ten electors, or *accoppiatori*, who appointed the *priori* for two-month terms, were favorable to Cosimo. Cosimo did not blatantly have these ten electors given permanent tenure, but as the years passed, the *signoria* repeatedly extended the length of their terms. By the time the *accoppiatori* were permanently dissolved in 1455 and a return to traditional methods of election was effected, the opposition to Cosimo was so weak as to pose no serious threat at all. Another constitutional device for the efficient control and operation of the government was the creation of a *balia* or executive council with broad powers to scrutinize the voter lists, pass tax bills, and appoint ministers of defense. At times these key officials of the state did not even bother to meet in the appropriate chambers of the Palazzo Vecchio, but met instead in the Medici palace on the Via Larga.

Another development may have been operating in favor of Cosimo's control of the city. Some historians have held that the general level of prosperity had declined below that of 1338, and that a larger percentage of the total wealth was concentrated in fewer hands than ever before. Seven *arti maggiori* in Cosimo's day held seven of nine positions in the *signoria*. These positions were largely preempted by a very few families, favorable to Cosimo. Of the 411 names on the scrutiny list of people from the *arti maggiori* who were eligible for the three highest offices in 1448, 240 were members of 25 families. Clearly the base of political power was narrowing. At the very center of political power was Cosimo, shrewdly assessing these developments and cleverly manipulating the controls of this delicate political machine. Maintaining stability among a population as volatile as the Florentines was a noteworthy achievement indeed.

Cosimo was a friend of learning and a patron of literature and art. It is said that on his deathbed he had Platonic dialogues read to him for comfort. He was given the title of *pater patriae* by his grateful countrymen. "I know my countrymen," Cosimo once commented cynically. "They will remember me a few years hence only for the buildings I have erected in Florence."

He married his son Piero to Lucrezia Tornabuoni, of a prominent Florentine family. But Piero, nicknamed "the Gouty," was not of his father's stature. He was a magnanimous man, but he was crippled by illness. Yet he surprised his enemies, such as Luca Pitti and Agnolo Acciaiuoli, by the energy he displayed in defending his interests. During Piero's brief rule (1464–1469) Florence had to defend itself against the Venetians, who used the death of Francesco Sforza as an opportunity to move against Milan and Florence. When Piero died he left behind two sons, Lorenzo (1449–1492) and Giuliano (1453–1478), who assumed the direction of the state with greater energy than their father and much more openly than Cosimo.

In 1471 Lorenzo had a *balia* formed for a five-year term, which was made up of the *signoria,* the *accoppiatori,* and 240 Medici partisans. Lorenzo was openly moving toward a position of power. In 1472 he launched a punitive expedition against the little city of Volterra, because of a quarrel over certain alum mines, and crushed it.

Fearing the growing strength of Florence and coveting Tuscan territories for the Papal States and his nephews, Pope Sixtus IV plotted against the Medicis. He seems at least to have had knowledge of the plot against their lives, though he may not have been personally involved in it. In 1478 the Pazzis too conspired against the Medicis. While Lorenzo and Giuliano attended mass and knelt before the altar rail in the cathedral, the assassins struck. Giuliano was killed. Lorenzo fled to the vestry on the right, where he barricaded himself with some retainers and fought for his life. The vengeance that Lorenzo and his followers took upon the Pazzis was fearful, and Lorenzo emerged from the crisis in a stronger position than before. Giuliano had not been particularly interested in political life, but it was Lorenzo's great love. Giuliano left behind one illegitimate son, Giulio, who later became Pope Clement VII.

Pope Sixtus IV was relentless. He excommunicated Lorenzo and joined with King Ferrante of Naples in a war on Florence. The unholy allies met with great resistance, but finally, after a number of indecisive battles, they won a victory over the Florentines at Poggio Imperiale in 1480 and threatened the city itself. At that moment of acute danger to the city, Lorenzo took a bold gamble. He believed that he could convince King Ferrante that it was not to the advantage of Naples to build up the Papal States against Florence. He hurried to Naples and appeared before the king in person to present his case and to ask for favorable terms. "He exposed his own life," wrote Machiavelli, "to restore peace to his country." Ludovico il Moro, who had just become regent of Milan with the help of Naples, urged Ferrante to make peace. After two months of diplomatic dickering, Naples made peace, and soon thereafter the triple alliance of Milan, Florence, and Naples was restored.

Lorenzo's keen political sense told him to seize the moment to consolidate his power. In April 1480 he formed a *balia* that appointed a council of seventy, made up of Lorenzo's friends, to rule the state. Although it was originally appointed for five years, the council remained a permanent institution. Lorenzo's enemies frequently accused him, not without justification, of fusing his personal fortune with public finance in order to increase his own wealth. Lorenzo was now clearly master of the state. "If Florence had had a tyrant," wrote the historian Guicciardini some years later, "she could not have found a better one than Lorenzo."

Posterity has bestowed upon him the sobriquet Lorenzo the Magnificent. This title is in part a misreading of the Italian *magnifico,* a term of honor used very generally in the *Quattrocento* and given to various of the Medicis. He was a patron of the arts and letters, although the actual extent of his generosity is still under dispute. He sponsored the artists Ghirlandaio and Botticelli, the poets Pulci and Politian, and the philosopher Marsilio Ficino, the great Platonist. He wrote vernacular poetry himself, *canzoni* and sonnets, and appreciated the Italian classics of the Renaissance. He wrote religious poetry with a Platonic cast to it, and even did a miracle play. At the same time, his *canti carnascialeschi,* or carnival songs, were extremely sensual. During his last years he came into conflict with Girolamo Savonarola, the moralistic Dominican preacher, who criticized him for his worldliness. A legend no longer accepted by historians, but intriguing nevertheless, is that when Lorenzo summoned Savonarola to his deathbed, Savonarola refused to grant him absolution for his sins, because he had destroyed the liberty of Florence and refused to restore it. When he died in 1492 at the age of forty-three, Lorenzo designated his son Piero, nearly a total misfit, to succeed him as ruler of Florence.

Lorenzo's reputation has suffered some from recent research. It is now clear that in his preoccupation with politics he neglected the family banking enterprise and allowed the Medici fortune to dwindle. Much of his energy was dissipated in handling the petty intrigues and constant threats of new hostilities from neighboring states. He sought by diplomatic marriages to ally his family with European royalty. He succeeded in placing one son, Giovanni, in the College of Cardinals at the age of fourteen, and Giovanni became Pope Leo X.

Lorenzo's elder son, Piero (1471–1503), was a wastrel and a lecherous youth with little character and even less political sense. When Charles VIII of France invaded Italy in his march on Naples, Piero allied himself with Naples, in spite of the traditional friendship of Florence and France. When Charles entered Tuscany, took Sarzana, and threatened Florence, Piero crept submissively to the French camp, begged forgiveness, and asked Charles to spare Florence. Charles agreed, but forced him to cede Leghorn, Pisa, and other Tuscan towns. The Florentines were furious, and when Piero returned to Florence on November 8, 1494, he was not admitted to the Palazzo Vecchio. Amid shouts of *"Popolo e libertà!"* the crowds frightened him away. He fled from the city with a few retainers, and his brother, Giovanni, soon followed him into exile. The first period of Medici rule in Florence was over. With the invasion of Charles VIII, domination by major foreign powers began and Italy entered its time of troubles.

Renaissance Diplomacy

Jacob Burckhardt proudly called Italy the first-born among the sons of Europe, for he believed that modern secular statecraft and the interstate diplomacy that has characterized European history first emerged during the Italian Renaissance. The metahistorian Arnold J. Toynbee finds in the Italian microcosm the very laws of interstate relations that have been characteristic of international relations in contemporary Europe. He finds in the Italy of the Renaissance a balance-of-power principle. This configuration of Italian city-states lay, however, in the very center, and was unable to expand territorially. Meanwhile, the giant states to the north, west, and east grew to outsized proportions. Toynbee sees an analogy to the situation in Europe before 1914. The small states of England, France, Germany, and Italy had achieved a balance of power and held each other at a standoff. France and Germany coveted tiny bits of territory such as Alsace and Lorraine. Meanwhile, on the periphery, Russia and the United States expanded eastward and westward until they became the giants that today overshadow little Europe. That there is mimicry involved and not merely coincidence is indicated by the fact that the instruments and language of diplomacy with which Renaissance statesmen directed interstate relations have been adopted and used in the same way by statesmen of modern Europe. This phenomenon Toynbee refers to as the Italianization of the West.

This style of Renaissance statesmen, the conceptions and the language of their diplomacy, make a fascinating study. In the fifteenth century an equilibrium did develop on the peninsula and the great powers did intervene to prevent Italy's domination by a single state or its possession by an outside force. Before the end of the century the term "balance of power" was used to describe the military parity of the two groups of allies among the city-states. This conception of the balance of power was the achievement of Cosimo de' Medici, who is usually credited with arranging the alliance that was the keystone of diplomacy in the second half of the century.

After the terrifying threats of Milan to Florence and the danger from Naples had passed, Cosimo brought Florence into an alliance with its recent enemies. He had hired the *condottiere* Francesco Sforza for the defense of Florence, and after Francesco's accession to power in Milan, Cosimo saw in him a potentially strong ally. In 1454 Florence and Milan signed the Peace of Lodi, which established a strong axis of power, joined also by Naples, as a counterpoise to the Papal States and Venice. The papacy and Venice, traditionally hostile because of territorial conflicts, now found cooperation to be to their mutual interest. The balance of power thus achieved facilitated an uneasy truce that lasted for forty years, until the invasion by Charles VIII in 1494. It seemed to the Florentines that Lorenzo the Magnificent was the master diplomatist who maintained peace. Lorenzo was a skilled manipulator and came through brilliantly, as in the crisis with Ferrante of Naples; but the Florence-Milan alliance was set well before Lorenzo took over the reins.

Throughout the second half of the fifteenth century the Italians were painfully aware of the fact that they were living under the shadow of the crescent. The steady advance of the Turks had not gone unnoticed earlier, with their victory at Nicopolis in 1396 and at Varna in 1444, but the fall of Constantinople in 1453 was nevertheless a traumatic event. The battle of Belgrade in 1456, the seizure of Negropont in 1470, the assault upon Rhodes in 1480, and a number of lesser raids on the Italian peninsula itself brought home to the Italians that the terrible Turk was not only at the gateway to the West, but was already marching through it. The news of

Constantinople's fall spread throughout the West during the summer of 1453. A monk at Agarathos wrote that "nothing worse than this has happened, nor will happen." Sensitive to developments in the East, the Venetians were thrown into near panic. The secretary to the *Dieci* read the news of the fall to a silent senate. The Venetians dispatched a letter the next day warning Pope Nicholas V that the Turkish triumph was as perilous as it was grievous. The West was becoming aware of the fact that the Turks now had a base for naval and military operations on the continent which posed a possibly fatal threat. The news was accompanied by rumors of the assassination of whole city populations and the abduction of Christian children into slavery.

The diplomatic response of the Italian states to the Turkish threat was anything but inspiring. The Peace of Lodi was to preserve the peace so that the Christian princes would be able to ward off the assaults of the Turks. Similarly the Holy League, formed in 1495 by Venice, the papacy, Emperor Maximilian, Ferdinand and Isabella, and Ludovico il Moro, was ostensibly intended for the defense of Christendom against the Ottoman Turks; but in reality it was directed against the French, who had invaded Italy a year before. It has even been said that the emissaries of Bayazid II listened to the discussions from behind a screen. The diplomats illustrated the myopia of most statesmen of nearly every age, who much prefer to meet short-term emergencies rather than plan policy beyond their particular interests at any given moment.

The development of a sophisticated urban culture in Renaissance Italy and the urgencies of interstate relations led to the creation of techniques and a language of diplomacy well ahead of those in use in other parts of Europe. A more secular concept of politics was essential to the new rational and calculating approach to diplomacy. The development of the resident ambassador was one of the most important innovations in Renaissance diplomacy. Traditionally an ambassador was sent by one state to another for a specific purpose and a limited time. William Durant defined a *legatus* or legate of the thirteenth century simply as "anybody sent by another." The Italians learned the advantage of having resident ambassadors who could represent the interests of their states at all times, gather and secretly transmit information about their host country, and even intervene in local affairs. Although a variety of names for these state representatives in residence was in use in the fifteenth century, such as *orator* or *nuntius* (messenger, for ecclesiastical ambassadors), it is significant that the Italian word *ambasciator* came into general use. The states soon recognized the diplomatic immunity, safe-conduct, and special protection that accompanied the post, although there were many violations and it was centuries before these special privileges were regularized and codified in international law.

"Ambassadors," wrote Guicciardini in his *History of Italy,* "are the eyes and ears of the state." They had more than a ceremonial function, for they served as intelligence agents for their states. The Venetian ambassadors were the most famous for their detailed reports. Their instructions were to send back day-by-day accounts of all the information they could accumulate about the comings and goings of political figures, whether or not it seemed significant to them, for only the "home office" had the whole picture. They reported on the political temper of the people, the likelihood of local disturbances, the condition of the market, and general economic developments. Needless to say, these *relazioni* of the Venetian ambassadors are today prize sources of information in historical research.

The diplomats were symbols of alliances and keepers of goodwill. An ambassador, according to an epigram falsely attributed to the seventeenth-century diplomat Sir Henry Wotton by a man who didn't like him very much, is "an honest man sent to lie abroad for the good of his country." Machiavelli, who represented Florence at the court of Cesare Borgia and held other assignments, once confessed, "I never believe what I say, or say what I believe." Secret dispatches soon were sent in code and the ciphering of messages developed into a fine art. Abbot Trithemius discussed the potentials of the art in his work *Polygraphiae libri sex.* Cesare Borgia heard of a cleric in Germany, Lorenz Behaim, who had many occult powers and secret devices. He sent him a letter in which he asked Behaim how to open a letter and seal it again without leaving any sign that it had been opened; how to write a letter with ink that in two weeks would turn white or with water that would turn black; how to write on skin, on a shirt, on iron; how to transmit a ciphered message by the use of dots; how to cause a message to disappear by chewing the letter; how to develop one's memory; how to secrete poisons in prison and introduce them into food; how to use slow-acting poisons so that their effects would be apparent only after four to six months; and how to induce a severe fever in a man and then give him relief again.

Behaim wrote in his own hand a recipe for a poison that gradually desiccates the body. On the reverse side of the recipe was an invocation to the devil asking his help in making the potion effective on both body and soul.

The invasion of Italy by the non-Italian powers led to the rapid spread of Italian diplomatic methods throughout the rest of Europe. Ferdinand of Aragon was the quickest to learn, and Machiavelli greatly admired both his ability and his success. Spain remained a leader in astute diplomacy. The routines of diplomacy were varied and irregular. The growth of the nation-states, each considering itself sovereign and recognizing no power as higher than its own, brought clearly into focus the need for international law, which had remained dormant as long as the unity of Christendom existed at least as a myth in the minds of men. Hugo Grotius in the seventeenth century, while not the first to write on the subject, understood the problem and urged the development of a law of nations for the good of the sovereign states themselves.

Jacob Burckhardt once ventured the opinion that the only remedy for Italy's ills would have been a union of the free cities. Such a union would have ended the costly and debilitating internecine warfare of the Italian city-states, and would also

EUROPEAN CIVILIZATION
During The Renaissance

MILES 0   50   100   200   300

———— Boundaries of approximately 1470

Location of School of Art → ⊕ ← Early printing press

Important church council → ⊕ ← Library

● Birthplace outside city

Florence Location of important Renaissance building

AGE OF HUMANISM

RENAISSANCE PAINTING AND SCULPTURE

CLASSICAL AND BIBLICAL STUDIES

FIRST PRINTED BOOKS

SCOTLAND

Edinburgh
John Knox, 1505

IRELAND
Dublin

North Sea

NORWAY

DEN

Coverdale, 1488

Cranmer, 1489

WALES
ENGLAND
Malory, 15th Cent.
Tyndale, 1490
Oxford
Colet, 1466
More, 1478
Hampton Court
London
Wyatt, 1503
Caxton, 1422
Canterbury
Linacre, 1480
Lefèvre d'Étaples, 1455

Rotterdam
Erasmus, 1466
Leiden
Leuven, 1520
Bruges
Van de Wyden
Van Eyck, 1381
Louvain
Malines, 1480
Cologne

DOMAINS OF
Coolnes, 1440
Gerlei, 1470

Ulrich von Hutten, 1488

Mainz
Gutenberg, 1397
Melanchthon, 1497

Trier
Nicholas Cusanus, 1401

Agricola, 1443
Bremen

Chartier, 1392

Noyon
Calvin, 1509

Paris
NATIONAL LIBRARY
COLLEGE OF FRANCE
Boccaccio, 1375
Charles of Orleans, 1391

Reuchlin, 1455

Pare, 1510
Fontainebleau
Blois
Rabelais, 1490
Azay-le-Rideau
Amboise
Tours
Jean Fouquet, 1415
Chambord
Moulins
Villon, 1430
Dijon

DUKES OF
BURGUNDY

Basel
Holbein

Zurich
Zwingli
Paracelsus, 1493
Geneva

Constance

Bay of Biscay

FRANCE

Angoulême
Marguerite d'Angoulême, 1492

Bordeaux
Garonne

Avignon

Milan

Genoa

Bologna

Pisa
Siena

Loyola, 1493

Pau
NAVARRE
Servetus, 1511

PYRENEES

Magellan, 1480
Duero
Ximénez, 1436

PORTUGAL

Madrid

CASTILE
Tagus

Lisbon

Vasco da Gama, 1450

Guadiana

Seville
Guadalquivir

ARAGON

Barcelona

CORSICA
(Genoa)

SARDINIA
(Aragon)

VATICAN
SOCIETY

Tyr

Marseille

BALEARIC ISLANDS
(Aragon)

GRANADA

Mediterran

20°   10°   0°   50°   40°   0°   10°

THE ITALIAN RENAISSANCE

have allowed them to build up a united defense force formidable enough to discourage other powers from their adventurous invasions of Italian soil. But the contemporary Italian historian Nino Valeri quite realistically concludes that the city-states were simply too small and too selfish to act as the times required. Sir Thomas More, whose *Utopia* appeared at about the same time as Machiavelli's *Prince,* found the problem to be human pride, which is deeply rooted in the nature of man himself. "This hell-hound," he wrote, "crept into man's heart and is so deeply rooted in man's breast that it cannot be plucked out."

Bibliography

General:

Bowsky, William. *Henry VII in Italy: The Conflict of Empire and City-State, 1310–1313.* Lincoln, NB, 1960.

Chamberlin, E. R. *Everyday Life in Renaissance Times.* New York, 1967.

Kohl, B. G., and R. G. Witt, eds. *The Earthly Republic: Italian Humanists on Government and Society.* Philadelphia, 1978.

Martines, Lauro, ed., *Violence and Civil Disorder in Italian Cities, 1200–1500.* Berkeley, 1972.

Salvatorelli, Luigi. *A Concise History of Italy.* New York, 1940.

Simeoni, Luigi. *Le signorie, 1313–1559,* 2 vols., 4th ed. Milan, 1950.

Sismondi, J. C. L. *History of the Italian Republics in the Middle Ages.* London, n.d.

Valeri, Nino. *L'Italia nell'età dei principati dal 1343 al 1516.* Verona, 1950.

Rome:

D'Amico, John F., *Renaissance Humanism in Papal Rome: Humanists and Churchmen on the Eve of the Reformation.* Baltimore, 1983.

Klaczko, J. *Rome and the Renaissance: The Pontificate of Julius II, 1503–1515.* Paris, 1926.

Partner, Peter. *The Papal State Under Martin V.* London, 1958.

———. *Renaissance Rome, 1500–1559: A Portrait of a Society.* Berkeley and Los Angeles, 1977.

Paschang, John L. *The Popes and the Revival of Learning.* Washington, 1927.

Paschini, P. *Roma nel Rinascimento.* Bologna, 1940.

Roscoe, William. *The Life and Pontificate of Leo the Tenth,* 2 vols., 7th rev. ed. London, 1878.

Wright, John, ed., *The Life of Cola di Rienzo.* Toronto, 1975.

Naples and Sicily:

Léonard, Émile G. *Les Angevins de Naples.* Paris, 1954.

Milan:

Bueno de Mesquita, D. M. *Giangaleazzo Visconti.* Cambridge, 1941.

Fondazione Treccani degli Alfieri. *Storia di Milano,* vols. 1–10. Milan, 1955–

Muir, Dorothy. *A History of Milan Under the Visconti.* London, 1924.

Pieri, Piero. *I Visconti e l'Italia del secolo XIV.* Turin, 1952.

Venice:

Bouwsma, William. *Venice and the Defence of Republican Liberty: Renaissance Values in the Age of the Counter Reformation.* Berkeley, 1968.

Cessi, Roberto. *Storia della Repubblica di Venezia,* 2 vols. Milan, 1944–1946.

Davis, James C. *The Decline of the Venetian Nobility as a Ruling Class.* Baltimore, 1962.

Labalme, Patricia H. *Bernardo Giustiniani, a Venetian of the Quattrocento.* Rome, 1969.

Lane, Frederick C. *Venice in History.* Baltimore, 1966.

McNeill, William H. *Venice, the Hinge of Europe 1081–1797.* Chicago, 1974.

Mallet, M. E., and J. R. Hale. *The Military Organization of a Renaissance State: Venice c. 1400–1617*. New York, 1984.

Molmenti, Pompeo G. *Venice: Its Individual Growth from the Earliest Beginnings to the Fall of the Republic*, 6 vols. Chicago, 1906–1908.

Pullan, Brian. *Rich and Poor in Renaissance Venice: The Social Institutions of a Catholic State to 1620*. Cambridge, MA, 1971.

Florence:

Ady, C. M. *Lorenzo de' Medici and Renaissance Italy*. London, 1955.

Albertini, Rudolf von. *Das florentinische Staatsbewusstsein im Übergang von der Republik zum Prinzipat*. Bern, 1955.

Becker, Marvin. *Florence in Transition*; vol. 1, *Decline of the Commune*; vol. 2, *Studies in the Rise of the Territorial Estate*. Baltimore, 1967, 1968.

Brucker, Gene. *Florentine Politics and Society, 1343–1378*. Princeton, 1962.

———. *Renaissance Florence*. New York, 1969.

———. *The Society of Renaissance Florence: A Documentary Study*. New York, 1971.

———. *Giovanni and Lusanna: Love and Marriage in Renaissance Florence*. Berkeley, 1986.

Gutkind, Kurt S. *Cosimo de' Medici, pater patriae, 1389–1464*. New York, 1938.

Martines, Lauro. *Lawyers and Statecraft in Renaissance Florence*. Princeton, 1968.

Najemy, John M. *Corporatism and Consensus in Florentine Electoral Politics, 1280–1400*. Chapel Hill, 1982.

Rodolico, Niccolò. *I Ciompi*. Florence, 1945.

Rubinstein, Nicolai. *The Government of Florence Under the Medici: 1434–1494*. New York, 1966.

Ruggiers, Paul G. *Florence in the Age of Dante*. Norman, OK, 1964.

Schevill, Ferdinand. *History of Florence*. New York, 1936.

———. *The Medici*. New York, 1949.

Lesser states:

Ady, C. M. *The Bentivoglio of Bologna: A Study in Despotism*. New York, 1937.

Brinton, S. *The Gonzaga Lords of Mantua*. London, 1927.

Brown, Judith. *In the Shadow of Florence: Provincial Society in Renaissance Pescia*. New York, 1982.

Cristiani, E. *Nobilità e popolo nel comune di Pisa*. Naples, 1962.

Gardner, E. *Dukes and Poets of Ferrara*. New York, 1904.

Gundersheimer, Werner L. *Ferrara: The Style of a Renaissance Despotism*. Princeton, 1973.

Herlihy, David. *Pisa in the Early Renaissance: A Study of Urban Growth*. New Haven, 1958.

———. *Medieval and Renaissance Pistoia: The Social History of an Italian Town*. New Haven, 1967.

Hutton, E. *Sigismondo Pandulfo Malatesta, Lord of Rimini*. London, 1906.

Hyde, J. K. *Padua in the Age of Dante: The Social History of an Italian City-State, 1256–1328*. New York, 1965.

Jones, P. J. *The Malatesta of Rimini and the Papal State*. New York, 1974.

Larner, John. *The Lords of Romagna*. Ithaca, NY, 1965.

Schevill, Ferdinand. *Siena: The History of a Medieval Community*. New York, 1964.

Renaissance diplomacy:

Mattingly, Garrett. *Renaissance Diplomacy*. New York, 1954.

Mowat, R. B. *A History of European Diplomacy, 1451–1789*. New York, 1928.

Petry, C. *Earlier Diplomatic History, 1492–1713*. New York, 1949.

Pieri, P. *Il Rinascimento e la crisi militare italiana*. Turin, 1952.

Pontieri, E. *L'equilibrio e la crisi politica italiana nella seconda metà del secolo XV*. Naples, 1946.

Queller, Donald E. *The Office of the Ambassador in the Middle Ages*. Princeton, 1967.

CHAPTER 5

The Rise
of Capitalism

Over the door of the beautiful Renaissance house of Jacques Coeur, "the money man," in Bourges is engraved a motto that is at the same time an egregious pun on the name Coeur (heart) and an expression of the verve of that early capitalist:

> TO THE VALIANT HEART
> NOTHING IS IMPOSSIBLE.

The men who built enormous fortunes under most hazardous conditions needed valiant hearts and iron constitutions. They were bold adventurers, but they could also be calculating and cautious. They were driven on by that desire to acquire which was a common characteristic of all the early capitalists.

The Origins of Capitalism

HISTORY IS NEVER INNOCENT, least of all when it offers a simple narrative or a single analysis as unadorned truth. There are a number of major theories about the origins of capitalism, theories so controversial that blood as well as ink has been spilled over them.

THE QUALITATIVE SCHOOL

The qualitative school of economic history held that the critical factor in the development of capitalism was a change in the mind and outlook of man. Whereas the medieval agrarian system had provided security, with a predetermined place for every man, and kept most people at the minimum subsistence level, capitalism resulted from the development of a strong acquisitive instinct. The desire to accumulate wealth, the self-restraint requisite for delayed satisfactions, and the mental discipline necessary for rationalizing economic activity were part of the new economic man imbued with the spirit of capitalism. One of the early leaders of this qualitative school, Werner Sombart, a German political economist writing in the early twentieth century, found this mentality in Leon Battista Alberti, the author of a work *On the Family,* which identifies and lauds the bourgeois virtues of sobriety, thrift, rational order, industry, and the desire to build a family fortune for future generations. Daniel Defoe's Robinson Crusoe was exemplary in husbanding the resources of his island, accumulating a store in his stockade, and putting his man Friday to work. Benjamin Franklin's *Poor Richard's Almanac* exuded the capitalistic spirit in its admonitions: "Time is money"; "A penny saved is a penny earned." In his *Household Book* Anton Tucher, a German capitalist, showed how accounts were to be kept to eliminate any frivolous spending and how money was to be carefully husbanded. Sombart believed that high churchmen, bureaucrats in the rising national monarchies, and aristocrats who collected rents on land, rather than tradesmen, were responsible for the primary accumulation of capital. He emphasized the importance of woman's role in the demand for luxuries and the effects of this demand on the growth of cities. He believed also that Jews were especially important to the rise of capitalism, for in accordance with the Mosaic laws they were industrious and lived orderly lives. Moreover, because of the ecclesiastical restraints upon usury, Christians left financial activity largely to the Jews.

The sociologist Max Weber, a contemporary of Sombart, argued that Protestantism and especially the ethic of Calvinism produced the kind of sober, hardworking men who pursued their vocations with zeal and considered material success a sign of God's favor. R. H. Tawney found these virtues to be a general Christian phenomenon and an inheritance from Judaism. Luigi Brentano traced the emergence of the acquisitive instinct to the early Middle Ages, and argued the futility of trying to pin down its actual beginning.

THE MARXIST SCHOOL

Karl Marx and Friedrich Engels theorized at great length on the nature, origin, and demise of capitalism. They stressed the separation of the ownership of the means of production and the producer or worker, the labor theory of value, and the rise of capitalism in the total setting of their historical dialectic. Since their day, knowledge of early economic history has so increased and economic analysis has become so refined that in contemporary scholarly discussion the views of more sophisticated Marxist theorists such as Maurice Dobb are given more weight than the historically interesting but superseded statements of Marx himself.

In his various studies of the rise of modern capitalism, Maurice Dobb raises a number of important questions. The question of causation brings up the Marxist assertion of the inefficiency of feudalism. In the onward movement of the historical dialectic, according to the Marxists, feudalism was bound to collapse because of its own internal contradictions, just as capitalism will do eventually. Dobb argues that the inefficiency of the feudal system was causally more important than blows from without, such as the incursions of merchant capitalism. He describes the money economy of the twelfth to the sixteenth centuries as a merchant capitalism, which should not be confused with industrial capitalism. The merchant capitalists were, as Marx described them, parasitical, not contributing to the total wealth by labor, but merely exploiting price differentials due to differences in market conditions. The Marxist analysis is highly complex and is not to be dismissed cavalierly, but a few questions can be raised. If the feudal agrarian economy was so inefficient, whence came the increment of value represented in the early accumulation of capital used to develop trade? If merchant capitalism was parasitical, merely siphoning off the surplus, could it have been the source of the capital that made possible the expansion of industry? If old feudal agrarian arrangements in England first declined in the counties far from the mercantile center of London and persisted near London, was this because the wealth of the city supported the inefficient agrarian system nearby? Why didn't the feudal agrarian economy decline first in Russia, far from the most active mercantile centers of western Europe? In general, most informed historians find that the Marxists do not give due consideration to multilateral causation and to mutually interdependent variables such as the effects of the money economy, the desire for luxuries, the breakup of the land-labor ratio, and the contribution of merchants in risk, labor, enterprise, and exchange of raw materials for finished products.

THE MERCHANT ENTERPRISE SCHOOL

The point of view that most Western historians find acceptable is much more complex and not compressed within a ready-made ideological structure. It is now well established on the basis of numismatic and other evidence that some trade between the West and the eastern half of the Roman Empire continued even during the Dark Ages of the Germanic invasions. Nor did the Moslem expansion and domination of much of the Mediterranean completely cut off trade and nonagrarian economic activity. From the eighth to the mid-eleventh centuries the proprie-

tary land organization was the predominant form of economic life, with the care
of the individual family as virtually the limit of its capacity. The businessmen
(*negociatores*) of those centuries were petty traders who operated on a small scale
and in limited localities. Even then towns were growing, some in the ruins of the
old Roman cities, the ancient administrative and trading centers. Urban centers
and small manufacturing enterprises developed first in Italy and the Netherlands,
in such towns as Bruges and Ghent. The general stability achieved during the
eleventh century made possible a striking recrudescence of trade and manufacturing during the twelfth century.

Commerce developed first along seacoasts and then at the confluence of rivers
and other natural centers. Peasants moved to the urban centers to work for wages
and to achieve more personal freedom. As the old German saying has it, "City air
makes one free!" (*Stadt Luft macht frei!*) The pioneers of commerce came from
the fringes of society: poor men, adventurers, floaters. St. Godric of Finchale was
a peasant who grew rich by successively larger trading operations. His aim was
profit and riches, not merely a livelihood. The merchants of the eleventh and
twelfth centuries organized into associations (*caritates*). Some of the wealthy *par-
venus* found security by investing in land, and made further gains in ground rents
and the sale of produce for cash in the growing towns. Many factors, interacting
and reinforcing, contributed to the rise of capitalism.

As cities grew, manufacturing increased, especially of textiles, and many sec-
ondary industrial localities developed. Some urban centers handled merely local
trade, but others developed a European market for their products. Many of the
instruments of capitalism that had developed during the Roman Empire were
preserved in Byzantium and transmitted back to the West. In the major urban
centers capitalistic techniques were now perfected, with banknotes, credit systems,
double-entry bookkeeping, and trade fairs, as at Champagne. The thirteenth century saw the raising of restrictions by the church, guilds, and city councils in the
interest of the collective welfare. New, aggressive capitalists entered the scene, and
new cities, such as Antwerp, less hampered by old limitations and regulations,
overtook the older urban centers and outstripped them. By the fourteenth and
fifteenth centuries banker-tradesmen had built enterprises that reached throughout all Europe and into the Levant, businesses that involved assets of millions of
dollars, all well before the advent of Protestantism in the sixteenth century.

This analysis of the origins of capitalism is usually associated with the name
of the great Belgian historian Henri Pirenne, who based his conclusions upon
archival research into the growth of Flemish cities. Other writers have objected
to the anticapitalist bias of the religio-sociological and Marxist schools and have
been eloquent in praise of capitalist virtues. H. M. Robertson argued that the new
bourgeois individualism was not merely a product of greed. He believed it incul-
cated a sense of honor and justice, of liberty to act in accordance with fair rules of

business. The members of the bourgeoisie held man to be sufficiently rational to prefer justice to injustice. They were sincerely convinced that the market would be more cheaply and better supplied by free competition than it would be in an economy heavily controlled by legislation. The most important school for economists in the sixteenth and seventeenth centuries was the school of business experience, Robertson held. The capitalist spirit was equivalent to the rise of economic rationalism.

In assessing capitalism in the Renaissance, it is useful to bear these varying interpretations in mind.

Capitalism in Italy

IN ITALY the first significant accumulations of capital took place in the seaport towns. Genoa has received the most attention, in part because it developed early and was a worthy rival of Venice, but in part for the very pedestrian reason that very fine sources for the study of this problem have survived in Genoa, such as the archives of Genoese notaries before whom contracts were registered. The Bank of St. George in Genoa was one of the most powerful financial institutions in the Mediterranean world by the early sixteenth century. It exercised great political power, and because of its large holdings in Corsica it directed and supported Genoa's efforts to hold the island against Aragonese and Neapolitan aggression. But the growth of capitalistic institutions can also be traced in Pisa, Siena, Pistoia, and other major Italian cities, and very much the same pattern emerges in all of them. A basic distinction can be made between speculative capitalism, in which financiers profited by taking advantage of the fluctuating value of currencies and bills of exchange from country to country, and methodical rational enterprise of a more stable kind. Finance capitalism was useful as an instrument of both trade and industrial development.

Historians have often conveniently forgotten one source of capital and manpower during the Renaissance: the slave trade. At the end of the Roman Empire and during the early Middle Ages the institution of slavery died out. It was no longer economically viable. Moreover, the moral force of Christianity and the conviction that it was wrong to enslave a human being worked against it. But the thirteenth century witnessed a resurgence of slavery as the merchants of Genoa and other Italian city-states, avid for profit, entered the lively slave trade in the East. Prisoners of war and the children of starving or greedy parents were bought up and sold in the markets of Egypt and in Italy itself. The Balkans and the Black Sea area provided most of the human flesh for this traffic. In Egypt slaves were bought to fill the harems and garrisons of the Mamelukes. Orientals and captured Turks were highly prized in Italy as house servants and for lowly tasks in industry. Their sale and their exploitation as a source of labor provided another source of capital. Still, although precise statistics are not available, the main source of capital remained profit gained through trade.

At first individuals traded on a very small scale. Then the "society" or simple partnership developed, with each partner supplying equal capital and participation. A more common arrangement was for one partner to supply two-thirds of the capital and stay at home, while the other partner invested only one-third of the money but personally undertook the voyage. A further development took the form of the "accommodation," an arrangement of a company of several investors who hired an agent or a factor to carry merchandise abroad for trade, an early anticipation of the joint stock company.

With this development an adjustment in legal interpretation took place. Aristotle, whose authority loomed large in the thirteenth century, had stated flatly that money is inert and cannot of itself bring forth money. The Old Testament injunction against "taking usury or increase" from a borrower was given a literal application by scholastic theorists such as Thomas Aquinas and canon lawyers. In the agrarian culture of the ancient Hebrews a man borrowed from his neighbor or family, and then only when he was in need. The extension of this command against charging interest to an impersonal situation, in which the borrower sought capital to be utilized for his own enrichment, was not really appropriate. But taking the historical situation into account was not one of the intellectuals' habits at that time. As the practice of charging interest evolved, theory adjusted to circumstances, and the scholastic philosophers developed a number of fascinating rationalizations for it. The lender could now charge interest, not on the money as such, but as just payment for his own loss in not having the use of the money while it was out on loan, for the risk he incurred in placing his money in the hands of the borrower, and for the opportunities for enrichment that he was transferring to the borrower.

In the late thirteenth century the courts ordered restitution when a man was proved guilty of usury. If the amount of usury involved was uncertain, either because the sum was indeterminate or the exploited party was unknown, then a gift to charity could be substituted for repayment. The merchant princes gradually brought about acceptance of the idea of usury and compelled a change in the prevailing social ethic. The great banking families endowed chapels, hospitals, and other foundations to redress the grievances that society or the church might have against them, at the same time magnifying their reputations as solid citizens. Later the compensation became increasingly secular, taking the forms of fountains and statues to enhance the city.

FLORENTINE BANKS

The Bardis and Peruzzis.   In the year 1254 the first florin was coined in Florence. On one side of the coin was impressed the lily of the city and on the other side John the Baptist, its patron saint. The florin became one of the most stable currencies in an epoch of economic instability.

The most prosperous of the early Florentine banking families at the end of the thirteenth and beginning of the fourteenth centuries was the Bardi family. They were basically engaged in trade, with a banking operation on the side that facilitated the mercantile activity and brought in easy profit by taking advantage of differentials in the rates of exchange. Pope Boniface VIII used the Bardi banks throughout Christendom for the collection of papal taxes from England to Poland and the transmission of money to Rome. The Peruzzis' operations were very similar to the Bardis'.

One of the Bardi agents, Pegolotti, who worked for the family for some forty years, wrote a fascinating business manual, the *Practica della mercatura*. The handbook, a useful compilation for Bardi agents, gives information on weights, the value of monetary units, and rates of exchange, and includes a discussion of the standard currencies of Italy. Pegolotti records transit tolls and taxes; describes how items are to be packed—sugar and rose water from Cypress, for example—in order to preserve them; discusses the standard weight of wool per sack in England, the gathering of wool from monasteries, and the least expensive and most efficient transit across France, down the Rhône, and across to Florence; lists all of the feudal dues collected from the merchant transporting goods overland; describes the routes across Asia to Cathay; and lists the factors and agents in charge of the Bardi trading posts in Syria, Greece, Spain, Bruges, Ghent, Antwerp, Poland, and elsewhere throughout the empire—some four hundred in all. It is fascinating to learn that when the Bardis went into receivership, Pegolotti was one of those who took over what remained of their assets. He knew the business extremely well.

Political loans proved to be the ruination of the Bardis, as well as of many other banking houses during the next two centuries. At the beginning of the Hundred Years' War England was well behind other countries in economic development. It served almost as a colony, producing raw materials for more advanced industrial areas, notably Flanders. The Bardi bank supplied huge loans to the feudal English monarchy, which had a very inefficient revenue system and was usually at least a year behind in its collection of taxes. The government adopted the practice of anticipating income from taxes and borrowing money from the bankers, who received the tax revenues at the end of the year, usually a good deal more than the loan had been. This easy money became a trap, for the escalation from small political loans to large ones was easily made, especially when the bank had become obligated for obvious windfalls. Pegolotti tells of precious cups and other treasures given to members of the royal family, sometimes as gifts and sometimes as payment in kind. Not until 1338 and 1339, during the reign of Edward III, did the Bardis float a really large loan, guaranteed by the wool taxes. Since the Bardis had at the same time made loans in France, Naples, and other countries, they were dangerously overextended.

In 1340 Edward III, in great financial difficulty because of the war, repudiated all of his debts except those to the Bardis, whom he considered essential to his war economy, but very shortly thereafter he threw the Bardi agents into prison as well. The default of England and the Bardis' general overextension brought them to bankruptcy. In the same year some less important members of the Bardi family planned a coup in Florence, in the hope that control of the city-state's foreign policy might enable them to achieve greater security for their foreign investments. Their plan failed, although various members of the Bardi family retained important status in Florentine society even after their bank collapsed. The city-state did not provide sufficient political leverage for economic enterprises that were extended far beyond its influence.

The Medicis. The Medici family learned from the experience of the Bardis and Peruzzis. Whereas the Bardis' operations were highly centralized, so that when the English branch went bankrupt, the whole bank suffered the loss, the Medicis organized their bank on a decentralized system. From 1434 on, under Cosimo, the Medici bank operated as a system of partnerships between the central bank, managed out of the main office to the left of the grand entrance of their palace, and agents in various cities. The arrangements varied, and were drawn up as individual contracts between the bank and the agents, with the main bank holding the controlling interest but with the agent making a large personal investment, which guaranteed his energetic participation and proper caution.

The Medici bank was involved in trade as well as banking—trade in bills of exchange and trade in goods. Although Giovanni de' Medici amassed a respectable fortune, the Medici bank entered its greatest period with Cosimo, who was the senior partner in eleven enterprises. Bound to the main bank by contracts were three industrial establishments in Florence and about eight banking houses in other major European cities. The branch managers were junior partners who took a share of the profits rather than drawing salaries. They made their day-to-day decisions with complete freedom. Although they usually dealt with other Medici branches, each managed his individual branch as though it were an independent concern. Control by the senior partners in Florence on matters of policy was firm but quite general. Of course, the senior partners (among whom the principal ones were members of the Medici family) contributed most of the capital to operate the branches and drew most of the profits.

The three Medici industrial operations in Florence were a silk factory and

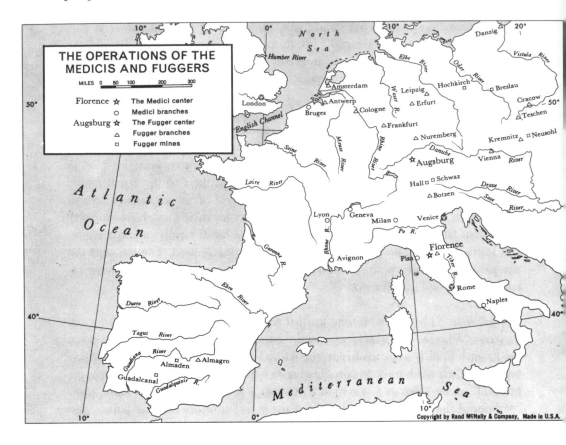

THE OPERATIONS OF THE
MEDICIS AND FUGGERS

MILES 0   50   100   200   300

Florence ★   The Medici center
        ○   Medici branches
Augsburg ★   The Fugger center
        △   Fugger branches
        □   Fugger mines

two woolen cloth factories, each operated by a separate Medici-controlled partner-ship. The word "factory" is really a misnomer, for there were no industrial plants, and production was organized on a putting-out system. Finished goods were sold to local exporters or shipped to foreign branches of the Medici bank. These indus-trial enterprises were not very important in the overall Medici operation.

The banking operation was not a simple matter of lending at interest, for interest charges were taboo on religious grounds. The bankers carried on a traffic in bills of exchange, devices by which merchants bought and sold merchandise in one currency in one locality and made or received payment in another currency at another locality. Hence banking was an indispensable adjunct of commerce. Its relation to industry was very slight. The profit derived from handling bills of exchange was derived not by discounting them in advance, but by a somewhat hazardous calculation on a favorable rate of exchange. Money-market watching was the favorite indoor sport of fifteenth-century bankers.

As we have seen, there has been much theoretical speculation on the source of capital, and the answer in the case of the Medicis is interesting. The profits accumulated through trading were in part added to the capital holdings of the company. Money was invested not only by the Medicis and their junior partners, but also by outsiders. Many of the investors were Florentines, but some were not. The French politician and chronicler Commynes invested in the Lyon branch. The Medicis paid interest to its outside investors.

The Medicis' banking operations served to facilitate their trading operations. The Bruges bank, for example, bought and sold commodities like any merchant firm: wool, silk, spices, olive oil, alum, nuts, currants, citrus fruits, Venetian glass, any item for which there was a market. Just like the Bardis in their day, the Medicis in Rome acted as fiscal agents for the papacy. For a time they managed the alum mines owned by the papacy in the Papal States.

During his last years Cosimo was unable to oversee the vast operation in his customary way. Piero was so ill and unsure of himself that he could not maintain firm control. Lorenzo was involved in the cares of state and in grand political designs, and so neglected the business. The third quarter of the fifteenth century saw several reverses and an overall decline due to general mismanagement and overextension. The Bruges branch, under a reckless and politically ambitious manager, lent money to the ill-fated Burgundian duke Charles the Bold, killed at Nancy in 1477. The Medicis themselves invested ever larger sums in culture, patronage of men of letters, and artistic monuments, and plowed increasingly smaller amounts of their profits back into the business. The branches went down like dominoes: London, Venice, Bruges. Then in 1494, the year of Charles VIII's invasion, the Roman branch folded and the home office in Florence closed down.[1]

The observation of the early capitalists during the Italian Renaissance suggests both the potentialities and the limitations of their position. The small city-state seemed to be a congenial environment as a base of operations, for the capitalists were able to assert control over the political power on the local level. The city-state, however, had definite limitations, for it lacked the power to offer real protection to its merchants abroad, even in enforcing contracts, to say nothing of fighting piracy and confiscation by larger states. Even Venice, the most successful in this respect because of its great naval power, was always subject to losses. In the long run the city-state could not provide sufficiently secure coverage for the continuity of an international financial operation. In the larger states the basis for a mercantilist national economic organization was already present in the fourteenth century.

A certain myopia on the part of these early capitalists is evident. They were often apologetic about their materialism on moral grounds, and frequently suffered pangs of conscience about usurious practices. Because of the precariousness of their whole operation, they tended to be very much on the defensive. They seem

---

[1] See Raymond A. de Roover, *The Medici Bank: Its Organization, Management, Operations, and Decline* (New York, 1948) and *The Rise and Decline of the Medici Bank, 1397–1494* (Cambridge, Mass., 1963).

not to have realized the full extent of the political power that their economic strength would have permitted them to wield. It may have required more time than they had to adjust psychologically to the new reality they helped to bring into being, the power of capitalism.

The Hanse

ALTHOUGH THE EARLY emergence of capitalism in Italy is particularly striking, it was a European phenomenon, and by the fifteenth century it was fully developed in many parts of the continent. The Hanse (League) in the north was a full-blown international organization of merchant capitalists whose operations reached from the Atlantic into Russia and whose naval power grew great enough to bring a king to his knees.

Two conditions made possible the organization of the Hanseatic cities. The first was the difference in economic life between western Europe and the Baltic area. The west, with its textile manufacturing, was industrially more advanced than the east, with its basic raw materials. The Hanseatic merchants provided the essential link between them, taking cloth and fine goods to the Baltic in exchange for such products as Swedish iron, lumber, herring, amber, and furs. Furs were especially prized by the upper classes, for castles and manor houses were even harder to heat than the small cottages of the peasants.

The second condition favoring the development of the Hanse was the freedom of the German commune in comparison with those states (England, France, Aragon, Castile) where the central government was stronger than the emperor. The Hohenstaufen emperors in the thirteenth century were preoccupied with Italian affairs, and in the fourteenth century the interregnum as well as the weakness of the emperors left the German cities free to go their own way. Whole colonies of merchants emigrated to new locations. The movement into the Baltic area by German merchants in the thirteenth and fourteenth centuries was much like the colonization of Sicily and other Mediterranean areas by the Doric Greeks in antiquity. Cologne merchants went to London, where they enjoyed special privileges and participated in guild activities and in city government. Known as Easterlings in London, they even minted their own silver coins, and gave their name to "sterling" silver. The Hanse had outposts in Pomerania, Königsberg, and Riga, and on the island of Gotland, where the German merchants at Visby developed a more elaborate form of corporate organization. Merchants of the Hanse traveled as far as Novgorod in search of furs and amber and were active as far west as the Iberian peninsula. Bruges was a Hanseatic "staple": a center for the sale of certain commodities, in which any ship arriving with such commodities

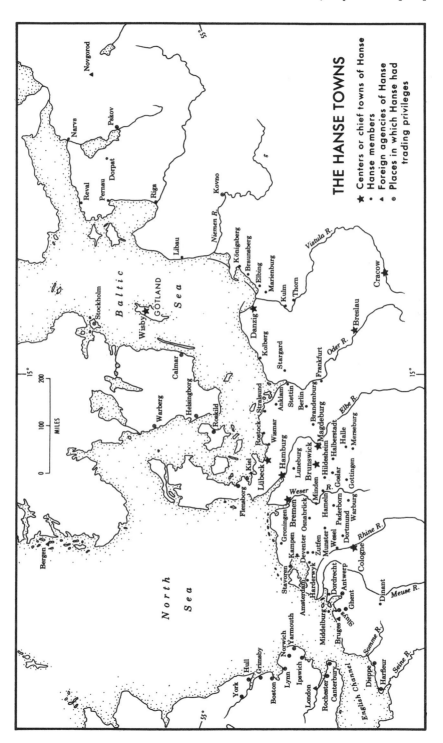

THE HANSE TOWNS

★ Centers or chief towns of Hanse
● Hanse members
▲ Foreign agencies of Hanse
⊙ Places in which Hanse had trading privileges

had to give the merchants of the Hanse the privilege of buying first, a very profitable advantage.

In the fourteenth century the Hanse rode the high tide of fortune. The Hanse met in a diet, usually at Lübeck. Visitors to Lübeck today can still see there the red-brick St. Mary's Church, the commerce building, the Hospital of the Holy Ghost for retired sea captains, and the city gate, endowed by the Hanseatic merchants in the city's heyday. The diet taxed its members and planned their military defense. The year 1370 marks the high point of Hanseatic power, for in that year, after a long contest with the Danish king, marked by naval battles and the invasion of Denmark, representatives of the Hanse dictated the terms of the Peace of Stralsund.

During the fifteenth century the Hanse declined under the pressure of larger states. As the duchy of Muscovy expanded, it took in Novgorod. In England, the Netherlands, Scandinavia, and Flanders the Hanseatic merchants encountered increasing restrictions and limitations. The tradition-bound conservatism of Hanseatic policies contributed to the decline of Bruges, which was finally ruined as a port by the silting up of the Zwyn estuary. The first great movement of foreign merchants from Bruges to Antwerp took place in 1442. Antwerp, unhampered by traditional restrictions and encouraged by Habsburg diplomacy, rose rapidly as the most important trade center in the Netherlands for silver, copper, alum, spices, and textiles. During the late fifteenth century a peculiar thing happened, still unexplained: The herring emigrated from the Baltic to the North Sea, which forced the reorganization of the fishing industry. But the main cause of the decline of the Hanse was the rise of competitive forces within a large national political structure.

Capitalism in France

A STRIKING EXAMPLE of an individual capitalist operating within the structure of a rising national state is the famous Jacques Coeur (1395–1456) of France.

Coeur was the son of a fur merchant connected with the Hanse. Young Jacques was trained for the French royal service. At an early age he took charge of the royal mint in Bourges. There he was arrested and tried for coin clipping. In the course of his trial it became clear that he had trimmed the precious metals from the coins with royal connivance, and he very conveniently escaped. He appeared next in the Near East, where he organized trade to supply the needs of the court. In a very short time Coeur had many agents and ships under his control. In the final period of the Hundred Years' War, Coeur lent money to the French king to finance his decisive victories in Normandy. He was rewarded with an appointment as the king's jeweler.

Suddenly Coeur suffered another reversal of fortune. He was arrested and tried on a number of serious charges: that he had poisoned Agnes Sorel, the king's mistress; that he had accepted gifts from the Ottoman Turks; and that he had impressed sailors into forced labor. Coeur escaped from prison and fled to the Turks, but after a time he turned against them and fell at last in a campaign mounted by the pope against the Turks after the fall of Constantinople. His beautiful Renaissance house still stands in Bourges, a tribute to the good taste of at least one of the *nouveaux riches*.

LYON

One cannot leave the French scene without taking note of at least one rising commercial center, which illustrates what the favor of the rising national monarchy could mean not merely to an individual, but to a whole city. The trading center of Lyon, even more than the international bourse in Antwerp, was the conscious and carefully tended creation of its country's rulers. After the fairs at Champagne went into decline early in the fourteenth century, France lacked a prominent trading center. King Charles VII was the first to give favorable treatment to Lyon, in order to build it up as a competitor to prosperous Geneva. Late in the fifteenth century, Louis XI, with a mercantilist economic approach, further strengthened Lyon in order to prevent the loss of bullion through trade in Geneva. Lyon developed a bourse, held four fairs, and became an important center for the new and fast-growing printing industry.

German Capitalists

LIKE ITALY, the empire was subdivided into many small states, including imperial and territorial cities with a great deal of freedom. These cities along the Rhine and especially in southern Germany became centers for feverish mercantile activity. The merchants of Augsburg, Nuremberg, Ulm, Regensburg, and other cities of southern Germany carried on a lively trade with the cities of northern Italy, through the Brenner pass and along other routes. In some places, such as Venice, part of the city was allotted to them as a center for their banking and mercantile operations. They served as a link between Italy and the Netherlands. In time they amassed such fortunes that through their international banking operations their activities reached through all of Europe.

THE FUGGERS

The growth of a family fortune through several generations is best illustrated by the fabulous Fuggers of Augsburg. Hans Fugger came to Augsburg from a small village as a fustian weaver. He became a trader on the side, selling his own textiles and those of his less enterprising neighbors, and accumulated a small fortune of three thousand florins. Jakob Fugger I, Hans's son, became master of the Guild of Weavers in Augsburg. Through his father-in-law, who was mintmaster in Tyrol, Jakob became interested in mining investments in the Tyrol, which became his second source of wealth. Jakob II, called "the Rich," began with a great deal of caution to make political loans. Since these paid a high rate of interest, his wealth grew rapidly. His loans to Maximilian I, for example, were guaranteed by the income from the royal salt mines. In an impudent letter to Charles V, Jakob Fugger once reminded the emperor that he owed his crown to the Fugger bank, which had lent the money with which he bought the votes of the electors. His marriage to a member of the Thurzo family of Austria, with mining interests in Hungary, the Tyrol, and the Sudeten mountains, increased his fortune. When urged by Thurzo to retire, Jakob Fugger made his famous statement: "I shall earn as long as I am able."

The heyday of the house came under Anton Fugger (1493–1560). During the Schmalkald War the house suffered losses by having holdings in Protestant as well as Catholic lands. (The Fuggers were Catholics.) The Fugger bank was caught again when the Spanish Habsburgs defaulted in 1575. In 1650 the Fuggers still had a claim of some 615,000 florins against the Habsburgs. The social settlement of 142 residents that Jakob II built for the poor in Augsburg, the Fuggerei, is still in service, and the indigent still pay only a few marks a month rent. He dedicated it "to the praise of God and in gratitude to Him." The chapel he built in the compound still stands. And in the rebuilt Fugger house, descendants of the family still operate a Fugger bank, though on a small scale.

The form of business combination used by the Fuggers was a family partnership, a link in a chain that led to the joint stock company. The business was centralized in the home office at Augsburg, but somewhat localized in the very distant cities such as Antwerp and Naples. Their policy was to keep control in the family, but to keep the leadership as virile and aggressive as possible. Jakob Fugger II has been called the first modern businessman, but since he did not specialize, he belonged to an order that has in the main disappeared.

OTHER GERMAN CAPITALISTS

The rapid development of the silver mines of the Tyrol around the middle of the fifteenth century induced the Fuggers and other families to leave the traditional paths of trade with Venice and to venture into mining operations. The Meuting family of Augsburg invested in Tyrolean mines as well as in silver mines in Saxony. The Paumgartner family of Nuremberg invested in Tyrolean copper mines.

The Welser family, which ranked next to the Fuggers in wealth, was an old Augsburg family. The Welsers joined with the Vöhlins to enter the Tyrolean silver business and played a prominent role in the great trade expeditions to the East Indies. They had active factories in both Antwerp and Lisbon, and eleven branch offices in leading cities. Conrad Peutinger and other humanists acted as agents for them. Like the Fuggers, however, they could not resist the temptation of easy profits on risky political loans. They made sizable loans to the Habsburgs, but regretted them during the Schmalkald War, when their money and land were confiscated by princes who grew suspicious of their imperial loans. The Welsers' claims on the French court and in the Netherlands remained unpaid. They fell into great difficulty during a credit crisis in 1562 and could scarcely meet the demands of their own creditors.

The Hochstetters were the third most important of the south German capitalist families. Ambrosius Hochstetter made a phenomenal rise and was one of the first to set up a branch in Antwerp. The Hochstetters were engaged in the East Indies trade and came very close to establishing a monopoly in quicksilver, but failed when new deposits were discovered in Hungary and Spain. They soon were beset with financial trouble with the Greshams in England and went broke in Antwerp. If their rise was rapid, their fall came early, for by around 1530 their house went into receivership.[2]

CAPITALISM AND CONSCIENCE

As time went by, the consciences of the early capitalists were bothered less and less by the charging of interest and monopolistic practices. They kept up certain pious pretentions, as when Francesco di Marco Datini headed his account book "To God and Profit." The Augsburg merchants and the Ravensburg trade association kept separate accounts captioned "Our Lord God's Capital." In their account book of 1511 the Fuggers included 15,000 florins for charity dedicated to St. Ulrich, the patron saint of Augsburg. Piety and profit were beautifully harmonized.

Preachers and moralizers might storm against them, but the merchant princes remained unperturbed and even hired propagandists to counterattack. The popular Alsatian preacher Geiler von Kaisersberg and the humanist Sebastian Brant, au-

---

[2] For a more detailed account of early German financiers, see Richard Ehrenberg, *Capital and Finance in the Age of the Renaissance* (New York, 1928), chap. 2, "The Other German Financiers," pp. 133–92.

thor of *The Ship of Fools,* boldly attacked usury and monopolies. The humanist Adelmann von Adelmannsfelden applied Plutarch's treatise *On Avoiding Usury* in a very obvious way to Jakob Fugger. The Fuggers supported the young Ingolstadt professor of theology Johannes Eck, who drew a distinction between interest and usury, and argued that the charging of interest was permissible. When the bishop of Eichstätt refused to allow a public disputation on the question, Eck traveled to Bologna, with a subsidy from the Fuggers, and there defended interest charges of 5 percent. The Dominicans adopted his position and the University of Paris favored his thesis. Although these intellectuals provided a theoretical basis for charging interest with arguments drawn from moral philosophy, the Catholic Church itself held officially to its absolute injunction against interest all through the Renaissance and Reformation period; in fact, down to the nineteenth century.

Industrial Development

IN EUROPE as a whole, the general economy picked up from the mid-fifteenth century on. The picture in Italy is unclear and is still debated. While many nineteenth-century historians believed that the great efflorescence of culture in the *Quattrocento* was a natural concomitant of a prosperous bourgeois society, some more recent historians have argued that the investments in culture were made despite hard times. It is fairly clear that in the second half of the fourteenth century the level of prosperity fell far below the heights reached around 1338. In the fifteenth century, Genoa, of course, went down, but Florence made a good recovery. It has been argued that fewer families were wealthy and that the aggregate wealth of a city like Florence was less than it had been early in the preceding century, but that is yet to be proved. Certain indices point to a higher general level of prosperity in fifteenth-century Florence. The manufacture of silk, for example, a real luxury item, increased markedly. We know, too, how the resourceful Venetians adjusted to the exigencies of the times, and that many of the most splendid palaces of the merchant princes along the Grand Canal were built during the seventeenth and eighteenth centuries. Yet with the foreign invasions from 1494 on, Italy's difficulties increased enormously, and the economies of Lombardy and Tuscany suffered.

Industry changed more slowly than commerce during the fifteenth and sixteenth centuries. Textiles had been very important during the medieval period, but from the mid-fifteenth century on other large industries developed, notably printing, mining, metallurgy, and silk manufacture. Although block printing had been in use for some time, the invention of the printing press by Johannes Gutenberg triggered the development of a major new industry. His original contribution, around the year 1450, was the development of an alloy that could be poured into molds to form letters that would not shrink or twist on cooling. This made feasible the use of movable type. From the thirteenth century on the supply of paper had increased, so that the mass production of books was now possible. Books now cost only one-twentieth as much as they had cost in manuscript. From Mainz printing establishments spread rapidly throughout Europe. In the printing establishments the owner of the press hired the printers and kept their apprentices, thus separating the workers from ownership of the means of production. They introduced standardization in production and rationalization in schedules, for they tried to time a book's production to meet set dates, such as the opening of the Leipzig and Frankfurt fairs. Labor troubles developed early in this industry, and the printers struck in Lyon. King Francis I published edicts ordering the suppression of labor disturbances and regulating the relationship of journeyman printers and apprentices. Some publishing centers had as many as five thousand of the new industrial proletariat.

Astonishing technological breakthroughs were made in the mining industry. Georg Agricola, in a treatise *On Metals,* described the new machinery and techniques for separating the metal from the ore and purifying it. Legal problems regarding the rights to underground resources had to be resolved. Theorists on Roman law held to the right of the monarch to the ownership and control of all underground minerals. But as the princes fell into financial difficulties, they transferred their titles to mineral rights to the bankers as security for loans. The financiers were quick to exploit these mineral resources, and copper, iron, and silver mining boomed.

One mining enterprise of special importance in this period was the production of alum, a sulfate that was used in textile manufacturing to fix dyes. During the Middle Ages most of the alum used in Europe came from Asia Minor. Western mining engineers and technicians had worked the deposits there, but as the Turks advanced they returned to the West, and frantic search for new alum deposits began. The ancient alum mines at Volterra were rediscovered in 1458 and at Tolfa in the Papal States in 1461. The papacy attempted to establish a monopoly on alum production as a source of funds for a crusade against the Turks. Papal agents actually used some of the funds to encourage Balkan leaders to resist. The Chigis and other bankers helped to finance and manage the papal mining enterprises. The mines employed eight to ten thousand workers.

The growth of the silk industry, especially in Italy and France, was another important industrial development of the time. Lucca in Tuscany was Italy's major silk center, but Florence and other cities also increased production of this luxury item.

From the end of the fifteenth century through most of the sixteenth century Europe experienced an inflationary spiral. The rise in prices served as a stimulus to industrial expansion, but wages, as always, rose much more slowly than prices. The laborers caught in this financial squeeze fought for better pay, and industrial relations throughout the century can hardly be described as tranquil. Europe, of course, has never been known for tranquillity in any case.

The rise of capitalism and the development of an urban society were necessary preconditions for much of the rebirth of culture during the fourteenth and fifteenth centuries. The economic factor was important for the emergence of the modern world. It helped to shape the political and social framework within which Renaissance cultural developments took place. Capitalism served as a solvent of the medieval agrarian economy by facilitating the transition from feudalism to larger territorial and national states. To state this is by no means to suggest economic determinism, for in addition to the economic component, many political, traditional, intellectual, aesthetic, and religious forces were at work which were often only remotely influenced by economic considerations. The human spirit is capable of great creative breakthroughs, and economic conditions can seldom be shown to be their prime cause.

Bibliography

General economic history:
Beaud, Michel. *A History of Capitalism 1500–1980.* New York, 1983.
Boissonade, P. *Life and Work in Medieval Europe: Fifth to Fifteenth Centuries.* New York, 1927.
Cambridge Economic History of Europe, 6 vols., vols. 1–3. Cambridge, 1941–1967.
Braudel, Fernand, *Capitalism and Material Life 1400–1800.* New York, 1967.
———. *Afterthoughts on Material Civilization and Capitalism.* Baltimore, 1977.
———. *Civilization and Capitalism 15th–18th Century,* 3 vols. New York, 1984.
Burke, Peter, ed. *Economy and Society in Early Modern Europe: Essays from Annales.* New York, 1972.
Chaunu, P. and H. *Seville et l'Atlantique.* 11 vols., Paris, 1955–1959.
Dobb, Maurice. *Modern Capitalism: Its Origin and Growth.* London, 1928.
———. *Studies in the Development of Capitalism.* London, 1946.
Elliott, John H. *The Old World and the New.* Cambridge, 1970.
Genicot, Léopold. "Crisis: From the Middle Ages to Modern Times." In *Cambridge Economic History of Europe,* 2nd ed., vol. 1, pp. 660–741. Cambridge, 1966.
Glass, D. V., and D. Everseley, eds. *Population and History.* Chicago, 1965.
Gras, N. S. B. *Business and Capitalism.* New York, 1939.
———. *A History of Agriculture in Europe and America,* 2nd ed. New York, 1940.
Heaton, Herbert. *Economic History of Europe,* 2nd ed. New York, 1948.
Jeannin, Pierre. *Merchants of the Sixteenth Century,* trans. Paul F. Hingoff. New York, 1972.
Kriedte, Peter. *Peasants, landlords and Merchant Capitalists: Europe and the World Economy 1500–1800.* New York, 1984.
Lopez, Robert. "Hard Times and Investment in Culture." *The Renaissance: A Symposium,* pp.19–34. New York, 1953.
———. and H. A. Miskimin. "The Economic Depression of the Renaissance." *Economic History Review,* 14 (1962):408–26.
Mauro, Frédéric. *Le XVIᵉ Siècle Européen. Aspects Économiques.* Paris, 1966.

Miskimin, Harry A. *The Economy of Early Renaissance Europe 1300–1460.* Englewood Cliffs, NJ, 1969.

———. *The Economy of Later Renaissance Europe 1460–1600.* London and New York, 1977.

Mols, Roger. *Introduction à la démographie historique des villes d'Europe du XIVᵉ au XVIIIᵉ siècle,* 3 vols. Louvain, 1954–1956.

Nef, John U. "Industrial Europe on the Eve of the Reformation." *Journal of Political Economy,* 44 (1941): 1–40, 183–224.

Nelson, B. N. *The Idea of Usury.* Princeton, 1949.

North, Douglass C. and Robert Paul Thomas. *The Rise of the Western World: A New Economic History.* Cambridge, 1973.

Pernoud, R. *Les villes marchandes aux XIVᵉ et XVᵉ siècles: Imperialisme et capitalisme au moyen âge.* Paris, 1948.

Pirenne, Henri. *Medieval Cities: Their Origins and the Revival of Trade.* Princeton, 1925.

———. *Economic and Social History of Medieval Europe.* New York, 1937.

Robertson, H. M. *Aspects of the Rise of Economic Individualism.* Cambridge, 1935.

Sée, Henri. *Modern Capitalism: Its Origin and Evolution.* New York, 1928.

Sombart, Werner. *Luxury and Capitalism.* Ann Arbor, 1967.

———. *The Quintessence of Capitalism: A Study of the History and Psychology of the Modern Businessman,* trans. and ed. M. Epstein. New York, 1967.

Von Martin, Alfred. *Sociology of the Renaissance.* London, 1944.

Italy:

Conti, E. *La formazione della struttura agraria moderna nel contado fiorentino.* Rome, 1965.

Davidsohn, Robert. "Über die Entstehung des Kapitalismus." In *Forschungen zur Geschichte von Florenz,* vol. 4, pp. 268f. Berlin, 1908.

Fanfani, Amintore. *Le origini dello spirito capitalistico in Italia.* Milan, 1933.

Goldthwaite, Richard A. *Private Wealth in Renaissance Florence: A Study of Four Families.* Princeton, 1968.

———. *The Building of Renaissance Florence: An Economic and Social History.* Baltimore, 1983.

Lane, Frederick C. *Venetian Ships and Shipbuilding of the Renaissance.* Baltimore, 1934.

———. *Andrea Barbarigo, Merchant of Venice, 1418–1449.* Baltimore, 1944.

Luzzato, Gino. *An Economic History of Italy.* London, 1962.

Molho, Anthony. *Florentine Public Finance in the Early Renaissance.* Cambridge, MA, 1972.

Origo, Iris. *The Merchant of Prato: The Life and Papers of Francesco di Marco Datini.* London, 1957.

Richards, Gertrude R. *Florentine Merchants in the Age of the Medici.* Cambridge, MA, 1932.

Roover, Raymond de. *The Medici Bank: Its Organization, Management, Operations, and Decline.* New York, 1948.

———. *The Rise and Decline of the Medici Bank, 1397–1494.* Cambridge, MA, 1963.

Sapori, A. *La crisi delle compagnie mercantili dei Bardi e dei Peruzzi.* Florence, 1926.

———. *Studi di storia economica medievale,* 3rd ed. Florence, 1955.

Northern Europe:

Andrews, Kenneth R. *Trade, Plunder and Settlement: Maritime Enterprise and the Genesis of the British Empire. 1480–1630.* New York, 1985.

Carus-Wilson, E. M. *Medieval Merchant Venturers.* London, 1954.

Dollinger, Philippe. *La Hanse (XIIᵉ–XVIIᵉ siècles).* Paris, 1964.

Ehrenberg, Richard. *Capital and Finance in the Age of the Renaissance.* New York, 1963.

Hering, Ernst. *Die Fugger.* Leipzig, 1939.

Kerr, A. B. *Jacques Coeur, Merchant Prince of the Middle Ages.* New York, 1927.

Martin, John E. *Feudalism to Capitalism: Peasant and Landlord in English Agrarian Development.* Atlantic Highlands, NJ, 1983.

Miskimin, Harry A. *Money, Prices, and Foreign Exchange in Fourteenth Century France.* New Haven, 1963.

Pagel, Karl. *Die Hanse,* 4th ed. Brunswick, 1965.

Planitz, Hans. *Die deutsche Stadt im Mittelalter.* Graz, 1954.

Power, Eileen. *The Wool Trade in English Medieval History.* London, 1941.

———— and M. M. Postan, eds. *Studies in English Trade in the Fifteenth Century.* London, 1933.

Roover, Raymond de. *Money, Banking, and Credit in Medieval Bruges.* Cambridge, MA, 1948.

Sée, Henri. *Histoire économique de la France.* Paris, 1939.

Strieder, Jakob. *Jacob Fugger the Rich.* New York, 1932; repr. Hamden, 1966.

Thrupp, Sylvia. *The Merchant Class of Medieval London, 1300–1500.* Chicago, 1948.

Van der Wee, H. *The Growth of the Antwerp Market and the European Economy,* 3 vols. The Hague, 1963.

Von Polnitz, G. *Jakob Fugger,* 2 vols. Tübingen, 1949–1951.

Wolfe, Martin. *The Fiscal System of Renaissance France.* New Haven, 1972.

CHAPTER 6

Renaissance Humanism

The most characteristic form of Renaissance intellectual life was the thought of the humanists. The term "humanism" was coined by a German pedagogue, F. J. Niethammer, who used it in 1808 to refer to a philosophy of education that favored classical studies in the school curriculum. Since then the term has been subjected to many varying interpretations. Early in the nineteenth century it was used for the so-called second humanism of Wilhelm von Humboldt and his contemporaries, who made reason and experience the sole touchstones of truth. In a very general way it was tied up with those rationalistic and humanitarian attitudes cultivated by the Enlightenment. The "new" or "third humanism" of the twentieth century, militantly anthropocentric and not infrequently antireligious, existential humanism, communist "progressive humanism," and a host of other varieties have in our day further complicated the use of the term.

Even if the historian succeeds in thrusting aside all these modern connotations and examines Renaissance humanism in its historical context, the task is difficult and dangerous, for he cannot and must not reduce such a complex phenomenon to a single formula. Renaissance humanism embraced many intellectual emphases. It was not a static thing, but underwent change and movement throughout the period. It can be understood only in relation to its historical situations in both Italy and northern Europe.

Despite the difficulties, it is possible to sketch a crude profile that will point up at least the most prominent and common features of Renaissance humanism. The German scholar Paul Joachimsen offered a clear and positive definition of it as "an intellectual movement, primarily literary and philological, which was rooted in the love of and desire for the rebirth of classical antiquity." Humanism was not merely an interest in antiquity, but a certain way of looking at antiquity and of relating it to the present. Antiquity provided the humanists not only with certain classical forms of thought, literary expression, and action, but with new norms for determining the suitability and rightness of the content of thought, word, and deed. The humanists were concerned with *humaniora,* or the humane studies. The concept of the *studia humanitatis,* the liberal arts, was taken over from Cicero, who believed that the poet or orator was best suited to communicate humane learning. These liberal arts embraced grammar, rhetoric, poetry, history, and moral philosophy. The Italian humanist Leonardo Bruni expressed a thought common to nearly all of them when he wrote to Niccolò Strozzi that these studies were best designed to perfect and ornament man. The term "humanist" was initially applied to the professional teacher of these liberal arts.

As a group of professionals the humanists were continuing the medieval vocation of the *dictatores,* men who taught the skills of letter-writing and proper style in written work and in speech. The humanists were more insistent upon the imitation of classical models, but they belonged to this medieval tradition. The twelfth-century renaissance had been an ecclesiastical affair, with its chief centers at the cathedral schools of Tours, Chartres, Laon, and Orléans in France, and to a lesser extent at Canterbury in England. The principal educational resources at hand were the Latin literary classics, late antique grammars, and the rhetorical tradition. The study of the liberal arts was the customary method of training the clerical administrators needed for the expanding ecclesiastical hierarchy. Thus John of Salisbury, perhaps the most famous humanist of his time, was bishop of Chartres at the time of his death in 1180.

In the thirteenth century the teachers of the *ars dictaminis,* epistolary techniques and skills useful to an ecclesiastical official, city secretary, or chancellor, developed rhetoric and classicism. Dante's teacher Brunetto Latini not only had an impressive knowledge of the Latin classics, but even undertook to teach the Florentines the lessons that Aristotle had to offer for running the state. To say that the Renaissance humanists stood in this older rhetorical tradition, however, is not to say that they did not differ from it. They were conscious of being different, and said so loudly, in their fervent love of the classics and in their cultivation of rhetoric as a guide to and expression of wisdom. They considered eloquence of great importance and seemed never to tire of Cicero's phrase from his treatise *On Oratory:* "For eloquence is nothing else than wisdom speaking copiously."

Wisdom must be brought to bear upon life in the most effective way possible. Wisdom must be given such rhetorical expression in language and tone that form and content fuse for maximum impact upon the hearer or reader. The Italian humanists rediscovered the ancient Greek definition of man as a "living being having the power of speech." They had tremendous faith in the power of the word. Classical languages were not merely philological tools, but living instruments that were used to give expression to man's highest culture.

Before the term "humanist" came to be used in the late fifteenth and early sixteenth centuries for the professional teachers of the humanities, they applied other names to themselves and their colleagues. The most common was "orator," for they frequently held chairs of rhetoric or spoke as advocates of their cities or princes. They also called themselves philosophers, poets, even prophets (*vates:* inspired poet-prophet). As professional rhetoricians they vied with the scholastic philosophers for the place of their discipline in the universities and even for endowed chairs. Not all of the conflict of the humanists and scholastics was intellectual. In fact, the humanists did not meet scholastic philosophy head on in debate; they declared scholastic problems trivial compared with their own pursuit of wisdom.

Two Trecento Humanists

PETRARCH, FATHER OF HUMANISM

Francesco Petrarca, or Petrarch (1304–1374), was the son of Florentine exiles, who as White Guelphs were driven from the city by the Blacks at the same time as Dante. He was born in Arezzo near Florence, but when he was still young his family moved to Carpentras, near Avignon. In the family circle his father, a notary, read Cicero's letters and orations aloud. Petrarch thought Cicero so wonderful that he had to wonder at those who did not wonder at him. Then as now, the most certain way to rise in public life was through a career in law. Petrarch spent four years at the University of Montpellier and another three at Bologna, the most famous center for the study of both civil and canon law. But the study of law failed to satisfy him and he studied classical literature assiduously on the side. When his father died in 1326, he returned to Avignon, then a lively intellectual center with the pope in residence. There he enjoyed the confidence and patronage of Cardinal Colonna and other high-ranking churchmen. He took minor orders, although he was never ordained. It was on April 6, 1327, that Petrarch first laid eyes on the woman we know only as Laura, in the church of Santa Chiara in

Avignon. She was married, a beautiful woman who became the angel of his dreams, the inspiration of his sonnets. He idealized this beauty, etherealized her, sublimated his passions. His Italian sonnets, which were greatly influenced by Provençal lyrics, established his renown. Until the second half of the fifteenth century they constituted his chief claim to fame, for his other writings were little recognized until then.

Laura, alas, was carried away in the Great Plague of 1348, and Petrarch could only await a happy spiritual reunion with her in heaven. Here on earth he fathered two illegitimate children by a less ethereal woman. Always torn between the active life and the contemplative life, he loved to withdraw to his villa in the nearby valley of Vaucluse to cultivate his studies and indulge his melancholy moods. He traveled in the Netherlands, the empire, and Italy. On the nomination of King Robert of Naples, the Roman senate crowned him poet laureate on the Capitoline Hill in Rome in April 1341, and King Robert granted him a commission "for reading [teaching], disputing, and interpreting the ancient writers both in the said poetic discipline and in the said historical discipline, and for himself composing new books and poetry." In 1347 he became a supporter of Cola di Rienzo. Petrarch accepted the hospitality and patronage of the Viscontis, the Correggios, the Carraras, and Venice, whose council gave him the use of a palace. During his last years he lived once again a life of solitude on a small farm at Arquà, where his daughter, Francesca, looked after him. He was recognized by the next generation as the founder of a new cultural period.

During the medieval centuries a strange sense of identity with the Roman Empire persisted. The political myth of the "translation of the empire" to the Germans, the religious presence of the Roman Catholic Church, and the lack of a sense of history contributed to this feeling of continuity. This conception was evident in medieval art, which portrayed Roman and biblical people in medieval costumes and ancient scenes in medieval settings. Petrarch developed a new sense of distance from classical antiquity, for he felt that the centuries preceding his own times were a dark age that broke the continuity from ancient times to the present.

Petrarch was fond of letters. His own correspondence, beginning in 1325, when he was twenty-one, rivals that of Cicero, Erasmus, and Voltaire in revealing insights into his age. He used a fictional correspondence as a literary device for expressing his inner feelings. In his *Letters to the Ancient Dead* Petrarch addressed familiar letters to his cultural heroes of antiquity: Cicero, Livy, Virgil, Horace. He reported to Cicero on the condition of Rome and the empire, and wrote an epistle to Livy, the Roman historian, expressing his wish that he could have lived in Livy's age, or Livy in his. He regretted the loss of so many ancient writings, and confided that he read Livy's histories in order to forget the present low estate of Italy and the customs of his age. "I am filled with bitter indignation," he wrote, "against the mores of today, when men value nothing except gold and silver and desire nothing except sensual pleasures."[1]

Petrarch failed to integrate the Roman virtues with his Christian values. In some treatises he celebrated the Roman values of piety, gravity, dignity, faith, probity, and honesty in the hope that they would help restore virtue "in the face of the miseries of the age." In "Concerning the Best Methods of Administering a State" (*Epistolae seniles,* book 14, epistle 1) he commended the injunction found in Roman law "to harm no one, to give to each his own, and to live honestly." Petrarch thought he would be best remembered for his *Africa,* in which he depicted Scipio as the apotheosis of republican virtues in contrast to Carthaginian malice, but it turned out to be an epic bore.

In a number of important treatises, such as *On the Solitary Life* and the *Secretum,* Petrarch developed as themes conventional Christian virtues, although not without some ambivalence. In the *Secretum,* subtitled *On the Contempt of the World,* which he had first entitled *Concerning the Secret Conflict of My Desires,* Petrarch developed his religious thought in three dialogues with St. Augustine. In the second dialogue Augustine explores Petrarch's feelings of sin and guilt. He probes the melancholy in his soul (*accidia,* melancholy; not *tristitia,* sadness). The way of despair leads to destruction. Using the analogy of a besieged castle, Petrarch depicts his soul engulfed in melancholy. His trouble, Augustine ventures to suggest, is that he has too low an opinion of himself, counsel that does not have an authentic Augustinian ring to it. The problem of melancholy runs like a black thread through the texture of Renaissance thought, much like the melancholy strain in Chateaubriand and romanticism in a later century. Perhaps melancholy was generated by the insecurity that resulted from the increased individualism of the period. Possibly it was the price paid for the broader cultural horizon, which now included a much greater knowledge and deeper appreciation of pagan antiquity. Then again, perhaps the recovery of so much material from the late classic period which was pessimistic and decadent in tone worked against the basic Christian optimism of the humanists. Certainly the famines, plagues, exilings, wars, and vendettas of Renaissance Italy were unsettling enough to infect all but the hardiest types with anxiety, fear, and melancholy.

Some of the ambiguities of Petrarch's position can be seen in his *Ascent of Mt. Ventoux,* which expresses both Christian and classical ideas. It used to be said that the *Ascent* illustrated the humanist's rediscovery of nature, after the long centuries of medieval neglect. But it is quite clear that the account is not a nature story, but rather a highly sophisticated literary piece. Petrarch describes the search for a companion attuned to his own psyche and intellect. He has difficulty finding a real

---

[1] Myron P. Gilmore, "The Renaissance Conception of the Lessons of History," in *Facets of the Renaissance,* ed. William Werkmeister (Los Angeles, 1959), p. 75.

soul mate, and so he chooses his own younger brother. They meander around the mountain rather than attempting a direct vertical ascent—apparently an allusion to the circuitousness of life. Finally he leaves his brother behind and climbs alone. On the mountaintop at last, far from merely drinking in the beauties of nature, Petrarch opens St. Augustine's *Confessions* to Book 10, in which Augustine discusses the lust of the flesh, the lust of the eyes, the pride of life, and what Christian continence prescribes for each. Christ the mediator can cure the sick soul. Petrarch has Augustine deplore the fact that "human beings go around admiring the mountain heights, the mighty tides of the seas, the broad streams of the rivers, the circle of the ocean, and the orbits of the stars, but do not care to look more deeply into themselves." In the *Ascent* Petrarch is ornamenting his own experience and transforming the whole literary treatise into an allegory.

Petrarch even wrote as an apologist for the Christian view of man and the humanists' appreciation of individual worth against certain Neo-Aristotelians whose doctrines he believed to be subversive. The Neo-Aristotelians, mistakenly referred to as Averroists, held that upon a person's death his soul is absorbed into a world soul or *intellectus,* thus being assured of immortality, but of an impersonal kind. This, plus the idea of the eternal self-sufficiency of matter, seemed to Petrarch, as it was to seem to the Platonists, to be contrary to Christian doctrine and to militate against the dignity of man. He questioned the validity of a philosophy that investigates "the nature of beasts, birds, fishes, and snakes but ignores or neglects the nature and destiny of man." For much the same reason Petrarch preferred the study of law, which is concerned with society, to medicine, which is concerned with the physical body. Petrarch touched upon some of these issues in *On His Own Ignorance and That of Many Others*. Spelling out the limitation of reason, he asserted that "the object of the will is to be good; that of the intellect is truth. It is better to will the good than to know the truth." He confessed quite frankly: "If to admire Cicero means to be a Ciceronian, I am a Ciceronian. . . . However, when we come to think or speak of religion, that is, of supreme truth and true happiness, and of eternal salvation, then I am certainly not a Ciceronian, or a Platonist, but a Christian."

In his political thought Petrarch was anything but clear and realistic. He had a vague conception of Italy as his motherland, movingly voiced in his poem *"Italia mia."* But his lack of realism could be seen in his support of Rienzo. While enjoying the patronage of Francesco di Carrara in Padua he wrote "Concerning the Best Methods of Administering a State," which expressed a sense of city loyalty. It was not a great republican document, however, for he urged the despot to mobilize the civic spirit in support of state projects. The ruler must justify his existence by ruling well.

Petrarch's conception of his own place in history was expressed in his *Letters to Posterity,* which form a kind of autobiography. Renaissance men were concerned about their reputation with posterity, for fame constituted one sure form of immortality. Boccaccio spoke of man's "great desire for perpetuating his own name." The generation of humanists at the end of the fourteenth century acknowledged Dante, Petrarch, and Boccaccio as the three founders of the new age; but during the course of the Renaissance, while Dante continued to have an important symbolic cultural significance for the Italians, he gradually came to be associated more with the Middle Ages, the "voice of ten silent centuries," as the romantic writer Johann Ludwig Tieck was to call him, because he wrote in the vernacular and in the *Divine Comedy* presented a poetic *summa* of the medieval world view. In his *Epistolae familiares* (Book 21, epistle 15) Petrarch himself, in a letter to Giovanni Boccaccio, made the gratuitous comment that from his youth he had avoided the attractions of Dante for fear they might make of him too a poet "applauded by innkeepers, dyers, and wool weavers." Petrarch was the self-conscious founder of neo-Latin literature.

When Petrarch and Dante are compared, several points of difference do stand out. Dante really was more medieval in his conception of hierarchy in political life, and in his whole world view. Petrarch's outlook was more fully integrated with classic viewpoints. The pyramidal social and political structures of Dante's conception fitted neatly into his Ptolemaic cosmology and Thomistic theology. Petrarch acknowledged the political particularism that existed in the city-state structure of Italy and the national patriotisms of the north. Dante used the vernacular and took many liberties in composition. Much of his prose and poetry, such as the *Vita nuova,* his spiritual autobiography in which he recounts his great love for Beatrice, is filled with dream visions and allegory of a spiritualized medieval cast. Petrarch used Latin for his "serious" writings and introduced classicism. Latin purists among the later humanists were highly critical of Dante for his linguistic flaws. Cardinal Bembo, an elegant Ciceronian Latinist, in his *Prose* (Venice, 1525) rebuked Dante for using base words. By the middle of the sixteenth century the judgment of the critics was entirely in favor of Petrarch and against Dante. Giraldi Cinthio compared the two in his *Discorsi* (Venice, 1554):

> But the law is not so strict for romances as not to permit more license in words than is customary for sonnets and *canzoni*. Long and serious subjects, if the conception is not to be warped, need such latitude, which must nevertheless be limited. Petrarch shows this clearly in his *Trionfi*. I will not cite Dante; for whether through the fault of his age, or because of his own nature, he took so many liberties that this liberty became a fault. Therefore I find quite judicious that painter who, to show us in a fair scene the literary value of the one poet and the other, imagined both in a green and flowery mead on the slopes of Helicon, and put into Dante's hand a scythe, which, with his gown tucked up to his knees, he was wielding in circles, cutting every plant that the scythe struck. Behind Dante he painted Petrarch, in senatorial robe, stooping to select the noble plants and the well-bred flowers—all this to show us the liberty of the one and the judgment and observance of the other.[2]

---

[2] Cited in Charles Sears Baldwin, *Renaissance Literary Theory and Practice* (New York, 1939), pp. 29–30.

Was Petrarch the first modern man, as Ernst Renan tagged him? The answer depends upon what is meant by "modern man." He was modern in his highly self-conscious individuality. This individualism was characterized less by egoism or bravado than by sensitive introversion. Even his love poems seem less concerned with the lady than with his own complicated state of mind and emotion. His self-searching dialogues reveal a concern with inner motives and questions of conscience that we commonly associate with highly psychologized modern man. In the medieval period only Abelard approaches this level of agonizing. It is telling that Petrarch chose as his partner in conversation St. Augustine, whom William James once called "the first man" because of his tendency toward sensitive introspection. Petrarch was constantly torn by the conflict between the active life and the contemplative life. The life of study, he came to believe, was really a life of action. This conflict posed problems for many of the humanists during the two centuries that followed.

Petrarch was the founder of humanism, the most characteristic expression of Renaissance culture, and as such became a symbol of the new and the "modern" element in that culture. "For who of you is unaware," wrote the sober Antonio Minturno in *De poeta* (Venice, 1559),

> that from the time when the Roman Empire, for all its power and eminence, began to totter and lean, literature was asleep, not to say overwhelmed and buried, till the time of Petrarch? From then on, it has been so steadily regaining the light that now it has been almost recalled from the rude and barbarous [medieval] teaching to its ancient cult.[3]

As a pioneer in literary culture, Petrarch was a spiritual guide and an inspiration to many generations of Western man. But he had many limitations, as do all men, and in a way he seems as far removed from our times as Cicero seemed from his. But distance in time did not prevent Petrarch from intensely admiring Cicero, just as Cicero in his day pointed to Plato, the divine mind who would free the intellects of his age. We can hardly withhold our praise from Petrarch.

BOCCACCIO, LITERARY HUMANIST

It is a mistake to make sharp distinctions among various categories of humanism, such as literary, civic, and metaphysical humanism. For some literary men—Petrarch was one—showed a modicum of civic concern and political interest, and some civic humanists, such as Coluccio Salutati and Leonardo Bruni, involved in the operation of the state, had keen literary, philosophical, and religious concerns, and even published in these areas. The labels literary, civic, educational, and philosophic humanists are introduced here for convenience in discussion, not as airtight distinctions.

---

3 *Ibid.*, p. 4.

The third man in the great *Trecento* triumvirate, together with Dante and Petrarch, was Giovanni Boccaccio (1313–1375), a friend of Petrarch's. The illegitimate son of a Florentine merchant and a French woman of Paris, Giovanni was educated for a career in business. His father sent him to Naples to work for the Bardi bank there, but he developed an intense dislike for business routine and bourgeois taste. He preferred the court with its chivalric and aristocratic way of life, brought from France by the house of Anjou. There he developed a burning passion for Maria d'Aquino, the illegitimate daughter of King Robert. Although she was married, she finally yielded to him, and thereby won a place in literature as the Fiammetta of Boccaccio's poems and romances. When Fiammetta at last turned away from him in 1341, Boccaccio left Naples for Florence, where he sought solace in the study of the classics.

Boccaccio's fame rests primarily on the *Decameron,* a collection of one hundred short stories. Three youths and seven young ladies have fled Florence to escape the Great Plague of 1348 and found refuge in a country villa. To pass the time away in their rural retreat they tell ten tales a day. The stories are drawn from the old chivalric romances and *fabliaux,* but Boccaccio has fun with them, mocks and ridicules. Bed-hopping is a major theme and the lasciviousness of monks and nuns he finds very amusing.

There was something of the antiquarian about Boccaccio in his zeal to recover ancient manuscripts. His biographer tells the story of his visit to the ancient Benedictine monastery of Monte Cassino in search of lost classics. The account may not be authentic, but it is true to Boccaccio's spirit:

> Desirous of seeing the collection of books, which he understood to be a very choice one, he modestly asked a monk to open the library, as a favor, for him. The monk answered, stiffly, pointing to a steep staircase, "Go up; it is open." Boccaccio went up gladly, but he found that the place, which held so great a treasure, was without a door or key. He entered, and saw grass sprouting on the windows, and all the books and benches thick with dust. In his astonishment, he began to open and turn the leaves of ancient and foreign works. Some of them had lost several sheets, others were snipped and pared all around the text. At length, lamenting that the toil and study of so many illustrious men should have passed into the hands of most abandoned wretches, he departed with tears and sighs.[4]

Boccaccio made some great finds while reconnoitering: a text of Ausonius, another of Martial, a minor work of Ovid, and an important Tacitus selection. Boccaccio authored a manual of classical geography, a book *On Famous Women,* and one *On the Fortunes of Great Men,* mostly Greeks and Romans.

The work of Boccaccio that merits the most serious attention was his *Genealogy of the Gods,* an encyclopedia of ancient mythology. In Book 4 he revives the Prometheus myth in a significant new form. Prometheus defied the gods by

---

[4] J. E. Sandys, *History of Classical Scholarship* (Cambridge, 1908), vol. 2, p. 13.

stealing fire from them and as punishment was chained to a rock, exposed so that an eagle could tear the flesh away from around his heart. Boccaccio knows of a second Prometheus—that is, the learned man. Learning "makes of natural man civil man, remarkable for morals, knowledge, and virtue, whereby it becomes obvious that nature produces man and learning then forms him anew." This is a telling humanist view of man, for his dignity does not consist in his human nature as such, but in that learning which first truly makes a man human.

Boccaccio was aware of the innovations the humanists were introducing into culture. In a letter addressed to Jacopo Pizzinghe around 1370 Boccaccio wrote:

> In our age, if I observe well, more illustrious men have come from heaven, generous spirits who wish to raise up again with all their strength the oppressed art of poetry, and to recall it from exile into its former abode; and not in vain. But we see . . . that in advance of others who are worthy of note, a famous man, our Dante Alighieri, who dwelt in the house of Philosophy, had drunk the honied waters at that fount which was lost many centuries ago. . . .
>
> Then, after Dante, his fellow citizen of Florence, that illustrious man, Francesco Petrarca, my teacher. . . . For Petrarca cleansed the fount of Helicon, swampy with mud and rushes, restoring its waters to their former purity, and reopened the Castalian cave which was overgrown with the entwining of wild vines. Clearing the laurel grove of briars, he restored Apollo to his ancient temple and brought back the Muses, soiled by rusticity, to their pristine beauty. Then he ascended to the topmost peaks of Parnassus.[5]

The Cult of the Classics

THE GREAT DUTCH cultural historian Johan Huizinga, in his *Homo ludens*, said of the Renaissance humanists, "If ever an elite, fully conscious of its own merits, sought to segregate itself from the vulgar herd and live life as a game of artistic perfection, that was the circle of choice Renaissance spirits." Although Huizinga exaggerated, as historians who are remembered are wont to do, he did in this sentence put his finger upon a very important feature of humanism. It was an upperclass phenomenon and the humanists were elitists.

With its medieval communes, Italy had never genuinely fitted into classical feudalism as it developed in France, the empire, and England. With the rise of the universities Italy was again out of phase, emphasizing law and medicine rather than theology as at Paris, Cologne, or Oxford. In literature chivalric poetry, which flourished in the north, and Provençal lyrics and sonnets found a home, and then only briefly, in the court life of Naples and Sicily. In architecture, Gothic had to be

---

[5] James Ross and Mary McLaughlin, eds., *The Portable Renaissance Reader* (New York, 1965), pp. 123–25.

artificially introduced, usually by northern architects, as happened in Milan. While medieval culture in the north reached its climax in the thirteenth century, Italy lagged behind.

The late thirteenth and early fourteenth centuries witnessed a basic change in this situation. For in those decades Italy reached a new height of prosperity and developed a secular urban culture more advanced than any Europe had seen since antiquity. The new humanism, with its nearly fanatical devotion to classical culture, suited the taste of the rich laymen who dominated urban society. The humanists catered to these men, for they provided support and an appreciative audience. Moreover, many of the humanists were drawn from this stratum of society, or worked their way up into it. The middle and lower bourgeois types had no appreciation of the aristocratic humanist culture. The shopkeeper Vespasiano da Bisticci, in a gossipy book on famous men of Florence, tells of these middle-class types not interested in learning and culture. Leon Battista Alberti observed that the Florentines did not care about the liberal arts, only in making money. "They say," Alberti observed, "that it is enough to be able to sign your own name and to be able to strike a balance in a ledger." The proletariat, of course, had no interest in the new literary culture at all. The humanists, for their part, were condescending to shopkeepers and artisans and disdainful of the ignorant masses.

A brief description of the socioeconomic aspects of the situation does not at all explain the rise of humanism as an intellectual and cultural phenomenon. A dominant wealthy class does not by itself guarantee the development of a specifically humanist culture. For that, powerful ideas must come into play. Men of intellect and dedication must serve as carriers and creators of the new culture. The humanists recognized each other as brothers joined in the battle against medieval barbarism and builders of a new world of thought. Their zeal for the recovery and study of the classics made them not only intellectual elitists but virtually devotees of a cult.

It is possible to trace a concatenation of people who transmitted Petrarchan humanism to all parts of Italy. Since Petrarch spent his last years in the lands of the Carraras, his influence was powerful in cities in their domain, such as Verona and Padua. At the University of Padua, Giovanni Conversini (1347–1406) was given a chair of rhetoric in 1392. An enthusiastic Ciceronian and great admirer of Petrarch, Conversini promoted the classics as professor and then as chancellor of the university. Among the students he inspired were Poggio Bracciolini, Francesco Filelfo, Guarino da Verona, and Vittorino da Feltre, who became major figures in Renaissance humanism.

Gasparino da Barzizza (1359–1431), author of the famous text *Orthographia*, having tried in vain to find support in Venice, opened a humanist school in Padua in 1408. Filippo Maria Visconti, who read Dante and Petrarch, as well as medieval chivalric romances, invited him to open a Latin school for boys in Milan in 1418.

And so the wandering humanists carried classical culture to new courts and cities.

Florence proved very early to be open to the new culture, for had not Dante and Petrarch been her own sons, though driven from home? In Florence an Augustinian monk, Luigi Marsigli (d. 1394), a friend of Petrarch, gathered a group of intellectuals·together at the Church of Santo Spirito and discoursed on the classics. Palla Strozzi (1372–1402), influenced by Petrarch and Conversini, became a patron-practitioner of humanist studies. He gave large sums of money to develop the *studia* or University of Florence. He encouraged the Greek scholar Manuel Chrysoloras (*c.* 1350–1415) to come to Florence to lecture, and founded the first public library in Florence in the Santa Trinità monastery. Very active in business and public life, he hurried home from the office in order to spend his evening hours reading the classics. Later he hired John Argyropoulos, a Greek refugee from Constantinople, to tutor him privately in Greek.

Another Florentine merchant who promoted the "new learning," as the humanists fondly called their studies, was Niccolò Niccoli (1363–1437). Niccoli showed less zeal for merchandise than for books, and attended Luigi Marsigli's lectures faithfully. He in turn opened his own house to students of the new learning. Although Niccoli became a fine classicist, he never published a line, for he was too inhibited by the glories of the classics and too firmly convinced that he was inferior to the ancients.

POGGIO BRACCIOLINI

Petrarch and Boccaccio began what was to become one of the favorite sports of the humanists, the search for ancient manuscripts. The most energetic and successful hunter was the unlovable egotist Poggio Bracciolini (1380–1459), who was a friend of Niccolò Niccoli and studied with Manuel Chrysoloras. His conduct was anything but exemplary, and when, to improve his station in life, he found it prudent to enter into the state of lawful wedlock, he was obliged to dismiss a mistress who had produced for him twelve sons and two daughters. His personal deficiencies did not keep him from being a severe critic of the institutions and ways of life of his times. An elegant Latin stylist, he served for many years as apostolic secretary and at the end of his life as Florentine chancellor. While in the service of Pope John XXIII he traveled to the Council of Constance in the papal retinue. When the hapless pope was deposed, Poggio was free to search for classical manuscripts in northern monasteries.

Poggio had a very low opinion of the monks, who had the reputation of ignorantly neglecting the precious manuscripts that had been so laboriously copied and stored in the monastic libraries from the days when Cassiodorus initiated the first *scriptorium* at Squillace in the last days of the Roman Empire. Actually the Carthusian hermits were the only monks who completely rejected nontheological or worldly learning. When the Cluniacs were asked for a pagan or secular book, they would scratch their ears like dogs, indicating their opinion that such books were lousy, but at least they preserved the books and made them available. It was in Cluny, as a matter of fact, that Poggio discovered several of Cicero's orations in the summer of 1415. The next year, in the great Swiss monastery of St. Gall, he made his greatest find, Quintilian's *Institutio oratoris,* which, together with Cicero's work on oratory, became the basis of the humanists' doctrines on rhetoric. Two years later he searched through the monasteries of Einsiedeln, Reichenau, and St. Gall once again. On this expedition he recovered copies of the work of Ammianus Marcellinus, the late Roman historian, and the skeptical poet Lucretius. Through the years Poggio also found the text of Vitruvius, whose theories were so important for Renaissance architects, nine new Plautus comedies, and the letters of Pliny the Younger. He helped recover some of the historian Tacitus' minor works, *Agricola,* the *Dialogues,* and the *Germania,* a work vastly exciting to the German humanists, for it was the only major literary source of information on the ancient Germans between Julius Caesar's *Gallic Wars* and the history of Ammianus Marcellinus. In addition to making these finds, Poggio wrote a description of the Roman ruins, *De varietate fortunae,* which revealed his appreciation of their aesthetic value as well as their importance for literary and historical documentation.

FRANCESCO FILELFO

Poggio's great rival as a collector was Francesco Filelfo (1398–1481), who studied Latin and rhetoric at Padua, and in 1417 was invited to teach moral philosophy and rhetoric in Venice. He made such an impression with his knowledge of Cicero and Virgil that two years later the Venetians made him secretary to their consul general in Constantinople. He studied Greek with John Chrysoloras, a relative of Manuel. In 1427 he brought back to Venice not only his Greek bride, John's daughter, but a very large collection of Greek manuscripts. Filelfo was a man of gross appetites and great physical energy, with a vile temper and wicked tongue. Exceedingly greedy, restless, and ambitious, he made his life into one constant chase after golden opportunities. From Venice he went to Bologna, from there to Florence. In Florence he lectured daily on major Greek and Latin authors and on occasional Sundays he discoursed on Dante in the cathedral. He also busied himself translating Greek authors: Aristotle, Xenophon, and the orator Lysias. When the Albizzis exiled Cosimo de' Medici in 1433, Filelfo urged the death penalty for him. When Cosimo later made a political comeback, there was no room in Florence for Filelfo. Filelfo even claimed that Cosimo had paid an assassin to murder him, though Cosimo really had bigger targets than this loud-mouthed professor.

Filelfo gladly accepted a post in Siena, where he lasted four years. Showered with tempting offers, he chose in 1440 to accept a lucrative position from Filippo Maria Visconti, duke of Milan, which paid seven hundred gold florins a year plus honoraria for special panegyrics and orations greeting visiting dignitaries and lamenting the honored dead. He continued university teaching, translating Greek, and heaping scorn and abuse upon Milan's political enemies and his own literary rivals in Florence. When Francesco Sforza destroyed the Ambrosian Republic, Filelfo ingratiated himself with the winner by producing a ponderous epic, the *Sforziad,* which fortunately was never published.

When Francesco died, Filelfo, now seventy-seven years old, cast about for greener pastures, and found them in Rome, where Pope Sixtus IV gave him a well-endowed chair of rhetoric. But he soon quarreled with the papal treasurer and made an ill-tempered attack on Sixtus IV himself, so that he found it prudent to return to Milan. He was ambitious, however, to make his mark in Florence. At the time of the Pazzi revolt Filelfo issued a harsh indictment of Pope Sixtus IV for his part in the plot. Gratified, Lorenzo the Magnificent invited Filelfo to teach Greek in Florence, but he died of dysentery just two weeks after he arrived. He was buried in the Church of the Annunziata at the age of eighty-three.

Filelfo was of great importance to the Renaissance, not for anything original he created, but as a wandering apostle of humanism. As a carrier of the new classical culture, he played a most important role with energy and conviction.

Humanist controversies were not always very elevating. Filelfo had attacked Cosimo de' Medici and rejoiced when Cosimo was imprisoned in the Palazzo Vecchio and exiled. With Cosimo's exile, Filelfo's rival Poggio lost his best patron and most powerful friend in Florence. Then when the Medicis returned, Filelfo became a professor in exile. In response to the invective of the jealous Poggio, Filelfo dipped his pen in gall and vilified Poggio in a bitter satire of one hundred verses:

> Poggio! ere long thy babbling tongue shall feel
> The keen impression of the trenchant steel;
> That tongue, the herald of malicious lies,
> That sheds its venom on the good and wise.
> What mighty master in detraction's school,
> Thus into knavery has matured a fool?[6]

Poggio responded in a fit of rage:

Thou stinking he-goat! Thou horned monster! Thou malevolent detractor! Thou father of lies and author of discord! May the divine vengeance destroy thee as an enemy of the virtuous, a parricide who endeavorest to ruin the wise and good by lies and slanders, and the most false and foul imputations. If thou must be contu-

---

[6] M. W. Shepherd, *The Life of Poggio Bracciolini,* 2nd ed. (Liverpool, 1837), p. 250.

melious, write thy satires against the suitors of thy wife—discharge the putridity of thy stomach upon those who adorn thy forehead with horns![7]

Poggio had a vocabulary to cover any occasion.

The Greek Revival

THE ROMAN POET Horace observed that captive Greece took her barbarian captors captive. During the fifteenth century the Renaissance too, initially a Latin literary phenomenon, experienced a reconquest by the Greeks. From Cicero, the most important single influence upon the early Renaissance, the humanists learned the keenest admiration for Greek culture. The church had not been unmindful of the value of the Greek language, and in 1312 the Council of Vienne provided for instruction in Greek at the Universities of Paris, Bologna, Oxford, and Salamanca, and at the Curial University. It also called for the study of Arabic, Chaldee, and Hebrew, but nothing came of these good intentions. The humanists took up the challenge.

Sicily and southern Italy, once known as Magna Graecia, had many Greek settlements in Petrarch's day. Even now Greek survives in the patois of some localities in Calabria. From Calabria came Petrarch's Greek teacher, Barlaam, whom he met in Avignon. Petrarch had developed a passion to read Homer and Plato in the original, but he actually made little progress in mastering the language. Boccaccio discovered the scholar Leontius Pilatus and arranged for a chair in Greek studies at Florence in 1360, but only Boccaccio and a few others came to hear his lectures. Simon Atumano, a very fine philologist, taught in Rome in 1380–1381, but he attracted only one student. Still absorbed in reviving Latin antiquity, the intellectuals of that generation had little energy in reserve for learning Greek.

There is a legend that when Constantinople fell in 1453, a stream of Greek refugees poured into the West, bringing many precious manuscripts saved from the Turks and initiating the Greek revival. It is quite clear, however, that by 1453 the humanists had already revived Greek studies in Italy, and that the refugees after the fall added little that was new, though they did lend them fresh impetus. In fact, nearly all of the important classical manuscripts that had survived the disastrous sack of Constantinople by the fourth crusade in 1204 had been brought to the West long before 1453, so that very little was lost to the Turks.

During the closing decades of the fourteenth century, the eastern emperor, under pressure from the Turks, had sought renewed contact with and aid from the

---

[7] *Ibid.*, p. 252.

West. An imperial expedition in 1374 and another in 1399 produced no help from the West. The distinguished Greek scholar Manuel Chrysoloras came to Venice in 1393. Niccolò Niccoli and Palla Strozzi asked the chancellor of Florence, Coluccio Salutati, to invite Chrysoloras to Florence, and he was appointed to lecture on the classics at the university there in 1387. In the years 1397–1399 Chrysoloras traveled with Manuel II Palaeologus through northern Italy and to Paris and London, but nowhere outside of Florence did he find a truly appreciative audience for his lectures.

One of Chrysoloras' most brilliant pupils was Leonardo Bruni (1374–1444), who succeeded Salutati as chancellor of Florence. In a moving passage Bruni tells of his excitement at the prospect of learning Greek.

> I was then studying the civil law, but . . . I burned with love of academic studies and had spent no little pains on dialectic and rhetoric. At the coming of Chrysoloras, I was torn in mind, deeming it shameful to desert the law, and yet a crime to lose such a chance of studying Greek literature; and often with youthful impulse I would say to myself, "Thou, when it is permitted thee to gaze on Homer, Plato, and Demosthenes, and other poets, philosophers, and orators, of whom such glorious things are spread abroad, and speak with them and be instructed in their admirable teaching, wilt thou desert and rob thyself? Wilt thou neglect this opportunity so divinely offered? For seven hundred years no one in Italy has possessed Greek letters, and yet we confess that all knowledge is derived from them. There are doctors of civil law everywhere, and the chance of learning will not fail thee. But if this one and only doctor of Greek letters disappears, no one can be found to teach thee." Overcome at length by these reasons, I gave myself to Chrysoloras, with such zeal to learn, that what through the waking day I gathered, I followed after in night, even when asleep.[8]

Bruni learned his Greek so well that he made valuable translations of Plato, Aristotle, Demosthenes, Plutarch, and St. Basil, the Greek church father.

In 1438 John VIII Palaeologus came to Italy with several hundred Greeks to beg the Council of Ferrara-Florence for help. He had to borrow heavily from Venice and the pope to gather the funds for the trip and to get his jewels out of hock for the occasion. Although the reunion of the churches was declared on July 6, 1439, the West sent no real aid to beleaguered Constantinople.

Among the Greeks to attend the Council of Ferrara-Florence was the Byzantine Platonist Gemistos Pletho, the author of a distinguished book on law. Pletho, together with Landino and others, played a role in the development of "theological poetry." At Cosimo's request he gave a speech on Plato in Florence and helped to inspire a Platonic revival. He urged Cosimo to establish an academy in Florence where Greek letters and Platonic philosophy would be cultivated. When Pletho

---

[8] Henry O. Taylor, *Thought and Expression in the Sixteenth Century* (New York, 1920), vol. 1, p. 36.

died in 1450 the Malatestas had his body taken to Rimini. The mortal remains of scholars were becoming as prestigious as those of saints and martyrs.

The chief negotiator for the Greeks at the council was John Bessarion (1403–1472), metropolitan of Nicea, another distinguished Platonist. He remained in the West and was elevated to the dignity of cardinal in 1439. Unlike Pletho, who was primarily interested in the pagan classics, Bessarion was a student of the Greek patristic writers.

Ambrogio Traversari (1386–1439), the prior of the Camaldese Convent of Santa Maria degli Angeli in Florence, turned the convent into a center for humanist learning and especially the study of the Greek church fathers, just as Luigi Marsigli had made the Santo Spirito a center for the study of the Latin classics. Traversari personally translated many of the Greek patristic writings. He worked for the union of the churches at the Council of Ferrara-Florence, and he influenced the pattern of Lorenzo Ghiberti's magnificent bronze doors for the Baptistery in Florence.

Meanwhile two manuscript collectors did for the East what Poggio, Filelfo, and others had done for the West. Cyriaco de' Pizzicolli of Ancona (*c.* 1391–1457), a merchant adventurer, gathered epigraphy, made drawings, and collected manuscripts, vases, and statues. His notebooks, containing descriptions of the Greek and Roman monuments he found in Greece, the Aegean islands, Syria, and Egypt, are still today a valuable source of information for classical archeologists. "I go," exclaimed Cyriaco, "to awake the dead!" Giovanni Aurispa (1374–1450) traveled to Chios in 1413 and brought home texts of Thucydides, Euripides, and Sophocles. He journeyed to Constantinople in 1421, and when he returned to Italy two years later he brought with him 238 codices, most of them containing Greek classics. After the fall of Constantinople, other Greek scholars—John Argyropoulos, Demetrius Chalcondylas, John and Constantine Lascaris—fled to the West, adding new impetus to the Greek revival and broadening the dimensions of philosophical discussion.

Education

POSSIBLY AT NO TIME in history previous to our own has so much attention been paid to educational theory as in the age of the Renaissance. The humanists had a high opinion of the rationality of the upper strata of human society and were generally optimistic about the educability of man.

Petrarch initiated the discussion of some of the issues involved with his argument about the superiority of law to medicine, for he believed that "Averroistic" science subverted moral philosophy. Salutati continued that particular debate in his discourse *On the Nobility of Law and Medicine,* in which he discussed the relative merits of studying law, which deals with human relationships, and medicine, which belongs to the world of nature. Law deals with the soul of man and involves questions of moral philosophy, whereas medicine treats man's body and is concerned merely with physical properties. Laws control medicine and the other sciences, while the reverse is not true. In the course of this rambling treatise Salutati came to the question of what constitutes true nobility. Nobility, he declared, does not depend upon relationship or blood, but upon virtue. Nobility of virtue is possible for slave and freeman, rich and poor, ruler and subject. This was, of course, a classic platitude, but for the chancellor of Florence, spokesman for the urban bourgeoisie, thus to reject openly the feudal conception of a man's worth was noteworthy. The question that such a definition of true nobility posed for educators was how to instill such virtue in the young, and how to help it develop.

Renaissance educators believed that the study of the liberal arts best served the purpose of developing true virtue in man. During the Middle Ages the liberal arts existed as a basis for later professional study in theology, law, or medicine. Little thought was given to the value of the liberal arts themselves in producing men of cultivation and character, fit to be leaders of society. Moreover, by the thirteenth century the study of logic and the authority of Aristotle had come to overshadow grammar and rhetoric and the other arts. The author of *The Battle of the Seven Liberal Arts,* a tedious medieval vernacular poem, lamented that "logic now has the students whereas grammar is reduced in numbers. . . . Aristotle strikes Priscian, our noble ancient authority, that he makes him drop to the ground. He wanted to trample him under his horse." Renaissance educators lifted grammar up out of the dust and elevated rhetoric to new dignity. The recovery of Cicero's *On Oratory* and Quintilian's *Institutes of Oratory* gave new impetus to the study of rhetoric and stirred new enthusiasm for the liberal arts.

PIETRO PAOLO VERGERIO

The most influential treatise on education during the Renaissance came from the pen of Pietro Paolo Vergerio (1370–1444). His *De ingenuis moribus* (On Morals Becoming a Free Man) drew heavily on Plato, Plutarch, and Cicero. He wrote it for Ubertino, son of the Carrara lord of Padua. Vergerio, a personal friend of Salutati and Bruni, was a student of Conversini and Chrysoloras. His career as professor of logic and rhetoric took him to Florence, Padua, and Verona. He put his Latin skill to work as secretary to Pope Innocent VII and to Cardinal Zabarella at the Council of Constance. He served later as orator at the court of Emperor Sigismund, and died in Buda.

In discussing the ideal curriculum, Vergerio spelled out the importance of the liberal arts for teaching the secret of true freedom and developing the individual to his full potential. This is the platform he laid down for higher learning:

> We call those studies liberal which are worthy of a free man, those studies by which we attain and practice virtue and wisdom. That education which calls forth, trains and develops those highest gifts of body and of mind which ennoble men, and which are rightly judged to rank next in dignity to virtue alone. . . . Amongst these [studies] I accord the first place to History on grounds both of its attractiveness and of its utility, qualities which appeal equally to the scholar and to the statesman. Next in importance ranks Moral Philosophy. . . . History then gives us the concrete examples of the principles inculcated by philosophy. The one shows what men should do, the other what men have said and done in the past, and what practical lessons we may draw therefrom for the present day. I would indicate, as the third branch of study, Eloquence. . . . By philosophy we learn the essential truth of things, which by eloquence we so exhibit in orderly adornment, as to bring conviction to differing minds.[9]

What Vergerio worked out in theory other educators put into practice.

VITTORINO DA FELTRE

The two greatest of these practical educators were Vittorino da Feltre (1378–1446) and Guarino da Verona (1370–1460), who founded schools based on the humanist educational philosophy at Mantua, Verona, and Ferrara. Vittorino lived in Venice and Padua at the time when Greek learning was coming in from Constantinople. He felt that insufficient attention was being paid by educators to the development of individual character. He grew impatient with dialectics and scholastic disputes that he thought frustrated the principal aims of education. Gian Francesco I Gonzaga, endeavoring to make of the little court of Mantua an important center of culture, invited Vittorino to set up a school there, and Vittorino resigned his chair at Padua and created in Mantua a model for teaching the liberal arts, well supported by Gonzaga.

Although Vittorino retained the formal structure of the medieval trivium and quadrivium, he gave them an entirely new emphasis. He aimed at building character by the study of classical literary masters, such as Plutarch and the historians. He also taught the Scriptures and the works of the church fathers, above all St. Augustine. He believed that a cheerful environment was important for good learning and named his school La Casa Giocosa, the Pleasant House. He introduced such novelties as coeducation, games, and physical education, including swimming, riding, fencing, and drill. His aim was to develop a sound mind in a sound body, and to develop in the student a proper sense of form, style, and decorum. Although the school served primarily the Gonzaga princes and Mantuan

---

[9] W. H. Woodward, *Vittorino da Feltre and Other Humanist Educators* (Cambridge, 1918), pp. 102, 106.

nobility, Vittorino also admitted children of the lower classes, to provide a multi-cultural experience. Possibly with reference to Vittorino's school the humanist pope Pius II wrote:

> As regards a boy's physical training we must bear in mind that we aim at implanting habits which will prove beneficial through life. So let him cultivate a certain hardness which rejects excess of sleep and idleness in all its forms. Habits of indulgence such as the luxury of soft beds, or the wearing of silk instead of linen next to the skin, tend to enervate both body and mind. Too much importance can hardly be attached to right bearing and gesture. . . . In ancient Greece we find that both philosophers and men of affairs—Socrates, for instance . . . or Philip of Macedon— deemed this matter worthy of their concern, and therefore it may be thought deserving of ours. Games and exercises which develop the muscular activities and the general carriage of the person should be encouraged by every teacher.[10]

Vittorino's pupils proved the value of the new pedagogy, for the alumni of his school included rulers of men and scholars as well. Ludovico Gonzaga succeeded his father, Gian Francesco, as marquis of Mantua in 1444. He retained his enthusiasm for the classics and even carried a copy of Caesar's *Gallic Wars* on his campaigns. He loved art and brought the painter Andrea Mantegna to Mantua. He commissioned the great architect Leon Battista Alberti to design the beautiful Sant' Andrea Church in Mantua. Vittorino's most famous pupil was Federico da Montefeltro, duke of Urbino, who turned his tiny court into a brilliant center of Renaissance art and literature. Vespasiano da Bisticci related that Federico had Livy read aloud in Latin during the midday meal, except during Lent, when he had the Scriptures read instead. Another pupil was Giovanni Andrea di Bussi, bishop of Aleria, who edited an edition of Livy's works that was published in Rome in 1469. In his preface the learned bishop dutifully acknowledged that he owed his knowledge of Livy to his genial mentor Vittorino.

GUARINO DA VERONA

Guarino da Verona was a pupil of Chrysoloras. He had studied Greek in Constantinople and brought back many Greek manuscripts when he returned. On the invitation of the Este family he set up a court school in Ferrara, not unlike that of Vittorino in aim and program. He and his somewhat less famous son, Battista da Guarino, composed important educational treatises.

LEONARDO BRUNI

The most potent statement of the power and practicality of a humanist education did not come from a professional educator, but from a man of ready discourse

---

10 *Ibid.*, pp. 137–38.

and action, Leonardo Bruni, chancellor of Florence in a time of crisis. He shall have the final word on the subject. In *On Studies and Letters,* written between 1423 and 1426, Bruni explained:

> That high standard of education to which I referred at the outset is only to be reached by one who has seen many things and read much. Poet, orator, historian and the rest, all must be studied, each must contribute a share. Our learning thus becomes full, ready, varied and elegant, available for action or for discourse in all subjects. But to enable us to make effectual use of what we know we must add to our knowledge the power of expression. These two sides of learning, indeed, should not be separated: they afford mutual aid and distinction. Proficiency in literary form, not accompanied by broad acquaintance with facts and truths, is a barren attainment; whilst information, however vast, which lacks all grace of expression, would seem to be put under a bushel or partly thrown away. Indeed, one may fairly ask what advantage it is to possess profound and varied learning if one cannot convey it in language worthy of the subject. Where, however, this double capacity exists— breadth of learning and grace of style—we allow the highest title to distinction and to abiding fame. . . . My last word must be this. The intelligence that aspires to the best must aim at both. In doing so, all sources of profitable learning will in due proportion claim your study. None have more urgent claim than the subjects and authors which treat of Religion and of our duties in the world; and it is because they assist and illustrate these supreme studies that I press upon your attention the works of the most approved poets, historians and orators of the past.[11]

With Leonardo Bruni we join the company of the distinguished civic humanists, who combined their love of learning with active participation in political affairs.

Civic Humanism

AFTER MANY CENTURIES during which men thought of Cicero as primarily a moral philosopher of the stature of Seneca, it came as a surprise to the humanists to discover the Cicero who was an active statesman and an apologist for the Roman Republic. With such authoritative sanction, the humanists could involve themselves with enthusiasm in the affairs of state and live the *vita activa* while cultivating the *vita studiosa* in their available leisure time. While the rhetorical discipline had been put into the service of the state by chancellors and orators long before the end of the fourteenth century, during the chancellorships of Coluccio Salutati and Leonardo Bruni in Florence a new element was added. During their terms in office Florence was involved in a struggle to the death for its freedom and for its very survival as an independent state. If Florence had become a provincial town in a Milanese territorial state there would have been no Renaissance in

---

[11] *Ibid.,* pp. 132–33.

Florence such as we know it. The humanist chancellors used their rhetorical skill and historical insight to strengthen the will of the people to defend the republic and resist tyrannous aggression.

From the time of Dante's *De monarchia* in the second decade of the fourteenth century to the treatises of Coluccio Salutati, Leonardo Bruni, and Alamanno Rinuccini (1419–1499), author of the anti-Medici dialogue *De libertate,* there is not a single work by a Florentine that can justly be called a work of political thought. The crisis of Florence galvanized the humanists into action; rhetoricians became civic humanists.

COLUCCIO SALUTATI

Florence was fortunate to have in Coluccio Salutati (1331–1406) a chancellor of superior quality, which was revealed as successive crises overtook the city. Salutati was born in Stignano, a small town in Tuscany, and spent twenty years in Bologna, where he studied law and became a notary. He worked as a notary for nearly a quarter of a century, at first in obscure posts, eventually for two years in Rome. Then in February 1374 he received an appointment as notary in the office of elections in Florence, and a year later he became chancellor, a position he held until his death, thirty-one years later. The chancellor not only played a major role in domestic decisions, but served as foreign minister as well.

Salutati showed his iron will by remaining calm during the Ciompi revolt in 1378. In spite of the street fighting and the attack on the Palazzo Vecchio, he denied that the revolt had caused much destruction or bloodshed, in a valiant though fruitless attempt to forestall excessive reaction against the defeated Ciompi. In that same year Pope Gregory XI accused him of heresy for making war on the papacy. Salutati responded with a skillful letter, done in his best Ciceronian style, declaring that Florence had not made war, but had merely defended its territory against papal attack. "In a fight for liberty," he wrote, "all will unite."

Salutati developed an intense love for Florence. He criticized all those who deserted the city in time of plague and refused to leave himself or to send his children away, for he was a fatalist and believed that no one would die before his appointed time. In an eloquent tribute to Florence he called her "the first in Tuscany, the most famous in Italy, known through all the world. Free herself, she is the mother of freedom and that is the glory of nations!" He was reelected to office again and again, with the gratitude and praise of the council and citizens.

The loyalty of the Florentines was put to the supreme test in the struggle with Gian Galeazzo Visconti, duke of Milan, who was determined to subdue the city and nearly encircled it. The war began in 1390, and Salutati rallied the people to the city's defense while he engaged in diplomatic maneuvering designed to frustrate Milan's designs. Gian Galeazzo said that a thousand Florentine horsemen did him less damage than the letters of Coluccio Salutati, and he sent assassins to kill the chancellor. When they failed, he tried a favorite trick and arranged for a forged letter, implicating Salutati in treason to Florence, to come into the possession of the council. By a similar ruse he had gotten the marquis of Mantua to behead his own wife. The marquis later used the same device against him, when the gullible duke was trapped into putting his own chancellor in prison, where he soon died. Fortunately, Salutati was able to persuade the council that the letter was indeed forged and that they were up against a ruthless and artful enemy. Though Salutati of course had nothing to do with the treasonous letter, he did write many others, and his correspondence, public and private, covering a period of fifty years, constitutes a major source of knowledge about the political and diplomatic history of the period.

Though less skilled than Petrarch and Boccaccio, Salutati had literary ambitions of his own. He wrote *On the Labors of Hercules,* an allegorical explanation of Seneca's play which was medieval in its use of allegory and in its moralizing but Renaissance in its use of quotations from the classics. In *On the World and Religion,* written about 1381, he offered arguments to persuade a monk to remain true to his calling. In another work, *On Fate and Fortune,* he took St. Augustine as his guide and assumed a basically orthodox position. But the work of Salutati that has stirred up the most discussion is his *Concerning the Tyrant,* because it seems to run counter to the republican sentiments of his civic humanism. In response to an inquiry from a young law student in Padua, Salutati wrote that a tyrant is a usurper who rules unjustly and therefore can justly be destroyed. Nevertheless, he argued, Dante was right in condemning Brutus and Cassius for assassinating Caesar, for Caesar's power had been legalized and he was therefore not a tyrant. Perhaps this specious defense of Caesar revealed a cleavage between Salutati the literary man, who felt driven emotionally to support Dante, and Salutati the civic humanist, who opposed tyranny. Then again, as a foreign minister Salutati may have wished to discourage anyone who might consider his argument as a license to attack the Carraras in Padua. Salutati was basically a very religious man, who was emerging from a medieval mentality into an early humanist frame of mind.[12] When Salutati died on May 4, 1406, he was honored with the laurel wreath. Poggio praised him as the haven and refuge of all scholars, the bright light of his fatherland, the glory of Italy.

LEONARDO BRUNI

During the decades after Salutati's death Florence was confronted by repeated crises in foreign relations. King Ladislas of Naples threatened from the south, but his designs were cut short by his death in 1414. Then Filippo Maria Visconti

---

[12] For a judicious assessment of Salutati's works, see Berthold L. Ullman, *The Humanism of Coluccio Salutati* (Padua, 1963), pp. 19–38; for a discussion of the medieval and humanistic elements in the man and his works, see *ibid.,* pp. 39–49.

took up Gian Galeazzo's ambitious plans for southward expansion from Milan at the expense of Florence. During much of this critical period the implementation of Florentine Policy was entrusted to Chancellor Leonardo Bruni Aretino (*c.* 1370–1444).

Leonardo Bruni was very much a self-made man. Born in nearby Arezzo in modest circumstances, he rose by sheer ability and determination to positions of prominence in the state and built up a sizable fortune. Early inspired by humanist culture, he caught the attention of Coluccio Salutati, who promoted his career. He was an eager student of Chrysoloras, mastered Greek, and became a tutor in the Medici household. In 1405 he became secretary to the papal chancery under Pope Innocent VII. In 1410 he was back in Florence for a brief tour of duty as chancellor. Then Pope John XXIII enticed him back to Rome by offering a career in the church. He accompanied the pope to the Council of Constance in 1414, but in March 1415 he returned to Florence, where he served as one of the *Dieci* and as a *priore* until in 1427 he again became chancellor, a post he kept until his death.

Bruni continued Salutati's application of humanist learning to social and political life, in contrast to Petrarch's constant urge to withdraw to the contemplative life. A member of the third generation of Florentine humanists, Bruni demonstrated a maturity and assurance not to be found in the early tentative phases. His dialogue *Ad petrum histrum* (1401) punned on the name of the educator Pietro Paolo Vergerio, who came from Istria; he may have intended the last word of the title to suggest "history" as well. This dialogue, a treatise on education, is an obvious imitation of the Platonic dialogues. It differs from most of the few attempts at dialogue in medieval literature in the way its characters stand out as individuals rather than as representatives of some type or class: the cleric, the knight, the scholar. The dialogue, which develops in a salon atmosphere, touches upon the value of learning and of conversation, the greatness of Cicero, the importance of Varro, and similar subjects. Near the close Bruni has Salutati speak as a representative of the old generation, venturing the opinion that Dante, Petrarch, and Boccaccio were the equals of the ancients. This opinion draws protests from three younger men, Niccolò Niccoli, Roberto de' Rossi, and Bruni himself, who prefer "a single letter of Cicero to all your moderns."

Bruni not only defended Florence diplomatically, but helped build up a patriotic tradition in order to deepen the loyalty of the upper classes to the city. His *Praise of the City of Florence* (1400) lauded the freedom of the republic, its security as an inland city, and its physical plan, with the tower of the Palazzo Vecchio in the center surrounded by four concentric circles. To Bruni, the beauty of Florence exceeded that of ancient Athens and Rome.

Bruni worked nearly three decades on his great *History of Florence*. He studied Livy, Polybius, Julius Caesar, and Thucydides, and absorbed the classic notion that history is philosophy taught by example. He could therefore introduce

Ciceronian rhetoric in driving home the lessons to be learned from historical events. He argued that Florence, a daughter of Rome, had not been founded by Caesar, as legend had it, but by Sulla, champion of the senate. From its very origins, therefore, Florence had a republican tradition. Liberty is perhaps the main theme of the *History,* freedom from tyranny and freedom from foreign domination. The twelfth and final book of this ambitious undertaking was still unfinished at the time of Bruni's death.

From the ancients he learned the legitimacy of contemporary history. In his *Commentary on Things Done in His Own Time* he explained that he felt an obligation to pass on knowledge of his age to posterity. He regretted that those who lived before his day had not done the same; if they had, men would not now find themselves in such a state of darkness and ignorance. The age of Cicero and the age of Demosthenes, he pointed out, were much better known than the period sixty years before his own time.

It is difficult to say whether Florence appreciated Bruni more as a man of action or as an intellectual. He himself had declared in 1433, "The greatest philosopher must give way to the greatest captain." When he died he was given a state funeral. As he lay upon the bier a copy of his *History of Florence* was placed upon his breast beneath his folded hands. The eloquent Giannozzo Manetti spoke the eulogy and laid upon his head the laurel crown. Bruni lies buried in the Santa Croce, where Galileo and other great Italians are enshrined. In front of the church stands a splendid statue of Dante, presiding over the noisy marketers and parking attendants.

CIVIC HUMANISM AS SOCIAL ACTION

The concept of civic humanism lends itself to a somewhat broader usage than an ideology of embattled republicanism. When it is understood as a life of action for the common good, such treatises as Leon Battista Alberti's *On the Family* and Matteo Palmieri's *On Civil Life* deserve to be included as representative expressions. But the most eloquent statement in praise of civic man's achievements came from the man who had delivered Bruni's funeral oration, Giannozzo Manetti (1396–1459), a man of a good Florence family, prominent as a statesman and diplomat. In the activist tradition of civic humanism, he once answered King Alfonso of Naples, who had asked what comprises the whole duty of man, "To understand and to act." It was to King Alfonso that he dedicated his most famous treatise, *On the Dignity and Excellence of Man.* He stressed man's achievements as evidence of his intrinsic worth. He rehearsed the triumphs of man from the building of the pyramids in ancient Egypt to the construction of Brunelleschi's dome in Florence.

> The genius of man is such that all these things, after that first new and rude creation of the world, seem to have been discovered and completed and perfected by us with

a certain unique and extraordinary acumen of the human mind. For things which are perceived are ours, that is, are human things, since they have been made by men, all houses, all towns, all cities, in short, all edifices on earth, which certainly are so great and such that they ought rightly to be considered the works of angels rather than of men, on account of this great excellence of theirs. Ours are the pictures, ours the sculptures, ours the arts, ours the sciences.[13]

Had Manetti known in 1451 and 1452, when he composed this exuberant piece, that he would soon be facing total ruin and disastrous flight from Florence, he might have felt in a somewhat less expansive mood. But if the civic humanists of the early *Quattrocento* could have known to what domestic tyranny and foreign oppression Florence would fall victim before the century was over, they might have lost their magnificent verve and become as cynical or despondent as Machiavelli and Guicciardini at the end of the Renaissance.

Humanism and History

THE HUMANISTS were keenly interested in history, especially in classical history, the history of their own times, and the place they would occupy in history yet to be written. Their beloved Cicero had declared: "History is the witness of the times, the torch of truth, the life of memory, the teacher of life, the messenger of antiquity." Paradoxically, it was the growing sense of their distance from classical antiquity, first seen in Petrarch, that contributed most to their deepened sense of history. From the classical historians, both Roman and Greek, they learned a view of history that differed from that of the medieval chronicler. A master such as Leonardo Bruni, whose *History of Florence* was a model and basic source for many later historians, derived from the reading of classic historians a feeling for coherent organization, literary style, and historical criticism. The contrast with even such late chroniclers as Matteo and Giovanni Villani is very noticeable, even though Bruni too could be needlessly detailed and tedious.

The humanists also learned from classic authors the pragmatic purpose of history. The rediscovered Tacitus, great Roman historian of the decline, had written: "The principal office of history I take to be this: to prevent virtues from being forgotten, and that evil words and deeds should fear an infamous reputation with posterity." History has the power to encourage good deeds and inhibit evil ones. It provides concrete examples for truths that moral philosophy teaches only in the abstract. The humanist historians were not at all embarrassed about introducing Ciceronian rhetoric in order to drive home a lesson suggested by the events they were narrating. They learned from the classic historians how history can serve a

---

[13] Giannozzo Manetti, *De dignitate et excellentia hominis,* in *Filosofi italiani del quattrocento,* ed. Eugenio Garin (Florence, 1942), p. 238.

patriotic cause, demonstrating the honorable course of their city-state or nation through the centuries. The writing of contemporary history, then, is respectable and a great service to posterity. But above all the humanist historians developed a sense of historical criticism, of the power of history as an instrument for the criticism of society and institutions. Educators provided an important place for history in the curriculum. It must be conceded, however, that the humanists did not contribute to what today would be known as the historical sciences, nor did they carve out a place in higher education for history as a discipline.

From Salutati to Machiavelli, author of a great *History of Florence,* and Francesco Guicciardini, author of a monumental *History of Italy* at the end of the Renaissance period, the humanists shared a wholesome respect for history. In 1392 Salutati wrote to the grand master of the order of St. John of Jerusalem praising his collection of books, especially of history. He commended him for having

> cherished the historians whose duty it is to hand down to posterity the memory of things done so that the examples of kings, nations, and illustrious men can be either equalled or exceeded by imitating them. . . . The knowledge of things done warns princes, teaches people, and instructs individuals. . . . It is the most certain basis for the conduct of affairs. History teaches us the doctrines of philosophy. What is rhetoric itself, one of the most beautiful of the sciences, but the conflict and opposition between things which have been done and things which ought to have been done?[14]

This understanding of the meaning and utility of history became so common during the Renaissance and Reformation periods as to become platitudinous.

ARCHEOLOGY

The search for ancient documents stimulated a search for ancient monuments. The founder of modern archeology was Flavio Biondo (1389–1463), who as papal secretary was well situated to study the Roman ruins. In two massive works, *Rome Triumphant* and *Rome Restored,* Biondo reconstructed the way of life and the political institutions of the ancient Romans, utilizing his knowledge of the topography of the city, its monuments, and its archeological finds. Then he broadened the scope of his studies to include all of Italy in a topographical-historical survey from ancient times and published an encyclopedic work entitled *Italy Illustrated.* These works not only were a great mine of information for historians and patriots in later years, but inspired similar efforts in other lands.

LORENZO VALLA

The man who demonstrated most powerfully the force of the new sense of history and the effective use of historical criticism was no historian at all, but a

---

[14] Myron P. Gilmore, *Humanists and Jurists* (Cambridge, Mass., 1963), p. 19.

philologist and rhetorician, Lorenzo Valla (1407–1457), perhaps the most brilliant critical mind of the Renaissance. The philosopher Leibniz, at any rate, considered Lorenzo Valla and Nicholas Cusanus to have been "the two most powerful spirits of the late Middle Ages."

Valla was born in Rome and was proud of being a Roman. A pupil of the famous pedagogue Vittorino da Feltre, he proved to be a student worthy of the great teacher. He became a superb Latinist and learned Greek so well that he did translations for the pope on commission. A real peripatetic, he moved about from Pavia to Milan to Genoa to Ferrara to Mantua, and then spent many years as secretary to King Alfonso of Naples. The last decade of his life he spent at home in Rome in the service of Pope Nicholas V, as a notary in the apostolic chancery, a position that left him a great deal of time for his literary activities.

Valla early gained a reputation as a pagan Epicurean with his dialogue *Concerning Pleasure and Concerning the True Good*. In this dialogue, directed against Boethius' quasi-Christian Stoic philosophy in *On the Consolation of Philosophy*, Valla reports the conversation of a Stoic, a Christian, and an Epicurean. The dialogue form makes it difficult to determine which of the three is expressing Valla's own opinions. The message, however, seems to be that if people could vote, they would choose happiness. For many years during the nineteenth century, when historians stressed the pagan nature of the Renaissance, they assumed that Valla was endorsing the Epicurean position. It seems, however, that he had a more subtle point to make. He was an ambitious student of the Greek church fathers, and many leading patristic thinkers held the position that Epicurus' stress upon true pleasure, which emphasized control over desire, not self-indulgence, was more readily harmonized than Stoicism with the Christian's belief in God's love for mankind and desire for man's true good and happiness. Valla was in harmony with the fathers of the Eastern church.

Valla's best-known work was the *Elegances of the Latin Language* (1444), which became a standard handbook for humanists south and north who were interested in philological precision and graceful style. Valla noted how two words could be synonymous, yet have quite different connotations. Thus the Latin words *gesta* and *acta* both mean a deed or an action, but *gesta* suggests the grand deed of a hero, a great man such as Alexander or Julius Caesar, while *acta* means any action of any man; the words *series* and *ordo* both mean a succession of things, but *series* merely suggests a sequence while *ordo* implies a grand and stable order of relationships. This work became an indispensable tool for stylists, but by scorning medieval Latin and insisting on classical precision Valla helped kill Latin as a living language.

Always a critical genius and independent thinker, Valla entered the arena of philosophy with his work *On Free Will*. He argued that predestination is not inconsistent with free will and that divine foreknowledge and human free will can be harmonized. He doubted that man has the capacity to bridge the natural and supernatural worlds intellectually or to harmonize reason and revelation rationally. "We stand," he concluded, "by faith, not by the probabilities of reason." He was here swimming against the humanist stream and speaking counter to the spirit of the times, for the theme of man's dignity and the power of his reason were shibboleths for many humanists. Small wonder, in view of his combative temperament, that his stormy career was filled with controversy, including a two-year feud with the rambunctious Poggio.

Three other works of Valla's touched upon problems that were to loom large in the controversies of the next century. His *Annotations to the New Testament* undertook to undo the textual mistakes of Jerome's Vulgate and even ventured to criticize exegetical interpretations of authorities like St. Augustine. In *Concerning the Profession of the Religious* he argued that the monastic life does not have a higher religious value than the good life of the layman, for the layman's good works spring from his own volition and do not consist merely of conformity to rules imposed from without. In his *Encomium of St. Thomas Aquinas* he subtly criticized St. Thomas for giving logic and metaphysics prominent places in theology, and for poor style, by praising the Latin and Greek church fathers. The fathers abhorred speculation and followed Paul's injunctions against following after philosophy and vain deceit, and not after Christ. In style the fathers modeled their writings after the great ancient authors and imitated Paul, a master stylist and rhetorician, whom Valla compared favorably with Demosthenes.[15]

Valla's most sensational work was his *Declamation Concerning the False Donation of Constantine,* in which he challenged the authenticity of the document that allegedly proved that Constantine, when he moved the capital to the east, had given the Lateran Palace and outlying provinces to Pope Sylvester. Valla held that this was the sole basis of the pope's claim to his temporal possessions, so that if it were discredited, the pope's worldly kingdom would collapse. Valla was in the pay at the time (1440) of King Alfonso of Naples, a foe of Pope Eugenius IV. In 1444 the pope commanded the Inquisition in Naples to bring Valla to trial, but the king frustrated its efforts.

Valla used rhetoric in this *Declamation* to appeal to his audience, playing on emotions and constructing fictitious speeches. His concern was with what one might reasonably assume to have taken place. Valla used a general historical argument: Constantine would scarcely have been likely to make the donation, nor would his sons have permitted it. What is more, Pope Sylvester would not have accepted such a gift, even if Constantine had offered it to him, for at that time the church was still pure and the saintly pope was concerned with his spiritual

15 Hanna H. Gray, "Valla's *Encomium of St. Thomas Aquinas* and the Humanist Conception of Christian Antiquity," in *Essays in History and Literature,* ed. Heinz Bluhm (Chicago, 1965), pp. 37–51.

office as shepherd of souls. The specific historical-critical and philological arguments that Valla used to prove that the document could not have been written in
the fourth century, but must have been of a later date, brought into play his remarkable linguistic talent. He showed that the word used for the papal crown was
not in use at the time of Sylvester. He pointed to the word "satraps" in the document, and exploded: "What do satraps have to do with this? Stupid! Dumbbell!
Do caesars speak that way? Has anyone ever heard of any reference to satraps in
the councils of the Romans?"

Valla was quite right, of course, for the document that was purported to have
been written by Constantine was an eighth-century compilation, backed up by
pseudo-Isidorian decretals and other documents. Wycliffe, Dante, and Cusanus
had all challenged the authenticity of the *Donation,* but they had done so from a
royalist, imperialist, or conciliarist point of view, and had used only general arguments. Valla employed the much more persuasive historical-critical method, and
he was in addition compellingly vehement and uncompromising. It is a tribute to
the tolerance of the Renaissance pope Nicholas V that he welcomed Valla to Rome
even after he had written his treatise on the *Donation.* In the Counterreformation
period Cardinal Bellarmine called Valla a precursor of Luther. Luther himself
acknowledged Wycliffe and Valla as his two great authorities. The Renaissance
and the Reformation movements had many such interconnections.

Bibliography

General:
Baker, Herschel. *The Dignity of Man.* Cambridge, MA, 1947.
Baron, Hans. *Humanistic and Political Literature in Florence and Venice at the Beginning of the
Quattrocento.* Cambridge, MA, 1955.
———. *The Crisis of the Early Italian Renaissance,* 2 vols., rev. ed. Princeton, 1966.
———. *From Petrarch to Leonardo Bruni: Studies in Humanistic and Political Literature.* Chi-
cago, 1968.
Bayley, Charles. *War and Society in Renaissance Florence.* Toronto, 1961.
Bentley, Jerry H. *Humanists and Holy Writ: New Testament Scholarship in the Renaissance.* Prince-
ton, 1983.
Bolgar, R. R. *The Classical Heritage and Its Beneficiaries.* Cambridge, 1954.
Burke, Peter. *The Renaissance Sense of the Past.* New York, 1969.
Chastel, A. *The Age of Humanism: Europe 1480–1530.* New York, 1963.
Dresden, Sem. *Humanism in the Renaissance.* New York, 1968.
Emerton, Ephraim. *Humanism and Tyranny: Studies in the Italian Trecento.* Cambridge, MA,
1925.
Fletcher, Jefferson B. *Literature of the Italian Renaissance.* New York, 1934.
Fryde, E. B. *Humanism and Renaissance Historiography.* London, 1983.
Garin, Eugenio. *L'Educazione in Europa, 1400–1600.* Bari, 1957.
———. *Italian Humanism, Philosophy, and Civic Life in the Renaissance.* New York, 1965.
Geanakoplos, Deno. *Greek Scholars in Venice.* Cambridge, MA, 1962.
Gilmore, Myron P. *Humanists and Jurists: Six Studies in the Renaissance.* Cambridge, MA, 1963.
Goldsmith, E. P. *The Printed Book of the Renaissance.* Cambridge, MA, 1950.

Grendler, Paul F. *Critics of the Italian World: Anton Francesco Doni, Nicolo Franco & Ortensio Lando.* Madison, 1969.

Holmes, George. *The Florentine Enlightenment, 1400–1450.* New York, 1969.

King, Margaret L. *Venetian Humanism in an Age of Patrician Dominance.* Princeton, 1986.

Kohl, B. G. and Witt, R. G., eds. *The Earthly Republic: Italian Humanists on Government and Society.* Philadelphia, 1978.

Kristeller, Paul Oskar. *The Classics and Renaissance Thought.* Cambridge, MA, 1955.

———. *Studies in Renaissance Thought and Letters.* Rome, 1956.

———. *Renaissance Thought and Its Sources.* New York, 1979.

Lind, Levi R., ed. *Lyric Poetry of the Italian Renaissance.* New Haven, 1954.

Martines, Lauro. *The Social World of the Florentine Humanists.* Edinburgh, 1963.

Molho, Anthony, and Tedeschi, John A., eds. *Renaissance Studies in Honor of Hans Baron.* DeKalb, IL, 1971.

Nelson, John C. *The Renaissance Theory of Love.* New York, 1958.

Rice, Eugene F. *The Renaissance Idea of Wisdom.* Cambridge, MA, 1958.

Rossi, Vittorio. *Storia letteraria d'Italia: Il Quattrocento.* Milan, 1945.

Roth, Cecil. *The Jews in the Renaissance.* Philadelphia, 1959.

Saitta, G. *Il pensiero italiano nell' umanesimo e nel Rinascimento,* 3 vols. Bologna, 1949–1950.

Sanctis, F. de. *History of Italian Literature,* 2 vols. New York, 1931.

Sapegno, N. *Storia letteraria d'Italia: Il Trecento,* 3rd ed. Milan, 1938.

Seigel, Jerrold E. *Rhetoric and Philosophy in Renaissance Humanism.* Princeton, 1968.

Speroni, Charles. *Wit and Wisdom of the Italian Renaissance.* Berkeley, 1964.

Struever, Nancy S. *The Language of History in the Renaissance: Rhetoric and Historical Consciousness in Florentine Humanism.* Princeton, 1970.

Trinkaus, Charles. *Adversity's Noblemen: The Italian Humanists on Happiness.* New York, 1965.

———. *"In Our Image and Likeness": Humanity and Divinity in Italian Humanist Thought,* 2 vols. Chicago, 1970.

———. *The Scope of Renaissance Humanism.* Ann Arbor, 1983.

Ullman, B. L. *The Humanism of Coluccio Salutati.* Padua, 1963.

Voigt, Georg. *Die Wiederbelebung des klassischen Altertums oder das erste Jahrhundert des Humanismus.* Berlin, 1859.

Watkins, Renée Neu, trans. & ed. *Leon Battista Alberti, The Family in Renaissance Florence.* Columbia, SC, 1969.

Weinberg, Bernhard. *Literary Criticism in the Italian Renaissance,* 2 vols. Chicago, 1961.

Weiss, Roberto. *The Spread of Italian Humanism.* London, 1964.

———. *The Dawn of Humanism in Italy.* London, 1959.

Wilcox, Donald. *The Development of Florentine Humanist Historiography in the Fifteenth Century.* Cambridge, MA, 1969.

Wilkins, E. H. *A History of Italian Literature.* Cambridge, MA, 1954.

Woodward, W. H. *Vittorino da Feltre and Other Humanist Educators.* Cambridge, MA, 1964.

———. *Studies in Education During the Age of the Renaissance.* Cambridge, MA, 1965.

Dante:

Barbi, Michele. *Life of Dante,* ed. P. Ruggiers. Berkeley, 1954.

Brandeis, Irma. *The Ladder of Vision: A Study of Dante's Comedy.* Garden City, NY, 1961.

Chubb, Thomas C. *Dante and His World.* Boston, 1967.

Croce, Benedetto. *The Poetry of Dante.* New York, 1922.

Fergusson, Francis. *Dante's Drama of the Mind.* Princeton, 1953.

Fletcher, Jefferson B. *Dante.* South Bend, IN, 1965.

Freccero, John. *Dante: The Poetry of Conversion.* Cambridge, MA, 1986.

Gilbert, Allan. *Dante and His Comedy.* New York, 1963.

Grandgent, C. N. *Dante.* London, 1920.

Singleton, Charles S. *Dante Studies,* 2 vols. Cambridge, MA, 1954, 1958.

———. *An Essay on the Vita Nuova.* Cambridge, MA., 1958.

Toynbee, Paget. *Dante Alighieri: His Life and Works,* ed. C. Singleton. New York, 1965.

Petrarch:

Bishop, Morris. *Petrarch and His World.* Bloomington, IN, 1963.

Nolhac, Pierre de. *Petrarque et l'humanisme,* 2 vols., 2nd ed. Paris, 1907.

Sanctis, Francesco de. *Saggio critico sul Petrarca.* Bari, 1954.

Tatham, E. H. R. *Francesco Petrarca: The First Modern Man of Letters, 1304–1347,* 2 vols. London, 1925–1926.

Whitfield, John H. *Petrarch and the Renascence.* New York, 1943.

Wilkins, Ernest H. *Studies in the Life and Works of Petrarch.* Cambridge, MA, 1955.

———. *Petrarch at Vaucluse.* Chicago, 1958.

———. *Petrarch's Eight Years in Milan.* Cambridge, MA, 1958.

———. *Petrarch's Later Years.* Cambridge, MA., 1959.

———. *Life of Petrarch.* Chicago, 1961.

Boccaccio:

MacManus, Francis. *Boccaccio.* New York, 1947.

Osgood, Charles G. *Boccaccio on Poetry.* Princeton, 1930.

Scaglione, Aldo D. *Nature and Love in the Late Middle Ages.* Berkeley, 1963.

CHAPTER 7

Renaissance Philosophy, Literature, and Science

Oswald Spengler, the twentieth-century historical pessimist, was wrong on many counts in his analyses and predictions, but he showed brilliant insight in characterizing Western culture as Faustian. That mysterious German Dr. Faust emerged from the shadows during the Renaissance period, willing to bargain away his soul in exchange for forbidden knowledge. The Faustian drive, the yearning for learning, the wish to sound the depths of wisdom and even to explore the arcane and occult impelled many men onward in a phrenetic search for knowledge, human and divine. "For men are from the earth," Cicero had written in *On the Nature of the Gods,* "not as inhabitants or dwellers but as spectators of the higher and heavenly things, a view of which things belongs to no other kind of living being."

Many major figures among the Italian humanists were gone by the mid-fifteenth century or died soon thereafter: Bruni, Vergerio, Poggio, Vittorino, Manetti, Valla. The cultural Renaissance moved on into a new metaphysical phase. The relatively uncomplicated moral philosophy of the humanists was superseded by an intense preoccupation with Neoplatonic, Neo-Pythagorean, Neo-Aristotelian, Hermetic, and Cabalistic philosophies and theodicies.

Social and political conditions in Florence were altered as the Medici family tightened its hold upon the state, restricting the expression of the republican leanings of the civic humanists. As the base of wealth narrowed, there were fewer and fewer opportunities for the professional humanists to participate in significant political action and to share in the economic prosperity of the upper classes, among whom they had once moved so freely. But even more important than these social and political changes was a progression of intellectual life into a new key, a nuance of the mind. For although no dramatic social change equivalent to Florence's took place in Milan, Venice, Rome, Naples, or lesser cities and courts, they too experienced a striking intellectual change. The most powerful factor in this mid-century intellectual and cultural change was the impact of the rediscovered Hellenic philosophy and theology upon minds sufficiently well schooled and sophisticated to respond to them.

The Patristic Revival

THE MASTERY of the language, the availability of a large body of philosophical literature, the enthusiasm of Roman authors for Greek philosophers, and the Platonic component in medieval thought all contributed to the readiness of Renaissance intellectuals for the "ancient theology." But there is one aspect of this development that needs special emphasis, because it has been largely neglected until recently. The Renaissance saw the revival of Christian antiquity as well as of classic culture. Ambrogio Traversari, Leonardo Bruni, John Bessarion, Lorenzo Valla, Egidio da Viterbo, Baptista Mantuanus, and many other scholars devoted tremendous energy to the study of patristic literature. Petrarch himself had pointed to the church fathers as models:

> The Romans may imitate as leaders the Camilluses, the Fabriciuses, the Reguluses, the Scipios. Philosophers may propose to themselves Pythagoras, Socrates, Plato, and Aristotle. Poets may emulate Homer, Virgil, Menander, Terence; historians Thucydides, Sallust, Herodotus, Livy; orators Lysias, the Gracchi, Demosthenes, Tully. And now we come to our own: the bishops and priests may have as an example the apostles and men of apostolic times. . . . We, moreover, have provided as our princes Paul, Antony, Julian, Hilary, Macarius, and, as we return to the truth of the Scriptures, our prince is Elijah, is Elisha, our leaders the sons of the prophets! Thus, brothers, those who were Jerome's leaders are your leaders; further we have Jerome himself, and Augustine and Gregory, and all those anywhere who for love of Christ, by leading a solitary and eremitical life, have been known to have been distinguished by religious leisure.[1]

The patristic revival was important not only because it provided a vision of

---

[1] Petrarch, *De otio religioso,* cited in Charles Trinkaus, "Humanist Treatises on the Status of the Religious: Petrarch, Salutati, Valla," in *Studies in the Renaissance,* ed. M. A. Shaaber (New York, 1964), vol. 11, pp. 16–17.

a golden age in the past, but specifically because of the positive attitude that the Greek and Latin church fathers took toward Greek philosophy. They looked for possibilities of synthesis and areas of agreement. They developed a theory that the divine *Logos,* or principle of wisdom, had inspired pagan philosophers long before becoming incarnate in Christ. Paul's sermon on Mars Hill in Athens had cited pagan poets with approval. One of the early apologists, Justin Martyr, declared, "Whatever has been well said belongs to us Christians." In his first *Apologia* he stated explicitly:

> We have been taught that Christ was first-begotten of God and we have indicated above that He is the Word of whom all mankind partakes. Those who lived by reason are Christians, even though they have been considered atheists: such as, among the Greeks, Socrates, Heraclitus, and others like them.

Gregory Nazianzen, St. Basil, who wrote an "Exhortation to Young Men on How They Might Derive Profit from Pagan Literature," and that great syncretist Clement of Alexandria believed that the *Logos* or the Holy Spirit had inspired the pagan philosophers before New Testament times. Philosophy, Clement argued, educated the Greek people for Christ, just as the law did the Hebrews. A few rigorists, such as Tertullian, opposed classical writings as lascivious and the antique gods as demons. Tertullian called the Greek philosophers "patriarchs of heresy" and Plato a "grocery store for all heretics," and declared that Aristotle had "introduced dialectic for the benefit of heresy."

In the West, St. Jerome was an avid student of the classics. St. Augustine, whose authority loomed so large in the fifteenth and sixteenth centuries, took a basically positive position toward the utility of the classics. In his *De doctrina christiana* he explained: "If perchance those who are called philosophers have spoken things true and agreeable to our faith, especially the Platonists, not only are they not to be feared, but they should be appropriated from them as from unjust possessors for our own use." With very few exceptions the philosophers of the Renaissance took their cue from Augustine. They were less interested in a pagan revival than in working out a grand new synthesis of Greek philosophy and Christian theology. They looked for the most ancient sources of wisdom and sought corroboration of the truth of Christianity in Greek and Hebrew sources.

Neoplatonism

PARTLY BECAUSE of its contrast to the Aristotelianism of the thirteenth century, so central to Thomist scholastic philosophy, Neoplatonism seems to be the most prominent and the most characteristic form of Renaissance philosophy. It lent itself readily to the endeavor of the "academicians" to fuse the "classical ideal of beauty and the Christian ideal of moral perfection." In the *Trionfo della fama* Petrarch assigned the first place to Plato and only second place to Aristotle, since, he said, Plato was praised by the greatest authors, Aristotle only by the greatest numbers.

From the time of Petrarch until the end of the Renaissance, Platonism won an ever larger place in Western thought. Egidio da Viterbo (1469–1532), prior general of the Augustinian order and a cardinal under Leo X, thought that Platonism would bring on a golden age. In his *Commentary on the Sentences* he exclaimed, "Oh, if only Plato rather than Aristotle had come into the hands of our theologians!" Egidio considered Plato a Christian before Christ, one who discovered the secret of the Trinity by means of natural theology. The Renaissance Platonists were concerned with the traditional theological problems: the existence and nature of God, the immortality of the soul, predestination, free will. Their way of thinking was not opposed to formal theology, but it was no longer merely in the service of official theology. The nature of Platonic thought can perhaps best be seen in the key ideas of the three most prominent philosophers of the Renaissance: Nicholas Cusanus, Marsilio Ficino, and Giovanni Pico della Mirandola.

NICHOLAS CUSANUS

Perhaps the most original and significant thinker of the fifteenth century was Nicholas Cusanus (1401–1464), a German churchman who spent a good many years in Renaissance Italy. Ernst Cassirer and other scholars have pointed to Cusanus as the great pioneer of modern thought who made the transition from a scholastic synthesis to a new relativistic approach, using mathematical symbolism to express and illustrate his ideas.

Born in Cues, a small town nestled on the bank of the Moselle River, he possibly went to school in Deventer and then studied Greek, Hebrew, mathematics, and astronomy at Padua. During the papal schism, as a representative of the archbishop of Trier at the Council of Basel, he was a convinced conciliarist, and wrote one of the great statements of conciliar thought. But he became disillusioned with the constant divisions and acrimonious bickerings of the conciliarists, and in 1437 he swung over to the papal side. He was entrusted with many missions by the pope, who sent him to Constantinople to work for the unity of the Eastern and Western churches. He was made a cardinal in 1448 and became Bishop of Brixen in 1450. The Habsburg archduke of Austria attacked him and even imprisoned him for his strong defense of the rights of the church. In 1460 he retired to Rome, where he spent his last four years writing his brilliant philosophical treatises.

Cusanus, a true man of the Renaissance, discovered several classic manuscripts and was a jurist, theologian, speculative thinker, and observer of nature. He was pacific and conciliatory toward Islam and other non-Christian religions. A great synthesizer of disparate viewpoints, he considered error to be merely insufficiency of truth. His own thought was very much conditioned by medieval Neoplatonism and mysticism, and by such authors as Dionysius the Areopagite, Duns Scotus, Erigena, the Neoplatonist Proclus, and the great mystic Meister Eckhart.

He employed the negative approach to knowledge of things divine, according to which one arrived at a closer knowledge of God by describing in ever more refined negative comparisons what he is not, rather than stating positively by analogy what he is. Thus the statement "God is not a stone" is more true than "God is not a soul." But Cusanus went well beyond medieval negative theology in the consistency and radicalism of his approach.

Cusanus' basic philosophical concern was the search for unity, for the infinite One that individualizes and reveals itself in the multiplicity of finite things. "Man has actually come into this world in order to seek God," he wrote. The differences and antitheses of all finite creatures coincide in the infinity of God. God is the *coincidentia oppositorum*, the coincidence of opposites, which reveals in the world something of the invisible spiritual world. The central thesis is *docta ignorantia*, learned ignorance, the insight that the most brilliant man of reason cannot by rational principles grasp the identity of unity and infinite multiplicity. God is the nexus of all things, which are in turn the explication or unfolding of God. Cusanus applied to the world such terms as *deus visibilis* and *deus creatus*, bringing down upon himself charges of pantheism. To him the world was a living totality with great worth and value.

Cusanus illustrated his metaphysical theories with mathematical and geometrical symbolism: God is the maximum and the minimum of all finite creation, just as a straight line may be thought of as the circumference of a circle having an infinite radius. A straight line coincides with an infinitely enlarged angle, with an infinitely enlarged curve. Cusanus broke with Aristotle's categories, which assumed that the universe was finite and that the earth was its stationary center. He conceived of the universe rather as an infinite sphere with its circumference everywhere and its center at no specific point. By denying the centrality of the earth or any other point in the universe, he introduced relativity into cosmology. He even taught the rotation of the earth on its axis. His thought was important for Copernicus and Giordano Bruno in the next century.

MARSILIO FICINO

Excited by the new Greek learning, Cosimo de' Medici chose his physician's precocious young son to become a master of Greek and a Platonic philosopher. Cosimo told the boy, Marsilio Ficino (1433–1499), that as his father had cared for his body, so Marsilio was to become "the curer of his soul." The young man was far from impressive physically, for he was small and hunchbacked, but he was a mental giant whose mind embraced and harmonized whole systems of thought.

Cosimo made available a villa, built for him as a summer home by Michelozzo at Careggi, for his "Platonic Academy." It was not really a formal academy, but rather a salon where Ficino presided over the scholarly discussions of friends and visitors. He had no students, Ficino once stated, only "conversation partners." The academicians burned a candle to Plato and faithfully celebrated his birthday each year with a banquet, for Plato was said to have died at eighty-one after such a celebration.

Ficino edited the complete works of Plato and they were published by the Aldine Press in Venice, a beautiful edition. He completed a translation of Plato's *Dialogues* before 1469, the year in which he wrote his commentary on Plato's *Symposium*. He also edited and translated various Neoplatonic works of Plotinus (*Enneads*), Proclus, Porphyry, and Dionysius the Areopagite. He translated from Greek to Latin various texts dating from the second and third centuries A.D. which were ascribed to Hermes Trismegistus (Hermes the Thrice Greatest) and were typical of the gnosticism of that age. And he went on to write many impressive volumes of his own in which he developed his "pious philosophy" or Platonic theology.

After a long period of melancholy, in 1473 Ficino became a priest and wrote a work entitled *De religione christiana*. Between 1469 and 1474 he worked on his masterpiece, the *Theologia platonica,* an elaborate statement of his Neoplatonic philosophy. Ficino considered himself to be a "fisher of men," like St. Peter, and used Neoplatonism to bind intellectuals to the Christian faith. His philosophy was too comprehensive to be presented here in detail, but we can consider at least its most prominent and characteristic features.

Ficino's "pious philosophy" or "learned religion" presupposed an epistemology of poesy and faith. Divine poetry and allegory serve as a veil for true religion. The rhapsodic and the mystical express religious truth, which cannot be encompassed in simple intellectual formulae. "I certainly prefer to believe by divine inspiration," he wrote, "than to know in human fashion." Truth has been transmitted through a long tradition from the ancient philosophers, and wisdom has been revealed in many forms. Plato and the Neoplatonists encompassed in their thought all the elements of the "ancient theology of the gentiles." Ficino did not draw a clear line between the revealed truth of Scripture and the inspired wisdom of the philosophers. The structure of his arguments even suggests that Ficino derived the authority of the Christian faith from its correspondence with the more ancient wisdom, rather than the reverse. Certainly Ficino tended toward a syncretistic universalism that recognized truth, goodness, and beauty in all religious sources, wherever they might be found.

Ficino and the Florentine Platonists, drawing heavily on Plotinus' *Enneads* and other Neoplatonic sources, envisioned the cosmos and everything within it as a great hierarchy of being. Plotinus described the "One" (God) as the absolute and uncontradicted original essence, prior to the plurality of specific individual beings. God is the ultimate unity of all things. The One, which embraces within itself numberless numbers, is related to the lesser creatures through a great chain of being. By emanations proceeding from the One, the lesser orders are brought into being. A stepladder of bodies, qualities, souls, and heavenly intelligences marks the way of ascent to the eternal One. Man is at the center of this great chain of being, linked to the world of matter by his body and to the realm of spirit by his soul, which enables him to rise to reunion with God. The supposition that man is a product of a divine emanation and that God is therefore immanent in him reassures man of his own divinity.

At this point Ficino introduces specifically Christian theology into his system. Plotinus had conceived of an intermediary, a demiurge, between the pure One and the subdivided spiritual and material world. Ficino identified this intermediary with the divine *Logos,* Christ, the Word that became flesh and dwelt among us. Christ is the intermediary between God and man, the mirror image of God the Father, who leads men to love and to enjoy God and who serves as an archetype and example of the perfect man. Christ demonstrates God's great love for man and frees man's soul for the ascent to God. The church, through her sacraments and her teaching, keeps man in contact with the spiritual world. Freed of the body, man's immortal soul will someday enjoy the beatific vision of God without mediation.

Ficino believed that all parts of the universe are held together by bonds of sympathetic love. He used the imagery of a "light metaphysic" to represent this cosmology:

> Man is the earthly star in a cloudy covering and the stars are heavenly people. . . .
> To the song of the joyous heavenly spirits, as the Pythagoreans believe, the spheres
> lead the dances. . . . When the stars laugh, everything in heaven and earth laughs.
> . . . Light is the laughter of heaven and expresses the joy of the heavenly spirits. . . .
> And from the laughing stars as from the eyes of divine minds friendly and happy
> rays travel, influencing the seeds of all living things.[2]

The light metaphysic lent itself easily to astrological theories. Due in part to the popularity of late classic writers such as Macrobius, who declared that "man's fate is controlled by the seven stars," astrology had a strong hold over many men in "the star-crossed Renaissance." The light metaphysic lent plausibility to astral influence and to the notion that men of an artistic and intellectual temperament come readily under the sway of Saturnine melancholy.

Ficino's Platonic theory of love harmonized smoothly with his light meta-

---

[2] Marsilio Ficino, *Opera* (Basel, 1576), vol. 1, pp. 659, 978.

physic. Love binds all men together in their common humanity. The highest form of love, Platonic love, leads the true lover to love the other for the sake of God. Love directs man in his choice of good over evil, of the beautiful over the unlovely. In Neoplatonism the value of beauty is intimately associated with qualities of goodness and truth. Aesthetics, ethics, and epistemology are intimately united in Neoplatonic metaphysics. The standard use of allegory to convey ideas not readily tied down by precise syllogistic expression made this system very congenial to poets and men of letters.

GIOVANNI PICO DELLA MIRANDOLA

The most brilliant young philosopher of the Renaissance was without a doubt Giovanni Pico della Mirandola (1463–1494), a friend and pupil of Ficino. Pico was the youngest son of Francesco Pico, count of Mirandola and Concordia, a small principality just west of Ferrara. At fourteen he went to study at Bologna, but after two years he struck out on a "student wandering" that took him to universities throughout Italy and France. In Paris he was engrossed in the study of scholastic theology. In addition to the usual Latin and Greek, he studied Hebrew, and he was interested too in Arabic and other Near Eastern languages. He nearly burned out his eyes, he relates, reading Hebrew texts belonging to a Jew who was leaving in a few days for Spain. His Hebrew teachers introduced him to the mysteries of the Jewish Cabala, which appealed to his theosophic and mystical interest.

As ambitious as he was charming, Pico went in 1486 to Rome, where he published nine hundred *Conclusiones,* a summation of all learning, which were to serve as theses for a public disputation. He even offered to pay the way for any worthy disputant who could not afford the trip to Rome for a debate. No debate took place, however, for several of the theses were declared to be heretical and the pope prohibited the distribution of the little book. Pico wrote an *Apologia* in his defense, and Pope Alexander VI subsequently vindicated Pico's orthodoxy.

As a rhetorical introduction to the *Conclusiones,* Pico composed an "Oration on the Dignity of Man," one of the most famous writings of the Renaissance. Pico held that man is truly the king of creation, not merely the middle link in the great chain of being, but the object of a special creation. He has the ability to rise upward toward the angels or to sink downward to the level of beasts by indulging sensate appetites.

A tall, blond Lombard nobleman, Pico was as handsome as he was wealthy. He lived a free and easy life, which included such conveniences as mistresses. But in his late twenties he took a more serious turn, and three years before his premature death he gave up his share of the Mirandola patrimony and planned to give away his personal property in order to take up the life of a poor preacher. At twenty-eight he published a mystical commentary on the creation story in Genesis entitled the *Heptaplus.* He also wrote a treatise on God and creation, *Of Being and Unity,* and somber commentaries on selected psalms and on the Lord's Prayer, in which he stressed man's dependence on God and his need for grace. He came under the influence of Savonarola, and remarked that his hair stood on end and chills ran down his back when he heard the friar preach. He died in Florence of a fever on November 17, 1494, just when King Charles VIII came to Florence during his invasion of Italy and Savonarola assumed rule over the city.

Pico's great tribute to the dignity of man is a representative statement of the positive humanism of the Renaissance. But since Pico also acknowledged the shadowy side of human life, a word may be in order at this point about the darker vision of humanist thought. Eugenio Garin, the well-known scholar at the University of Florence, has remarked that the Renaissance was a splendid but not a happy age. Manetti, Fazio, and Pico, drawing upon classical sources and upon such church fathers as Nemesius of Emessa and Lactantius, the Christian Cicero, could write about the dignity of man and attempt to refute Pope Innocent III's dour treatise *On the Contempt of the World.* But the humanists were usually also acutely aware of mankind's miseries. Salutati's treatise *On the World and Religion* devoted one book to the evils of secular life and a second book to the joys of the monastic life. Leonardo Bruni penned an *Introduction to Moral Discipline* which emphasized the difficulty of achieving happiness, while allowing for the possibility of doing so. Poggio, as an old man of seventy-two, composed a work *On the Misery of the Human Condition,* which complained about everything the world might offer man. It has been argued with some plausibility that Manetti's optimistic declaration on man's dignity and excellence was just a shade removed from a fundamental pessimism, for the arguments seemed to grow from a search for reassurance rather than from conviction. Renaissance intellectuals and artists were frequently overwhelmed by a sense of melancholy. The humanists were hopeful for man, but not unrealistic about the human condition.

Neo-Aristotelianism

In ADDITION to humanism and Neoplatonism, a third vigorous school of philosophy flourished during the Renaissance, Italian Aristotelianism or Neo-Aristotelianism, which dominated the professional circles of philosophers in the universities.

ARISTOTLE IN ITALY

Aristotelianism rose in the second half of the twelfth century and was a major influence on philosophers for four centuries. Its rise carried learning beyond the basic trivium and quadrivium of the earlier Middle Ages. Scholars such as William of Moerbeke translated texts of Aristotle, pseudo-Aristotelian writings, and the commentaries of Averroës (d. 1198) and other Arabic philosophers. The rise of modern Aristotelianism coincided roughly with the rise to prominence of the universities.

By the mid-thirteenth century Aristotle and his commentators, including Averroës, were studied in Paris and at other universities in the north. Philosophy was an independent discipline, but it was most often studied in conjunction with the liberal arts, as a preparation for theological studies. Thomas Aquinas made the great synthesis or *summa* of theology and Aristotelian philosophy, drawing immediately upon the thought of the Jewish Aristotelian Maimonides. In contrast to the northern universities, the universities of Italy cultivated medicine and law rather than theology. Where Aristotelianism became associated with medicine, as at Salerno in the late twelfth century, it served as a form of natural philosophy. During the course of the thirteenth century Aristotelianism penetrated Bologna, became well entrenched at Padua, and spread to other universities. Only at the University of Pisa did Platonism achieve official status.

The Greek revival during the Renaissance added new impetus to the interest in Aristotle and broadened its scope from his logic and natural philosophy to his moral philosophy, especially the *Nichomachean Ethics,* and rhetoric. The Byzantine Aristotelian John Argyropoulos lectured on moral philosophy at the University of Florence in 1457. His disciple Donato Acciaiuoli (1428–1478) represented an Aristotelian perspective in Florence during the years of Neoplatonist Marsilio Ficino's prominence. George of Trebizond and Theodore of Gaza further promoted Aristotle, against the resistance of such Platonists as Bessarion, who defended the divine Plato "against his calumniators."

Pietro Pomponazzi.   In *The Pickwick Papers* Charles Dickens tells about a man who prepared to write about Chinese philosophy by looking up "Chinese" in the encyclopedia under *C* and "metaphysics" under *M*. The historian who undertakes to describe Renaissance Aristotelianism soon discovers that there is no such simple solution. Various schools of interpretation flourished—Averroist, Alexandrian, Thomist, and eclectic varieties. More can possibly be gained by considering the thought of a typical Aristotelian of Padua, one of the most prominent schools, than by trying in brief compass to cover the distinctions among the varieties of Aristotelians.

Born in Mantua, Pietro Pomponazzi (1462–1525) took his degree at the University of Padua, where he became a professor in 1488. He knew the writings of Pico and Ficino, read such classical works as those of Cicero and Plutarch, but was preoccupied above all with the study of Aristotle, the famous Greek Aristotelian commentator Alexander of Aphrodisias, and the Stoic philosophers.

His writing has a tortured scholastic style, with only occasional humanist elegance and subjective personal outbursts. In his *On Incantations* he offered natural explanations for strange phenomena popularly ascribed to spirits and demons. In his treatise *On Fate,* he wrestled with the problems of free will, fate, and predestination, and concluded by trying, with the Stoics, to reconcile determinism and human responsibility. His most famous work was *On the Immortality of the Soul.* After considering the opinions of Averroës, Plato, and Thomas Aquinas, Pomponazzi took a position that he identified with that of Alexander of Aphrodisias. The human soul, having only one nature, is absolutely mortal, and only in certain respects immortal. He held that the human intellect needs the body for its object and cannot act without the help of sense images. It is therefore clearly mortal. But the human intellect does not use the body as its subject, as animals do, and therefore in this respect it participates in immortality. The immortality of the soul, Pomponazzi confessed, can be neither proved nor disproved on empirical or rational grounds, but must be accepted on the authority of the church.

The excellence of man, Pomponazzi asserted, consists not in contemplation but in his moral virtue. Man cannot think outside of the sensible world and can understand his life only from within the world. What he thinks has only a relative value, therefore, and not an absolute value. Theoretical speculations must always remain unsatisfying. Man can build a harmonious existence only by limiting himself to those things that he is capable of achieving. The mark of the measured man is to be satisfied with what comes to him and with what he can have. It is vain to fear the inevitable, and a man should therefore "thank God and nature and always be ready to die and not to fear death."[3]

Sixteenth-Century Neo-Aristotelianism. Three Italian philosophers of the sixteenth century who merit special mention are Bernardino Telesio, Francesco Patrizzi, and Giordano Bruno. Telesio was most interested in physical and biological phenomena. In his work *On the Nature of Things* (Naples, 1565) he discarded traditional concepts of matter and form in favor of a dynamic theory of antithetical forces, such as heat and cold, brought into balance. He struggled to free himself from Aristotelian philosophy and to develop his own thought independently. Francesco Patrizzi was truly eclectic, drawing on Plato, Proclus, and Hermes Trismegistus, and translating Philopon's commentary on Aristotle's *Metaphysics* (1583). He wrote treatises on history and poetry, and held a chair of Platonic philosophy in Rome.

The most brilliant and original of the three was Giordano Bruno (1548–1600), who has been called the martyr of the Renaissance. A member of the Dominican order at eighteen, he developed grave doubts about the faith. When his deviation-

---

[3] On Neo-Aristotelianism and Pomponazzi, see Paul Oskar Kristeller, *Eight Philosophers of the Italian Renaissance* (Stanford, 1964), pp. 72–90.

ism became known while he was in Rome in 1576, he was charged with heresy. He escaped and began a long pilgrimage that took him through northern Italy to Geneva, Paris, Marburg, Wittenberg, Prague, Helmstedt, Frankfort, and then back to Padua and Venice. The Inquisition seized him in 1592 and transferred him to Rome, where, in spite of his attempts to recant, he was imprisoned for seven years and finally tried for heresy and burned at the stake in the Campo de' Fiori in February 1600.

Bruno's thought was very much influenced by the mysticism of Hermes Trismegistus. He derived his theory of heroic love, expressed in his work *Eroici furori,* from Ficino's doctrine of Platonic love. While one of the charges against Bruno was that he espoused the Copernican system, his ideas about the universe were actually more imaginative than Copernicus'. From Cusanus he derived the concepts of relativity and of an infinite universe containing an infinite number of solar systems. God is related to this infinite universe as its vital principle, in the same way in which the soul is related to the body.

With Telesio, Patrizzi, and Bruno, however, we are carried into the second half of the sixteenth century, after the impact of the Reformation and Counterreformation had made itself felt in Italy. Throughout the Renaissance both the humanists and the Platonists were basically hostile to the Aristotelians and often overtly critical of them. They believed that the Aristotelian philosophy militated against the dignity of man in denying the person immortality of the individual soul, in holding to the eternity of matter rather than to a special creation that places man above all other creatures, and in having a depersonalized concept of God, who is seen as prime mover rather than as divine father. The impetuous young Pico della Mirandola undertook to write *On the Harmony of Plato and Aristotle,* but he died without realizing his ambition. The endeavor to harmonize the two was not lost sight of, however, and was taken up again by Melanchthon and other intellectuals in the north.

Metaphysics and Literature

FOR A PHILOSOPHY that was not institutionalized, Platonism showed tremendous staying power and had a widespread, subtle influence. After Ficino's death, a friend and pupil of his, Diacceto, carried on the tradition of Platonic studies, and about 1540 a second "Platonic Academy," meeting in the Rucellai Gardens of Florence, developed as a kind of literary club dedicated to the cultivation of pure Tuscan Italian and Platonic studies. Platonism in Renaissance Italy remained a rather fashionable drawing-room body of ideas that colored the thought of poets and artists, theologians and scientists.

Lorenzo de' Medici not only was a grand patron of humanists and artists, but was a prolific poet himself. His volume of verse *Selva d'amore* was inspired by the Platonic theory of love and has received rather high praise from literary critics. Certain members of the Medici circle were excellent poets, especially Cristoforo Landino (1424–1504), author of the *Questiones camaldulenses,* and Politian (1454–1494), a philologist as well as a man of letters. A very metaphysical poet, Girolamo Benivieni, in his "Song of Divine Love" gave a highly religious form to the Neoplatonic thought of Pico della Mirandola, emphasizing the immortality of the soul and the final reunion of man, a noble creature, with God.

In the latter part of the fifteenth century a cult of Dante developed in the Medici circle. Dante's *Vita nuova* embodied several basic Platonic ideas, such as regeneration by love. The circle of Dante cultists stressed his mysticism and developed it in Neoplatonic terms. Matteo Palmieri, Giovanni Nesi, and Luigi Pulci reflect this tendency. Luigi Pulci also had a mischievous side, however, for he delighted in mockery and in exposing the comic aspects of grave institutions and pretentious beliefs.

Poetry flourished also at the court of Naples. Giovanni Pontano (1426–1503) gained renown for his excellent lyrics. Jacopo Sannazzaro (1456–1530) created a pastoral idyll, "Arcadia," which moved Renaissance artists to portray the simplicity and virtues of pastoral life. In a poem "On the Birth of the Virgin" he presented the life of the Virgin Mary in a classical poetic style.

The great master at presenting Christian themes in classical dress was Baptista Mantuanus (1448–1516), the prior general of the Carmelite order. He favored constructive religious poetry, ornamented with classical figures of speech, to counteract the pagan influence of Greek and Latin literature. He was widely hailed as a second Virgil, and Pico called him the most learned man of the period. He was avidly read in the north because of the very religious nature of his poetry.

During the sixteenth century love literature became popular, vulgarized, and often very sensuous. The only really excellent love poem of this period was Leone Ebreo's *Dialoghi d'amore,* which showed philosophical depth and genuine originality. Michelangelo's lyrics, like his art, reflected a strong Neoplatonic influence. Neoplatonic ideas reached their culmination late in the sixteenth century and early in the seventeenth century in the works of Giordano Bruno and Tommaso Campanella (1568–1639). Campanella's philosophical outlook was strongly influenced by Cusanus, Ficino, and Telesio. He accepted the authority of the church in matters of faith, but, not unlike St. Augustine, he built his philosophy upon the certainty of individual consciousness. His most famous writing, *City of the Sun,* was in the area of political philosophy. In it he portrayed an ideal communism, based upon the closed society of Plato's *Republic.* He advocated a community of wives and property, universal military training, and population control by the state. Administrators, whose authority was to be in direct proportion to their knowledge, were to direct every detail in the lives of the happy citizens, so that the individual welfare corresponded to the collective good. Some Renaissance verve still comes through in Campanella's ecstatic vision: "The novelties of ancient truths, of new worlds, new systems, new nations are the beginning of a new era. Let God not make delay, and let us for our part do all we can."

Renaissance thought is frequently described as a steppingstone toward the Enlightenment. In reality, many features of Renaissance philosophy and literature are reminiscent of late eighteenth- and early nineteenth-century romanticism. Particularly striking is the tendency to spiritualize nature and to idealize thought. The stress on inner freedom, ecstatic theories of love, and an instinctive or intuitive approach to truth, a product of Platonic epistemology based on the doctrine of innate ideas, are romantic notions very prominent in Renaissance thought.

Science

IN THE GREAT DEBATE on the relation of the Renaissance to the modern world, the place of science in the Renaissance is of critical importance, for surely natural science is one of the most important aspects of modern culture. Its rise is usually dated from the seventeenth century. Historians who clearly see a renaissance in literature and art therefore have difficulty in discovering a similar renaissance in science. Some historians, in fact, argue that the Renaissance was a low period for science and that humanism retarded science by directing the attention of intellectuals away from nature and back to classical antiquity and "the pale imitation of the past." They see such scientific progress as was made during the Renaissance as the achievements of craftsmen and technicians, of artists who stood low on the social scale and used the vernacular rather than learned Latin to record their discoveries. On the other hand, some Renaissance scholars believe that the humanists' development of a critical mentality in their philological studies was very important for the rise of science. Thus Valla's textual and historical criticism and Machiavelli's social-scientific approach to politics helped to prepare the Western mind for a critical study of nature.

The humanists, it is true, were more interested in books than in nature, and in understanding man than in rediscovering the world. Petrarch typified their attitude when he spoke with scorn of popular bestiaries and travel books:

> And even if these things were true, they contribute nothing at all to a blessed life. For what, I ask, does it profit us to know about the nature of animals, birds, fishes, and serpents if we remain ignorant of the nature of mankind, to which we belong, and neither know nor care whence we came or whither we are going?[4]

---

[4] Petrarch, *Le traité De sui ipsius et multorium ignorantia*, ed. L. M. Capelli (Paris, 1906), pp. 24–25.

Natural science, like medicine, seemed to the humanists to belong to the preserve of the Aristotelians and scholastics.

FRANCISCAN AND PADUAN PHYSICISTS

The scholastics did indeed make significant contributions to science in the area of theoretical physics. Seventeenth-century scientists were so prone to think and speak of themselves as pioneers and innovators that their own great debt to earlier centuries is sometimes lost from view.

The basic idea of an experimentally grounded science appeared in Arabic Alexandrine science, based upon the study of the ancients. During the second half of the twelfth century and during the thirteenth century Aristotle's physics predominated in the West. In the area of dynamics the key axiom of Aristotle was that "no movement can continue unless it is acted upon by the continual power of a mover directly and immediately applied to it." Aristotle believed, for instance, that the power that sustained an arrow in flight was the movement of the air produced by the hand or implement that discharged it. Nearly all antiquity accepted this notion. The one exception was Philopon (John of Alexandria), who suggested that the arrow continued to move without any mover because the string of the bow generated energy that played the role of the moving force. The Arabic philosophers, true to Aristotle, had nothing but scorn for Philopon.

In 1277 the bishop of Paris, Étienne Tempier, pronounced against a number of Aristotle's theses that seemed to be antithetical to sound theology. This criticism weakened Aristotle's authority and prepared the way for a critique of his physical theories also. William of Occam attacked Aristotle's theory of motion, but he did not replace it with a positive theory of his own. Some followers of Duns Scotus, however, revived Philopon's theory, "energy" appearing now as "impetus."

Jean Buridan (d. 1358), rector of the University of Paris and a "modernist," took up this theory and founded a dynamics that "accorded with the phenomena." He believed that uniform laws apply to movement of any kind. The role that Buridan gave to "impetus" accorded very nearly with that which Galileo attributed to "impetus" or the "moment," Descartes to the "quantity of movement," Leibniz to the "living force." The correspondence was so exact that many centuries later, when Torricelli explained the theories of Galileo, he used the reasoning and almost the exact words of Buridan. The resistance of the surrounding medium counteracts impetus and explains variations in acceleration and the arc of a projectile.

Two of Buridan's pupils, Albert of Saxony (d. 1390), who taught in Paris and Vienna, and Nicolas Oresme (d. 1382), adopted and taught his theories of dynamics and kinesthetics. Albert of Saxony proposed two hypotheses: (1) the speed of a falling body is proportional to the time that has elapsed since it began its fall; (2) the speed of the fall is proportional to the path traveled. Nicolas Oresme, whose intellectual interests ranged from monetary theories to magic and astrology (he opposed them), worked out the essential principles of analytical geometry. Nicholas Cusanus in the fifteenth century knew the works of these men of the Paris school and summarized their position. Leonardo da Vinci was an avid reader of Albert of Saxony and adopted his principles.[5]

The Spanish Dominican Dominique Soto, a pupil of the Occamists, wrote in *Questions on the Physics of Aristotle* (1545) that the fall of a body or the vertical rise of a projectile is uniformly accelerated or decelerated, clearly anticipating Galileo's laws.

The essential link between the Franciscan theorists and Galileo was provided by the school of Padua, which made important contributions to the development of scientific method. During the first decade of the fourteenth century Pietro d'Abano formulated the problem of method, struggling with the two main kinds of proofs, effects through causes and causes through effects. Around 1413 Jacopo da Forli adopted these two "doctrines." Hugo of Siena defined two modes, resolution and composition, similar to Aristotle's analysis and synthesis. Paul of Venice, who around 1390 had developed an interest in scientific theory at Oxford, defended this two-step demonstration against the argument that it is circular. He and Gaetano da Thiene (d. 1465) knew and taught the theories of the Franciscan physicists at Padua. Jacopo Zabarella (d. 1589), a professor of logic, marked the culmination of the Paduan concern with scientific method, his greatest weakness being his failure to appreciate the importance of mathematics in quantitative analysis.[6]

The revival of interest in Neoplatonism, Pythagoreanism, and the Cabala quickened interest in numbers and mathematics, the indispensable and universal language of the physical sciences. Cusanus, Georg Peuerbach (d. 1461), and Regiomontanus (Johannes Müller, d. 1476) contributed to the development of mathematics. Finally the great mathematician Niccolò Tartaglia (*c.* 1506–1559), who taught at Verona and Venice, discovered the solution of cubic equations, and translated Euclid into Italian.

Recently historians of science have stressed the limitations of the Franciscans and the Paduan Aristotelians. They point out that they theorized and made observations, but were not systematic, since they did not do controlled experiments or refine their findings by a series of negative demonstrations. Nevertheless, Galileo learned essentials from them, and his work is in the Paduan tradition. He taught in Padua from 1592 to 1610. The application of the laws of physics to the universe as a means of explaining the movement of the heavenly bodies, in perpetual motion and

---

[5] The basic work on the Franciscan theorists remains Pierre Duhem, *Études sur Léonardo de Vinci* (Paris, 1906–1913), 3 vols.

[6] See John Herman Randall, Jr., "The Development of Scientific Method in the School of Padua," *Journal of the History of Ideas*, 1 (1940):177–206.

controlled by the necessary balance of forces, was one of the astounding achievements of early modern science. "Nature is very patient," Alfred North Whitehead observed wryly, "and lets us formulate whatever laws about her happen to interest us at the moment."

LEONARDO DA VINCI AS SCIENTIST

When in 1481 the brilliant artistic genius Leonardo da Vinci (1452–1519) applied to Ludovico il Moro for a position in Milan, he recommended himself first of all as a military engineer, secondly as a civil engineer, and only incidentally as an architect, painter, and sculptor. For military engineering was the great technical profession of the age, much in demand. As a military engineer for Ludovico, as well as for Cesare Borgia and King Francis I of France, Leonardo planned devices for protecting walls from assault, designed breech-loading cannons, built catapults, and plotted the courses of artillery projectiles. His most important contribution to architecture was the analysis of stresses for various kinds of materials.

As an artist Leonardo was interested not only in design and the laws of perspective, but in the anatomy of human beings and of animals, especially of horses. "The singular things of nature are finite," Leonardo wrote, "and the work the eyes order the hands to do is infinite; the painter reveals this in his representation of the infinite forms of animals and vegetables, plants and places." Leonardo illustrates the contributions to natural science made by the artist and craftsman of the Renaissance. He wrote in the vernacular, and it has been remarked that his genius was spared by the fact that he did not attend a university. On the other hand, Leonardo acquired a great deal of classical and religious learning in Florence and in the court circles of Milan and France, and he counted among his friends such learned humanists as Paolo Toscanelli and John Argyropoulos.

Leonardo's *Notebooks* are studded with fascinating observations on natural phenomena, for he was interested in irrigation, lightning, statics, dynamics, geometry, and anatomy. He performed autopsies, observed hardening of the arteries in old people, and came close to discovering the circulation of the blood. He discovered the relation between the rings in a tree trunk and the age of the tree. Leonardo's notes are scattered and fragmented. The entries were never revised or edited, and few dates are given. One cannot call him a precursor of Copernicus just because he once made a brief entry: "The sun does not move." We really do not know what he meant by that. In his book *On Divine Proportion* he was concerned with the mathematical relation of things in space. He was strongly influenced by Neoplatonism and Pythagoreanism. He constantly searched for some simple general rule that would serve to unify all parts of natural science, but of course he never found one.

Ernst Cassirer, a noted twentieth-century cultural historian, was mistaken when he spoke of Leonardo as the first man to have determined with precision the methodological foundations of experimental science. Nor did Leonardo's quest for the proportions of sensory phenomena and the rules that govern them contain implicitly the scientific idea of natural law, as Cassirer argued. Leonardo was neither so systematic in method nor so consequential in his conclusions as modern scientific method requires. He was far from the standards even of Galileo. But he was of great importance to science as a symbol of genius and as an inspiration, and some of his work did enter the body of cumulative knowledge that has come to make up modern science. In the seventeenth century Nicolas Poussin included some twenty of Leonardo's drawings in a book of anatomical drawings. And what fledgling scientist of our time has not marveled at Leonardo's designs for an airplane, a parachute, a helicopter, screw propellers, locks for canals, double-deck streets, rolling mills, multibarreled weapons, and other ingenious devices?

Leonardo's self-portrait as an old man shows deep worry lines. He was only sixty-seven at the time of his death. Vasari relates in his *Lives of the Painters* that on his deathbed Leonardo reproached himself for not having done his duty to God and man in his art. He thought that he had left too many things unfinished and had accomplished too little. Actually, Leonardo was a victim of his own brilliance. As André Gide once remarked, "When one has talent one does what one wishes; when one has genius one does what one can."

The Renaissance was not, like the seventeenth century, a great age of scientific discovery. It was important, however, for the transmission of the medieval advances. Above all the Renaissance saw the development of a secular society and an urban culture concerned with this world. The humanists contributed to the maturation of culture and of Western man's mentality, an important preparation for modern science.

The Spread of Learning

THE RENAISSANCE produced two great boons to learning that put all subsequent ages in its debt. The first of these was the invention of printing and the second was the endowment of libraries. The great Venetian publisher Aldus Manutius spoke for several generations of scholar-printers when he declared in 1490:

> I have resolved to devote my life to the cause of scholarship. I have chosen in place of a life of ease an anxious and toilsome career. Cato compared human existence to iron. When nothing is done with it, it rusts. It is only through constant activity that polish is secured.

Aldus was the first to develop Greek fonts and he was the inventor of italic type.

The Aldine Press published the beautiful edition of Plato's works edited by Ficino and did fine editions of all the major Greek authors. In the course of two decades Aldus published 126 works that had previously existed only in manuscript.

The spread of printing during the half century following Gutenberg's invention was astonishing. By the end of the century there were fifty-one presses in Germany, a fact that was to be of crucial importance for the success of the Reformation. France had thirty-nine, Spain twenty-four, the Netherlands fifteen, Switzerland eight. And Italy—an important index to the vitality of Renaissance culture—had seventy-three printing establishments.

Linen paper had been introduced into Europe from the Far East and was in general use by 1300. It was cheaper than parchment and more durable than papyrus. Without it mechanical printing would not have been practicable. Paper and the press made printing big business. The great book fairs in Leipzig, Cologne, and other centers dictated publishers' deadlines. The whole syndrome of modern publishing problems and possibilities came into being. The invention of printing, Francis Bacon declared, changed "the appearance and state of the whole world." He urged men to "take note of the force, effect, and consequences" of Gutenberg's great invention.[7] It changed men's mental processes, altered communications radically, and was a major factor in making a mercantile and eventually an industrial society a practical possibility.

Information storage in great public libraries marked another important cultural advance. Vespasiano reported that the first Renaissance pope, Nicholas V, had accumulated five thousand volumes in the Vatican library, which he refounded after a lapse of many centuries. St. Mark's library in Venice contained Petrarch's library. Cardinal Bessarion enriched its holdings with a bequest of some five hundred Greek manuscripts. Cosimo founded the famous Medici library in Florence. He employed forty-five copyists, who completed two hundred volumes in less than two years. Vespasiano describes its contents as the Bible, Greek and Latin patristic writers, the major medieval authors, including the scholastic doctors, and classical Latin authors. Most libraries contained many books of devotion and other religious materials. Private libraries of individual humanists and men of wealth were impressive, from a few dozen books to over a thousand. A full-blown interlibrary loan traffic went on, with the humanists sending books along with the post, purloining books, procrastinating in returning them, and developing all the other trials of the modern world of books.

The elder Aldus expressed the feelings of all men of letters when he exclaimed, "What joy to see these volumes of the ancients rescued from the book-burners, and given freely to the world!"

---

[7] Francis Bacon, *Novum organum*, aphorism 129.

Bibliography

Philosophy:

Allen, Don Cameron. *The Star-Crossed Renaissance: The Quarrel About Astrology and Its Influence in England.* Durham, NC, 1941.
──── . *Doubt's Boundless Sea: Skepticism and Faith in the Renaissance.* Baltimore, 1964.
Bett, Henry. *Nicholas of Cusa.* London, 1932.
Cassirer, Ernst, et al., eds. *The Renaissance Philosophy of Man.* Chicago, 1948.
──── . *The Individual and the Cosmos in Renaissance Philosophy.* New York, 1963.
Festugière, A. M. J. *La philosophie de l'amour de Marsile Ficin et son influence sur la littérature française au XVIe siècle.* Paris, 1941.
Garin, Eugenio. *La filosofia,* 2 vols. Milan, 1947.
──── . *La cultura filosofica del Rinascimento italiano.* Florence, 1961.
──── , ed. *Filosofi italiani del Quattrocento.* Florence, 1942.
Gentile, Giovanni. *Il pensiero italiano del Rinascimento,* 3rd ed. Florence, 1955.
Gilbert, Neal W. *Renaissance Concepts of Method.* New York, 1960.
Klibansky, R. *The Continuity of the Platonic Tradition.* London, 1950.
Kristeller, Paul Oskar. *The Philosophy of Marsilio Ficino.* New York, 1943.
──── . *Eight Philosophers of the Italian Renaissance.* Stanford, 1964.
──── . *Le Thomisme et la pensée italienne de la Renaissance.* Montreal, 1967.
Levao, Ronald. *Renaissance Minds and Their Fictions.* Berkeley, 1985.
Marcel, Raymond. *Marsile Ficin (1433–1499).* Paris, 1958.
Nardi, Bruno. *Saggi sull' aristotelismo padovano dal secolo XIV al XVI.* Florence, 1958.
──── . *Studi su Pietro Pomponazzi.* Florence, 1965.
Radcliff-Umstead, Douglas. *The Birth of Modern Comedy in Renaissance Italy.* Chicago, 1969.
Robb, Nesca. *The Neoplatonism of the Italian Renaissance.* London, 1935.
Rüegg, Walter. *Cicero und der Humanismus.* Zurich, 1946.
Ruggiero, G. de. *Rinascimento, riforma e controriforma,* pt. 3 of *Storia della filosofia,* 2 vols. Bari, 1937.
Secret, François. *Le Zôhar chez les chrétiens de la Renaissance.* Paris, 1958.
──── . *Les Kabbalistes chrétiens de la Renaissance.* Paris, 1964.
Seigel, Jerrold E. *Rhetoric and Philosophy in Renaissance Humanism: The Union of Eloquence and Wisdom, Petrarch to Valla.* Princeton, 1968.
Singer, Dorothea. *Giordano Bruno: His Life and Thought, with an Annotated Translation of His Work "On the Infinite Universe and Worlds."* New York, 1950.
Stinger, Charles. *Humanism and the Church Fathers: Ambrogio Traversari (1386–1439) and Christian Antiquity in the Italian Renaissance.* Albany, NY, 1977.
Walker, D. P. *Spiritual and Demonic Magic from Ficino to Campanella.* London, 1958.
Yates, Francis. *Giordano Bruno and the Hermetic Tradition.* Chicago, 1964.
──── . *The Art of Memory.* Chicago, 1966.

Science:

Boas, Marie. *The Scientific Renaissance, 1450–1630.* New York, 1962.
Burtt, Edwin A. *The Metaphysical Foundations of Modern Physical Sciences,* rev. ed. Garden City, NY, 1954.
Butterfield, Herbert. *The Origins of Modern Science, 1300–1800.* London, 1951.
Crombie, A. C. *Augustine to Galileo: The History of Science, 1400–1650.* London, 1952.
Duhem, Pierre. *Études sur Léonardo de Vinci,* 3 vols. Paris, 1906–1913.
──── . *Le système du monde, histoire des doctrines cosmologiques de Platon à Copernic,* 5 vols. Paris, 1913–1917.
Fierz, Markus. *Girolamo Cardano, 1501–1576: Physician, Natural Philosopher, Mathematician, Astrologer, and Interpreter of Dreams.* Trans. Helga Niman. Boston, 1983.

Jammer, Max. *Concepts of Space.* New York, 1960.

Koyré, A. *From the Closed World to the Infinite Universe.* New York, 1958.

Randall, John H. *The School of Padua and the Emergence of Modern Science.* New York, 1960.

———. *The Career of Philosophy: From the Middle Ages to the Enlightenment.* New York, 1962.

Sarton, George. *On the History of Science,* ed. Dorothy Stimson. Cambridge, MA, 1962.

Shumaker, Wayne. *The Occult Sciences in the Renaissance. A Study in Intellectual Patterns.* Berkeley and Los Angeles, 1973.

Singer, Charles, et al., eds. *History of Technology,* vol. 2. New York, 1955.

Stace, W. T. *Mysticism and Philosophy.* New York, 1960.

Thorndyke, Lynn. *A History of Magic and Experimental Science,* vols. 3 and 4. New York, 1934.

Wightman, William. *Science and the Renaissance,* 2 vols. New York, 1962.

Printing:

Berry, W. T., and H. E. Poole. *Annals of Printing: A Chronological Encyclopedia from Earliest Times to 1950.* London, 1966.

Butler, Pierce. *The Origin of Printing in Europe.* Chicago, 1940.

Chaytor, H. J. *From Script to Print: An Introduction to Medieval Literature.* Cambridge, 1945.

Chrisman, Miriam Usher. *Lay Culture, Learned Culture: Books and Social Change in Strasbourg, 1480–1599.* New Haven, 1982.

Eisenstein, Elizabeth L. *The Printing Revolution in Early Modern Europe.* New York, 1984.

Febvre, Lucien, and H. J. Martin. *L'Apparition du Livre,* vol. 49 of *L'Évolution de l'humanité.* Paris, 1958.

Goldschmidt, E. P. *Medieval Texts and Their First Appearance in Print.* London, 1943.

———. *The Printed Book of the Renaissance.* Cambridge, MA, 1950.

Hay, Denys. "Literature: The Printed Book." In *The New Cambridge Modern History,* ed. G. R. Elton, vol. 2, pp. 359–86. Cambridge, 1958.

Hirsch, Rudolph. *Printing, Selling, Reading, 1450–1550.* Wiesbaden, 1967.

McLuhan, Marshall. *The Gutenberg Galaxy: The Making of Typographical Man.* Toronto, 1962.

McMurtrie, Douglas C. *The Invention of Printing: A Bibliography.* Chicago, 1942.

———. *The Book: The Story of Printing and Bookmaking,* 3rd ed. New York and London, 1943.

Ruppel, Aloys. *Johannes Gutenberg: Sein Leben und sein Werk,* 3rd ed. Nieuwkoop, 1967.

Schutte, Anne Jacobson, *Printed Italian Vernacular Religious Books 1465–1550: A Finding List.* Geneva, 1983.

Steinberg, S. H. *Five Hundred Years of Printing,* rev. ed. Bristol, 1961.

CHAPTER **8**

The Fine Arts

Many points of similarity unite the visual arts of the Renaissance with the great literature and philosophy of the age. "A picture," Horace declared, "is a poem without words."

Giotto and the Birth of Renaissance Art

THE PERCEPTIVE POET Dante saw a decisive change taking place in his own day, as Giovanni Cimabue, the man who was held to have revived painting, gave place to the even greater Giotto:

> In painting Cimabue thought indeed
> > To hold the field; now Giotto has the cry,
> > So that the fame of the other few now heed.[1]

Before the thirteenth century Italy had been in low estate. "Greek" or Byzantine conventions held sway. Before there was serious talk about the revival of classi-

---

[1] Dante Alighieri, *Il Purgatorio,* canto 11, lines 94–96, in *The Portable Dante,* ed. Paolo Milano (New York, 1947), p. 243.

cal antiquity, Giotto (1266–1336) introduced a new naturalism into painting. When Giotto painted a madonna, he did not surround her with a host of saints and martyrs in order to emphasize her role as mother of God; rather he showed her as a lady of feeling and true virtue, worthy of veneration for her great spiritual quality. The world in which Dante and Giotto lived was conditioned toward Franciscan piety by the powerful preaching of the friars. Following in the tradition established by St. Francis, the Franciscans cultivated an intimate relationship with nature, which was reflected in Giotto's art. The Franciscan influence on Giotto is made explicit in his many portrayals of St. Francis. In the Church of St. Francis in Assisi, built above his tomb, Giotto painted twenty-eight frescoes depicting scenes from the life of the saint. His fresco of *The Death of St. Francis* in the Bardi Chapel of the Santa Croce in Florence is a masterpiece of composition and emotional expression.

But Giotto reserved his most moving artistry for the life of Christ. He sought to make his images of the Virgin Mary, of the Christ child, even of the angels real and palpable, showing love and compassion. His pictures were far more natural than the stiff and stylized icons of the Byzantine tradition. In his great masterpiece in the Arena Chapel at Padua, *The Lamentation*, he portrayed the love and anguish of Mary and the disciples over the death of Christ so passionately that all nature seemed lost in deepest mourning.

Giotto was indeed the founder of a new naturalistic approach to art. Boccaccio declared that Giotto could portray nature so realistically that a painting of Giotto's seemed to be not an image, but the thing itself. "Where was the painter's art," asked Matteo Palmieri in his *On Civil Life,* "till Giotto tardily restored it? It was a caricature of the art of human delineation! Sculpture and architecture, for long years sunk to the merest travesty of art, are only today in process of rescue from obscurity; only now are they being brought to a new pitch of perfection by men of genius and erudition."[2] The artist and critic Giorgio Vasari, in his monumental *Lives of the Painters,* stated as dogma that the artistic renaissance began with Giotto, for he led art back to "a path which may be called the true one."

Giotto made a beginning, but his naturalism had its limitations. He devoted himself exclusively to religious themes, and most of these were of a somber nature. Moreover, for decades after his break with tradition, although many artists tried to follow in his footsteps, none matched his achievements. His own assistant, Taddeo Baddi (*c.* 1300–1366), imitated the lively and novel aspects of Giotto's style, but could not handle the larger problems of complex spatial patterns and unity of total composition. The artists of Siena, such as Simone Martini (*c.* 1285–1344), produced more stylized work, in the manner of Gothic illuminations, with great beauty of color and line. The Sienese style influenced Florentine painters in the

---

[2] Denys Hay, *The Italian Renaissance in Its Historical Background* (Cambridge, 1961), p. 11.

Cimabue. *The Death of St. Francis.* Bardi Chapel, Santa Croce, Florence.

half century after Giotto. Gentile da Fabriano (*c.* 1370–1427), who decorated the Strozzi Chapel, and Antonio Pisano, called Pisanello (*c.* 1395–1455), reverted to an older style and took over relatively little of Giotto's naturalism. Pisanello became famous for his medals in bronze depicting John Palaeologus and other rulers, thus renewing the ancient practice of striking off commemorative plaques and medals which has continued down to the present day.

The Artist in Practice and Theory

IN VIEW of the adulation bordering on worship bestowed upon the artistic geniuses of the Renaissance in later centuries, it comes as a shock to moderns to learn that during the Renaissance artists were the social equals of leather workers and other artisans, and could barely be considered lower middle class. As men who worked with their hands, they were socially far beneath the aristocracy and the bourgeoisie.

Artists received their training as apprentices in the workshops of the masters. Leonardo da Vinci, for example, learned his craft in the workshop of Andrea del Verrocchio (1435–1488), and Michelangelo trained for a time in the workshop of Domenico Ghirlandaio (1449–1494). The workshops or studios produced paintings and other works of art on commission for the churches of the mendicant orders, for the private chapels of wealthy families, and for private patrons who wanted murals or altar paintings to donate to churches or to ornament their homes; late in the *Quattrocento*, family portraits also became popular. The master would sometimes sketch out the scene and have the apprentices fill in the parts. In due course the beginners themselves became masters. Filippo Villani included a number of artists among his *Famous Citizens of the City of Florence* at the end of the fourteenth century. By the end of the fifteenth century, great artists kept company with renowned men of letters and were a familiar sight at the courts of Mantua, Rimini, and Milan, in the circle of the Medicis in Florence, and at the papal court in Rome.

It is easy to trace the growth of lay patronage through commissions and the migrations of the artists, but it is considerably more difficult to be specific about the influence of lay patronage upon the substance and form of art itself. Since Renaissance society was at least formally very pious, the subject matter of most Renaissance art remained religious, but secular influence was to be seen in increasing naturalism. Attempts to correlate the styles of individual paintings with the social views of the patrons who commissioned them have met with only limited success.

CENNINO CENNINI

No book affords the modern student of art a better insight into the technical methods of the Renaissance artist than Cennino Cennini's *Il libro dell'arte*. Written in the fifteenth century, this craftsman's handbook summarized the tricks of the trade and was actually used as a manual by Piero della Francesca, Leonardo da Vinci, and other artists. The book opens with a charming introduction:

> Here begins the Craftsman's Handbook, made and composed by Cennino of Colle, in the reverence of God, and of the Virgin Mary, and of St. Eustace, and of St. Francis, and of St. John the Baptist, and of St. Anthony of Padua, and in general of all the saints of God; and in the reverence of Giotto, of Taddeo and of Agnolo, Cennino's master; and for the use and good and profit of anyone who wants to enter this profession.[3]

Cennini explains that painting combines theory with skill of hand, and deserves to be enthroned next to theory and to be crowned with poetry. The poet, with his theory, is free to compose and bind together or not, as he pleases. In the same way the painter is free to compose a figure standing or seated, half man and half horse, as his imagination prompts him. Some painters are moved by a lofty spirit; others pursue art for profit, driven by poverty or domestic need. Beginners must submit themselves to the direction of a master for instruction and must deck themselves out in the attire of one who would learn: enthusiasm, reverence, obedience, and constancy.

Cennini, an "unimportant practicing member of the profession of painting," then instructs the novice in the techniques of the trade. He explains how to make glue from goat hoofs. He tells how to make life masks by smearing oil on the eyelids, inserting tubes into the nostrils, putting a frame around the face, and the like. He warns against the use of cosmetics, for they cause the loss of a good complexion, wither the skin, turn teeth black, and induce premature aging in women. He describes methods of casting statues and offers a summary of the best techniques available to the artist.

Whereas the architects of the great Gothic cathedrals of the north had introduced large glass windows that greatly reduced the wall space available for painting, most Italian churches provided ample space for "sermons in pictures." For these wall paintings, or murals, the artists painted with water colors on a layer of wet plaster (fresco), so that the pigment soaked in and became fixed as the plaster dried. While the medium did not determine the message, it did influence the style; for fresco painting lent itself well to the portrayal of large figures, but was not suited for delicate detail.

For smaller paintings, Renaissance painters applied a mixture of plaster of Paris and glue to wooden panels. The mixture filled the pores in the wood and provided a smooth, dry, nonabsorbent surface. Until the introduction of oil paints in the fifteenth century, the whites or yolks of eggs were used as binders for pigments. Panel painting allowed for finer work than was possible in murals, and

---

[3] Cennino d'Andrea Cennini, *The Craftsman's Handbook* (New Haven, 1933), p. 1.

made possible the introduction of detail reminiscent of medieval manuscript illuminations, which had so strongly influenced Flemish art. Moreover, it freed painting from its architectural setting. When paintings became mobile, artists were able to extend their techniques to portraits, nature scenes, and other subjects not appropriate to churches.

DIVINE PERSPECTIVE

Renaissance artists were excited by their discovery of a new principle in art, linear perspective. Leonardo da Vinci and other great artists were so intrigued by the laws of perspective that they wrote theoretical treatises about it. We do not know who was the first to discover the laws of perspective, but certain artists, preeminently Brunelleschi (1377–1446), by precept and practice became important exponents of the new approach.

Renaissance artists frequently conceived of the painter and the observer as existing within the space of the scene represented in the painting, rather than at some point outside of it. Linear perspective makes this illusion possible by portraying objects upon a flat surface just as they are seen by binocular vision, without reference to their relative size. A man in the background may be larger than a woman in the foreground, but he appears smaller to the eye, so the artist gives him smaller dimensions in his painting. The whole scene is valid from the observation point of the individual spectator. Mathematical proportions and rationalized geometric patterns are essential to the design of a painting done in perspective. Linear perspective ("clear seeing") brought about a clean break with the flat, floating arrangements characteristic of medieval art. Renaissance painting was far different from the static forms of thirteenth-century Byzantine mosaics and even from the more traditional Italian painting of the fourteenth century. The painter Paolo Uccello spoke for his whole generation when he exclaimed, "How sweet is perspective!"

LEON BATTISTA ALBERTI

A great genius of the Renaissance, Leon Battista Alberti (1404–1472), came closer than anybody before Leonardo to being a "universal man," the Renaissance ideal who excelled in many fields. He was not only a man of letters and learning, an artist, and an architect, but a brilliant theoretician as well. Jacob Burckhardt called Alberti the "first universal genius."

Alberti belonged to a noble Florentine family that had acquired a fortune in the wool trade. In 1387 his grandfather was banished from Florence, and in 1401 his father too was exiled. In Genoa, where the family had a branch bank, the father married a wealthy Bolognese widow, who gave birth to two sons, Carlo and Leon

Battista. In 1428 the family was allowed to return to Florence and in 1434 the last legal restrictions were removed from the family. In the preface to the Italian edition of his book on painting, Alberti expressed his surprise at seeing Florence for himself.

At twenty Alberti wrote a Latin play, *Philodoxius,* and deceived Aldus Manutius the Younger, the learned Venetian printer, into believing that it was a lost work of Lepidus. Like Michelangelo when one of his early sculptures was successfully passed off as a rediscovered antique work, Alberti found that the veneration for antiquity dulled the critics' judgment. The versatile Alberti was one of the best organists of the time. Interested in engineering problems, he developed a device for raising a sunken Roman ship. Vasari relates that in 1457 Alberti invented a device similar to Gutenberg's printing press. He studied art and architecture in Rome, where he explored the ruins for examples of classical forms. Brunelleschi was just closing the dome of the Florence cathedral, and Alberti was excited by the new trend in architecture. A canon in the metropolitan church in Florence, Alberti had leisure to devote to art, architecture, and theory. In his later years he associated with the Platonic circle at the court of Lorenzo de' Medici.

As an architect Alberti introduced classical motifs in practice and in theory. In Rome he helped to restore the papal palace for Nicholas V and to ornament the Trevi Fountain. In Rimini between 1450 and 1460 he remodeled the thirteenth-century Church of San Francesco for Sigismondo Malatesta. The tyrant of Rimini intended the church to be a hall of fame where the classical scholars in his academy and his mistress Isotta were to be buried. Alberti covered the brick building with a marble veneer. The façade featured three rounded arches and four semidetached Corinthian columns; if the upper part had been completed, the whole design would have formed an arch of triumph in the ancient Roman style. The design was, in fact, adapted from a Roman gate in the walls of Rimini. In Florence the Rucellais commissioned him to build them a palace, and also to design the principal façade of the marvelous Church of Santa Maria Novella. But even more important than his own designs were his theoretical writings on architecture, painting, and social thought.

As a humanist Alberti was captivated by the architectural theories of Vitruvius, a Roman of the first century A.D. whose major work was discovered in 1414 in the monastery of St. Gall. Alberti's own book *On Building,* which he finished around 1452, reflected Vitruvius' influence. Alberti's theory was that creative design should utilize classical forms, not merely by copying them, but by applying the proven principles they embodied. He praised architecture as a social art, for it is concerned with the health and welfare of the people. Alberti held that no structure should be designed as an isolated unit; each building should be planned in relation to its social function and its entire urban setting. He proposed that cities be planned with large squares for open space and with various foci or centers. The city planning of later centuries, important for Washington, D.C., and later for Paris, was influenced by a tradition of urban design going back to Alberti.

Alberti's treatise *On Painting* (1435) reflected Neoplatonic influence. It was the first such study done in a scientific fashion and became a prototype for a host of later theoretical studies. Dedicated to Brunelleschi, the treatise discusses problems of mathematical analysis in design and the place of geometry in painting. Alberti considered mathematical proportion to be symbolic of divine harmony and order. He analyzes the spectrum, the use of color, and the effect of reflected light rays. He discusses the "one-point perspective system" and the elements of composition. The painter, according to Alberti, should bring out the beauty implicit in the object. He should not merely reproduce nature; he should idealize it, for nature of itself is not always beautiful. Thus he should paint the eye of a king in such a way as to bring out a look of strength and dignity. The ideal painting should tell an elevating story. Figures should be sculptured rather than linear. They should be grouped in geometric forms, and the groups should be related to each other in such a way that the total composition forms a geometric design. Alberti's theories were applied by Piero della Francesca and other artists, and are clearly in evidence in Raphael's *School of Athens*. In aesthetic theory Alberti pioneered a tradition that reached down in time through Leonardo da Vinci to Sir Joshua Reynolds. Alberti's treatise *On Sculpture* was less influential.

A lifelong bachelor, Alberti nevertheless wrote a famous four-volume treatise *On the Family* (1443), in which he presented his version of home economics. In these four books of dialogues Alberti has the younger members of the family discuss life with the more experienced and mature members. He stresses the virtue of saving to build up the economic strength of the family, contrasting bourgeois thrift with the spendthrift ways of the nobility. He considers a rational ordering of one's affairs of utmost importance, even going so far as to suggest a list of activities for each day and a systematic checking off of accomplishments each night. He acknowledged that men vary greatly in knowledge and attainments, and that there will therefore always be great differences in wealth; but he held that government should minimize the harmful effects of such differences.

Alberti's whole philosophy of life, in fact, reflected all the virtues of civic humanism. "Nothing is better or more suited to the acquisition of virtue and good ethics than to read learned authors," declared the scholarly artist. "Man is born in order to be useful to man," he asserted. Man is fully developed only when he directs all his efforts toward the welfare of "the fatherland, the public good, and the benefit of all citizens." Alberti was a typical Renaissance man in his restless energy and his titanic enterprise. "I am pleased," he said, "not in the man of leisure and cessation, but of operation and action!"

Quattrocento Painting

MASACCIO

If Giotto was properly honored as the creator of Renaissance art, Masaccio was the "second Prometheus" who carried Renaissance painting into a new phase in the fifteenth century. In his brief life Masaccio (1401–1428) introduced exciting innovations to fresco painting. A master at twenty, the young Florentine painter, son of a notary, moved to Rome in 1426 or 1427, and a year later passed away in obscurity.

Masaccio was a nickname like "Sloppy Joe," given him because of his slovenly habits and careless dress. His real name was Tommaso Guidi. According to Vasari, he was not fully appreciated as an artist during his lifetime, but he was a great innovator all the same and made an important impact upon the development of Renaissance painting.

His renown rests chiefly upon the frescoes in the Brancacci family chapel of the Church of Santa Maria del Carmine in Florence. In *The Tribute Money* he depicted the disciples clustered around Jesus waiting to hear his answer to the question "Is it lawful to pay tribute to Caesar?" Among the spectators Masaccio included portraits of himself and a friend. Perhaps his most famous fresco is *The Expulsion of Adam and Eve from the Garden,* in which the grief-stricken nude figures reveal the awful pathos of the moment. Masaccio pioneered in the use of perspective, going far beyond Giotto in this respect. His figures show a true naturalism in the manner of Giotto, but they are even more individualistic, and they are related to each other and to their setting in a much more realistic fashion. Masaccio achieved a modeling and a spaciousness that excelled those of his predecessors and contemporaries. Vasari tells how the giants of the high Renaissance, Leonardo, Michelangelo, and Raphael, came to the chapel to study Masaccio's technique of perspective, his skill in composition and psychological expression.

FRA ANGELICO

Not all of Masaccio's contemporaries were ready for his innovations. Fra Angelico (1387–1455) employed naturalistic techniques, but he treated his religious subjects with a delicate other-worldliness reminiscent of an earlier period. He sought to express the inner life of the soul in the countenance of the subject. He did not simply employ traditional iconography in order to convey his spiritual message, however. His beautiful landscapes, his mastery in the use of delicate colors, his love of flora, all proved him to be an authentic Renaissance artist in the new mode.

MASACCIO. *The Rendering of the Tribute Money.* Brancacci Chapel, Santa Maria del Carmine, Florence.

FRA FILIPPO LIPPI

Like Fra Angelico, Fra Filippo Lippi (1406–1469) concentrated on religious subjects, but he gave them a new cheerful earthly reality. His madonnas, done in brilliant colors, are very real and credible young ladies, and his children are quite human. Filippino Lippi (*c.* 1457–1504), his son, also treated religious subjects in a worldly way. This approach is to be seen later in the paintings of Ghirlandaio (1449–1494), and in the works of the Umbrian painters Pietro Perugino (1441–1523) and Bernardino Pinturicchio (1454–1513), who were decorative illustrators.

PIERO DELLA FRANCESCA

The most worthy successor to Masaccio was the Umbrian painter Piero della Francesca (*c.* 1416–1492), who was born and lived most of his life in the little town of Borgo San Sepolcro. He was impressed by the principle of perspective expounded by Alberti and Brunelleschi, and even wrote a mathematical treatise himself: *On Perspective Painting.* He was inspired by Masaccio's frescoes in the Brancacci Chapel and went on to perfect the union of the spiritual and the natural in his own masterpieces. Piero's work was restrained and discriminating, learned and yet full of feeling. He did a series of masterful frescoes in the Church of San Francesco in Arezzo that still capture the attention of the viewer. But his most powerful work is probably *The Resurrection.* The risen Christ stands erect and imperious in the center against a dawn-gray landscape. Beneath his feet the armed guards slumber on, as though to suggest the dreamlike and transient nature of the power of this world compared with the triumphant life of the spirit and the world beyond.

SANDRO BOTTICELLI

An artist whose work seems to be strangely out of phase with the tendency toward realism in Renaissance art as developed by Giotto and Masaccio was Sandro Botticelli (1444–1510), a Florentine who enjoyed the continuous patronage of the Medicis as long as they remained in power. The son of a tanner, Botticelli ("little barrel") was apprenticed at fourteen to Fra Filippo Lippi and spent nearly a decade in his studio learning the trade. When Botticelli painted his earliest picture still extant, *The Adoration of the Magi,* he was so much under the master's influence that it was long ascribed to him. But once Fra Filippo left Florence for Spoleto, Botticelli developed greater independence in style. From the school of Pollaiuoli he gained a measure of realism, precision in linear representation, and a more exact knowledge of the human body and its movement. He became a favorite of the Medicis and through them came into contact with the circle of Neoplatonic philoso-

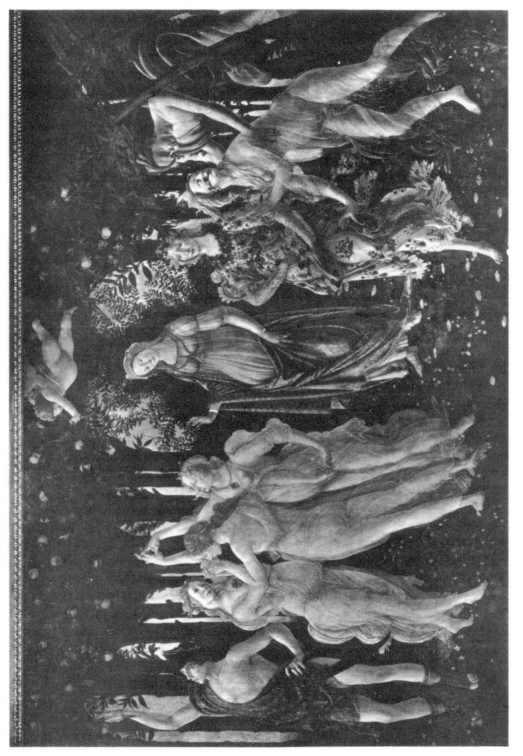

BOTTICELLI. *Primavera.* Uffizi Gallery, Florence.

phers and poets that they supported and encouraged. The poet Politian influenced him strongly and possibly inspired that dreamlike, evanescent quality of his mature work.

Botticelli did his two most famous paintings for the Medicis. Around 1477–1478 he painted the *Primavera,* or "Spring," for the younger Lorenzo's villa at Castello. Inspired by a poem of Politian as well as by the classical poets Horace and Lucretius, the *Primavera* portrays Venus, draped in a flowing translucent gown, standing in a grove of myrtle and orange trees awaiting the coming of spring. Mercury, messenger of the gods, heralds the advent of spring as Florus and Zephyr, the gentle west wind, encourage her entrance. Above Venus hovers Cupid, for spring is the season for love. In his other masterpiece, *The Birth of Venus,* Botticelli pictures the goddess of love emerging on a shell from the sea. The painting combines elements of medieval mysticism, Neoplatonic allegory, and Renaissance naturalism in a delicate and enchanting fantasy. Botticelli's great skill at linear representation and the delicacy and charm of his work, which suggests a highly spiritual quality, come to full expression in this masterpiece.

Botticelli did a number of religious paintings (his beautiful *Virgin with the Pomegranate* is outstanding), but he also did earthier pictures. When the Medicis had crushed the Pazzi revolt in 1478, they commissioned Botticelli to paint the rebels hanging by their necks on the walls of the Palazzo del Podestà, as a reminder to the people of the fate of traitors. When the Medicis were driven from power, the painting also perished. Botticelli also spent some time in Rome, decorating the walls of niches in the Sistine Chapel with papal portraits.

Botticelli's poetic fantasy, his increasingly intense religious sentiment, and his fascination with eschatological prophecy all conditioned him for Savonarola's message. He had done eighty-five illustrations for an edition of Dante's *Divine Comedy* just prior to Savonarola's emergence as a power in Florence. Thus mentally prepared, he was swept away by the somber preaching of the earnest Dominican. His *Nativity* is the painting that best illustrates the strong emotion and deep religious feeling of this final period.

ANDREA MANTEGNA

One of the greatest non-Florentine painters of the century, Mantegna (1431–1506) studied art in Padua. He had notable masters to emulate, for Giotto's frescoes in the Arena Chapel were an inspiration to him, and the sculptor Donatello worked in Padua for years and his monumental equestrian statue of the Venetian condottiere Gattamelata was already a city landmark. Mantegna was completely captivated by the art of antiquity and loved to portray in his paintings figures reminiscent of classic statuary and the columns and arches of Roman architecture. *The Circumcision,* an altar painting (1464), showing Mary and the Christ child in the temple with the priest at the moment of the cutting, tells the story dramatically. It illustrates Mantegna's special talent for precise detail that serves as a support for the major figures and the central theme.

PAOLO UCCELLO

The long-lived Paolo Uccello (1397–1475) turned his art to secular subjects. He still did a great number of religious paintings, but he also did hunting scenes and painted three battle scenes for Cosimo de' Medici celebrating "triumphs" of Florence over Siena. He did the first equestrian portrait of the period, of the English condottiere Sir John Hawkwood, who fought and died for Florence.

Renaissance art following Masaccio was marked by an increase in naturalism and in the number of secular subjects. Portraiture as such became more popular, and the inclusion of portraits of patrons and other contemporaries in large religious scenes became a very common practice. It may not be extravagant to suggest that bourgeois self-consciousness and a new individualism were here in evidence.

Sculpture

UNLIKE PAINTING, of which few classical examples had survived, ancient sculpture was represented by a multitude of models. Most examples came from the third and fourth centuries A.D. They were not the best that ancient sculptors had produced, for the most striking masterpieces of classical sculpturing, such as the Laocoön group and the Apollo Belvedere, were not unearthed until the sixteenth century. Still, those that were available to Renaissance sculptors served them well. Renaissance sculpture was not, however, merely an imitation of ancient art, but a living expression of the feeling, thought, and aspirations of a dynamic society. French sculpture of the thirteenth century reflected a decline in Gothic ideals, as sculptured figures were separated from their architectural settings and given artificial expressions and poses. Italian sculpture of the fourteenth to sixteenth centuries, while drawing on a strong classic tradition, expressed the growing naturalism, the psychological depths, and the intellectual currents of a vital Renaissance culture.

THE PISANS

The new naturalism found its first notable expression in the work of Nicola Pisano (1220–1278), whose pulpit in the Baptistery at Pisa (1260) pioneered in the new directions sculpture was to take. Vasari reports that Pisano had studied a Roman sarcophagus in the *campo santo* in Pisa, but his figures of men and animals prove that he was also a close student of nature itself. He decorated the hex-agonal pulpit with a set of panels portraying scenes from the New Testament, beginning with the nativity. His deeply engraved figures had the posture and expression of Roman statuary. The Virgin Mary, for example, lies on a couch like a Roman matron. Her head resembles that of an ancient Juno. The angel of the annunciation is wearing a toga, and in the foreground stands an antique basin. The crowded composition and the subject matter suggest that Pisano's work was still basically medieval, but the seeds of the future are in evidence.

His son, Giovanni Pisano (1250–1317), worked with him on the pulpit in the Siena cathedral, but gradually asserted independence in style. Giovanni moved toward greater realism and naturalism, replacing static figures with dynamic ones. In his nativity scene on a panel of the pulpit in Sant' Andrea at Pistoia, he por-trayed the agitation of the angel, the maternal tenderness of Mary, the wonder and reflectiveness of Joseph, and the concern of the busy midwives in a moving, human fashion. The vertical lines used by Nicola are replaced with diagonal lines. Nature is no longer merely symbolic of the spiritual world above it. Emotions are given freer expression. Sculpture is released to serve as a vehicle for the artist's highly individual interpretation of experience and reality as he understands it. Renaissance sculpture developed along the lines indicated by Giovanni Pisano's creations, not in imitation of them but as the original and vital expressions of a great age and of artistic geniuses such as the world had never seen before and has not equaled since.

LORENZO GHIBERTI

After a lag that lasted most of the fourteenth century, Renaissance sculpturing picked up again at the very beginning of the fifteenth century with the work of Lorenzo Ghiberti (1378–1455). Florence had a virtual monopoly on sculpture in the fifteenth and early sixteenth centuries. It was fitting, therefore, that its leader-ship in this field should be spotlighted by a contest for the commission to create the bronze doors of the Baptistery of San Giovanni in Florence.

The Guild of Wool Merchants endowed a pair of bronze doors for the Bap-tistery in thanks to God for saving the city during the plague of 1400, and the city staged a competition in 1401 to select the artist who should receive the commission. The task set was to prepare a panel on the sacrifice of Isaac by Abraham. The seven competitors were given a year in which to prepare their models. The choice was finally narrowed to the entries of Ghiberti and Filippo Brunelleschi. Ghiberti's panel revealed beautiful linear effect, clarity of composition, and rhythmic move-ment, all done with restraint; Brunelleschi's displayed an almost frightening sense of realism. Ghiberti was the victor, and it is said that this defeat was responsible for Brunelleschi's decision to devote himself to architecture, a field in which he was to gain great renown. The learned humanist Ambrogio Traversari prepared the program for Ghiberti's remaining panels. Ghiberti completed the doors in 1423 and won fame and acclaim for his efforts. The next year he won a commission for a second set of doors, which he completed in 1447. The first pair was then placed in the south entrance and the second pair on the east portal. Ghiberti said he had done his very best to imitate nature, and his best, as represented by the second pair of doors, has never been equaled. A lesson in bronze, they have instructed generations of artists in the achievement of naturalism and the demands of technical perfection. Michelangelo declared the doors in the east portal worthy to serve as "the gates of paradise."

JACOPO DELLA QUERCIA

Compared with the work of Ghiberti, that of Jacopo della Quercia (1371–1438) seems to lack precision and refinement. He too had entered the Baptistery competition and lost. He imitated the classical pattern more closely than Ghiberti, virtually eliminating the background detail in order to emphasize the figures themselves. Jacopo learned much from his study of classical models, but his inadequate knowledge of human anatomy marred his work. His sculptured reliefs were not truly appreciated by his contemporaries, who failed to see in them the potential for further development of free-standing nude figures. Not until Michelangelo was this art form fully realized.

DONATELLO

The undisputed master of sculpture in the first half of the *Quattrocento* was Donato Bardi (1386–1466), best known by the affectionate diminutive Donatello. Donatello received his early training in a goldsmith's shop and worked for a time in Ghiberti's studio. When Brunelleschi left Florence for Rome after losing the Baptistery competition to Ghiberti, Donatello accompanied him. While Brunelleschi measured the Pantheon dome and other classic buildings and ruins, Donatello examined Roman statuary and fragments. His scientific study of human anatomy helped him to resolve many of the problems of portraying the human body in various poses. The true sign of his genius was that the inner quality and spirit of his subject shone through the technical perfection of the form. Michelangelo said of his St. Mark, done for one of the fourteen exterior niches of the Or San Michele, the church of the Florentine guilds, "I have never seen a figure that so thoroughly represents a man of probity."

The first two figures that Donatello did upon his return to Florence, for the north portal of the cathedral, were still Gothic in style, but he was soon experimenting with classical forms and a new realism. For the campanile he did marble statues of St. John the Baptist and Jeremiah, and the *Zuccone* or "pumpkin head," presumably of Habakkuk. As has often been the case in literature, the unlovely is emphasized in the early strivings for realistic effects. The *Zuccone* is a typical example of this phenomenon. Donatello reproduced his homely, almost repugnant model precisely, without in any way ennobling the features as Leonardo da Vinci was later to do, when he brought out the beauty in even a wrinkled old face.

The most famous achievement of Donatello's classic period was his bronze David, now in the Bargello in Florence. The David was the first (*c.* 1430) nude statue of the Renaissance. Conceived in the round, the David is a free-standing figure, independent of any architectural surroundings. David is presented as a slender youth wearing a Tuscan shepherd's hat. The figure is relaxed, resting on one leg, and has the angular boniness and awkwardness typical of adolescence. It may reflect Etruscan or Gothic influence.

In 1442 Donatello was invited to Padua to decorate the high altar of San Antonio. His bronze crucifix on the high altar was acknowledged as a masterpiece. But his greatest triumph was an equestrian statue, the Gattamelata. In the very year in which Donatello came to Padua, the powerful Venetian condottiere Gattamelata died and left a huge bequest to Padua on the condition that the city erect an equestrian statue in his memory. Donatello received the commission and remained in Padua for ten years executing it. In 1453 the Gattamelata was finished, and stands today, imperious, like a Roman emperor, dominating the square. Donatello studied the anatomy of the horse with scientific precision—the nostrils, veins, neck, and heavy frame of the armor-bearing war steed. The condottiere himself displays confidence and near repose. The understatement conveys a sense of his real strength.

Donatello returned to spend the last years of his life in his native Florence. He did the repulsive, emaciated Mary Magdalen in the Baptistery in Florence and the Judith group for the courtyard of the Medici Palace. His last important commission was the bronze reliefs for the pulpit of San Lorenzo, about 1460, which an assistant finished after his death. His efforts as an architect were not very successful, for he was overliteral in imitating antique form and style and crowded his surfaces with too many details borrowed directly from classical models.

THE LATE QUATTROCENTO

During the second half of the fifteenth century, sculpture followed three tendencies: the expression of a sweet lyric sentiment, the realistic recognition of ugly aspects of life, and a scientific emphasis worthy of Donatello himself.

The most striking examples of the lyric sentiment are to be found in the works of Desiderio da Settignano (1428–1464), who studied with Donatello. His finest productions were linear low reliefs, like large cameos, of the Madonna and child. Luca della Robbia (1400–1482) is most famous for his glazed terra cotta plaques, often done in blue and white, of Mary and the Christ child.

Antonio Rossellino (1427–1478) pursued the trend toward stark realism evident in some of Donatello's work. His bust of the humanist Matteo Palmieri presents the gross features of the unfortunate man just as he was, with a wide mouth, prominent nose, and head of unruly curly hair. Roman "unheroic" busts may well have served as models for Rossellino's work.

The two leading representatives of the scientific technique were Andrea Verrocchio (1435–1488) and Antonio Pollaiuolo (1432–1499). Verrocchio, a pupil of Donatello, was master of a workshop in Florence, made famous not only by his own work, but by the fact that Leonardo da Vinci was an apprentice there. He did many casts of live and dead subjects. Verrocchio painted the *Baptism of Christ* and produced jewelry, objects in silver plate, and dozens of statuettes in precious metals. But his personal renown rests upon his sculptures, especially his David and an equestrian statue in Venice. His bronze statue of David, which was to stand in the courtyard of the Medici Palace, is reminiscent of Donatello's David. It shows a thin lad, ribs visible, sword in one hand, the other resting on his hip in a gesture of triumph; the head of Goliath lies at his feet.

In 1479 the city of Venice commissioned Verrocchio to do an equestrian statue of the Venetian condottiere Bartolommeo Colleoni. It took Verrocchio until the year of his death to complete the model, which was then cast and unveiled in 1496. Colleoni stands in his stirrups astride his magnificent steed. His right shoulder is drawn back, but his cold, stern, commanding face is turned slightly to the left. He is alive, nervous, moving—in command. As a work of art, scientifically accurate and flawlessly executed, this equestrian statue surpasses even the ancient Roman monument of Emperor Marcus Aurelius on his mount.

Antonio Pollaiuolo's scientific interest led him to explore the problems of stress and strain in the human body. His treatment of muscular movement reveals his astonishingly close observation of human anatomy. His best-known work is his statuette of Hercules and Antaeus, representing that dramatic moment when Hercules lifted Antaeus into the air—for Antaeus received strength only from contact with the earth—and squeezed the life out of him as he writhed in mortal agony.

The achievements of the fifteenth century in painting and sculpture were praiseworthy in themselves, but beyond this they contributed to that accumulation of ideals and supporting skills that made possible the magnificent achievements of the high Renaissance during those golden opening decades of the sixteenth century.

Architecture

DURING THE FOURTEENTH CENTURY Italian architecture was somnolent, devoid of creativity and innovation. There was a great deal of building, *palazzi* for the wealthy families, public buildings, fortifications, chapels and churches. But no distinctive Italian style evolved. Byzantine and Gothic elements were intermingled with a traditional Romanesque base in an eclectic jumble that all but defies analysis. This situation changed radically during the course of the fifteenth century. The humanists envisioned an ideal city, peopled by men of high morals and civic virtue, men of learning and impeccable taste, living the good life. This model of an ideal citizenry was accompanied by an aesthetic vision of a material city worthy of such men. Leonardo Bruni idealized Florence and Matteo Palmieri described the need for spacious edifices for free citizens, suited to the needs of church and state. Alberti's great treatise on architecture had a powerful influence upon building design in the Renaissance. The prime mover in actually establishing a new style was a man of unusual genius, Filippo Brunelleschi, an architect suited to the world of humanism.

FILIPPO BRUNELLESCHI

The man who pioneered a new Roman or classic style in architecture was extremely versatile, skilled in many of the arts. Filippo Brunelleschi (1377–1446), the son of a notary, served as an apprentice in a goldsmith's workshop and joined the guild. Interested in geometry, he developed a theory of linear perspective in painting. Vasari relates how he left Florence in a huff after he lost out to Ghiberti in the Baptistery door competition in 1401. In Rome he measured the Roman Pantheon and other ancient structures to determine their mathematical proportions. He sketched arches, cornices, pillars, half-barrel vaults, and other devices of the ancient Roman architects. From classical architecture, he once observed, he learned to place empty space above empty space and solid mass above solid mass, arch above arch, pillar above pillar. In his own designs he followed the spirit rather than the letter of classical architecture. He used earlier Florentine models and examples from the territory of Venice.

Thus prepared, he returned to Florence in 1407, at the very time when the city council had decided to complete the construction of the dome on the great cathedral of Santa Maria del Fiore. Brunelleschi's plans called for a double-shelled cupola, similar to those found in earlier constructions in the East. It was not until 1419, after endless wrangling, that he was entrusted with the actual construction. He erected the vault without scaffolding, a fantastic engineering feat, pushing the dome upward to a height of approximately ninety feet. The dome—it is not actually a pure rounded classical structure, but is made of triangular sections pointing upward with a somewhat Gothic effect—is larger in some of its dimensions than that of the later St. Peter's in Rome. Unfortunately Brunelleschi did not live to see the completion of his masterpiece.

In 1435 Brunelleschi designed a palace for Luca Pitti, built across the Arno

BRUNELLESCHI. *Florence Cathedral.*

River from the Palazzo Vecchio. This huge structure, erected largely by slave and prison labor, became a model for other Tuscan *palazzi* during subsequent centuries. He designed the churches of San Lorenzo and Santo Spirito, but as in the case of the cathedral, he had to adapt classical Roman motifs to the medieval cruciform floor plan. The Pazzi Chapel was the first church structure that was Renaissance in style both inside and out, with rounded arches and all other classic effects. His Hospital of the Innocents is considered by some critics to be the most thoroughly individual, and hence the most successful, of his buildings.

MICHELOZZI

Michelozzo Michelozzi (1396–1472) deserves to be remembered forever for his splendid design of the Medici Palace in Florence. The son of a tailor, Michelozzi began his artistic career as a sculptor, working in bronze, silver, and marble. Cosimo de' Medici, impressed by his skill, moderation, and good taste, took Michelozzi with him to Venice during his exile, and upon his return to Florence commissioned the young sculptor to design a palace for him. In its graceful proportions and relatively modest design it is superior to Brunelleschi's massive Pitti Palace. Gothic influence is still in evidence, for the round arches are marked off by a smooth line rather than being keyed into the stones of the surrounding wall in a typically classical way. He built or rebuilt numerous other structures in Florence, repaired the Palazzo Vecchio, and reconstructed the Monastery of San Marco, where he himself now lies, honored by a grateful city.

BRAMANTE

Not all of the great architects of the Renaissance were Florentines. Bramante (1444–1514) was born in Urbino, apprenticed there as a painter, worked in Milan from 1476 to 1499, and around the year 1500 moved to Rome to enter the service of the popes. He painted murals in Rome, but continued an early interest in architecture by a close study of ancient Roman buildings and ruins, and served as artistic consultant in papal building projects. For Julius II he designed the two corridors joining the Belvedere and the papal palaces. But his most important assignment was his design for St. Peter's Basilica, the capitol of Christendom. Although he died before he was able to complete the design, he did see the four central pillars rise with their connecting arches and vaults. He also finished the main chapel. But later other architects, preeminently Michelangelo, developed new and even more grandiose plans for St. Peter's.

The High Renaissance

THE CUMULATIVE EFFECT of the contributions of many individuals is less continuous and irreversible in the arts than in the sciences. Nevertheless, the pioneering work of the fifteenth-century artists, in creativity of conception as well as in the mastery of technique, did contribute directly to the supreme achievements of the geniuses of the high Renaissance.

By the end of the fifteenth century Italian artists had absorbed the technical skills of Flemish artists such as Jan van Eyck (*c.* 1380–1441), considered the founder of Flemish painting, his brother Hubert van Eyck, and Roger van der Weyden. Their mastery of minute detail, learned in part from medieval manuscript illuminations, their portraits, their interest in commonplace scenes such as domestic interiors, all impressed the Italian artists of the later *Quattrocento*.

But by the turn of the century the tide of influence was turning. Renaissance art drew northern artists to Italy, and Italian artists invaded the north. Among the northerners who came to Italy to look and to learn were Quentin Metsys (1466–1530), Lucas van Leyden (1494–1533), Bernaert van Orley (1493–1541), and the greatest of all, Albrecht Dürer (1471–1528). Dürer, of Nuremberg, was a master of woodcuts, copper etching, silverpoint, charcoal, watercolors, and oil painting. He spent two years in Venice (1505–1507), where he learned to know Giovanni Bellini and absorbed the Renaissance spirit of inquiry as well as Italian style. He was intrigued by the proportions of the human body, anatomy, and flora and fauna, and wrote treatises on *The Doctrine of Proportion* and *The Art of Measurement*. He was fascinated by the problems of linear perspective, and adopted an Italianate style during his early and most productive years.

But the rightful heirs of the rich artistic inheritance of Italy were the great Italian artists of the early sixteenth century. In Leonardo da Vinci, Raphael, Michelangelo, and Cellini, Renaissance art came into full flower. Ironically, this full bloom came during the decades of Italy's humiliation by foreign conquerors and its political disintegration.

LEONARDO DA VINCI

Vasari tells the story that while Leonardo was an apprentice of Verrocchio, he did an angel for one of Verrocchio's paintings that was so beautiful that the master, deeply impressed, resolved never to paint again. The story is demonstrably not true, for later work by Verrocchio is still extant. But the myth conveys the truth that Leonardo was a giant who towered high above his teachers.

Leonardo da Vinci (1452–1519) was the son of a Florentine lawyer named Piero and a woman of humble birth in Vinci, a fortified hill village outside Florence. His parents were married shortly after his birth, but not to each other. Piero, in fact, married four times, and had nine sons and two daughters by his last two wives. Piero raised Leonardo in his house in Florence and then apprenticed him to Verrocchio's studio, where he studied from 1470 to 1477. He became a friend of the painters Perugino and Botticelli, and at twenty he entered the painters' guild. Lorenzo the Magnificent became his patron from 1477 to 1482 or 1483, and Leonardo also received commissions from monasteries and other sources.

Leonardo had an enormous curiosity, and he made intensive studies of nature for his landscapes and of human anatomy for his paintings and sculptures of human figures. He wished to "learn the causes of things," and his early art reveals his love of nature. He painted calm, strange shapes, caves, rock formations, rare plants, faces, and was especially intrigued by the property and power of water. He excelled at *chiaroscuro,* the subtle treatment of light and shade. His early Adam and Eve in tempera reveals an exact knowledge of botany, such as Albrecht Dürer showed in his engravings three decades later. He used a bug as a model for a dragon he painted for a shield.

Unlike the moody Michelangelo, a solitary man who often withdrew into seclusion, Leonardo was relatively open and genial. He was a skilled horseman and loved good horses. Biographers have idealized him as a youth, describing him as a golden-haired lad who bought birds in the market to set them free. In Florence his friends included learned humanists and the Neoplatonic poets of the Medici circle.

At the age of thirty Leonardo left Florence for Milan to serve Ludovico il Moro, the Sforza tyrant. This first Milanese period (1483–1499) was an extremely productive one, although much of Leonardo's energies went into civil and military engineering projects. He became an apologist for Ludovico. When the mother of Gian Galeazzo, whose position Ludovico had usurped, attempted to assassinate Ludovico, Leonardo painted a political allegory in his behalf: a fierce stag, attacking Milan, is beaten off by the prudence and justice of Ludovico.

Ludovico commissioned a gigantic equestrian statue of Francesco Sforza to honor the double marriage in 1491 of Ludovico and Beatrice d'Este and of Alfonso d'Este and Anna Sforza. Leonardo did dozens of studies of horse heads and bodies (now in the Windsor Castle collection of drawings) by way of preparation. The statue was planned on a scale even grander than the equestrian statues of Donatello and Verrocchio, but it was never completed.

In Milan Leonardo painted some of his immortal masterpieces. Outstanding are *The Virgin of the Rocks* and *The Last Supper,* a fresco in the refectory of the convent of Santa Maria delle Grazie which illustrates the perspective and geometric arrangements (four groups of three disciples each) so characteristic of Renaissance art. With Pacioli, in fact, Leonardo later wrote a treatise entitled *On Divine Proportion.*

LEONARDO DA VINCI. *The Virgin of the Rocks.* National Gallery, London.

Then came for Leonardo a time of exile and wandering. He was in Milan for a while when the city was under French control, and it just may be that the Italians forced him to leave as a collaborator. At any rate, he left Milan in 1499, and in 1502 he was serving Cesare Borgia in the Romagna as chief engineer. He returned to Florence just before Cesare's fall. Over a four-year period (1503–1506) he perfected *La Gioconda*, a portrait of the twenty-four-year-old wife of an Italian gentleman, better known as the Mona Lisa. King Francis I paid 4,000 florins for the painting, and she has since smiled enigmatically upon millions of visitors to the Louvre in Paris. In Florence in 1503 the Soderinis commissioned two great battle scenes, one by Leonardo and one by Michelangelo. In Rome Leonardo served Leo X and did work for the Belvedere Palace in the Vatican. When at last he went to the court of Francis I in France, where he spent his last years, he took along three paintings: *John the Baptist; Anne, Mary, and the Christ Child;* and presumably the Mona Lisa. He also took along his notebooks and anatomical drawings, most of which he left to Francesco Melzi, his young assistant. He died in France and lies buried in a Gothic tomb in Amboise, a final irony.

RAPHAEL

When the "divine" Raphael journeyed from Urbino to Florence in 1504, he carried with him a letter from Giovanna Felicia Feltria, the sister of the duke of Urbino, introducing the young painter to Piero Soderini, *gonfaloniere* of Florence:

> Most Magnificent and Powerful Lord—
> He who presents this letter to you is Raphael, a painter of Urbino, endowed with great talent in art. He has decided to pass some time in Florence in order to improve himself in his studies. As the father, who was dear to me, was full of good qualities, so the son is a modest young man of distinguished manners; and thus I bear him an affection on every account, and wish that he should attain perfection.
> Giovanna, Duchess of Sora[4]

Raphael was a handsome young man, known for his charm and kindliness. Beloved in his own lifetime, he has remained the most universally popular artist, and is still acclaimed by many as the preeminent painter of all time. In the seventeen or eighteen working years he enjoyed before his early death, he produced a prodigious amount of work. He seemed to work calmly and with great ease, in contrast to such a tortured soul as Michelangelo.

Raphael Sanzio (1483–1520) was born in Urbino in Umbria, a lively cultural center. His father, a painter, died when Raphael was only eleven, but the boy had already learned from him much of the technical skill necessary for his calling. He studied then for five years in the studio of Perugino in Perugia. Perugino is said

---

4 Regina Shoolman and Charles Slatkin, *The Story of Art* (New York, 1940), p. 101.

to have exclaimed upon seeing Raphael's drawings, "Let him be my pupil! He will soon become my master." From Perugino he learned the soft, gentle grace of Umbrian art and in his workshop he developed a sense of spatial relationships. Inevitably he was drawn to Florence to further his development. There from 1504 to 1508 he studied the works of Fra Bartolommeo, Leonardo, Michelangelo, and other masters. While he learned from their technique, he created his own mature ideal of beauty.

With the fall of the Medicis and the other ills that befell Florence, the city on the Arno began to lose its leadership in the arts. In 1508 Pope Julius II invited Raphael to Rome, where he remained until his death at the early age of thirty-seven.

Raphael's name will forever be associated with his beautiful madonnas. Raphael was desperately in love with the beautiful Margherita, his mistress, who served as the model for his madonnas and whom he celebrated also in his lyric poetry. In 1516 Raphael painted his *Madonna of the Chair,* in which Mary holds the round and fleshy Christ child affectionately on her lap while the little John the Baptist looks up at them in adoration. In 1517 he did his most famous painting, the Sistine Madonna, for the monastery of San Sisto in Piacenza. The Virgin Mary, a majestic maiden of great beauty, framed by green draperies and standing upon billowy white clouds, holds the infant Jesus. To the right St. Barbara and to the left St. Sixtus kneel in worship, while below two dreamy *putti* lean upon the bottom frame of the panel. The museums of the Western world are studded with Raphael madonnas (the Esterházy Madonna in Budapest is especially fine), but the Sistine Madonna remains his masterpiece.

Raphael's mastery of Renaissance artistic theory is powerfully demonstrated in his frescoes *The School of Athens* and the *Disputa,* which he did for the walls of the papal signature room in the Vatican. The two frescoes portray the classical and the medieval philosophers who contributed to Western thought. The perspective, geometric groupings, and total spatial arrangement make of *The School of Athens* a perfect exemplar of Renaissance artistic theory and technique.

In the year 1519 Cardinal Giuliano de' Medici commissioned a painting of the Transfiguration for the cathedral of Narbonne. The scene shows Christ on Mt. Tabor with three of his disciples, Peter, James, and John, while others of his followers wait below. At Christ's side are Moses and Elias. The painting catches the moment when a bright cloud overshadows them and a voice out of the cloud says: "This is my beloved son, in whom I am well pleased; hear ye him." It was Raphael's last painting. Shortly after completing it he was struck down by a fever that raged for ten days and finally caused his death. The grief-stricken Romans carried the painting behind Raphael's body to the Pantheon, where he lies buried in a simple tomb.

His early death cut off the career of one of the world's greatest masters. The esteem in which he was held by his fellow artists is attested to by Bramante's death-

bed request in 1514 that Raphael be appointed to succeed him as chief architect of St. Peter's. But Raphael's own premature death kept him from exercising any great influence upon the construction of the great cathedral.

MICHELANGELO

The Titan Michelangelo was a genius in nearly every medium of art. His creative triumphs marked the culmination of the Renaissance and a transition to the new age of mannerism and the baroque. In sculpture, painting, architecture, drawing, and lyric poetry, Michelangelo showed himself a giant in a race of tall men. His achievements were the products not of a tranquil life of ease, but of a tortured spirit and a stormy career that would have broken the will of a lesser man.

Michelangelo Buonarroti (1475–1564) was the son of a petty nobleman who could barely eke out a living on the family estate, and had an aristocrat's disdain for labor. Michelangelo's nineteen-year-old mother left her sickly infant to be nursed by the wife of a stonecutter or marble worker of Settignano. Michelangelo was fond of saying that he had sucked in a passion for art with this mother's milk. The boy showed great talent for drawing and was apprenticed to study for three years in the studio of Domenico Ghirlandaio. Upon observing Michelangelo's talent, the master commented, "This youth understands more than I do myself." After only a single year had passed, during which he devoted much time to learning the technique of fresco painting, Michelangelo was sent with another beginner to the Medicis in response to Lorenzo's request for two young sculptors.

There in the circle of the Medicis Michelangelo encountered that grandeur of spirit and high style in thought which was so important for his intellectual and artistic development. A student of Donatello served as director of the school for sculpture that Lorenzo maintained in the Medici gardens. There Michelangelo heard discourses on Neoplatonic philosophy that influenced his aesthetic theory in art and poetry. And he carried away from Lorenzo's academy yet another mark that stayed with him through life: in response to a critical remark, which came easily for Michelangelo, one of his fellow students smashed his nose so badly that it was disfigured for life. "You will be remembered," Michelangelo prophesied, "only as the man who broke my nose." And so with a single blow the sculptor Torrigiano Torrigiani made his mark on history.

Michelangelo was always given to melancholy, dark brooding, and apprehensive presentiments. He sent almost all the money he received for his commissions to his father and three ungrateful brothers, whom he set up in business. His father even warned him in a letter against damaging his health and spirit by living in want. He poured all of his strength and energy into his artistic creations. But his wretched diet and Spartan life may have contributed to his psychological difficulties. Savonarola's dark prophecies moved him to despondency and near despair.

In June 1496 Michelangelo took the well-traveled road to Rome. The occasion for his trip was trivial enough, but the move to Rome was fateful in its consequences. An agent had paid Michelangelo thirty ducats for a sleeping Cupid, and suggested that they bury it in the earth to give it the appearance of age. Michelangelo thought the idea amusing; it never occurred to him that the agent was contemplating fraud. When he learned that the agent had taken the statue to Cardinal Raffaele Riario San Giorgio, a collector of antiques, and sold it as an antique for two hundred ducats, Michelangelo traveled to Rome to adjust the matter. Once there, he stayed for five years, winning ever greater commissions and fame. He received 450 ducats from Cardinal St. Denis, the French ambassador to the Vatican, for a beautiful Pietà.

But his native city offered a new challenge. In 1501 a prominent citizen of Florence, Piero Soderini, commissioned a statue of David to be done from a block of Carrara marble eighteen feet high. Some forty years earlier another sculptor had begun work on the stone, but had given up the task, and the block had stood there ever since. Michelangelo went into seclusion with the stone and for two years devoted most of his conscious moments to the creation of his David. His Neoplatonic notion was that the beautiful form was already there, imprisoned in the marble, waiting to be liberated by the artist as he chipped away the waste material around it. Then in 1504 came the unveiling of the Giant, as the people called it. Michelangelo portrayed the young hero of Israel as a shepherd boy, frowning earnestly, as well he might, watchful, eying his adversary, sling in hand, but with no sign of fear. The David stood thereafter outside the Palazzo Vecchio as a symbol of the *signoria* and the people of Florence.

This Florentine period lasted only five years. In 1506 Michelangelo returned to Rome, where he spent the three most productive decades of his life in the service of four popes. The warring Julius II lived a spectacular life and wished to lie buried in an equally dramatic tomb. He chose Michelangelo to do a monstrous mausoleum, three levels high, to be adorned with myriad statuettes of saints and apostles, cherubs and sybils. "Let it cost any amount and you shall have it," Julius II assured him. For eight months Michelangelo supervised the selection and cutting of the best marble in the Carrara quarry. It was transported to the square behind the Vatican, and there Michelangelo began his work on the tomb. Julius II occasionally came by to see how he was getting on. Then quite suddenly the pope ordered him to suspend his work on the tomb and to begin instead to paint frescoes on the ceiling of the Sistine Chapel. Michelangelo attributed this change of plan to his jealous rival Bramante, who saw a chance to disrupt the sculpturing project and force Michelangelo into another medium in which his brilliance was not yet tested. But his genius triumphed here also, and his Sistine Chapel frescoes came to be numbered among the most famous paintings in the world.

For years Michelangelo labored on his back on a high scaffold, assisted only by paint mixers and plaster grinders. He covered over ten thousand square feet of the depressed barrel-vault ceiling with nine huge panels. The first panel depicts the dividing of light and darkness at the time of creation; the second portrays the creation of the heavenly bodies; the third, the creation of the waters; the fourth, the moment when God's hand reaches out to Adam, his new creature; the fifth, the creation of woman; the sixth, man's fall into sin and the expulsion from Eden; the seventh, the sacrifice of Noah; the eighth, the deluge; and the ninth, the drunkenness of Noah. The puzzling feature of this sequence is the fact that the seventh, eighth, and ninth panels do not stand in the chronological sequence of the biblical account. One plausible theory offered by art historians is that the whole ceiling is intended to represent the Neoplatonic theory of the ascent of man from the spiritual abyss of drunkenness and shameful nakedness through the purgation of the deluge upward to the final moment of reunion with God, depicted in the scene showing Adam's hand reaching out to touch the finger of God. Michelangelo read Dante religiously and his Neoplatonism had a medieval mystical cast. No doubt this deep piety, combined with his egoism and will to triumph, kept him at his arduous task, which left him crippled and hunched the remainder of his life.

The restless, assertive warrior pope could not even let this great work proceed uninterrupted. When Julius II had triumphed over his enemies, cleared the Romagna of foes, and entered Bologna victorious, he summoned Michelangelo to Bologna to do a colossal bronze figure of the pope, seated, robed, and mitered, with the keys of the kingdom in one hand and the other held out in a gesture of benediction. It was placed over the main door of the Church of St. Petronius, but three years later the Bolognese revolted against the papal rule and destroyed the image of their conqueror.

During this period of his life Michelangelo was at his most dynamic, restless, forceful, and tempestuous. His art reflected his *furia* and *terribilità*. With the completion of the Sistine ceiling, he returned to work on Julius' tomb. At this time too he did his immortal Moses, the stern lawgiver, and the two *Captive Slaves*. Julius died just as the chapel was completed, but the grandiose tomb had to be abandoned. Michelangelo labored on at it in later years, but on a much reduced scale.

The two Medici popes, Leo X and Clement VII, recognized Michelangelo's special genius and put him to work in their honor. Leo X commissioned him to do a statue to his own glory for the Church of San Lorenzo in Florence, but when four years later the pope died, the project was abandoned. Clement VII had Michelangelo design the Laurentian Library next to San Lorenzo. The structure illustrates how the artist's Neoplatonic philosophy could influence even architectural design. The great sweeping flight of stairs has a swirl-back effect on each side, as though the staircase symbolized a series of stages in the upward ascent of man.

Michelangelo was not enamored of his Medici masters, and during the restoration of the republic he was put in charge of the city's fortifications. But with the

MICHELANGELO. *The Last Judgment*. Sistine Chapel, Rome.

return of the Medicis, Michelangelo reluctantly entered the service of the tyrannous family once again. In this period of disillusionment and disappointment he worked on the tombs in the Medici Chapel. There emerged from the marble the four giant mysterious figures *Day, Night, Dawn,* and *Twilight,* which still today hold the reflective viewer spellbound under their magnetic power.

Pope Paul III, who succeeded Clement VII in 1534, had other plans for Michelangelo. He assigned him the task of painting on the front wall of the Sistine Chapel *The Last Judgment,* one of the best-known paintings in the world. Michelangelo labored for years, reading his beloved Dante for recreation. When the giant fresco was at last opened to public view, it overwhelmed the spectators, and it still keeps tourists gaping in astonishment today. With over three hundred figures, each in its own right a work of art, the grand design presents a panoramic view of the day of wrath, when the Son of God will sit in judgment upon the world.

As an architect Michelangelo undertook several challenging projects during the pontificate of Paul III. He built for his family the Farnese Palace in Rome and designed a cluster of buildings to adorn the Capitoline Hill, but his proudest achievement was his success as the chief architect of St. Peter's. He reworked all the designs of his distinguished predecessors and supervised the construction of the supports and the lower sections of the giant dome, which stands today as the loftiest monument to the universal genius of Michelangelo.

Now a man of sixty, Michelangelo turned to less strenuous and physically demanding labors. He did drawings and composed lyrics and metaphysical love poems. He cultivated an intimate friendship with a handsome young Roman aristocrat, Tommaso dei Cavalieri, to whom he addressed passionate sonnets. For twelve years he was also devoted to a young widow, Vittoria Colonna, a woman of great piety and intellectual power. The poetry he poured out in her honor reflected his Christian faith, his Neoplatonic mystical bent, and the tender affection of his heart. It was as though his personal emotions, so long repressed and sublimated in the interest of his art, now came into full flower in the autumn of his life. Vittoria's death was a blow that struck him at a time when he was least able to bear it. Heartbroken and physically spent, he lived out his years to an infirm old age.

BENVENUTO CELLINI

Michelangelo once called his fellow artist Benvenuto Cellini (1500–1571) "the greatest goldsmith of whom the world has ever heard." Cellini was in complete agreement with this assessment, for he was a supreme egotist, self-serving and assertive. Afflicted with a violent temper, vengeful and reckless, he made countless enemies, was involved in brawls and murders, and was often either in prison or in full flight from the law. A passionate man, he fathered eight children, only one of them legitimate, and recounted coolly how he abandoned a young French girl when he returned to Italy. He and a conjuror, he related, summoned up a legion of demons in the Colosseum in Rome in order to take revenge when one of his mistresses was spirited away by her mother. But he was such a brilliant artist and consummate craftsman that people made many allowances for his extravagant behavior. "Men like Benvenuto," Pope Paul III commented, "unique in their profession, stand above the law."

Cellini was born in Florence, the son of a musician and instrument maker, and was apprenticed to a goldsmith. From an early age he traveled about, often in flight from the police, to Siena, Bologna, Pisa, and Rome. He happened to be in Rome when the imperial troops sacked the city in 1527. In his autobiography he recalls his own heroic role in the defense of the city. He claims that he personally shot the imperial commander, Constable de Bourbon, and later killed Philibert, prince of Orange. He returned to Florence for a productive period and then for a time served at the court of the duke of Mantua. He went back to Florence and then to Rome, where in 1529 he avenged his brother's death by killing his murderer. He himself had to flee the city after wounding a constable. He was accused, probably falsely, of stealing jewels from the papal tiara. He was imprisoned, escaped, was recaptured, tortured, and threatened with hanging. Finally he put a safe distance between himself and Rome, entering the service of Francis I of France in Fontainebleau and Paris. Back in Florence he became involved in more legal difficulties when he was charged by an enemy with gross immorality. At the same time it must be noted that he supported his widowed sister and her six children. When he died, the citizens of Florence gave him a magnificent funeral and buried him with honor in the Church of the Annunziata.

Although many of his masterpieces have disappeared, perhaps because of the precious metals and jewels he used, those that remain testify to his genius. Some of his works are extravagantly ornate, but a few of them are very satisfyingly balanced. The masterpiece that the world knows best is the gold and enamel saltcellar he made for the French king. In a setting of waves, dolphins, and other creatures of the sea, a nude Neptune and a sea nymph recline. The cups on either side, intended to hold salt and pepper, are ornate and exquisitely detailed. The work is a bit grand and flamboyant for so prosaic an object as a saltcellar, even a saltcellar for a king. Art critics have suggested that the figures were modeled after Michelangelo's stone statues for the Medici tomb. But Michelangelo's figures were monumental in conception and cannot be reduced to small scale without loss of meaning. Cellini was not so great as he imagined. But Francis I was delighted, and that was of crucial importance for Cellini. When he had shown him the wax model, the king cried out, "This is a hundred times more divine a thing than I had ever dreamed of!" And when at last he saw the saltcellar itself, Cellini recounted, "He uttered a loud cry of astonishment and could not satiate his eyes with gazing at it."

The Venetian School

IN THE FINE ARTS Venice, the proud queen of the Adriatic, not only arrived upon the scene relatively late, but then developed a unique style. A materialistic and sensuous society, Venice reached a high level of prosperity in the mid-fifteenth century. Its citizens loved fine dress, sumptuous meals, elaborate state ceremonies, pageantry, and processions. Each year the symbolic marriage of Venice to the Adriatic was reenacted. The doge arranged for a weekly public religious procession to one of the city's great churches. For centuries every merchant returning from the Near East was required to bring with him an object of art with which to adorn St. Mark's Cathedral, in the heart of the city, until it was a veritable jewel box glittering with treasures from the Levant. So intent were the Venetians on their commerce and then so preoccupied with the naval defense of their eastern empire, as the Ottoman Turks increased their pressure after the fall of Constantinople, that they were slow to appreciate the new Renaissance culture in either literature or art.

THE BELLINIS

Gentile da Fabriano, an Umbrian painter, came to Venice in 1408. He so impressed a Venetian artist, Jacopo Bellini, that Jacopo accompanied him to Florence as his assistant. Jacopo broke with the conservative Siena tradition, which earlier Venetian artists had followed quite literally, and developed a new naturalism. The remarkable Bellini family established Venetian painting as an independent force.

Two innovations in Venetian art proved to be important for the development of a distinct school. The first was Venetian artists' rather early adoption, around 1475, of oils as binders for their pigments, rather than the egg whites and yolks that had been used earlier, and were still being used by artists elsewhere. The second was painting on canvas instead of on plaster-covered walls, since the dampness in Venice made plaster peel, or on wooden panels, since wood warps and cracks so readily in a humid climate. Canvas was well suited to the portable paintings done to adorn the *palazzi*, churches, and public buildings of the republic. The Bellinis made good use of both of these new techniques.

Gentile Bellini (*c.* 1429–1507), Jacopo's elder son, loved to depict the pomp of Venetian public life and religious tradition. Among his better known works are *The Procession of Corpus Domini; Miracles of the True Cross;* and *The Preaching of St. Mark.*

His brother Giovanni (*c.* 1430–1516), however, not only produced paintings of greater fame, but exercised a more powerful influence upon such leading Venetian artists as Giorgione and Titian. At the outset Giovanni was himself very much influenced by the severe linear style and austere classicism of Mantegna, who had married the sister of Gentile and Giovanni and enjoyed considerable authority

as an accomplished master. But soon Giovanni's independent genius asserted itself. His love of color, his taste for glowing tones in the glitter of jewels and rich adornment brought vibrancy to his canvases. Many of his themes are religious, but they are handled in a frankly sensuous and earthy way. Among his most famous masterpieces are the *Madonna and Saints*, the *Transfiguration*, the *Resurrection*, and the mysterious mythological *Feast of the Gods*.

Vittore Carpaccio (*c.* 1523?) learned from the Bellinis to employ luminous coloring and to portray even angelic beings as undeniably human. A perfect example is his *Angel with Lute*, which also reveals his careful attention to detail.

GIORGIONE

The short-lived Giorgio Barbarelli (1477–1510), known as Giorgione, exemplified the most distinctively Venetian traits in Renaissance painting. In his *Sleeping Venus*, *The Tempest*, and *Fête Champêtre* he placed full-bodied human figures in gorgeous landscapes. He strove for an Arcadian pastoral effect. He so blurred distant objects, while presenting natural objects in the foreground in exquisite detail, that his compositions had a unity and coherent impact unrivaled by those of other artists of the period.

TITIAN

The long-lived Tiziano Vecelli (*c.* 1477–1576), better known as Titian, is known for his voluptuous Venuses and beautiful landscapes. He was a master of perspective, coloration, shading, and composition. He was less concerned with religious, moral, patriotic, or historical messages than in the intrinsic beauty of a painting. His *Danaë* is truly representative of this aspect of his work. In 1516 he succeeded Giovanni Bellini as official state painter. In that role he received assignments to do paintings for the city's churches, such as *The Assumption of the Virgin* in the Franciscan church and the massive *Martyrdom of St. Lawrence*. He was also called upon to paint official portraits, the most celebrated of which is no doubt his Charles V, victorious astride his steed on the field at Mühlberg. For the Vatican he did the famous paintings of Pope Paul III, Cardinal Alessandro, and Duke Ottavio Farnese, thus documenting the history of the period as well as creating things of beauty.

TINTORETTO AND VERONESE

Tintoretto (1518–1594), the "little dyer," and Veronese (1528–1588) carried on the special Venetian characteristics in painting—rich colors, fleshy human bodies, gorgeous landscapes, and worldly emphases—deep into the sixteenth century.

During those decades the transition to mannerism and the baroque was already under way.

Music

IN A STRIKING PASSAGE in his *Book on the Art of Counterpoint* (1477) the Flemish musical theorist Johannes Tinctoris, who spent the greater part of his life at the court of Naples as a singer, composer, teacher, and writer, remarked: "Although it seems beyond belief, there does not exist a single piece of music, not composed within the last forty years, that is regarded by the learned as worth hearing."[5] Tinctoris, then, dated the beginnings of modern music about the year 1435. "The fountain and origin of this new art," Tinctoris explains, "lies with the English, whose leading master was Dunstable. His French contemporaries were Dufay and Binchois, who were immediately succeeded by the moderns." He held that the English had subsequently stagnated, using the same style in composition, whereas the Franco-Netherlandish composers "freshly create new works day by day."

Composers of the Netherlands dominated the scene during the third decade of the fifteenth century and for a hundred years thereafter. The rich Flemish commercial cities such as Antwerp and Cambrai and the Burgundian court could afford the luxury of professional musicians. From 1410 on the cathedral chapter in Antwerp paid skilled singers for their services with incomes from endowed prebends, even though they were not clerics. Most of the composers and performers received their training in choir schools. Famous teachers taught and inspired the rapidly growing number of composers, singers, and instrumentalists.

Although in the Middle Ages a great many musical theorists were mathematicians, and music was often controlled by "Pythagorean" mathematical considerations, most Renaissance theorists were themselves practical musicians, concerned about the pleasing quality of sound. Tinctoris himself referred repeatedly to the aural impact of the music he was discussing: such a procedure "offends the sophisticated ear"; in this procedure "the ear of the listener finds a modicum of sweetness"; "in the judgment of my ears . . . " The effect on the listener is the important criterion for the success of the composition.[6]

Choirs of skilled professional singers were a necessary precondition for the evolution of the new complicated polyphonic music with its counterpoint and harmony. In the classical medieval technique, one voice part was completed before another was added to a composition, which meant that the harmonic result turned out to be haphazard (not to say accidental). In the new Renaissance technique,

---

[5] Johannes Tinctoris, "Liber de arte contrapuncti," trans. Olive Strunk, in *Source Readings in Music History*, ed. William Oliver Strunk (New York, 1950), p. 199.

[6] Edward E. Lowinsky, "Music of the Renaissance as Viewed by Renaissance Musicians," in *The Renaissance Image of Man and the World*, ed. Bernard O'Kelley (Columbus, O., 1966), p. 136.

the composer planned the euphony of the whole piece in advance. For the first time dissonance was deliberately introduced to achieve a special effect. Modern counterpoint is the art of combining two, three, four, five, or more voices in such a way that each individual voice achieves optimum melodic and rhythmic freedom in a carefully regulated texture of harmonic sound. "Modern harmony is the art of concord based on the triad."[7] These conceptions of musical composition and choral performance have been dominant to the present time, just as Renaissance art and architecture established the basic norms down to the twentieth century.

In comparison with the Netherlands, Italy contributed little to musical innovation and enrichment. During the *Quattrocento* there were no Italian composers who compared with the Flemish masters. Musical performance was thought to be essential for a well-rounded man. Alberti was an excellent organist, Cellini performed on the flute for the papal court, and Pietro Bono, a brilliant lutist, was a favorite in several Renaissance courts. Musical performances became important features of gracious living at the refined courts of Mantua, Ferrara, Urbino, and other centers. Singers not only gave recitals to the accompaniment of the lute or some other instrument, but entertained with songs between the scenes or acts of the humanist plays performed at court.

Sunny Italy was given to song: popular love songs, moving religious songs, secular carnival songs, courtly songs. The *frattola,* the characteristic form of Italian Renaissance music, was a poem set to music. These *frottole* were simple songs, compared with the complex polyphony of Flemish compositions. The upper voice carried the melody and the other voices supported it with block chords in four-part harmony. The choral style, familiar from religious music, was carried over into secular songs toward the end of the fifteenth century.

The fifteenth and especially the sixteenth centuries witnessed a musical revolution. Several generations of extremely productive composers brought to society a new world of beauty. The composers seemed to be most attracted to keyboard music, in part because of the demand for organ music in the churches and in part because the range of the keyboard was enlarged at that time to allow fuller scope for music. The printing press had a tremendous impact upon music, for it made possible greater precision in the reproduction of scores and the distribution of thousands of copies.

The Renaissance in the Fine Arts

THE FINE ARTS are most certainly not peripheral to man's existence or merely an ornament to his "real life." They come close to being at the very heart of his hu-

---

[7] *Ibid.,* p. 142.

manity, at the vital center where his religious faith, his appreciation of the world, and his affection for his fellows define him as a man. In our own day Albert Camus expressed something of this feeling when he wrote: "I know with certainty that a man's work is nothing but the long journey to recover, through the detours of art, the two or three simple and great images which first gained access to his heart." The magnificent effort of the Renaissance men of art and letters to define and express their essential humanity was one of the most superb undertakings the world has ever witnessed.

The romanticist Victor Hugo declared the Renaissance "the setting sun all Europe mistook for dawn." He believed that the Renaissance had succeeded so well in establishing classical norms for the arts that the subsequent centuries merely reiterated what they saw there until all became moribund. In architecture there was merely a restatement, by classic column, entablature, and pediment, of the themes of a foreign culture that had died long ago. The truth of the matter, however, is quite different from what Victor Hugo imagined or such modern critics as Frank Lloyd Wright have been willing to acknowledge. For the fine arts during the Renaissance were not merely restatements of what the artists and theorists found in classical models. Their finest achievements expressed creatively the ideal, the highest aspirations, and the aesthetic feelings of their own age.

Their times are not ours, and we must not be guilty of merely imitating even the greatest triumphs of their intellect and skill. Still, we are not so far removed from the Renaissance that we cannot thrill to the beauty its artists created, or contemplate without a twinge of sorrow the inroads of time and trouble on the masterpieces of that great age.

Bibliography

Art, general:

Artz, Frederick B. *From Renaissance to Romanticism: Trends in Style in Art, Literature, and Music.* Chicago, 1962.

Baxandall, M. *Painting and Experience in Fifteenth Century Italy.* Oxford, 1972.

Chambers, D. S. *Patrons and Artists in the Italian Renaissance.* Columbia, SC, 1971.

Cole, Bruce. *The Renaissance Artist at Work.* New York, 1983.

Gombrich, E. H. *The Story of Art.* London, 1956.

Hauser, A. *The Social History of Art,* 4 vols. New York, 1960.

Janson, H. W. *History of Art.* Englewood Cliffs, NJ, 1962.

Lassaigne, J., and G. C. Argan. *The Fifteenth Century, from van Eyck to Botticelli.* New York, 1955.

Mâle, Émile. *Religious Art: From the 12th to the 18th Century.* New York, 1958.

Panofsky, Erwin. *Studies in Iconology.* New York, 1939.

———. *Renaissance and Renaissances in Western Art,* 2 vols. Stockholm, 1960.

Sewall, John Ives. *A History of Western Art,* rev. ed. New York, 1961.

Seznec, Jean. *The Survival of the Pagan Gods: The Mythological Tradition and Its Place in Renaissance Humanism and Art.* Princeton, 1972.

Singleton, Charles E., ed. *Art, Science, and History in the Renaissance.* Baltimore, 1967.

Strong, Roy. *Art and Power: Renaissance Festivals, 1450–1650.* Berkeley and Los Angeles, 1985.

Sypher, Wylie. *Four Stages of Renaissance Style.* Garden City, NY, 1955.
Venturi, L. *The Sixteenth Century, from Leonardo to El Greco.* New York, 1956.
Wölfflin, Heinrich. *Principles of Art History.* London, 1932.

Art in Italy:
Antal, Frederick. *Florentine Painting and Its Social Background.* London, 1948.
Berenson, Bernhard. *The Italian Painters of the Renaissance.* New York, 1952.
Blunt, Anthony. *Artistic Theory in Italy, 1450–1600.* Oxford, 1940.
Chastel, André. *The Age of Humanism: Europe, 1480–1530.* New York, 1964.
———— . *The Flowering of the Italian Renaissance.* New York, 1965.
———— . *Styles and Studies: Italy, 1460–1500.* New York, 1966.
Clark, Kenneth. *Leonardo da Vinci: An Account of His Development as an Artist.* Cambridge, 1939.
———— . *Piero della Francesca.* London, 1950.
Clements, Robert J. *Michelangelo's Theory of Art.* New York, 1962.
Cole, Bruce. *Giotto and Florentine Painting, 1280–1375.* New York, 1976.
———— . *Sienese Painting in the Age of the Renaissance.* Bloomington, IN, 1985.
Dvořák, Max. *Geschichte der italienischen Kunst im Zeitalter der Renaissance,* 2 vols. Munich, 1927–1929.
Forster, Kurt. *Pontormo: Monographie mit kritischem Katalog.* Munich, 1966.
Gadol, Joan Kelly. *Leon Battista Alberti: Universal Man of the Early Renaissance.* Chicago, 1969.
Gombrich, E. H. "The Early Medici as Patrons of Art," in E. F. Jacob, ed., *Italian Renaissance Studies.* London, 1960, pp. 279–311.
Gould, Cecil. *An Introduction to Italian Renaissance Painting.* London, 1957.
Hathaway, B. *The Age of Criticism: The Late Renaissance in Italy.* Ithaca, NY, 1962.
Larner, J. *Culture and Society in Italy 1290–1420.* London, 1971.
MacCurdy, Edward. *The Mind of Leonardo da Vinci.* New York, 1928.
Meiss, Millard. *Painting in Florence and Siena After the Black Death.* Princeton, 1951.
Pope-Hennessey, J. *Italian Renaissance Sculpture.* New York, 1928.
Popham, A. E. *Catalogue of the Drawings of Parmigianino.* London, 1969.
Salinger, Margareta. *Michelangelo: The Last Judgment.* New York, 1963.
Thode, Henry. *Franz von Assisi und die Anfänge der Kunst der Renaissance in Italien,* 2nd ed. Berlin, 1904.
Tietze, Hans. *Tintoretto.* London, 1948.
Tolnay, Charles de. *Michelangelo,* 5 vols. Princeton, 1943–1960.
Vasari, Giorgio. *Lives of the Most Eminent Painters, Sculptors, and Architects,* 6 vols. London, 1878–1885.
Wind, Edgar. *Bellini's Feast of the Gods: A Study in Venetian Humanism.* Cambridge, MA, 1948.
———— . *Pagan Mysteries in the Renaissance.* London, 1958.
Wölfflin, Heinrich. *Classic Art: An Introduction to the Italian Renaissance,* rev. ed. New York, 1952.

Art in Northern Europe:
Benesch, Otto. *The Art of the Renaissance in Northern Europe: Its Relation to the Contemporary Spiritual and Intellectual Movements.* Cambridge, MA, 1945.
Boyd, Catherine E. *The French Renaissance.* Boston, 1940.
Burkhard, Arthur. *Matthias Grünewald: Personality and Accomplishment.* Cambridge, MA, 1936.
Conway, William. *The Woodcutters of the Netherlands in the Fifteenth Century.* Hildesheim, 1961.
Dehio, Georg. *Geschichte der deutschen Kunst,* 4 vols. Berlin, 1923–1934.
Dimier, Louis. *French Painting in the 16th Century.* New York, 1911.
Fraenger, Wilhelm. *The Millennium of Hieronymus Bosch.* Chicago, 1951.
Friedländer, M. J. *Early Netherlandish Painting, from van Eyck to Bruegel.* London, 1956. (All 14 vols., 1962–76.)
Ganz, Paul. *Hans Holbein the Younger.* London, 1950.
Mâle, Émile. *The Gothic Image.* New York, 1958.

Panofsky, Erwin. *Albrecht Dürer,* 2 vols., 3rd ed. Princeton, 1948, 4th ed., 1 vol., 1955.
———. *Early Netherlandish Painting: Its Origins and Character,* 2 vols. Cambridge, MA, 1953.
Pevsner, Nikolaus, and Michael Meier. *Grünewald.* New York, 1958.
Waetzoldt, Wilhelm. *Dürer and His Times.* London, 1950.

Architecture and Urban Planning:
Ackerman, James. *The Architecture of Michelangelo,* 2 vols. London, 1961.
Anderson, William J. *The Architecture of the Renaissance in Italy,* rev. ed. London, 1927.
Blunt, Sir Anthony. *Art and Architecture in France, 1500–1700.* Baltimore, 1953.
Giedion, Siegfried. *Space, Time, and Architecture,* 3rd ed. Cambridge, MA, 1954.
Goldthwaite, Richard. "The Florentine Palace as Domestic Architecture" *American Historical Review,* 77 (1972), 977–1012.
Murray, Peter. *The Architecture of the Italian Renaissance.* New York, 1963.
Pevsner, Nikolaus. *An Outline of European Architecture.* New York, 1948.
Ricci, Corrado. *Architecture and Decorative Sculpture of the High and Late Renaissance in Italy.* New York, 1923.
Scott, Geoffrey. *The Architecture of Humanism,* 2nd rev. ed. London, 1947.
Westfall, Carroll W. *In This Most Perfect Paradise: Alberti, Nicholas V, and the Invention of Conscious Urban Planning in Rome, 1447–55.* University Park, PA, 1973.
Wittkower, Rudolf. *Architectural Principles in the Age of Humanism.* New York, 1965.

Music:
Apel, Willi. *The Notation of Polyphonic Music, 900–1600,* 4th rev. ed. Cambridge, MA, 1949.
Besseler, Heinrich. *Die Musik des Mittelalters und der Renaissance.* Potsdam, 1931.
Bukofzer, Manfred. *Studies in Medieval and Renaissance Music.* New York, 1950.
Einstein, Alfred. *The Italian Madrigal,* 3 vols. Princeton, 1949.
Geiringer, Karl. *Musical Instruments: Their History in Western Culture.* New York, 1946.
Haar, James. *Chanson and Madrigal, 1480–1530.* Cambridge, MA, 1964.
Harman, Alec. *Medieval and Early Renaissance Music.* Fair Lawn, NJ, 1958.
Hughes, A., and G. Abraham, eds. *Ars Nova and the Renaissance,* vol. 3 of *New Oxford History of Music,* ed. J. A. Westrip et al. New York, 1960.
Lang, Paul H. *Music in Western Civilization.* New York, 1941.
Leichtentritt, Hugo. *Music, History, and Ideas.* Cambridge, MA, 1938.
Lowinsky, Edward E. *Tonality and Atonality in Sixteenth-Century Music.* Berkeley, 1961.
Reese, Gustave. *Music in the Renaissance.* New York, 1955.

CHAPTER 9

The Dwarfing
of Italy

Living through Italy's "time of troubles," the Renaissance historian
Francesco Guicciardini confided in his *Ricordi:*

> Three things I would willingly see before I die. And yet, though I were to live to a
> great age, I fear I shall see none of them. I desire to see a well-ordered republic
> established in Florence; Italy free from all her barbarian invaders; and the world
> delivered from the tyranny of these rascally priests [Series I, no. 14].

Writing the history of his own times, Guicciardini had the depressing task of recording the collapse of the Florentine republic, the intervention of the great powers
in Italian affairs, and the disruptive role of a secularized papacy and shocking corruption in the church. The Italian microcosm, which had enjoyed some forty years
of relative peace (1454–1494) and had developed a false sense of its own security,
was suddenly engulfed by the forces of the European macrocosm, the great powers
beyond the mountains and across the sea. The experience of foreign invasion gave
the Italians a traumatic shock from which they did not fully recover until their own
risorgimento in the nineteenth century.

Charles VIII Invades Italy

THE PEACE OF ITALY during the second half of the fifteenth century depended
upon the delicate balance of power among the five major city-states. This precarious

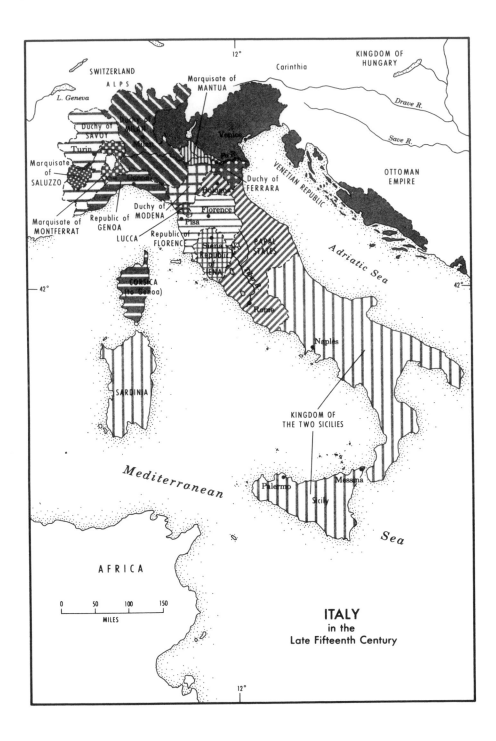

ITALY
in the
Late Fifteenth Century

equilibrium was jeopardized during the final decade of the century by the increasing rivalry and hostility of Naples and Milan. King Ferrante of Naples, a wise and crafty old man, recognized the hazards of an open break, but his son Alfonso pressed for action against Milan. Alfonso's daughter was married to Gian Galeazzo Sforza of Milan, who was suppressed by the regent, Ludovico il Moro. When Ferrante died, on January 25, 1494, Alfonso threw caution to the winds. He lined up Pope Alexander VI and Piero de' Medici of Florence against Ludovico il Moro and prepared to deliver the coup. At this juncture Ludovico called on the French king for aid.

Young King Charles VIII of France was eager for high adventure and fascinated by the grand designs of state. From the last Palaeologue emperor he had received authorization to save the East from the Turks and to free Constantinople. He saw himself as a great crusader and considered Naples a suitable port from which to set sail for the reconquest of Jerusalem. Propaganda tracts were scattered about, depicting him as the liberator of the Holy Land. This was heady stuff for a young man of twenty-four. It blurred his vision so that he did not see how heavy a price he would have to pay for his ambition. To secure his rear and his lines of communication, he had to depart from the wise policy of Louis XI, who had worked to build up a solid territorial state and was more interested in the possession of Artois, Comté, and Roussillon than in claims to far-off lands. Charles was prepared to make concessions to his neighbors in order to free himself for adventure. He pacified Emperor Maximilian in the Treaty of Senlis (May 23, 1493), and was ready to move when Ludovico appealed to him for aid against Alfonso of Naples.

Charles built up an army at Lyon and gathered a large fleet to support the invasion. It was one of the largest French armies ever fielded up to that time. More than half the force was made up of French cavalry, knights who were professional fighting men. The infantry was largely made up of Swiss mercenaries, who had developed a formidable new tactic. They grouped into tight phalanxes with long pikes and advanced against an opposing line with the force of a battering ram. The French army was well equipped with heavy artillery as well. Despite the efforts of the Italian military engineers to strengthen the stone walls and to build up the tops of the parapets so that they slanted more obliquely and thus would deflect cannonballs more effectively, the citadels were increasingly vulnerable to attack by big guns. The Italians were thoroughly cowed, and Charles's march on Naples turned out to be a triumphal procession. Charles, described by a contemporary as "small, with a large head, visibly credulous and without malice," rode through Italy like a conquering hero.

Once the scalpel had cut in, all the rot in the Italian body politic lay exposed. On October 15, 1494, Ludovico il Moro arrived in Pavia to greet his deliverer and cheer him on his way. On October 21 Gian Galeazzo died suddenly—there were whisperings of poison—leaving his uncle Ludovico as uncontested master of Milan.

Venice found it prudent to remain neutral for the time being. Giovanni Bentivoglio of Bologna had warned Ludovico's ambassador against bringing the French into Italy. Now that the Pandora's box had been opened, he vacillated so long that he missed the chance to make any effective resistance against the French. Charles moved south into Tuscany.

Florence was caught in an impossible predicament. It had a long tradition of friendship with France, based in part on commercial ties. These suffered, to be sure, when Charles ruined the Medici agents in Lyon, and Lorenzo de' Medici had based his foreign policy upon an alliance with Naples. Now Piero de' Medici, dull-witted and a wastrel, had to make a critical decision, and he blundered. Initially he decided to honor his obligation to Naples, but as the French army rolled into Tuscany, Piero hurried to prostrate himself before Charles. He surrendered Pisa and the key fortresses to Charles in return for the safety of the city. When he returned to Florence he found it in open rebellion. His enemies barred his entrance, and he fled for his life to Venice, disguised as a liveryman. The republic then sued for peace and allied itself with the conqueror. On November 17, 1494, Charles entered Florence, just one week after Piero's flight. He was received with all respect, for he was the personal fulfillment of the Dominican friar Savonarola's prophecy that a king would be sent by God to give a new birth to Italy. Florence remained a French vassal until 1512, when the French were expelled from Italy.

Charles announced his intention of spending the Christmas of 1494 in Rome. The Romans, who had heard of the brutality of the French soldiery, were terrified. The Colonnas, allies of the French, occupied Ostia and threatened to starve out the city. Pope Alexander VI, who had recognized Alfonso as king of Naples, now attempted to conciliate Charles by sending him Djem, the sultan's brother, as a hostage. On December 25 the king's envoys arrived before Rome and on December 31 Charles himself led his army into the Eternal City, riding at the head of the column with his lance at rest on one side. Taking along Cesare Borgia, the pope's son, to assure the pontiff's continued cooperation, Charles marched toward Naples.

King Alfonso abdicated and left his throne to his popular son, Ferrantino. On February 22, 1495, Charles rode triumphantly into Naples, without having fought a single serious engagement. But his prize quickly slipped through his fingers. The French quickly alienated the people of Naples. The soldiers terrorized the citizenry, and an epidemic of syphilis, known to the Neapolitans as the "French disease" and to the French as the "Neapolitan disease," spread like wildfire. The French monopolized all the best public offices. King Ferdinand of Aragon, a crafty schemer who was also king of Sicily and felt his vital interest in the Mediterranean threatened by the French, organized the League of Venice (March 31, 1495) to resist them. In addition to Ferdinand, the league included Pope Alexander VI, Ludovico il Moro, who now saw the danger of French claims to Milan, Emperor Maximilian, and the republic of Venice itself. That the Spanish king and the emperor were members of the league was an ominous sign for Italian independence. Charles realized that he was overextended, and returned with the main part of his army toward France. On July 6, 1495, he fought a brief and bitter battle at Fornova with the forces of the league under Francesco Gonzaga. Both sides claimed victory, but Charles disengaged his troops and escaped to the north. The Italians had demonstrated their ability to do battle with the French and Swiss. With the aid of Spanish troops, King Ferrantino drove out the garrisons Charles had left behind and took possession of his capital. On April 7, 1498, Charles VIII died. His great adventure had come and gone, but Italy would never be the same again. Henceforth the major states of Europe were to use it as a battleground and claim its treasures as their spoils of war.

Savonarola in Florence

VERY RADICAL CHANGES in Florence resulted from the coming and going of the French. The sophisticated city on the Arno fell under the spell of a charismatic leader, the Dominican friar Girolamo Savonarola (1452–1498). So strange is this phenomenon, and so instructive, that a close look at the man and his role in Florentine life will be rewarding.

This gaunt ascetic leader of men was born in Ferrara into a family of modest means. He was to become a doctor, like his grandfather, in the hope of building up the family's prosperity. But as a youth he showed signs of nonconformity. He was given to walking alone along the banks of the Po River. He read St. Thomas and the Arabic commentators on Aristotle. Although he was brought up in a courtier household and observed at firsthand the grandeur of Borso d'Este's Renaissance court, he held only disdain for the vanities of such a life. His love for a Strozzi daughter was frustrated when her family rejected him because of his lower social status. He prayed each day, "Lord, teach me the way my soul should walk." Then, at twenty-two, he fled to the Dominican monastery in Bologna, where he wrote a treatise *On the Contempt of the World*.

Savonarola made no particular impression on Bologna and Ferrara during his early years as a preacher there. In 1482 he was transferred to San Marco in Florence, a Medici foundation, where a circle of literati who called themselves "Martians" gathered to study the classics. His reaction to Florence was both sweet and sour, for he loved its beauty but was shocked at its worldliness. In 1483 he delivered the Lenten sermons in San Lorenzo, but the multitude went to hear the elegantly rhetorical Fra Mariano da Genazzano in the cathedral. Savonarola now began to have visions of divine wrath and great tribulation soon to overtake the sinful, worldly city.

From 1487 to 1490 he was away from Florence in nearby San Gimignano, where his preaching first began to attract attention. When he was recalled to Florence, his first sermon in San Marco, on August 1, 1490, called for repentance and conversion, and was full of vague apocalyptic prophecies. His reputation grew steadily until he was the most famous preacher in Florence. He criticized tyrants and predicted they would come to a bad end. Lorenzo had no great love for this gadfly, and Piero could not abide his sharp thrusts. Savonarola became a bold advocate of the poor and oppressed. Elected prior of San Marco and invited to preach in the cathedral, the eloquent friar became a greater and greater force in the city. His *Triumph of the Cross* was a rhetorically powerful writing.

In 1494 his Lenten sermons called for the building of another Noah's ark against the floods to come. In one of his visions he saw a hand bearing a flaming sword inscribed with the words "The sword of the Lord over the earth swift and speedy." He saw the coming of Charles VIII as the fulfillment of his prophecies that the Lord would send an avenger. When news reached Florence in September 1494 that the French king had crossed the Alps and had arrived in Genoa, Savonarola resumed preaching a series of sermons on Genesis, choosing as his text Genesis 6:17: "Lo, I shall loose over the earth the waters of the flood." The terrified congregation in the cathedral burst out in sobs and cries of despair. Pico della Mirandola told later how shivers ran up his spine and his hair stood on end, and as an old man Michelangelo said that Savonarola's voice still haunted him. On November 1, with the French army nearing the gates, Savonarola mounted the pulpit and preached to a packed cathedral:

> You know that some years ago, before there was any hint or rumor of these wars which have now come from beyond the mountains, great tribulations were foretold to you. You know, too, that less than two years ago I said to you: *Ecce gladius Domini super terram cito et velociter*. Not I, but God gave you this prediction, and now it has come. It is now approaching.[1]

With Charles VIII's entry into Florence on November 17 it seemed that the flood had come. Twice Savonarola intervened with the king, and though at times it looked as though he might sack the city, Charles marched out of the gates for Naples eleven days later without having done any deliberate damage. Now that Piero and Charles were both gone from Florence, it seemed to Savonarola that divine grace had intervened in favor of the city. He now announced "this good news to the city, that Florence will be more glorious, richer, more powerful than she has ever been." Glorious in the sight of God and man, Florence would have temporal and spiritual power over all of Italy. These cheery prophecies inaugurated the new republic, which Savonarola dominated for several years.

---

1 Roberto Ridolfi, *The Life of Girolamo Savonarola*, tr. Cecil Grayson (New York, 1959), p. 80.

Savonarola urged the adoption of a republican constitution similar to that of Venice. There was to be a grand council with some three thousand members to represent all the people, a third of the membership sitting for six months in turn. This council was empowered to create lesser councils for specific purposes. There was to be an upper council consisting of eighty members, which was to discuss delicate and confidential matters in consultation with the *signoria*. The system worked surprisingly well as long as Savonarola kept his hold on the people. He could sponsor legislation in the interest of moral improvement and convince the populace it was for the common good. In 1496 at carnival time he inspired the great "burning of the vanities," when the people made a great bonfire of their gambling equipment, jewelry, cosmetics, false hair and pads, lewd books, and trinkets. The story that many Renaissance art treasures were lost in an iconoclastic holocaust is pure fabrication. Such events and the unifying effect of the war with Pisa kept the Florentines in line for two or three years, but gradually Savonarola's hold over them weakened.

Savonarola was a severe critic of the secular interests and the gross immorality of the popes. He had even implored Charles VIII as a Christian prince to convene a council to depose the pope. He declared the independence of the Tuscan Dominican houses from the Lombard congregations, in order to purify them while they were free from the control of worldly officials. The infamous Alexander VI was unhappy over Florence's pro-French policy and its persistence in thwarting his expansionist designs northward. The pope forbade the "meddlesome friar" to preach, but Savonarola not only continued his attacks on the papacy, but intensified them. In 1497 papal emissaries excommunicated Savonarola and threatened to place Florence under an interdict if he were permitted to preach again. Although Savonarola denied the validity of the ban, since, he said, it was imposed by a pope who was the representative not of God but of Satan, the people were not convinced. Moreover, the oligarchical clans, who were accustomed to rule the city, were impatient with his theocratic rule.

The end came quickly, once the fickle populace turned against him. A conniving Franciscan challenged Savonarola to an ordeal by fire. Pressed by his fellow Dominicans, who had absolute faith in him, Savonarola accepted the challenge. But when the day of the ordeal arrived and the fires were prepared, the Franciscans managed to delay the proceedings until a rainstorm struck and they were able to hustle their champion away in the general confusion. Savonarola barely made it safely back to San Marco through the hostile crowd, angry and frustrated at missing the show. They were soon to have a bloody spectacle to their taste, for the city government arrested him and condemned him to death. On May 23, 1498, after days of torture, he and two young supporters were publicly hanged. The spot is still marked by a bronze plaque. Their bodies were burned and the ashes tossed into the Arno. It was reported that a member of the *Dieci* said on Savonarola's execution day, "Praise be to God, now we can practice sodomy."[2]

Louis XII Invades Italy

THE ITALIAN QUESTION was becoming increasingly a European question. The major states of the north and west saw their vital interests involved in the political affairs of the peninsula, and they promoted them with the two standard weapons, war and marriage. The Italian princelings in turn found it to their interests to marry their sons and daughters into wealthier and more powerful houses beyond the Alps. A Borgia married the sister of the king of Navarre, a Sforza daughter married Emperor Maximilian, a Medici daughter became the queen of France.

When Louis XII of France invaded Italy, the whole enterprise was different from the adventure of Charles VIII. Precedents had been set and the city-states could calculate their responses in advance in accordance with their particular interests. Moreover, the other major powers, especially Spain, could estimate with fair precision the counterforce necessary to clear the French out again.

Savonarola fell the day after Charles VIII died. The news of the king's death had of course not reached Florence yet, but the coincidence dramatically emphasized the dependence of the friar upon the king, of the Florentines upon the French.

Charles's successor was Louis XII, of the house of Orléans, who reigned from 1498 to 1515. Louis XII had married Jeanne, the daughter of King Louis XI, in order to establish a firm claim to the succession. But now that he was king, it seemed more useful for him to marry the widow of Charles VIII, Anne of Brittany, in order to keep her province securely attached to the French realm. Such a marital maneuver required church sanction, however, and the need for an annulment of the first marriage and dispensation for the second obligated the king to the pope. Alexander VI, seeing an opportunity to aggrandize his own family, sent his son Cesare Borgia to France as his emissary in 1498.

Cesare Borgia gave up his cardinalate in order to build up the papal territories as a frankly secular state. When he sailed for France aboard a French ship, he went as the duke of Valentinois, bringing with him the dispensation sought by Louis XII and a red hat for Georges d'Amboise, an influential churchman-politician. Cesare had marriage plans of his own, for he hoped to wed Carlotta, the daughter of King Federigo of Naples, who was being brought up at the French court. By marrying the princess, Cesare could unite southern and central Italy, a formidable

---

[2] *Ibid.*, p. 288. A fascinating sociopsychological analysis is T. C. Price Zimmermann, "Girolamo Savonarola: A Study in Mazeway Resynthesis," *Soundings*, 1 (1968):45–59.

base for even grander designs. But Carlotta found the idea of marrying the ex-cardinal repugnant. Her father did something most unusual for those days: he honored Carlotta's wishes and refused to force her into the marriage. This bit of paternal sentiment, as it turned out, cost him his kingdom. For, denied Carlotta, Cesare Borgia married Charlotte d'Albret, sister of the king of Navarre, and then joined Louis XII in an invasion of Italy that toppled Federigo from the throne of Naples.

Louis XII was not unmindful of the need to strengthen his central government and to control the feudal lords. But the lure of Italy was strong, and he could not refrain from asserting his dynastic claims to Naples and Milan. At last Ludovico il Moro was to pay the price for his folly in bringing the French into Italy. On the departure of Charles VIII, the Italian courts had returned to business and pleasure as usual. Ludovico was a big spender, for he loved tournaments and carnivals, and kept up a very elaborate and expensive court. Now that he needed financial reserves to hire mercenaries, he was nearly bankrupt.

In September 1499 Ludovico sought refuge in the Habsburg lands of the Tyrol. The following spring, when he thought conditions more favorable, he made his way back to Milan with an army of Swiss mercenaries. The people opened the gates of the city to him and received him with cheers. But the French held the mighty Castello, which a traitor had surrendered to them shortly after Ludovico's first flight. The French built up their forces, and at Novara on April 8, 1500, they captured Ludovico's army, for his Swiss soldiery would not fight against the Swiss mercenaries in the French army. Ludovico's mercenaries turned him over to the French, who shipped him off to France, where he lived out his days in a dungeon.

Louis XII moved on toward Naples. In the secret Treaty of Granada (November 1500) he and Ferdinand of Aragon agreed to partition the kingdom of Naples. Federigo was unaware of this deal until the French invasion was under way. When he realized that the Spaniards were not coming to his aid, he had to agree to an unconditional surrender. Soon the French fell out with the Spaniards and Sicilians over disputed territory. By January I, 1504, the Spaniards had driven them completely out of Neapolitan territory and Naples once again belonged to Aragon.

The French adventure in Italy worked to the immediate advantage of the papacy. Cesare Borgia used Milan as a base from which to conquer the Romagna, using Swiss infantry and French cavalry. In three campaigns he laid low the petty principalities within the papal estates which had dared to maintain or assert their independence. After Alexander VI's death and Cesare's departure from the scene, the French supported Julius II in his conquest of the north, and with their aid he even took Bologna. In 1508 the French, Pope Julius II, Emperor Maximilian, and Ferdinand of Spain formed the League of Cambrai against haughty Venice, and in 1509 defeated her decisively.

Having subdued all the papal states except Ferrara, which was a French protectorate, Julius II found it to his advantage to turn against the French, and in 1510 he helped to organize the Holy League of major powers to expel them from Italy. The Swiss meanwhile had been organized by Cardinal Matthias Schinner for an attack on the French. They came down through the Brenner Pass, put the French to flight, and in 1513 at Novara decisively defeated them. Ludovico's son, Massimiliano Sforza, was made duke of Milan, but the Swiss kept control over the duchy themselves in order to secure their mercantile interests.

After Savonarola's death the Florentine republic fumbled along with its cumbersome governmental machinery. From 1502 on, Piero Soderini served as *gonfaloniere,* which made him a kind of titular head of state, for there was to be no doge or duke. In August 1512 the Spaniards took little Prato, not far from Florence. Soderini was deposed, the republic fell, and the Medicis were restored to power in Florence. There was a brief republican revival from 1527 to 1530, but with Spanish support Duke Cosimo I de' Medici then became ruler of Florence and the call for liberty was silenced until a later century.

Machiavelli

IN THE YEAR of Charles VIII's invasion and Piero de' Medici's flight into exile, Niccolò Machiavelli entered public life. He was born in 1469, the year Lorenzo de' Medici came to power, and he was to die in 1527, the year of the invasion by the troops of Emperor Charles V and the sack of Rome. He lived through the years of Italy's ordeal and the times made a deep impression upon him.

Machiavelli belonged to a Florentine family of poor nobility. His father, Bernardo, was a jurist, who owned some landed property in addition to the modest house that still stands today at 16, via Guicciardini. Niccolò's education included a knowledge of the Latin and Italian classics, although he knew no Greek, and enough grammar and law to make him serviceable to the state. His first position was modest enough; he served as a clerk in the second chancery of the commune under Marcello Virgilio Adriani, who had taught him grammar. When in 1498 Adriani became chancellor of the republic, Machiavelli moved into his post with the title of second chancellor and secretary to the *Dieci.* The *Dieci* had independent power over war and diplomacy, as well as certain internal matters, although it was subordinate to the *signoria.* Machiavelli retained this position until the fall of Piero Soderini and the republic in 1512.

His life was totally absorbed in the affairs of his office, which included a voluminous correspondence, diplomatic missions of varying importance, and the inspection of fortifications and reforming of the militia. His more interesting assignments included a diplomatic mission to France in 1500 to negotiate with Louis XII about the problem of Pisa, for Soderini was determined that Florence should conquer Pisa and Máchiavelli urged on the war until Pisa fell in 1509. From October 1502 to January 1503 he served as an emissary to Cesare Borgia, to observe his conquest and pacification of the Romagna. In 1506 he was with Pope Julius II on his campaign through Perugia into the province of Emilia. In December 1507 he was dispatched to the court of Emperor Maximilian, who was planning an expedition to be crowned in Rome. Machiavelli traveled through Switzerland and the Habsburg Tyrol to Bolzano, and returned to Florence in June 1508.

This diplomatic experience served Machiavelli as a laboratory for political science, where he could observe men and governments in action. He used his journey to France as an opportunity to observe the vigor of the northerners. Although he did not get far into German lands, he made some very shrewd observations on the Germanic peoples. After observing Cesare Borgia in action, he prepared a discourse encouraging Soderini to spend freely in defense of the state, and wrote a book on military affairs. During 1506 and 1507 he organized a new "national militia" for Florence. He divided the country districts into departments, which were to provide levies of foot soldiers for a standing army. He had a low opinion of fortresses and thought artillery relatively ineffective; infantry was the critical force, for only infantry could hold the country surrounding a city, and if the countryside fell, the state could not long survive. When the Spaniards sacked Prato in 1512, however, Machiavelli's national militia proved ineffective against Spain's professional army of mercenaries.

Machiavelli was not an imposing man. He was of medium height, with a small head, a receding hairline, and a slightly aquiline nose. The only portrait of him, by Santi di Tito, probably done from his death mask, shows him with bright dark eyes and a wary, alert look, his thin lips ready to curl back in a sardonic smile. In 1502 he married Marietta Corsini and fathered several children. They were reasonably happy, despite his frequent infidelities. He was not a strong and secure person, and consequently he was given to posturing. In 1521, when he was sent to the monastery of Carpi on a petty mission, he arranged to have armed messengers ride up to the monastery at a gallop and ostentatiously deliver to him "urgent" dispatches that required his immediate attention. The monks were enormously impressed.

When the Medicis returned to power and the republic collapsed, Machiavelli lost his position. Worse, he was unfairly implicated in the anti-Medici conspiracy of Piero Paolo Boscoli in February 1513 and was tortured on the rack and thrown into a dungeon. When Giovanni de' Medici was elected to the papacy, the Medicis released Machiavelli from prison as a gracious gesture. He retired to his small farm near San Casciano, and in a famous letter to a friend he described his life there. In the morning he did menial chores, such as supervising the cutting of wood and dickering for its sale. Then he went to the village inn to gossip and play rustic games with the townsmen. Back home in the evening, however, he took off his muddy shoes and rough clothes, put on silken slippers and fine robes, in which he had once appeared before kings and princes, and turned to reading and writing. He felt more at home communing with the ancient dead, men of quality, than with the contemporaries who were available to him as companions. "I am welcomed kindly," he confided, "and fed on that fare which is mine alone, and for which I was born; where I am not ashamed to address them and to ask the reasons for their actions."

Machiavelli was a real intellectual, reacting creatively to all that he read as well as to all that he experienced and observed. He wrote three books, three plays, a volume of poems, and a short story. His *Mandragola* is a wild, witty, and lascivious farce in which a lusty adventurer, assisted by a cynical companion, a greedy confessor, and the indulgent, worldly-wise mother of a young married woman who has caught his eye, has the girl delivered to him, reluctantly yielding, by her own cuckolded husband. The comedy played to packed houses even in the rival city of Venice. In his serious work on political science and history, he showed respect for Livy and other ancient authors, but he always weighed what they had to say against reality as he had learned to know it. "I do not know," he once wrote to Francesco Vettori, "just what Aristotle says about countries that have been destroyed. What interests me more than theory is what is, what has been, and what may reasonably happen."

"You have always been at odds with the conventional, and an inventor of new and unexpected things," wrote Guicciardini to Machiavelli in 1521. Machiavelli pioneered as a "retrospective sociologist," analyzing statecraft and military power on the basis of historical case studies and his own observations. Rodolfo de Mattei has commented that Machiavelli is still "one of the poles of . . . scientific interest in the field of political thought." In his *Discourses on the First Ten Books of Livy* Machiavelli wrote: "I have decided to enter on a path which has up to now been trodden by no one, and if it brings me labor and difficulty, it may also bring me a reward. . . ." He believed that in statecraft the examples of the ancients were more admired than imitated. If lawyers considered the precedents of Roman law and if doctors could learn from ancient medicine, then men who governed states should learn from the political experience of rulers by reading history and applying its lessons to their own situations. His discourses took the form of commentaries on Livy's history, but in reality they provided the opportunity for Machiavelli to develop his own theories about the genesis and maintenance of states. "Whoever desires to found a state and give it laws must start with assuming that all men are bad and ever ready to display their vicious nature," Machiavelli observed in the *Discourses* (53). "If their evil disposition remains concealed for a time, it must be attributed to some unknown reason."

Machiavelli's most notorious book was *The Prince,* written with great fervor and a strong sense of urgency. His intent was to instruct a prince in ways to maintain the state in desperate times. The prince must be prepared to act amorally, even immorally, to lie, dissemble, and kill in the interest of the higher good, which is the security of the state. The prince must not even trust friends, for enmity is the norm. "It is much safer to be feared than loved," he counseled, "if one of the two has to be wanting." The prince must not trust treaties, for rival princes are held in check only by threat of war. Fortune "will not help those who will not help themselves, nor will the heavens—nor can they—sustain a thing that is determined to destroy itself." Machiavelli has therefore been accused of introducing the doctrine of *raison d'état,* that where the welfare of the state is involved, the end justifies any means. In *The Prince* the rules of power have priority over normal standards of good and evil, which are reduced from absolute to very relative categories. He dedicated the book to Lorenzo de' Medici, duke of Urbino, in an effort to ingratiate himself with the Medicis and enter once again into the service of his beloved Florence.

Judgments on Machiavelli's *Prince* have differed widely. In 1576 the French Huguenot Gentillet published a collection of Machiavelli's maxims which did much to blacken his reputation. On the Elizabethan stage Machiavelli appeared as a furtive, sinister figure. Englishmen, including Francis Bacon, read Machiavelli's own works, of course. The Spanish Jesuits in the sixteenth and seventeenth centuries judged him to be very wicked. The philosopher Spinoza suggested that Machiavelli had written it as a warning, to show how evil a prince can really be. Machiavelli was not blind to personal moral standards, but the situation in Italy appeared so desperate that realism divorced from moral considerations seemed to be called for. He seems less shocking to men who have seen the degradations of the twentieth century than he seemed to men in earlier times, when the restraints theoretically imposed by religion were more seriously considered. Men no doubt will continue to debate the question. Benedetto Croce once observed that "the puzzle of Machiavelli is one that will perhaps never be solved."

Machiavelli's third major work was *The History of Florence,* to which he devoted his declining years. Many habits of thought developed during his long years of work on the *Discourses* carried over to his historical writing. At times the narrative seems essentially a work of analysis and instruction, a pragmatic use of history. He had been commissioned to do the work in 1520, and when he died in 1527 it was still incomplete. But he had dedicated it to Pope Clement VII, and had already received 120 gold ducats as a reward for this gesture of esteem to a Medici. According to his son Piero, his fatal illness was brought on by a medicine he had taken.

Machiavelli's primary concern was for the security of the state. As Leopold von Ranke observed, he wished above all to see Italy freed of barbarian invaders.

Although he was an ardent republican, he saw that under some circumstances participation of the people in the government was less vital than the survival and security of the state itself. Thus the republican Machiavelli could counsel a Medici prince on how to save the state and possibly all Italy. He conceived of *virtù* as the leader's ability to conceive a plan and carry it through: intelligent will in action. He saw religion as a vital force in early Rome, a symbol of order and a support for public morals. The people's willingness to serve the state, in the Roman army and otherwise, made it stable and strong. Machiavelli seemed to feel that there is a limited amount of *virtù* available in any given historical epoch, and that its dispersion leads to decline. Just as Tacitus contrasted the *virtù* of the strong , simple German tribes with the decadence of the imperial Romans, so Machiavelli saw in his own day the *virtù* of the barbarians outside Italy—the Spaniards, French, Germans, and Turks— as overpowering corrupt Italy, now at the bottom of history's great cycle. In these last days, he saw some hope in a prince who might unite all Italy against the foreigners. Even while acknowledging the powerful forces of fate and fortune, Machiavelli remained an activist, believing that by superhuman effort it is possible to build the dams that can keep the river's torrent out of the city. Fortune, he writes in *The Prince,* is "ruler of half our actions, but she allows the other half or thereabouts to be governed by us." It was fitting that such a patriot of the republic should be buried in the Santa Croce, not far from Leonardo Bruni, the great civic humanist. The times in which the two men lived differed more than the two men differed from each other.

Guicciardini

MACHIAVELLI'S LIFE crisscrossed the life of another great Florentine, the statesman-historian Francesco Guicciardini (1483-1540). Pope Clement VII commissioned Machiavelli to inspect the fortifications of Florence in the spring of 1526. That summer he was ordered to attend Guicciardini, the pope's commissioner of war in Lombardy. In August Guicciardini sent him to Cremona to negotiate with Venetian officials. They were together later that year in Bologna. In the spring of 1527 Guicciardini sent him to Città Vecchia, but not long after his return Machiavelli died. The political scientist and the historian had seen together the tragedy of Renaissance Italy and had been involved in some of the same political maneuvering.

The scion of a prosperous and venerable Florentine family, Guicciardini was educated in the civil law in Florence, Ferrara, Padua, and Pisa. His professional life was bound to the service of the Medicis. He began his diplomatic career in 1512, when the *signoria* sent him as its emissary to the court of Ferdinand of Aragon, and he represented the Medicis there for two years. In December 1515 he served as the Florentine envoy to Pope Leo X at Cortona. In 1518 he entered the service of Leo X as papal governor of Modena and Reggio. In 1521 he became governor of Parma. The second Medici pope, Clement VII, made Guicciardini vice-regent of Romagna in 1523. On June 6, 1526, he became lieutenant general of the papal forces.

His military career was not exactly brilliant, for he failed to prevent the sack of Rome in 1527 and was unable to rescue Clement VII from the imperial troops besieging the Castello di Sant' Angelo. That same year he failed to suppress a popular revolt against the Medicis and was expelled with them for trying. Despite this record of failure, the pope continued to rely on him. He sent him to reinstate the Medicis in Florence in 1530, which he did "by cruel but effective means," as he himself wrote in his *Ricordi*. In 1531 Guicciardini became governor of Bologna, and had to suppress a popular revolt there on the death of Clement VII in 1534. He then cast his lot with the Medicis. As a member of the Council of Forty-Eight in Florence he promoted the cause of Cosimo I de' Medici, but once Cosimo was in, the senators, including Guicciardini, were out. Guicciardini retired to his villa to write his *History of Italy*. Three years later, at the age of fifty-eight, he was dead.

In his *Ricordi,* maxims of prudential wisdom which he compiled for future generations of his family, and an eighty-page commentary on Machiavelli's *Discourses,* Guicciardini was candid and articulate, if aphoristic, about his political views. A lifetime spent in the service of the Medicis destroyed whatever republican sentiment he might have had. "To speak of the people," he wrote, "is in truth to speak of a beast; mad, mistaken, perplexed, without taste, discernment, or stability." He cynically counseled princes, "Bind the people to the ruler; employ the younger men in the service of the ruler; let men forget the responsibilities of government and concentrate on their own pleasure and profit; give men who might be troublesome honor and office and ease." Some of his passages make Machiavelli look like a naïve idealist.

His personal failures, or possibly the whole experience of Italy's debasement, developed in Guicciardini a strong pessimistic streak. "It is scarcely possible to find anything that has not somewhere imperfection or blemish," he wrote. "We must therefore be content to take things as they are, and to reckon the least evil as good." Human life as such is short, brutal, and miserable. "When I consider how many accidents and perils of infirmity, of chance, of violence, and in infinite ways, the life of man is subjected to . . ." he wailed, "I marvel all the more to see an old man or a fruitful year." When a disillusioned realist, not to say cynic, turned to write the history of those times, the result is instructive.

Guicciardini's *History of Italy* covered the period from 1492 to 1534. In his *Ricordi* he had declared that a historian should "write in such a way that men born in a distant age should have every event as much before their eyes as those in whose presence it happened; for this is the true object of history." This desire to present each event as it actually happened led him to detailed descriptions of political happenings and diplomatic situations. He wrote virtually nothing on intellectual and cultural history, but excelled at analyzing personal motivations. His assumption that history could serve the pragmatic purpose of instructing future generations rested upon his conviction that human nature remains basically the same. "Past events," he wrote, "throw light on future ones, because the world has always been the same as it is now."

He wrote his contemporary history with a remarkable detachment, almost as though it were a history of another time. The famous French historian Henri Hauser believed that modern historiography begins with Guicciardini's *History of Italy*. But the famous English historian Macaulay related that a Florentine criminal, offered a choice between the galley and Guicciardini's *History*, thankfully chose to read Guicciardini, but when he reached the point in the narrative where Guicciardini rehearses in detail the history of the wars against Pisa, he changed his mind and asked to be sent to the galley instead.

In times such as our own, we can perhaps appreciate better than the Victorians those pessimistic realists Machiavelli and Guicciardini. Looking back on the collapse of Florence and the dwarfing of Italy, Guicciardini lamented:

> All cities, all states, all kingdoms are mortal, since either by nature or by accident everything in this world must at some time come to an end. But the citizen who happens to be living when his country is in its own decline should not so much lament over its unhappy fortunes as over his own. For his country only suffers what it was fated to suffer. His is the infelicity of being born at such a time when his country has to fulfill its doom.

Bibliography

General:
Cavaignac, Eugène. *Politique mondiale, 1492–1757.* Paris, 1934.
Clark, George. *Early Modern Europe: From About 1450 to About 1720.* New York, 1960.
Ercole, F. *Da Carlo VIII a Carlo V: La crisi della libertà italiana.* Florence, 1932.
Grant, A. J. *A History of Europe from 1494 to 1610,* 4th ed. London, 1948.
Laven, Peter. *Renaissance Italy, 1464–1534.* London, 1965.
Pieri, P. *Il Rinascimento e la crisi militare italiana,* 2nd ed. Turin, 1952.
Stephens, J. N. *The Fall of the Florentine Republic, 1512–1530.* Oxford, 1983.

Savonarola:
Bedoyère, Michael de la. *The Meddlesome Friar and the Wayward Pope.* Garden City, NY, 1958.
Naccari, Giuseppe. *Girolamo Savonarola.* Milan, 1955.
Ridolfi, Roberto. *The Life of Girolamo Savonarola.* New York, 1959.
Soranzo, Giovanni. *Il Tempo di Alessandro VI Papa e di Fra Girolamo Savonarola.* Milan, 1960.
Villari, Pasquale. *La Storia di Girolamo Savonarola e de suoi tempi,* 2 vols., 2nd ed. Florence, 1910.
Weinstein, Donald. *Savonarola and Florence: Prophecy and Patriotism in the Renaissance.* Princeton, 1971.

Machiavelli:

Butterfield, Herbert. *The Statecraft of Machiavelli*. London, 1940.

Cassirer, Ernst. *The Myth of the State*. New Haven, 1946.

Chabod, Federico. *Machiavelli and the Renaissance*. London, 1958.

Fleisher, Martin, ed. *Machiavelli and the Nature of Political Thought*. New York, 1972.

Gilbert, Allan H. *Machiavelli's Prince and Its Forerunners*. Durham, NC, 1938.

Gilmore, Myron P., ed. *Studies on Machiavelli*. Florence, 1972.

Hale, John R. *Machiavelli and Renaissance Italy*. New York, 1960.

Hexter, J. H. *The Vision of Politics on the Eve of the Reformation: More, Machiavelli, and Seyssel*. New York, 1973.

Hulliung, Mark. *Citizen Machiavelli*. Princeton, 1984.

Meinecke, Friedrich. *Machiavellism: The Doctrine of Raison d'État and Its Place in Modern History*. New Haven, 1957.

Ridolfi, Roberto. *The Life of Niccolò Machiavelli*. Chicago, 1963.

Villari, Pasquale. *Niccolò Machiavelli and His Times*, 4 vols. London, 1878–1883.

Whitfield, J. H. *Machiavelli*. Oxford, 1947.

Guicciardini:

Gilbert, Felix. *Machiavelli and Guicciardini: Politics and History in Sixteenth-Century Florence*. Princeton, 1965.

Ridolfi, Roberto. *The Life of Francesco Guicciardini*. New York, 1968.

CHAPTER 10

Renaissance
and
Reconnaissance

On the oldest surviving terrestrial globe known, made in Nuremberg in 1492, the geographer Martin Behaim inscribed the words: "Be it known that on this globe here present is laid out the whole world according to its length and breadth in accordance with the art of geometry ... wherefore let none doubt ... that every part may be reached in ships, as is here seen."[1] The discovery of a wider world that dwarfed not only Italy but Europe itself was an achievement of the Renaissance. There was great excitement about the new sea routes to the East and the New World, although more than a century was to pass before the ethnocentric Europeans began to appreciate the full implications of their new global horizons.

West Meets East

THE RELATIVE ISOLATION of Latin Christendom during the high Middle Ages began to break down during the thirteenth and fourteenth centuries as the Europeans

---

[1] Charles Singleton, ed., *Art, Science, and History in the Renaissance* (Baltimore, 1967), p. 187. D. W. Waters' essay "Science and the Techniques of Navigation," pp. 189–237, discusses the importance of portable sundials, mechanical clocks, and other instruments for navigation.

established promising contacts with the Far East. The West reacted with fear to the spread of the great Mongol Empire across Asia and part of Europe. Genghis Khan (1206–1227) seemed irresistible as his barbarous hordes, reportedly clad in skins, rolled across the great land mass of Asia. But the Mongol Empire soon fell apart as the leadership fragmented, and the threat to Europe subsided. In fact, the Mongols soon were thought of as a blessing in disguise, for they had attacked the Moslem caliphate from the rear and relieved pressure on eastern Europe from that source. They proved to be quite open to cultural and even religious influence from the West, and the possibility of trade with China beckoned.

For about a hundred years, from the mid-thirteenth to the mid-fourteenth centuries, the Far East was open to Europeans. In 1245 the council of Lyon and the pope sent a Franciscan friar, John of Plano Carpini, to the khan at his headquarters in Karakorum in what is now Outer Mongolia. In 1253 a Flemish Franciscan friar, William of Rubruck, was sent by King Louis IX of France to the Mongols. The king, St. Louis, was planning a crusade against the Moslems. Recalling the quick conversion of whole Germanic and Baltic tribes in the early Middle Ages, he hoped to win over the Mongols to Christianity in the same way and thus to box in the Moslems by encircling them from behind. William of Rubruck gave a long account of his mission (1253–1258), including his religious discussions with the great khan in Karakorum. He was impressed by the high moral standards of the Chinese. The scholars of that period tried to connect the Chinese with the true faith through their common descent from Noah, and stressed Nestorian Christian influence.

In 1256 two merchants of Venice, Niccolò and Matteo Polo, made a long trip in search of trade, which took them eventually to Peking, which the Tatar khans had made their permanent capital. The great khan, Kublai, was a man of great curiosity and philosophical flexibility, and before the Polo brothers turned toward home he asked them to come again to China and bring some churchmen who could teach him about their religion. In 1271 they returned to China with Niccolò's son Marco, then seventeen years old, and two Dominicans. Marco had an extraordinary talent for close observation, and after a journey he would relate unusual details and matters of special interest to the khan. The appreciative ruler therefore used him often as an emissary and thus afforded him many opportunities to see distant places. When the Polos at last returned again to Venice, they had been away twenty-five years. The account of Marco's travels we owe in part to the Venice-Genoa war, for he was captured by the Genoese in 1298, and while he was in prison in Genoa he had the leisure to write his famous book. Some of the more fantastic tales, and the report on Cipangu (Japan), far out to sea, he related from hearsay. He even included some legends from Greek mythology. But most of what he wrote from his own experience, such as his account of the "black rocks" that the Chinese burned for heat, proved to be quite reliable. His reports of the wealth of the East stirred great interest in Europe, and the geographical information he brought back was incorporated into the Catalan Atlas and was of great use to mariners and other travelers.

The relative reliability of Marco Polo's *Travels* becomes evident when his account is compared with Jehan de Mandeville's widely read *Book of the Wonders of the World*. This book of fantasies was supposedly written by a noble medical professor who was born in England and died in 1371 in Liège. It was a spurious work based on travelers' hearsay accounts, replete with stories of dog-headed islanders and other ancient myths. It appeared in many manuscript editions and was printed in Italian and French around 1480. It did much to popularize the idea that a ship could reach the East by sailing around the world toward the west.

In the early fourteenth century still more churchmen traveled to the Far East. John of Monte Corvino was commissioned in 1315 to establish contact with the Nestorian Christians in Asia. He accommodated himself beautifully to Chinese customs, was well received in Mandarin circles, and became bishop of Peking. Odoric of Pordenone traveled to India as well as to China. In a book about his travels he gave a very superior account of Chinese customs and spiced his story with interesting oddities and marvels. Other missionaries journeyed to the East and wrote accounts of their experiences. Merchants as well as missionaries were keenly interested, and their handbooks, such as that of Pegolotti around 1340, frequently gave quite precise descriptions of the main trade routes to India.

This promising intercourse was cut off by a series of historical developments. The Ilkhans of Persia were converted to Islam and thereby acquired a rationale for attacking Christendom. Farther east, the Ming dynasty overthrew the Mongol dynasty in 1368. Hostile to foreigners, they shut off the cultural communication and trade routes to Peking. Most ominous of all was the emergence of the Ottoman Turks, who posed a threat not only to the routes to the East, but to Europe itself.

The Osmanli or Ottoman Turks occupied a small state wedged between the Mongols and the Seljuk Turks. In the mid-fourteenth century they emerged as a major military power. Responding to Mongol pressure, they built a major base of power in Asia Minor and then proceeded to conquer the Balkans. In 1356 the Osmanli emirate set up a capital at Adrianople and pressed on through Macedonia to the west and through Bulgaria to the north. In the decisive battle of Nicopolis in 1396, the Turks defeated the Christian army. Only the city of Constantinople and a bit of territory around it still held out. The Turks suffered only one major setback, when around 1400 the terrible Tamerlaine, a Persian Mongol, attacked them from behind and slowed down their westward movement. By 1430, however, they pressed on into Greece, moved up the Adriatic coast, and threatened to take the whole Danube valley. Even Italy felt exposed and vulnerable. It was then that the Council of Florence, in 1439, declared the reunion of the Eastern and Western churches.

In 1453, after a terrible siege, Mohammed II rode into Constantinople on his white horse through a breach in the city walls pounded out by artillery. He is said to have ridden into Justinian's thousand-year-old cathedral, the Hagia Sophia, on his horse and commanded that it be whitewashed and converted into a mosque. The Turks still show a handprint on a stone pillar where Mohammed is said to have leaned against it. During his long reign (1451–1481) the Turks moved into Serbia (1459), Bosnia (1463–1464), and Morea (1458–1460), and seized the Genoese colonies on the Black Sea and the Venetian strongholds in the Aegean.

After a long war (1463–1479) with the Venetians, the Turks took Negroponte and other Venetian trade and naval centers in the eastern Mediterranean. Sultan Bayazid II (1481–1512) resumed the war with Venice in 1499 and continued it for four more years. The Ottomans had a well-developed bureaucracy and trained special shock troops for their armies, the dreaded janissaries, made up of captured Christian children indoctrinated as fanatical Moslems. Under Selim I (1512–1520) the Turks were temporarily diverted eastward. Selim fought and defeated the Moslem shah of Persia in 1514 and fought the Mamelukes in 1516–1517, conquering Syria and Egypt. Under Suleiman the Magnificent (1520–1566) they pressed up the Danube to the gates of Vienna and all the way across North Africa to the Atlantic Ocean. It is to be noted, however, that they did not cut across all the trade routes to the Far East until long after the Portuguese had begun their search for new ways to reach India.

Ancient Cosmology

CERTAIN COSMOLOGICAL SUPPOSITIONS and technical advances were essential preconditions to oceanic reconnaissance. Much of the information as well as fortunate misinformation available to explorers in the fifteenth century was inherited from classical antiquity. Questions about the shape of the cosmos, the distance around the globe, astronomical determination of position, and the like were crucial to mariners who ventured far from land or established sea lanes. The Arabs had stayed close to shore and within the Mediterranean, or had sailed in a straight line across the Indian Ocean with the prevailing winds and back again when the winds reversed. The Europeans who braved the Atlantic confronted a whole new set of navigational problems, and on their solution depended the success of the age of exploration.

The ancient Greeks had already speculated about the shape and size of the earth. In earlier centuries they thought of the earth as a round disk tilted to the south and floating upon an immense cosmic sea. This conception was not unlike the Hebrew notion of the "four corners" of the earth; only the shape differed. The

Pythagoreans in southern Italy seem to have first suggested that the earth was a sphere. Aristotle, like Plato, believed the cosmos to be spherical, but he envisioned the solid land mass as extending a relatively short distance from the north to the uninhabitable tropics, and stretching out very far from east to west. Again like Plato, he believed that there were islands in the antipodes. The astronomer-geographers Eratosthenes, Strabo, and Ptolemy held the earth to be a sphere.

All through the Middle Ages scholars with a minimum of learning held the earth to be round like a ball. In the works of St. Augustine and that great compiler and transmitter of Latin lore Isidore of Seville (d. 636) they could read about the round earth. In a widely used schoolbook Martianus Capella had taught that the earth is round. The Venerable Bede, in his treatise *On the Nature of Things,* spoke of the world as round. John Holywood (Sacrobosco) of Halifax, a mathematician and astronomer who taught in Paris in the thirteenth century, wrote immensely popular elementary treatises in which he declared the earth to be round. When a ship approaches land, he pointed out, a man on shore sees the top of the mast first; therefore the earth's surface must be curved. In the *Divine Comedy* Dante spoke of the earth as a sphere. By the fifteenth century the idea was taken for granted.

The ancient world drew the very logical conclusion that it was possible to reach eastern Asia by going westward. The Stoic philosopher Seneca wrote: "How far is it from the farthermost coast of Spain to that of India? With a good sailing wind only a few days' sea journey." The Hellenic scientists had made some very close estimates as to the size of the earth. Eratosthenes (275–195 B.C.) calculated the circumference of the earth at 250,000 stades, which was nearly accurate.

Living in Alexandria during the second century A.D., the Hellenized Egyptian Ptolemy summarized a great store of Greek learning in his two major works, the *Astronomy* or *Almagest,* which in Arabic means "the greatest," and the *Geography.* The *Almagest* was available from 1175 on in the Latin translation by Gerard of Cremona, working in Toledo. Ptolemy went beyond Aristotle's simple picture of the planets moving in concentric paths about the earth and introduced the more complex theory of spheres and epicycles in planetary motion which was widely held until the time of Copernicus.

Ptolemy's *Geography* was also a great compilation of Hellenic learning. It served as a major source for the Arabic scholar Edrisi, who spent fifteen years making a map of the world in the mid-twelfth century and wrote a text to accompany it, the *Book of Roger,* so named because he produced it while he was in residence at the court of Roger II of Sicily. But Ptolemy's work had its major impact through a translation made around 1406 by a pupil of Manuel Chrysoloras, Jacobus Angelus. Ptolemy divided the earth into 360 degrees of latitude and longitude, and from his calculation of the length of the equator he arrived at a figure for the length of a meridian. He explained how to construct a grid of parallels and meridians for maps drawn on a conical projection, and offered a method of adjusting the length of a degree of longitude for any given latitude.[2] The problem of projection in cartography was not really solved, of course, until Mercator produced his world chart in 1569. In the second part of his *Geography* Ptolemy offered a small atlas of regional maps and a map of the world. His work contained major errors that were uncritically accepted down to the fifteenth century. He attached southern Africa to Asia, making the Indian Ocean an inland sea. His estimate of the distance around the world was one-fourth too small. He extended the land mass of Asia too far to the east, making the westward route from Europe to Asia much shorter than it really is. But it was these very errors that encouraged the Renaissance explorers in their bold attempts to round Africa and to sail westward to Asia.

The leading theoretical geographer of the fifteenth century was the famous conciliarist Pierre d'Ailly. His *Imago mundi* (*c.* 1410) was an immense storehouse of knowledge in which he brought together biblical, classical, and Arabic cosmological lore. He followed Roger Bacon's *Opus majus* (1264) in holding that both Africa and Asia extended southward across the equator and that the tropics were habitable, an opinion held in antiquity by both Polybius and Ptolemy. He also held the common error that Asia extended much farther to the east than in fact it does. The geography and cosmography of the fifteenth-century Europeans left much to be desired and were in many respects inferior to the knowledge of some of the best scientists and navigators in antiquity.

New Technology

As LONG AS the ancient mariners stayed inside the Mediterranean Sea or hugged the coastline when passing through the Strait of Gibraltar to reach England and Flanders, navigational problems were relatively simple. In the Mediterranean they seldom sailed more than twenty-four hours without sight of land. They estimated their distances by dead reckoning, their speed by watching a floating chip pass by, and their location by familiar landmarks, which were shown on the increasingly accurate regional sea maps, the *portolani*. Sailing out onto the ocean, however, required astronomical navigation and instruments of relative precision.

In antiquity the astronomers of Alexandria worked out a catalog of the stars which gave their positions within the twelve signs of the zodiac throughout the year. The astronomer Hipparchus constructed an astrolabe that enabled a navigator to measure the height of a star and thus to arrive at the latitude. The astrolabe was the first instrument available for sidereal navigation.

---

[2] J. H. Parry, *The Age of Reconnaissance* (Cleveland, 1963), p. 11.

The Arabs transmitted Greek astronomy, as well as Persian and Indian lore, and handed on the knowledge of the astrolabe and charts of the stars. Massala in the eighth century and Aben Assafar in the eleventh century described the construction of the astrolabe and its use. Their treatises were translated into Latin and incorporated into Christian manuals. The astronomer Azarquiel (d. 1100), who worked in Toledo and Córdoba, worked out detailed tables of the positions of the stars which were still used by Portuguese and Spanish navigators in later centuries. King Alfonso X commissioned a group of court astronomers to prepare an almanac of the heavenly bodies (1248–1252). The Spanish Jew Zacuto of Salamanca prepared an *Almanac perpetuum* published in 1496. In 1475 in Nuremberg the mathematician-astronomer Regiomontanus published the *Ephemerides,* tables showing the daily positions of the heavenly bodies in relation to the celestial equator. His work was widely known in Spain and Portugal.[3]

The mechanics and craftsmen of the late medieval period were tremendously ingenious and inventive. They greatly improved upon the precision of the astrolabe and developed the quadrant, a simple instrument for measuring the altitude of the heavenly bodies, which in modern times was replaced by the sextant. It consisted of a graduated arc of 90 degrees, or of 45 degrees graduated to measure 90 degrees, with a movable radius carrying sights. The use of mechanical clocks became widespread during the fourteenth century. They were used on shore for recording tidal bearings, and at sea for checking the bearing of the sun. Another instrument developed during this period was the nocturnal, for telling the time at night. It consisted of movable circles, the larger having a handle, the lesser rotating around a hollow tube with a radial arm. On the larger the months and days of the year were engraved and on the smaller the hours, so that the navigator could tell the time by the positions of the pointer stars of the Little Bear or the Great Bear relative to the polestar.[4]

No doubt the most important nautical instrument was the compass. It was discovered in China, perhaps as early as the tenth century, although the first description of it dates from 1080. By the end of the eleventh century it was in use for navigation. The earliest European reference to it was made by Alexander Neckam in 1190. In the thirteenth century the magnetic sea compass evolved from a simple iron needle and lodestone indicator into an efficient, self-registering instrument. During the Renaissance the Mediterranean eight-rayed compass card, based upon the names of the eight prevalent Mediterranean winds, was replaced by the northern system of dividing the card into thirty-two points based upon the four cardinal points, north, east, south, and west.[5]

---

[3] Richard Konetzke, "Überseeische Entdeckungen und Eroberungen," *Propyläen-Weltgeschichte* (Berlin, 1964), vol. 6, p. 547.

[4] Waters, "Science and the Techniques of Navigation," p. 194.

[5] *Ibid.,* p. 195.

The Portuguese pilots, who first used sidereal navigation around 1480, measured their location against the position of the polestar. This was not only awkward, but actually impossible if the ship was moving south toward the equator, leaving the polestar behind over the northern horizon. They switched later to determining their position in relation to the place of the sun at high noon. Astronomical navigation was not adopted in the Mediterranean until the sixteenth century. Such were the technical demands of the new improved navigation that in 1508 King Ferdinand established the office of *piloto mayor* in the *Casa de la Contratación* of Seville. No pilot could steer a ship across the Atlantic unless he had first passed an examination given by the *piloto mayor*. The first man named to this important office was the Florentine navigator Amerigo Vespucci.

As important as the instruments and the navigators who used them were the ships in which they sailed. The ships with which the Europeans braved the seas at the beginning of the fifteenth century were inferior in structure and design to those in use in east Asia. But by the end of the sixteenth century the Europeans had the fastest, sturdiest, most maneuverable ships in the world. They borrowed ideas, but contributed important improvements of their own. Living on a peninsular continent surrounded by the ocean and several seas, they took readily to a seafaring way of life.

At the end of the fourteenth century and the beginning of the fifteenth an improved ship design was introduced by the Portuguese and Castilians, the caravel, familiar to every schoolboy, for this was the type of ship used by Columbus. The lateen caravel was a small, fast sailing vessel with a high, narrow poop and three-cornered sails. Borrowing freely from Arab designs, the Iberian shipbuilders continually improved the caravel and adapted it for ocean voyages. A caravel weighed fifty to a hundred tons. The number of masts was increased from two to three in order to enlarge the sail area. On some the middlemast was equipped with a square sail, while the masts fore and aft were rigged with three-cornered lateen (Latin) sails. The caravel did not have a raised forecastle; that space was used for ropes and gear. Most caravels had full decks, where the crew slept, except when storms drove them below. Tar, foul bilge water, unwashed bodies, cockroaches, and rats must have made the stench below overpowering. The crew ate ship's biscuits, salt pork and beef, chickpeas and beans, and after the water stored in the casks was no longer potable they drank wine.

The crew worked a two-watch system, with the pilot (navigator) and sailing master alternately in charge. Light artillery was mounted on the bows and on the poop. Sometimes guns were lined up along the waist to fire over the gunwales. In the late fifteenth century embrasures were cut into the gunwales, like slits in the parapet of a castle, through which the guns could be fired. During the sixteenth century, with the development of heavier naval artillery, the guns were given permanent mounts between the decks and portholes through which they could shoot.[6] The object of naval warfare came to be sinking the enemy's ship, not killing his men, apparently a Portuguese innovation first used against the Arab fleet in the Indian Ocean. The caravels used in exploration were not, then, the discarded tubs legend would have them, but the best designed ships the technology of the time could provide.

Societal Forces Toward Expansion

INDIVIDUAL MEN in sturdy ships explored, discovered, colonized, but their actions expressed the drives of their whole society. The development of a capitalistic society and strong central governments was a necessary precondition of Europe's outward thrust. Chinese junks were strong, seaworthy ships. Between 1405 and 1433 the Ming emperors sent seven expeditions westward down the east coast of Africa, but after assembling animals, black men, and other curiosities, the fleets returned to China without rounding the southern tip of the continent or otherwise following up on this promising beginning. The aggressive, competitive, acquisitive nature of Western society gave impetus to the drive for overseas expansion.

GOLD

Travelers' accounts of the fabulous wealth of the Indies and Cathay stirred the imagination of the Westerners. The 25 percent customs duties charged by the Mamelukes and the threat to trade routes posed by the Turks drove them to seek new routes to the Far East. Since the goods that the Europeans had to trade hardly compared with the value of the spices, silks, and other luxuries of the East, they were obliged to pay large amounts in gold and silver to acquire them. The need for precious metals led to intensified mining at home and the search for bonanzas abroad.

The arrival of Sudanese gold during the thirteenth century had aroused curiosity about the treasures of Africa. But the interest it stirred was mild compared with the gold fever that struck in the fifteenth and sixteenth centuries. During the reign of King Manuel I of Portugal (1495–1521) twelve ships were said to have arrived in Lisbon from Guinea laden with gold. The reports of gold attracted Flemish adventurers to the African coast and Italian and German bankers to Iberia. In 1459 the cortes in Lisbon indulged in a bit of xenophobia, urging Alfonso V to expel the Florentine bankers and other foreign parasites. But the monarchs usually brushed such nativism aside and protected and used the foreigners to their own advantage.

---

[6] J. H. Parry, *Europe and the Wider World, 1415–1715* (London, 1949), pp. 21–28.

SLAVES

Africa promised black gold as well—the lucrative slave trade. After the fall of Constantinople, the price of Eastern white and yellow slaves rose, and traders turned to Africa and its blacks. The Arabs had been trading in black slaves for some time, and now the Portuguese began shipping blacks to the European slave markets. It has been estimated that one to two thousand black slaves, bought from black slave dealers, were shipped out of Rio de Oro and Guinea between 1441 and 1448. During the next few years Portuguese slave traders shipped some 3,500 human beings as slaves from Senegal and Sierra Leone. From 1450 to 1505 a total of some 140,000 slaves was shipped out of Guinea alone.

Around 1460 a trader could get twenty-five or thirty slaves for a good Moroccan horse in Rio de Oro, although in Senegal he could get only ten or twelve. On the Gold Coast the tsetse fly made horses useless, so slaves were exchanged for woolen cloth instead. They were at first sold in Portugal, Spain, and Italy, but soon a new market opened up in the Spanish colonies across the Atlantic. In 1496 Ferdinand and Isabella forbade the sale of Indians and in 1500 forbade their importation to Spain. The truth was that Indians made poor slaves. In the hot lowlands of Spanish America they sickened and died in vast numbers under the harsh conditions of slavery, and in the cooler uplands, which in any case were less suited to slave labor, they disappeared into the mountains, where it was all but impossible to find and control them. And so Africans were shipped to the New World to work the new plantations.

COLONIZATION

The drive to colonize set in early, for large landowners, frustrated in attempts to expand in Europe, sought to aggrandize themselves abroad. In 1270 the Genoese Lancelot Malocello rediscovered the Canary Islands, which had been known to antiquity. In 1402 the Norman nobleman Jean de Béthancourt conquered three of the Canary Islands, built a church and a fortress, and placed himself under the protection of the Castilian throne. Three years later he brought 160 French colonists to settle his holdings and turn them into landed estates. Through the centuries that followed the European monarchs rewarded national heroes and court favorites with patents to landed estates in newly discovered lands, and poor townsmen and villagers flocked to seek their fortunes in the New World.

MISSIONS

In most men motives are curiously mixed. In the age of European expansion the missionary zeal of the high-minded, self-sacrificing mendicants was shared at least in some small part by the grossest and most secular materialists. It is a commonplace in histories of early modern Europe to describe the overseas expansion of Spain and Portugal as a natural extension of the Catholic crusade for the reconquest of Granada and the suppression of the Moors. But the reconquest of Portugal was completed by 1250, and a mission motive is more in evidence than a hateful crusading spirit as the Spaniards explored lands free of their old Islamic foes. The mendicant orders participated in the explorations and settlements from the very beginning. Their role can be seen as an extension of the thirteenth- and fourteenth-century missions to Asia. The spirit of St. Francis quickened the devotion of many devout Latin explorers as they literally went "into all the world."

The power of myth came into play in quickening the religious zeal of Catholics. The legend of Prester John stirred the imaginations of dreamers and offered hope to adventurers of receiving a friendly reception in some fabulously wealthy Christian kingdom in Africa or Asia. The belief that St. John, the "beloved disciple" of Christ, had not died, but had lived on in some lost corner of the world, presiding over a Christian realm, rested upon a popular interpretation of John 21:21–22:

> Peter seeing him [John] saith to Jesus, "Lord, and what shall this man do?"
> Jesus saith unto him, "If I will that he tarry till I come, what is that to thee? Follow thou me."

The story of Prester John's kingdom appeared in the chronicle of Otto of Freising and was very much alive in the fifteenth century. According to an early version, Prester John was the Christian emperor of Ethiopia. The emperor was invited to attend the Council of Florence in 1439 and his emissaries actually did arrive, though two years too late. Another account held that Prester John was king of a sub-Saharan realm, possibly in the Congo. Yet another variant was that he reigned as a potentate of a (Nestorian?) Christian state in India. In minds made feverish by Franciscan mysticism, the legend of Prester John found a ready reception.

MONARCHY

One very essential precondition of the age of European expansion was the development of powerful centralized monarchies. The transformed states of Portugal, Spain, France, and England took the lead in building empires overseas. The Italian city-states contributed skilled navigators, ancient learning, maps, instruments, and capital, but they did not play major roles in the unfolding drama. The Holy Roman Empire lost prestige and power relative to the rising Atlantic states. Its bankers provided capital for financing expeditions and its cities supplied learned geographers and astronomers, but it played no other part in the outreach to India or the discovery of America. The importance to exploration of the new monarchies is brought home forcefully by the work of Prince Henry the Navigator.

Henry the Navigator and Portuguese Voyages

THE PORTUGUESE completed the reconquest of their lands from the Moors more than two centuries before the Spaniards cleared their territories. But they had internal problems and trouble with their Spanish neighbors, so that they did not embark upon overseas adventures so promptly as they might have. In 1411 Portugal ended a twenty-year war with Castile and was thus at last freed for action. But the moving force and guiding spirit for its entrance upon the world scene was its young prince Henry, known as "the Navigator." An ascetic, scholarly youth, Henry (1394–1460) spent long hours in his secluded study and in his chapel. He was impelled by a great curiosity about this marvelous world and felt a missionary urge to Christianize it. Gomes Eanes de Zurara relates in his chronicle that Henry desired "to spread the holy faith of our Lord Jesus Christ and to lead all souls to it, who wish to be saved." Henry became the grand master of the Crusading Order of Christ.

Henry was a peculiar mixture of knight in shining armor and stay-at-home mission organizer. In 1415 he took part in King John I's capture of Ceuta, a Moorish stronghold across the Strait of Gibraltar. At twenty-one he was knighted on the battlefield. Ceuta was an important trade center for the Mauritanians, a marketplace for the sale of the wares of Africa and India. The city had palaces and other beautiful public buildings, and was said to have even more bazaars and warehouses than Venice. After plundering the city and slaughtering many of its inhabitants, the Portuguese made it the first overseas outpost of their mercantile empire. The use of Ceuta established the Portuguese pattern: a trade center would be captured, then held as a key to the mercantile nexus it served.

From the Arab traders Prince Henry learned of the precious metals and other treasures brought by caravans from the heart of Africa. It is doubtful that he thought primarily, if at all, of finding a new route to India as he sponsored the nearly annual expeditions down the west coast of Africa after 1415. At Sagres, east of Cape St. Vincent on the southwest coast of Portugal, Prince Henry assembled the best cartographers, geographers, and experienced seamen he could find and founded a school for navigators, from which the African explorations were directed. In 1434 one of his men, Gil Eannes, sailed around Cape Bojador. By 1445 his ships had discovered and colonized Madeira and the Azores, rounded Cape Verde, and pressed far down the coast of Africa. By 1471 the Portuguese caravels reached upper Guinea and began a profitable trade in gold, slaves, ivory, and precious woods. In 1483 they reached the Congo and Diago Cão set up a supply and trading post at the mouth of the river.

As the Portuguese voyaged farther and farther down the African coast, the problems of supply grew acute. When Bartolomeu Dias set out from Lisbon on his great expedition in 1487, he took along a storeship to supply his two caravels. About Christmastime he transferred supplies to the caravels and left the storeship and a few men behind in Walvis Bay. The caravels then sailed south, out of sight of land, until they reached 40 degrees south latitude, well beyond the southernmost point of Africa, where they picked up the prevailing westerly winds. Sailing then north and east in search of land, they struck the southern coast on February 3, 1488, having rounded the tip of Africa. They continued eastward until the northward trend of the coast was unmistakable, and warm-water currents indicated that the way to India lay open. But the crew and officers alike were weary of travel now and insisted on turning back. It was on the return voyage that they first sighted the cape that Dias named the Cape of Storms, which King John II later renamed the Cape of Good Hope. Farther north Dias picked up his storeship, with only three men on board still alive. The three ships arrived back in Lisbon in December 1488. Because of the reports of Columbus' success, the death of King John II in 1495, and Dias' discouraging reports of the contrary winds east of Africa, the rounding of the cape was followed up only a decade later when Vasco da Gama undertook his long voyage to India.

In *The Wealth of Nations* (1776) the political economist Adam Smith pronounced the discovery of America and the journey to India around the Cape of Good Hope the two most important developments of which human history had to tell. Vasco da Gama set sail in 1497. He was a diplomat-soldier rather than a professional navigator. His fleet of square-rigged ships, equipped with twenty cannon, was outfitted under the supervision of Dias, who accompanied him part of the way in a caravel. He set sail southwest from the Cape Verde Islands, crossed the equator, and then picked up the westerly trade winds, which carried him east again. After thirteen weeks at sea out of sight of land, he reached the coast of Africa about a hundred miles north of the Cape of Good Hope. He ran into the same trouble as Dias with storms at the cape, and then worked his way up the eastern coast. Owing to Arab influence, he was received in an unfriendly and even hostile manner in most ports. But at Malindi he was fortunate in gaining the services as pilot of Ahmed ibn Majid, a skillful navigator, who knew the Indian Ocean well. On May 20, 1498, the fleet anchored off Calicut on the Malabar coast—India at last!

Vasco da Gama began immediately to negotiate with the local ruler for permission to trade, which was vigorously opposed by the Arab merchants. But in spite of their hostility, and the fact that the cloth and hardware he had brought along to trade were of little interest to the Indians, he did manage to get together a cargo of pepper and cinnamon, with which he sailed for home. The entire voyage took two years and cost the lives of half his men, but the returns on the spices he brought back and the appreciation of King Manuel richly rewarded Vasco da Gama for his efforts.

Determined to follow up on this sensational success, King Manuel the Fortunate sent out a merchant-war fleet of thirteen ships under Pedro Álvarez Cabral in 1500. Bartolomeu Dias was a member of the expedition. They sailed to the southwest on the now proven theory that they needed to catch the westerlies south of the equator to round Africa. But they crossed the equator too far west of the Cape Verde meridian and ended up in Brazil, which Cabral claimed for his king. Caught in storms, Dias and the captains of three other ships were lost at sea. Cabral eventually rounded the Cape of Good Hope and reached Calicut, India, where his reception was anything but friendly. The Arab merchants stirred up a murderous mob against him, and forty of his men were killed. But at Cochin and Cannamore he was able to trade. When he returned to Lisbon, despite the loss of five ships, he made a 100 percent profit on the voyage.

In 1505 King Manuel appointed Francisco Almeida as first viceroy of East India. An ominous combination of foes was beginning to coalesce: the Arab traders, who feared the competition of the Portuguese; the Mamelukes of Egypt, who felt the loss of custom revenues on goods transported through Suez and Alexandria; and the merchants of Venice, who saw the lucrative eastern trade slipping through their fingers. Venetian spies in Lisbon sent word east so that Arab pirates could be ready to intercept Portuguese ships as they entered the Indian Ocean. In 1509 Almeida fought a naval battle with a large Arab fleet off Diu in the Mohammedan sultanate of Gudjarat. Portuguese gunners concentrated on sinking the Arab ships rather than on trying to grapple and board them or shoot down their men. The Arab ships lacked maneuverability and the Portuguese victory was decisive. Almeida and the able Alfonso d'Albuquerque, who succeeded him as viceroy, established the Portuguese empire in India and eastward.

Columbus and the Spanish Voyages

A WEATHER-BEATEN MARINER stood among the crowd watching the return of Dias to Lisbon in 1488. He was a widely traveled Genoese sailor named Christopher Columbus, who was already dreaming of surpassing Dias' feat. If he was not the first European to see the New World, his was the discovery that had the greatest consequences.

There are many theories about pre-Columbian explorations of the New World. There is a Chinese tale of a trans-Pacific expedition in the fifth century and there are advocates of Phoenician and African claims. But European claims have been

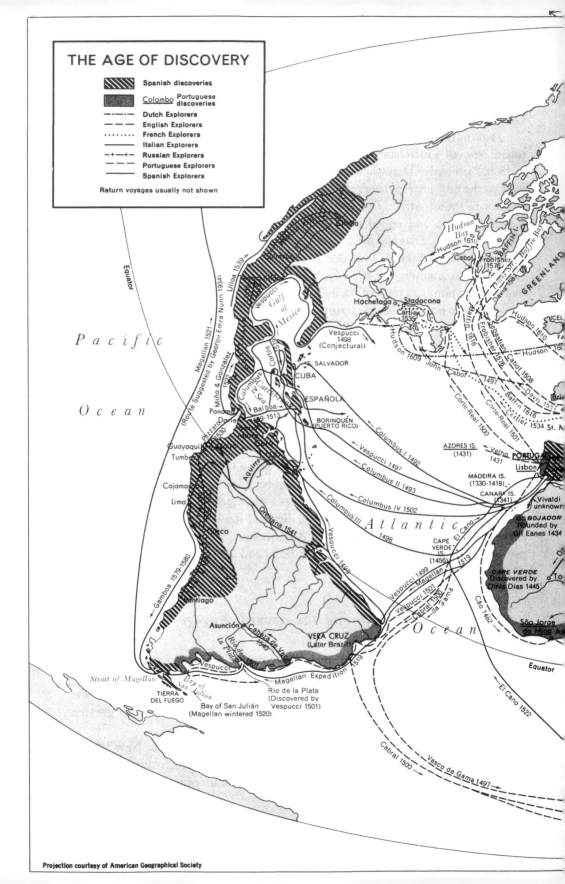

THE AGE OF DISCOVERY

Spanish discoveries

<u>Colombo</u> Portuguese discoveries

Dutch Explorers
English Explorers
French Explorers
Italian Explorers
Russian Explorers
Portuguese Explorers
Spanish Explorers

Return voyages usually not shown

Equator

Pacific

Ocean

Hudson
Bay
Hudson 1610

Cabot Frobisher
1576

GREENLAND

BAFFIN I.

Baffin 1616

Davis 1587

ICEL.

FA.

Hochelaga Stadacona
Cartier
1535

Hudson 1610

Vespucci
1498
(Conjectural)

Hudson 1609
Cabot 1508
John Cabot 1497
Davis 1527
Bri.

Sebastian Cabot 1508

Corte-Real 1500
Corte-Real 1501
Cartier 1534 St. M.

Gulf
of
Mexico

Vespucci

S. SALVADOR

CUBA

ESPAÑOLA

Columbus
Carib. IV Sea
Panama Balboa
Darien 1509-1513

BORINQUÉN
(PUERTO RICO)

Columbus I 1492

AZORES IS.
(1431)

Velho
1431

PORTUGAL
Lisbon

Vespucci 1497

Columbus II 1493

MADEIRA IS.
(1330-1418)

CANARY IS.
(1341)

Vivaldi
unknown

Columbus IV 1502

Columbus III
1498

Atlantic

BOJADOR
Rounded by
Gil Eanes 1434

Guayaquil
Tumbe

Pizarro 1530

Miño & Gonzalez
1522

(Route Suggested by George Emra Nunn 1934)

Magellan 1521

Ulloa 1539

Cortés

Cajama

Lima

Cuzco

Aguirre

Orellana 1541

Vespucci 1499

CAPE
VERDE
IS.
(1456)

El Cano

1519

CAPE VERDE
Discovered by
Dinis Dias 1445

Cão 1462

São Jorge
da Mina

Gamboa 1579-1580

Santiago

Vespucci 1499

Vespucci 1501

Magellan

Cabral 1500
da Gama

Ocean

Equator

Asunción Cabeza de Vaca
1540

La Plata

VERA CRUZ
(Later Brazil)

Magellan Expedition 1519

El Cano
1522

Vespucci 1501

Strait of Magellan

TIERRA
DEL FUEGO

Bay of
San Julián

Rio de la Plata
(Discovered by
Vespucci 1501)

Bay of San Julián
(Magellan wintered 1520)

Cabral 1500

Vasco da Gama 1497

Projection courtesy of American Geographical Society

Atlassov 1697

Kolyma

Nizhne

Okhotsk

NOVAYA
REMLYA

Yakutsk
Lena
Poyarkov
Amur

JAPAN

LADRONES
(MARIANAS IS.)

GUAM

Magellan 1521

Equator

Enisei
L. Baikal
(Discovered
1643)

RYU KYU
IS.

Mota 1542

FORMOSA

Perhaps visited by
Europeans before Magellan.
Spanish conquest began
under Miguel Lopez
de Legaspi, 1565.

Vilalobos

1542

NEW
GUINEA
(PAPUA)

Ob

Peking

Pires
1517

CHINA
(Ming Empire)

Canton
Macau

LUZON

PHILIPPINE
IS.

Alvares 1513

MINDANAO

GILOLO
TERNATE
TIDORE
MOLUCCAS

BANDA
IS.

Moscow
Chancellor 1553
Volga

After Magellan's death
his expedition wandered
aimlessly for months.

Goes 1602-1607

TIBET

Brahmaputra

Mandalay

SIAM

Pegu

Serrao
1512

BORNEO

Conti

Abreu 1511

Astrakhan
1474
Jenkinson
Koffa
Derbend
Black Sea
Tiflis
Tabriz
Ispahan

Bokhara

Caspian
Sea

Jenkinson

PERSIA

Delhi
Goes
Agra

Ganges

Conti

INDIA
(Mogul Empire
after 1526)

Indus

Conti

Mota 1513

Malacca

Conti

SUMATRA

Conti

JAVA

AUSTRALIA
(Undiscovered)

Baghdad
Basra
Ormuz
Damascus
Jerusalem
*Persian
Gulf*
Cairo
exandria

Conti

Muscat

Damão
Diu
Bassein
Chaul
Goa
Canonor
Calicut
Cochin

Mailapur
Vijayanagar

CEYLON

Colombo

Sequeira 1509

Red Sea

Covilha
Cabral
Covilha
Vasco da Gama 1498
Covilha

Indian

Ocean

El Cano commanding Victoria (Magellan) Expedition

Aden

ABYSSINIA

Covilha
1491

Malindi
Mombasa

Covilha ?

Kilwa

Zaire and
Mani Congo
discovered by
Diogo Cão
1482-1483

Covilha ?

Mozambique

MADAGASCAR
Discovered by Diogo Dias
(Cabral Expedition 1500)

Sofala

Vasco da Gama 1498
Cabral

CROSS
vered by
Cão 1485

scovered by
Dias 1486

Diogo Dias 1500

taken most seriously. Certain islands on Battista Beccario's map of 1435 were once thought to represent the Antilles, but it was later decided that they were the Azores, moved west. Martin Behaim, the geographer, reported a voyage of western discovery in 1415. A claimant for Portuguese priority alleges that Portuguese sailors reached Newfoundland in 1452. A Copenhagen scholar tried to demonstrate that the Danes visited America around 1472–1474. But the Portuguese and Danish advocates lack any tenable evidence.[7]

On the other hand, material evidence for the claims of an earlier Viking exploration is building up in an impressive fashion. The Norse sagas relate how a party led by Bjarni Herjulfson was driven off course while sailing from Iceland to Greenland around the year 986. Blown west and south, they saw a wooded shore, and during subsequent days saw land repeatedly. They made no landing, but when they had made their way back to Greenland they recounted their experiences to Bjarni's friend Eric the Red and his son Leif. Around 992 Leif Ericson set out in Bjarni's ship with thirty-five men to search for the coast Bjarni had seen. They came first to Helluland (Stoneland), then sailed south till they came to an inviting wooded land. They found many wild grapes, and so named the new land Vinland. Fish and game were plentiful. After wintering there, they returned to Greenland. The Norsemen, including Leif's brother Thorwald, made several subsequent voyages to the New World in the years—perhaps centuries—that followed. As recently as 1963 archaeologists discovered the remains of a Norse settlement in Newfoundland. A 1440 map now in Yale University's library shows North America and refers to the expeditions of Bjarni and Leif Ericson. The map, however, is probably fraudulent. The Kensington Stone, found on a Minnesota farm in 1898, bearing runes that purport to tell of a Norse expedition from Vinland into the interior, has been discredited. In any case, no Norse settlement led to permanent colonization or changed the history of the world. The honor for this must go to Columbus.

Sources for the first forty-one years of Columbus' life are very sparse and are questioned on nearly every point. He was born in Genoa in 1451, the son of a wool weaver, Domenico Colombo. A Spanish historian has recently asserted that the family name, Colón in Spanish, is Jewish, and that his parents were probably Spanish Jews who emigrated to Genoa. Another theory, recently advanced by the Spanish historian Fernando del Valle Lersundi, is that Columbus was the nephew of the French Basque freebooter Guillaume de Casenove-Coullon, a vice-admiral of Louis XI. Casenove-Coullon may well have been a relative, for Columbus is said to have fought under him in the service of Portugal against a fleet of Genoese ships off Cape St. Vincent, near Lisbon, in August 1476—an incident that, if true, certainly suggests no patriotic ties to Genoa. Other sources claim that he was fighting with

---

[7] Charles E. Nowell, "The Columbus Question," *American Historical Review*, 44 (1939):802–22.

the Genoese. At least there is agreement that he was there. Columbus' second son, Ferdinand, born to Beatriz Enríquez de Arana, a Spanish woman with whom Columbus had a love affair, wrote a biography of his father which was published in Venice some thirty-two years after Columbus' death, but its authenticity has been questioned on the ground that it may have been largely written by Luis de Colón, Columbus' dishonest grandson. The account of Columbus' life written by the Spanish bishop Bartolomé de Las Casas in his *Historia de las Indias* agrees with Ferdinand's biography, but there is no way of knowing whether this agreement brings Las Casas into question or supports Ferdinand. Enough has been said to suggest that we are far less well informed about Columbus than we would like to be. The great authority on naval history Cecil Jane thought Columbus to be illiterate at least as late as 1492, but this seems very unlikely, for he was a well-traveled man, could converse effectively with kings and scholars, and had a collection of very learned books, so that if he learned to read after forty, he must have been remarkably talented.

Although Columbus began as an apprentice in his father's shop, at fourteen he took to the sea. His first voyages were in the Mediterranean, but he soon sailed into the Atlantic. In the battle off Cape St. Vincent his ship was lost and he clung to an oar until he reached land. The fact that he was not detained suggests that he was probably not fighting on the side of Genoa. He made his way to Lisbon, where his brother Bartolomé had settled and had a small shop in which he sold maps. Columbus signed up shortly thereafter with a Portuguese ship that sailed north to England or Ireland; some sources say Iceland. He may also have sailed south to Africa on a Portuguese trading vessel. In 1478 he married a Portuguese woman, who bore his first son, Diego.

During this period of his life Columbus thought out his plan to reach the Far East by sailing west. One cannot with certainty establish that the books in the Columbus library in Seville which bear careful marginal notations in Spanish in the hands of the Columbus brothers were actually read prior to 1492, but it seems likely that he would have studied the authorities before rather than after his voyage. He knew Ptolemy's theories about the small circumference of the earth and the great extension of Asia eastward. He annotated Marco Polo's *Travels* in detail and thought the great island of Cipangu to be located about where Florida actually is. He also annotated extensively Cardinal Pierre d'Ailly's *Imago mundi*. A very controversial matter is the business of the Toscanelli letters. The learned Florentine humanist, physician, and geographer Paolo Toscanelli (1397–1482) prepared a map of the world and sent it with an accompanying letter to the Portuguese cardinal Fernâs Martins de Roriz. The letter tells of the islands on the way to Guinea and the way across the ocean to "India and the islands." Martins may have handed it on to Columbus, for when Ferdinand was preparing his father's biography, he found it among his papers. Ferdinand claimed that Toscanelli had sent a duplicate of this letter to Columbus. In any case, if Columbus did see it prior to 1492, Toscanelli's message must merely have reinforced an opinion he already held. A second "Toscanelli letter" is clearly forged.

Columbus' motivation was primarily glory and gold, but many of his statements suggest that he was also a religious visionary with a sense of mission. He once wrote to the Spanish monarchs that whoever has gold can do what he wants in the world, and can even bring souls into paradise. He invested in his own voyage, paying an eighth of its costs, which he borrowed from Italian bankers in Seville and from the Pinzón brothers, seamen and shipowners of Palos, who had befriended and encouraged him when it seemed no one would back the voyage he proposed. He offered to send the Spanish rulers as many Indians as they should demand, and actually did several times send Indians for sale as slaves. On the other hand, he had a considerable measure of Catholic piety. According to Las Casas, he was "especially devoted to the honor of St. Francis." He spoke of "Prester John of India." He wrote of his first voyage that he wished to tell about the princes and people of India in order to show how to "spread our most holy faith abroad there." Before his second voyage the Spanish rulers instructed him to be concerned about bringing "the inhabitants of the named islands and lands in all ways and by every means to the point of converting to our holy Catholic faith." He suggested that the Catholic monarchs could use the profit from the Indian spice trade to finance a crusade for the liberation of Jerusalem. Perhaps misled by older maps that showed Jerusalem at the center of the world, he believed that if he kept going west, he could arrive at Jerusalem and strike at the Moslems from behind. It is impossible to tell how much of all this was conventional piety and how much was personal zeal.

Columbus was completely obsessed by his great idea and carried it to the thrones of Portugal and Spain. King John II of Portugal heard him patiently and sympathetically, then referred the matter to a commission for study. When the commission reported unfavorably, the king dismissed him. In Spain Queen Isabella granted him an audience. She received him graciously and listened sympathetically, but then she too referred the matter to a commission, which also reported unfavorably. The Spanish monarchs, however, were intrigued by the dream and fascinated by the earnest conviction of Columbus. Since Portugal could claim control of the eastward route to India, a westward route seemed to be Spain's only chance of sharing in the wealth to be found there. Ferdinand and Isabella put him on a pension to hold him in Spain until they were in a position to do something further about his project. Years passed, but when in January 1492 they completed the conquest of Granada, they were free to take up Columbus' project again. They decided in his favor.

On August 3, 1492, Columbus set sail from Palos as admiral of a fleet of three ships: the flagship *Santa María,* under Columbus; the *Pinta,* under Martín Alonso Pinzón, with Martín's brother Francisco as pilot; and the *Niña,* under another

Pinzón brother, Vicente. They sailed to the Canary Islands and then headed straight west. Columbus used an astrolabe, a quadrant, and a compass as navigational aids, and he proved to be an expert sailor. The complement of ninety men was not the crew of criminals and cutthroats of legend, but able and experienced seamen who had fallen on hard times and hoped to win or recoup their fortunes. But their faith in Columbus' great idea began to fail after several weeks at sea with no sight of land, and on October 10 they demanded and received Columbus' promise that if they did not sight land within three days, they would turn back. Two days later Rodrigo de Triana on the *Pinta* sighted land. The island was very likely the one known today as Watling Island. That very morning Columbus dressed in his finest and, accompanied by the Pinzón brothers and most of the crew, carried ashore the flag of Spain. They knelt upon the shore, kissed the ground with tears of joy, gave thanks to God for the great mercy received, named the island San Salvador, and took possession of it in the names of Ferdinand and Isabella.

When they reached Cuba, Columbus believed he had reached China, and sent a party ashore to greet the great khan. When he was not to be found, the expedition sailed on and next discovered Hispaniola, the island now divided by Haiti and the Dominican Republic. On November 21 the *Pinta* disappeared before a strong wind, and on Christmas Day the *Santa María* was wrecked on a reef, so Columbus decided to return to Spain with news of his discovery and as many of the men and stores as he could crowd aboard the *Niña*. The rest—some forty men—were left behind to establish a settlement called Villa de la Navidad (Christmastown).

On the return voyage the *Pinta* was sighted, and although the two ships were later separated again, both of them arrived back in Palos on the same day, March 15, 1493. Five days later Martín Pinzón died.

Columbus' reception by the Spanish court in Barcelona was all he could desire. He displayed his trophies—six Indians, gold trinkets, cotton, unknown plants and birds, and other curiosities—and received from Ferdinand and Isabella the titles of Admiral of the Ocean Sea and Viceroy of the Indies, a coat of arms bearing royal symbols, and wealth appropriate to these honors.

On September 25, 1493, he set sail on his second voyage with three galleons, fourteen caravels, and a complement of 1,500 men. The search for China in the West Indies continued to be fruitless. He found the settlement of La Navidad wiped out, and established a new settlement at another site on Hispaniola. After sailing among the islands for two and a half years, accomplishing little beyond the stirring up of anger among the Spaniards and the enmity of the Indians, he returned to Spain in 1496 and was kindly received by the Spanish monarchs.

On his third voyage, in 1498, he reached the mainland of South America, but, still clinging to the illusion that Cuba was the Chinese mainland, decided that this was Marco Polo's great island to the southeast, and without exploring further sailed back to his colony on Hispaniola. The complaints of the colonists reached the ears of the monarchs back in Spain and Columbus lost favor, especially with Ferdinand. The king appointed a new governor, Francisco de Bobadilla, who arrived in Hispaniola on August 23, 1500, to find Columbus and his brothers Bartolomé and Diego engaged in hanging those Spaniards who were displeased with Columbus' rule. Bobadilla freed the prisoners not yet hanged and returned the Columbus brothers to Spain in irons.

But by the time Columbus appeared in court on December 17, 1500, the tide had turned once more in his favor, and he was received with honor. On his third voyage he had heard of the ocean to the west of Panama, and now he persuaded the monarchs to send him on a fourth voyage to find a passage through the "islands" to the sea beyond. On May 9, 1502, he sailed with four caravels and 150 men. After profitless reconnoitering in the Caribbean and a fruitless attempt to found a colony, he returned in November 1504 for the last time, ill and disoriented. On May 20, 1506, he died without ever realizing the magnitude of his accomplishment. Unable to admit his failure to find Asia, he could not appreciate his achievement in discovering a new world. After many removals and reinterments, he now lies buried in the cathedral of Seville.

In May 1493 the Spanish pope Alexander VI, at the urging of Ferdinand and Isabella, laid down a line of demarcation between the Portuguese and Spanish possessions. He gave the Spaniards everything that lay one hundred leagues or nautical miles "west of the islands of the green foothills," or the Cape Verde Islands and the Azores. Portugal was less than happy with this demarcation, and opened direct negotiations with Spain. These negotiations culminated in 1494 in the Treaty of Tordesillas, which moved the line to 340 miles west of the Cape Verde Islands. They were thinking less of dividing up the newly discovered land than of defining and limiting the two ways to India—south and east for Portugal, west for Spain. Effectively this secured Brazil to Portugal and the rest of the New World to Spain.

So great is the fame of Columbus that other illustrious men and glorious deeds are sometimes forgotten. Thus Amerigo Vespucci (1451–1512), a Florentine merchant sent to Spain as a Medici agent around 1491, became inspired by Columbus and in 1497 joined an expedition to the Indies, serving as navigator. In 1499 and 1500 he sailed along the coast of Central and South America until he reached the Amazon. In 1501 he sailed again, this time with a Portuguese expedition. In a series of letters written in 1504 he described these lands as a continent, as though he fully realized the true nature of the discovery. It is not entirely unfair, then, that the New World came to be known as America rather than Columbia. In 1507 Martin Waldseemüller, a German cartographer, published Vespucci's letters in Latin in a volume entitled *Introduction to Cosmography*. On a map of the newly discovered lands he labeled the South American continent "America," a name that came very quickly to be used for North America as well.

Other explorers followed, notably Vasco Núñez de Balboa, who crossed the Isthmus of Panama and in 1513 discovered the Pacific Ocean. Ferdinand Magellan, a Portuguese navigator in the employ of Spain, set sail westward in 1519 on a journey that led to the circumnavigation of the globe. He passed through the straits at the southern end of South America and sailed across the Pacific. Unfortunately he was killed by the natives of the islands later named the Philippines, in honor of the Spanish king Philip II, but one of his ships sailed on and finally arrived home again. There could now be no doubt about the nature of Columbus' discovery. Moreover, Europeans now had a clear idea of the size of the earth and the relation of the major continents to each other. By a treaty in 1529 Spain took possession of the Philippines but confirmed the Portuguese claim to the Moluccas or Spice Islands.

The Spaniards' first attempts at colonization were very modest, but with the adventures on the mainland of such *conquistadores* as Hernán Cortés, Francisco Pizarro, and Juan Ponce de León, Spanish overseas expansion entered a new phase of conquest and colonialism.

The Ancient and the New Worlds

IN THE DAYS when Jacob Burckhardt's description of the rediscovery of the world and of man in the age of the Renaissance was still taken quite literally, it was possible to see the voyages of discovery as but one more expression of the spirit of the Renaissance. Yet it is quite obvious that the contributions of Italy, the home of the Renaissance, were very modest compared with those of "medieval" Portugal and Spain. The humanists helped to revitalize the knowledge of the ancients and enthusiasm for their learning, but the texts crucial for exploration, such as those of Ptolemy, owed scarcely anything to the humanists for their great influence, nor did the technological advances that made it possible. Much more important were the societal factors, the economic drives of a competitive capitalism, the expansive impulses of the national dynasties, the missionary drive still operative in the kingdoms of Iberia. Italy supplied mapmakers and navigators, Vespucci and Columbus, but they had to make their fortunes with the Portuguese and Spaniards.

The new discoveries caused some stir, but in retrospect it seems strange that those sensational finds did not arouse greater excitement than they did. It was more than a century before the full implications of the new geography and ethnography were fully appreciated. Engrossed in their studies of the ancient world, some of the most powerful intellects of the day scarcely took note of the new. Yet a few did get into the spirit of the modern world. The Italian humanist Pietro Martire d'Anghiera exclaimed, "What has been done and written since the beginning of the world is still little, as I see it, when we compare it with these new lands and seas, those manifold peoples and languages, those treasures of precious metals and discoveries of pearls!"[8] But Pietro had already emigrated to Spain and had no intention of ever returning to Italy.

On May 4, 1503, Johann Kollauer, royal secretary to Emperor Maximilian and member of the Augsburg sodality of northern humanists, wrote a letter from Antwerp to Conrad Celtis, the German humanist who was titular head of the Rhenish and Danubian sodalities, about the exciting reports he had heard from Portuguese sailors who had returned from voyages of discovery, and urged Celtis to join him there so he could hear for himself of the wonders of the New World from men who had actually seen them. But Celtis was no more interested in the New World than were Marsilio Ficino, Niccolò Machiavelli, Desiderius Erasmus, or Martin Luther.

Bibliography

Abbott, W. C. *The Expansion of Europe,* 2 vols. New York, 1918.

Andrews, Kenneth R. *Trade, Plunder and Settlement: Maritime Enterprise and the Genesis of the British Empire, 1480–1630.* New York, 1985.

Arciniegas, Germán. *Amerigo and the New World.* New York, 1955.

Baker, J. N. L. *A History of Geographical Discovery and Exploration.* London, 1931.

Baker, Nina. *Amerigo Vespucci.* New York, 1957.

Beazley, C. R. *Prince Henry the Navigator.* New York, 1894.

———. *The Dawn of Modern Geography,* 3 vols. London, 1897–1906.

Blake, J. W. *European Beginnings in West Africa, 1454–1578.* New York, 1937.

Boxer, Charles. *Four Centuries of Portuguese Expansion, 1415–1825.* Johannesburg, 1961.

Cipolla, C. *Guns and Sails in the Early Phase of European Expansion, 1400–1700.* London, 1965.

Hakluyt, R. *The Principal Navigations, Voyages, Traffiques, and Discoveries of the English Nation,* 3 vols. London, 1599–1600. Republished in the Edinburgh and Everyman editions.

Hart, Henry H. *Sea Road to the Indies.* London, 1952.

———. *Marco Polo: Venetian Adventurer.* Norman, OK, 1967.

Hay, Denys. *Europe: The Emergence of an Idea.* Edinburgh, 1957.

Heers, J., et al. *Les grandes voies maritimes dans le monde (XVᵉ–XIXᵉ siècles).* Paris, 1965.

Jane, Cecil, trans. *The Journal of Christopher Columbus.* New York, 1960.

Jensen, De Lamar, ed. *The Expansion of Europe: Motives, Methods, and Theory.* Boston, 1967.

Morison, Samuel E. *Portuguese Voyages to America in the Fifteenth Century.* Cambridge, MA, 1940.

———. *Admiral of the Ocean Sea: A Life of Christopher Columbus,* 2 vols. Boston, 1942.

———. *The European Discovery of America: The Northern Voyages.* Oxford, 1971.

Newton, A. P., ed. *The Great Age of Discovery.* London, 1932.

Parry, John H. *The Spanish Theory of Empire in the Sixteenth Century.* Cambridge, 1940.

———. *The Establishment of the European Hegemony, 1415–1715.* New York, 1961.

———. *The Age of Reconnaissance.* Cleveland, 1963.

———. *The Spanish Seaborne Empire.* New York, 1966.

Penrose, Boies. *Travel and Discovery in the Renaissance, 1420–1620.* Cambridge, MA, 1952.

Pohl, F. H. *Amerigo Vespucci, Pilot Major.* New York, 1944.

Prestage, E. *The Portuguese Pioneers.* London, 1933.

---

[8] Konetzke, "Überseeische Entdeckungen," p. 538.

Sanceau, E. *Henry the Navigator*. New York, 1947.

Sauer, C. *The Early Spanish Main*. Berkeley, 1966.

Schwoebel, Robert. *The Shadow of the Crescent: The Renaissance Image of the Turk, 1453–1517*. Nieuwkoop, 1967.

Williamson, J. A. *Maritime Enterprise, 1485–1558*. New York, 1913.

——— . *The Voyages of the Cabots and the English Discovery of North America Under Henry VII and Henry VIII*. London, 1929.

Wroth, Lawrence C. *The Voyages of Giovanni da Verrazzano, 1524–1528*. New Haven, 1970.

CHAPTER 11

Humanism
Beyond Italy

"Thank God we are out of the Gothic night!" *exclaimed François*
Rabelais, the French wit and humanist. It took northern Europe longer than
southern Europe to emerge from medievalism precisely because the Gothic culture
was northern. Gothic architecture and scholastic philosophy had to be artificially
introduced into Italy, and that very late. Conversely, the Renaissance, based on a revival of classical learning, could hardly have occurred spontaneously in a land
where classical learning had never flourished. In the lands that had once been the
northern provinces of the Roman Empire and in the other areas that had lain
beyond the borders of ancient Rome, there was less a genuine renaissance in the
fifteenth and sixteenth centuries than the development of a humanist literary culture and some artistic adaptation. It seems more appropriate to speak of northern
humanism than of a northern renaissance.

Social change came slowly to northern and western Europe, and urbanization
was limited in comparison with the growth of cities in northern and central Italy.
The feudal nobility was not so easily absorbed into the moneyed mercantile class in
other areas as it was in Italy; it retained its hereditary cast and social status longer in
the wooded north. As the military and political power of the feudal lords ebbed
away, they clung all the more tenaciously to their traditional way of life.

The northern humanists poured scorn upon the nobles who took greater pleasure in drink and the hunt than in learned discourse and books. The rich merchants of the northern cities adapted themselves to the literary standards of the feudal aristocracy, preferring chivalric romances and lyrics to classical works or humanist writings. Moralizing treatises, golden legends, lives of saints, and other traditional materials suited the taste of the provincial nobility and of the urban middle class. Even after the invention of the printing press, many of the books issued in the second half of the fifteenth century were of the chivalric and devotional kind. But that half century saw the beginnings of the new humanist culture as well.

"A man who has not been in Italy," Dr. Samuel Johnson pronounced three centuries later, "is always conscious of an inferiority." He was reflecting a convention of high society formed during the Renaissance. In 1549 the English author William Thomas commented in his *History of Italy* on the number of foreigners in that country, "specially of gentlemen, whose resort thither is principally under pretense of study." During the late fifteenth and the sixteenth centuries there was a two-way traffic of men and ideas. Italian humanists and artists traveled north as diplomatic emissaries, ecclesiastical legates, secretaries to northern princes and cities, lecturers in the universities, or business representatives. Northerners went to Italy either as students, primarily of law and medicine, or simply as admirers of the learned Italians, whose wisdom they hoped to absorb.

As capitalism grew and the cities of the north developed, an atmosphere more congenial to humanist culture evolved. The princes and courts gradually learned to admire the elegance of the Italian Renaissance courts, the wit and charm of their ladies, and the skill of their humanist chancellors in diplomacy and domestic politics. Even the ecclesiastical potentates, the prince-bishops, began to emulate the fashions of Italian courts and churchmen. Humanism, promoted by poets and orators, began at last to penetrate even the universities.

Once humanist culture began to take hold in the north, enthusiasm for the classics sometimes went wild. When a second-rate Italian humanist, Aleander, gave a series of lectures on a third-rate Roman poet, Ausonius, in Paris one hot summer, two thousand culture seekers listened for two and a half hours to his initial lecture, and on the third day the house was packed at eleven for a lecture that was not scheduled to start until one. But humanist culture was not the same in northern Europe as in Italy, for humanism fused with the indigenous cultures of the various peoples that embraced it, producing in each area a unique cultural amalgam.

There might very well have been an efflorescence of culture in northern Europe in the late fifteenth and early sixteenth centuries even without Italian influence. The Hundred Years' War over, relative peace returned. As trade expanded, the urban centers prospered and an economic base strong enough to support higher culture developed. But even more important than political and economic factors was the emergence in the north of an educational movement of major importance.

The Brethren of the Common Life, founded by Gerard Groote (d. 1384), were concerned essentially with deepening inward religious faith and with cultivating practical Christian living, but they saw education as the major instrument for promoting these concerns. They established schools, opened hospices for indigent students in university towns, and operated printing presses for the publishing of devotional literature, grammars and textbooks, Bibles, and the moral treatises of classical philosophers. Since they found the "safe classics," such as the ethical treatises of Cicero and Seneca, to be of great value in instructing the young and favored a pure Latin style, they became instrumental in promoting a classical revival in the north. The houses of the Brethren spread from Deventer and Zwolle in the Netherlands along the Rhine through Westphalia, Hesse, and Württemberg, and along the North and Baltic seas into Saxony and as far as Kulm. Many famous men of letters were either directly educated or supported by them. Alexander Hegius (1433–1498), the learned master at Deventer, was a friend and correspondent of Agricola and the teacher of Erasmus. But while there might well have been a flowering of culture in those decades in any case, without Italian influence it would not have taken the classical form it did.

German Humanism

IN THE YEAR 1507 Nicholas Gerbellius, a young humanist, wrote, "I congratulate myself often on living in this glorious century in which so many remarkable men have arisen in Germany." The first two decades of the sixteenth century marked the high tide of German humanism. The new culture came earlier to the Germanies than to the other countries of the north. There were many close political ties between the empire and Italy, and a lively trade prospered between the Italian cities and the German cities along the Danube and the Rhine. The old medieval tradition of student wandering brought literally thousands of German students to the Italian universities each year. The "German nations" at the universities of Bologna, Padua, and Pavia were large and active. The transition from wandering student to roving humanist was not hard to make.

PIONEERS AND MORALISTS

The migratory birds of German humanism appeared in the north during the second half of the fifteenth century. Peter Luder (*c.* 1415–1474) was a typical pioneer of the movement. He went as a cleric to Rome, wandered around Italy, and joined the German students in Padua. In 1444 the elector of the Palatinate appointed him a lecturer in classical languages and literature at the University of Heidelberg. An aggressive, free-wheeling, hard-drinking man, Luder battled conservative professors for a larger place in the curriculum for classical rhetoric and poetry. A combination of academic hostility and the plague drove him away from Heidelberg, and he returned to study medicine in Italy and later taught at Basel and Vienna. Besides loose-living poets such as Luder, there were schoolteacher humanists like Johannes Murmellius and Rudolf von Langen, scholastic humanists like Conrad Summenhart and Paul Scriptoris, and moralistic critics of society like Heinrich Bebel and Jacob Wimpfeling.

Jacob Wimpfeling (1450–1528), the cathedral preacher at Speyer, stood in an ambivalent relationship to Italian humanism, for he admired classical form but disliked pagan morals. Invited to join the Rhenish sodality of humanists, he responded with the shy demurrer that he would only be a crow among nightingales or an owl among falcons. He attacked simony and concubinage, and his major work, *De integritate,* was designed to help priests learn to abhor the pernicious love of women. As an Alsatian, Wimpfeling was a strong German patriot, and he warned against the designs of the French king on the pearl of the empire. He founded in Schlettstadt a small sodality of humanists. Two of his friends, Sebastian Brant (1457–1521) and Johann Geiler von Kaisersberg (1445–1510), were the same sort of reformers. Brant's popular book of satiric poetry, *The Ship of Fools,* holds up to ridicule lazy students, pedantic professors, and the high and the mighty. Geiler von Kaisersberg, a powerful penitential preacher, carried the same earnest message to the people from the pulpit.

RUDOLF AGRICOLA

Rudolf Agricola (1444–1485) was clearly the most important representative of the older generation. "It was Rudolf Agricola," Erasmus declared, "who first brought with him from Italy some gleam of a better literature." He believed that "Agricola could have been the first in Italy had he not preferred Germany." Agricola's power lay not in his pen, but in his personality. He wrote relatively little, but he inspired many younger humanists, especially at Heidelberg, and became a symbol of the new wave of humanism.

Born near Groningen in Frisia, Agricola studied at Erfurt, Louvain, and Cologne. He spent ten years in Italy, from 1469 to 1479, and while there wrote a *Life of Petrarch* to honor the "father and restorer of good arts." "We are indebted to Petrarch for the intellectual culture of our century," he wrote. "All ages owe him a debt of gratitude—antiquity for having rescued its treasure from oblivion and modern times for having with his own strength founded and revived culture, which he has left as a precious legacy to future ages." Drawn homeward in 1479, he found, as Albrecht Dürer was to do when he returned from Italy, that he "froze after the sun." He lamented to Alexander Hegius that he was losing his capacity for thought and ornamented style. His spirit would not respond.

Bishop Johannes von Dalberg and the Palatine elector brought Agricola to

Heidelberg, where he presided informally over a circle of young humanists. "I have the brightest hope," he said, "that we shall one day wrest from haughty Italy the reputation for classical expression which it has nearly monopolized, so to speak, and lay claim to it ourselves, and free ourselves from the reproach of ignorance and being called unlearned and inarticulate barbarians; and that our Germany will be so cultured and literate that Latium will not know Latin any better." His major work was an introductory manual, *On Dialectical Invention,* primarily intended for teachers in the arts, in which he sought to demonstrate that the true function of logic, as an element basic to rhetoric, was to produce conviction through straight thinking and effective style.

CONRAD CELTIS

Among Agricola's disciples at Heidelberg was a young student named Conrad Celtis, who became the best lyric poet among the German humanists. Celtis (1459–1508), a runaway son of a peasant, studied at Cologne, Heidelberg, Rostock, and Leipzig.

On April 18, 1487, Emperor Frederick III crowned Celtis the first German poet laureate of the empire at Nuremberg. "O sacred and mighty work of the poets," Celtis declaimed, "you alone free all things from fate and lift up mortal ashes to the stars!" In the four volumes of his *Amores* he celebrated four of his loves, symbolizing the four parts of Germany. In his *Odes* he wrote eloquently of life, love, and learning. From Cicero and Horace he learned the sophist-rhetorical theory of the art of poetry as a passionate and rousing power, the motif of poetic madness and intoxication. He liked to think of himself as a *vates,* a term restored to favor by Virgil, meaning a poet-philosopher, a prophet or sage.

Later in 1487 he crossed the Alps for a rapid trip through Italy, visiting Venice, Padua, Bologna, Florence, and Rome. After unpleasant encounters with the "superior" Italians, he hurried back to Cracow, where he studied mathematics and poetry, and moved on from there to Nuremberg and then to Ingolstadt, where he became a professor of rhetoric.

In his inaugural address at the University of Ingolstadt he summoned his fellow Germans to cultural rivalry with Italy. "Take up again, O German men," he cried, "that old spirit of yours with which you so many times were a terror and specter to the Romans!" Romantic cultural nationalism was one of the major themes of German humanism. To demonstrate that the Germans too had a literary past, he published the plays of Roswitha, a tenth-century nun of Gandersheim, and the epic poem *Ligurinus* in praise of Frederick Barbarossa. Celtis organized the Rhenish and Danubian sodalities, loose associations of local societies of humanists which sprang up under his aegis in Linz, Ingolstadt, Augsburg, and other cities, and recruited their members as contributors to his *Germany Illustrated,* a topographical-historical work modeled on Biondo's *Italy Illustrated* and on his own *Norimberga*, which described the past and present glories of Nuremberg.

In 1497 he accepted Emperor Maximilian's invitation to the University of Vienna. There he founded the College of Poets and Mathematicians, wrote poems and plays, and taught until he died of syphilis at the age of forty-nine. He was buried in St. Stephen's Cathedral.

COURTS AND CITIES

By 1520 humanism had penetrated the courts of Germany to a much greater extent than historians have realized. This was true not only of the imperial Habsburg courts in Linz and Vienna, but of the courts of the many territorial princes and the powerful ecclesiastical prince-bishops in Mainz, Trier, and Cologne. The advantages of having a skilled Latinist as secretary and a rhetorician as orator came to be recognized, and with the introduction of Roman law, legists who coupled a humanist interest in letters with a knowledge of civil law became commonplace.

Aeneas Silvius Piccolomini spent the years 1442 to 1445 at the court of Emperor Frederick III (1440–1492) as a member of the imperial chancery. His description of Germany, blessed by the presence of the Roman church, helped to kindle national pride among the German humanists, while Sabellicus and other Italians who ridiculed the Germans as barbarians stimulated their competitive instincts. The humanists looked to young Emperor Maximilian (1493–1519) as the hero who would restore the empire to greatness and introduce a new golden age. Celtis and the rest wrote plays to ornament his court and poems in his honor. Maximilian himself sought immortality as a patron of poets and artists. He commissioned a long poetic allegory, the *Theuerdank,* to celebrate his courtship of Mary of Burgundy, and he dictated *Der Weisskunig,* or *The White King,* which related his own daring deeds. For Maximilian the Nuremberg artist Albrecht Dürer did the woodcut *Triumphal Arch* and a portrait.

The prosperous cities of south Germany served as focal points of humanist and artistic activity. In Augsburg, home of the Fuggers, Welsers, Paumgartners, and other wealthy families, Conrad Peutinger (1465–1547) became a highly influential legist and humanist. While studying law in Italy he developed a passion for classical learning, and he collected coins, artwork, and classical manuscripts. His stylistic ability made him of special value to the city government and he served as a privy counselor for Emperor Maximilian as well. He owned the important *Tabula Peutingeriana,* a military map of the Roman Empire which Celtis had discovered and presented to him.

The historian Johann Turmair, known as Aventinus (1477–1534), served in Ingolstadt as tutor to the two younger sons of the duke of Bavaria. Encouraged by

Duke William IV, he undertook to write *The Annals of Bavaria,* which he completed in 1521.

In Nuremberg the city councillor Willibald Pirckheimer (1470–1528) presided over humanist intellectual life. A friend of Celtis and of Albrecht Dürer, Pirckheimer was a scholar in his own right. He was educated in Italy, read and wrote Greek, composed a history of the Swabian-Swiss war, and took part in the sacramental controversy during the Reformation period. Luther was a guest in his home on one occasion, but Pirckheimer remained within the Catholic Church. His sisters, especially Caritas, a nun, were so well educated that Erasmus compared them in his *Colloquies* with the brilliant daughters of Sir Thomas More.

Conrad Mutianus Rufus (1471–1526) held that there is divine revelation in every religion and that Christ is the universal spirit.

THE REUCHLIN CONTROVERSY

The humanists were virtually unanimous in their attack upon scholastic theology. They believed the language to be barbarous, the dialectic religiously ineffective, the emphasis upon logical formulation and demonstration of dogma misplaced. They favored an ethical interpretation of Paul and a spiritualization of dogma. One of the humanists most concerned with reinvigorating Christian doctrine by exploring new sources of religious knowledge was Johannes Reuchlin, a pioneer in Hebrew studies. In his *Rudimenta hebraica* he wrote, "I reverence St. Jerome as an angel, I prize Nicholas de Lyra as a great master, but Truth I worship as God."

Johannes Reuchlin (1455–1522) was educated at northern universities. On two trips to Italy he came to know Marsilio Ficino and Giovanni Pico della Mirandola, and he was an avid reader of Nicholas Cusanus. A professional lawyer, he served most of his life as chancellor to the duke of Württemberg, but spent his last years as a professor at Ingolstadt and Tübingen.

Reuchlin believed that Hebrew brought him closer to God than any other language. Moses, after all, was more ancient than the Greek philosophers. Reuchlin's *Rudimenta hebraica* was the first fairly reliable manual of Hebrew grammar by a Christian scholar. But through the years, as his knowledge of Hebrew deepened, he became intrigued by Jewish mysticism. He believed that Moses and the prophets had transmitted many divine truths orally through the seventy wise men in unbroken tradition until they were embodied by the medieval Jewish mystics in the Cabala. Because of the references in the Cabala to the Messiah, Reuchlin believed that the Cabala corroborated Christian revelation. From Pico he received the suggestion that the ideas of the Cabalists paralleled the philosophy of the Pythagoreans. "Marsilio [Ficino] produced Plato for Italy. Lefèvre d'Étaples restored Aristotle to France. I shall complete the number and . . . show to the Germans Pythagoras reborn through me!" he boasted. The numerological mysticism of the Cabalists was related, he held, to the mysterious power and quality of numbers which Pythagoras developed in the mid-sixth century B.C. He wrote two major works, *On the Wonder-Working Word* and *On the Cabalistic Art*, in which he sought to demonstrate the way in which Pythagoreanism and Cabalism harmonize with and support Christian revelation.

Ironically, this Christian apologist became the target of a vicious obscurantist attack. In 1506 a Jew named Pfefferkorn had renounced Judaism for Christianity. With the zeal of the convert he wrote *A Mirror for Jews*, in which he argued that all Hebrew books should be confiscated. The Dominicans of Cologne backed his outrageous demand, and in 1509 the emperor issued a decree ordering the Jews to turn in their books. In response to an inquiry from the archbishop of Mainz, Reuchlin offered the opinion that Hebrew books should not be destroyed. Pfefferkorn attacked Reuchlin in a scurrilous pamphlet entitled *The Hand Mirror*, accusing him of ignorance. Reuchlin loathed controversy, but he felt that he must defend his position, and did so in *The Eye Mirror*. He also published a collection of testimonials in his favor under the title of *Letters of Famous Men*. The case dragged on until in 1520 the pope finally condemned Reuchlin's *Eye Mirror*.

This attack on the humanists' idol was more than they could bear in silence. While the controversy was at its height, two young students, Crotus Rubeanus and Ulrich von Hutten, published *Letters of Obscure Men*, a biting satire on the "obscurantists" of Cologne and the would-be book-burners who supported them. It set Europe to laughing on the very eve of the Reformation.

ULRICH VON HUTTEN

Ulrich von Hutten (1488–1523), a militant critic of scholasticism and of abuses in the church, was a fighter. A German knight, he belonged to a class that was rapidly losing its social utility. When the Reformation broke out and Luther was summoned to appear before the diet at Worms in 1521, Hutten called to him, "Long live liberty!"

Hutten was born in the fortress of Steckelberg, on the border of Franconia and Hesse. At the age of eleven he was sent to the ancient monastery of Fulda to begin life as a religious. At seventeen he fled from the monastery, only a few weeks before Luther entered one at Erfurt. He studied at Cologne, Erfurt, and Frankfort on the Oder, where he took his A.B., then went on to Leipzig, Greifswald, and Rostock. During the course of his wanderings he became an enthusiastic humanist, and he dedicated his life to poetics and polemics. "Behold, posterity," he wrote, "the songs of Hutten the poet, whom you are rightly able to call your own."

He saw the hypocritical priests and superstitious monks as the implacable foes of learning. Only gradually did he come to regard the pope as the *bête noire* leading the forces of reaction. His goal was to free the fatherland of the forces of ignorance and to elevate culture in Germany above that of Italy. Hutten was an angry young man who poured out polemical tracts from the depths of a choleric soul. In his *Trias Romana* Hutten had a character named Ernholdus offer what really was his own program: "Truly it is a great and excellent deed to bring it about by persuading, exhorting, inciting, driving, and impelling that the fatherland come to recognize its own debasement and arm itself to win back its ancient liberty." "Even if it cannot be attained," Hutten responds in the dialogue, "there is merit in having tried!"

Hutten's writings were like a barrel of grapeshot, all the more devastating for being fired at close range. He attacked the whole catalog of evils in the church—simony, nepotism, benefice-hunting, immorality, neglect of duty, clerical pride and insolence. He called for the abolition of celibacy, and caricatured Cardinal Cajetan as a dissolute papal lackey who pretended to be collecting money for defense against the Turks when he had really come to cheat the Germans out of their money so that the Romans could live in luxury. He attacked the sale of indulgences as exploitation.

Hutten's attitude toward the papacy became increasingly hostile. At first he considered the pope to be an enemy of the emperor, but finally he pronounced him to be an enemy of Christ himself. In 1517 he published a new edition of Lorenzo Valla's *On the Donation of Constantine*, which exposed the false foundation of the papal claim to temporal power. In a letter to Pope Leo X in December 1520 he concluded with the biblical phrase: "Let us break their chains asunder and cast their yoke from us."

Hutten died in August 1523 of syphilis, the same disease that had claimed the life of his foe Pope Julius II. He was buried on the island of Ufenau in Lake Zurich. His only remaining possession was his most powerful weapon, his pen.

Humanism in Eastern Europe

HUMANISM PENETRATED rather feebly into eastern Europe. King Matthias Corvinus of Hungary invited Italian humanists to Buda, built up a sizable library, and ornamented his court with Renaissance art; John Vitez, nephew of the archbishop of Buda, a doctor of canon law from Bologna and an ambassador of Matthias in Rome, was in close touch with Celtis, who made him the patron of the *Sodalitas Litteraria Danubiana*. Celtis visited Buda from Vienna in 1490, and he came with much fanfare. Marius Nizolius contributed to rhetorical theory. But the advance of the Turks up the Danube and their conquest of Hungary cut off this promising beginning of Hungarian humanism.

Bohemia was so torn up by the Hussite wars during the fifteenth century that it could not participate very fully in the Renaissance. Fierce nationalism and its separation from Italy by the territory of the empire had a further negative influence. The nobleman Bohuslav Hasištein of Lobkovice (1460–1510) spent seven years in Italy and upon his return organized a literary circle. Some of the writings of Petrarch and Erasmus were translated into Czech. But that is about all there is to say about humanism in Bohemia, which in the days of Emperor Charles and Cola di Rienzo had been a cradle of Renaissance culture in the north.

Students traveled to Italian universities from Poland as they did from Germany, but in much fewer numbers. The Italian humanist Philip Buonacorsi, known as Callimachus (1438–1496), came to Poland as an exile. He had belonged to the Roman Academy of Pomponius Laetus, which Pope Paul II suspected of pagan proclivities and closed down. Callimachus became tutor to the children of King Casimir and taught at the University of Cracow. Largely because of his influence, Cracow became an important center for mathematics, astronomy, and humanistic studies. But the most important developments took place in western rather than eastern Europe as the Renaissance moved over the Alps into new territory.

French Humanism

VESPASIANO DA BISTICCI remarked disparagingly of the northerners, "These *ultramontanes* generally have little spirit." From an Italian point of view, this observation was essentially true of fifteenth-century French humanism, but it hardly did justice to the major figures of the sixteenth century. The French Renaissance showed most of the general characteristics of the German movement, including its deep religious concern, although romantic cultural nationalism was less in evidence and criticisms of ecclesiastical abuses were less pronounced.

The flowering of neoclassical culture in France was delayed by the Hundred Years' War and by France's duel with Burgundy. Only two major figures truly qualify as humanists in the first half of the fifteenth century. The chancellor Jean de Montreuil (1354–1418) acquired from his many Italian contacts an enthusiasm for Petrarch and Renaissance culture, and the great preacher Nicholas de Clemanges (1367–1437) admired Cicero and was mindful of the utility of rhetoric in his calling. But these promising beginnings were not followed up until the very end of the century.

Historians at one time liked to date the French Renaissance from the time of Charles VIII's invasion of Italy. We now appreciate more fully that ideas, books, and men such as Pico della Mirandola had made their influence felt in France before the troops returned from Italy. But no doubt the adventures of Charles VIII, Louis XII, and Francis I did focus renewed attention upon Italy. Local styles of art and architecture flourished, particularly in the Loire valley; outstanding examples can be seen in the châteaux of Amboise and Blois. Flemish and German artists, Jan van Eyck and Hans Memling in particular, were important influences on French art until the time of Francis I. But during Francis' long reign (1515–1547) Italian influence became much more pronounced. The king brought Italian artists to France as a regular policy: Leonardo da Vinci, Benvenuto Cellini, Andrea del Sarto, Il Rosso, and Francesco Primaticcio. The Flemish artist Jean Clouet and his son François also came, and combined Flemish realism with French delicacy. The palace of Fontainebleau, built during Francis' reign, betrays Italian neoclassical design in many of its features, but the Château de Chambord, also built for Francis I, is an interesting composite of the Italian and French traditions.[1]

During the reign of Francis I French literary culture came alive. In his *Commentaries on the Latin Tongue* Étienne Dolet (1508–1546) boasted of the progress literature was making and appealed for increased support from the court, the aristocracy, and other men of means. Dolet himself lived in Lyon and was a friend of François Rabelais. He placed his hope in the power of secular scholarship, believing that if men know the truth, they will act in accordance with it. He was burned as a freethinker in Paris, the "martyr of the Renaissance."

GUILLAUME BUDÉ

The man whom Dolet called the chief captain of the French humanists, Guillaume Budé (1468–1540), was indeed a scholar of substantial achievement, an intellectual of many serious interests, and an indefatigible worker. He represented all the basic motifs of French humanism: devotion to the classics, religious thought, and the reformation of society.

Budé's family had a tradition of government service, and he seemed destined for a government career himself. But he left the study of law at an early age, captivated by the classical revival, and at twenty-six took up the study of Greek with such zeal that the story went around that he spent several hours on his wedding day studying Greek grammar. When a servant burst into his study one day to tell him the house was on fire, he was said to have replied, "Tell my good wife *she* is in charge of housekeeping!" If these stories are apocryphal, it is at least true that Budé often stayed up all night reading and writing Greek. He wrote a good many letters in Greek to Erasmus and to others less able to reply in kind.

Budé's literary career was notable for the breadth of his interest. He wrote a commentary on the *Pandects* or digest of Justinian's law (*Annotationes,* 1508). In 1515 he published *De asse,* a treatise on coinage and money in which he applied historical analysis to the study of the ancient monetary system. His most important work, however, was his *Commentaries on the Greek Language* (1529), in which

---

[1] Catherine Boyd, *The French Renaissance* (Boston, 1940), pts. 1 and 2.

he offered several thousand critical analyses of grammatical and syntactical questions, providing examples from Greek texts. His work was rambling and undisciplined, but readers of that century were patient with savants who felt a compulsion to display all the erudition at their command.

Francis I esteemed Budé highly and considered him an ornament to his court. Budé and Jean du Bellay, bishop of Narbonne, persuaded the king to found the Collegium Trilingue (1530), which developed into the Collège de France. Budé also induced the king to establish a library at Fontainebleau, from which grew the Bibliothèque Nationale in Paris. After his death he was suspected of having had Protestant leanings, for his widow retired to Geneva and openly professed the Reformed faith. Erasmus declared Budé to be the "marvel of France"—but Erasmus was given to easy compliments.

LEFÈVRE D'ÉTAPLES

Lefèvre d'Étaples (1455-1536) had tremendous influence on the course of events in the Reformation period. He took his doctorate at Paris, dutifully made an intellectual pilgrimage to Italy, and studied at Florence, where he encountered Ficino's Neoplatonism, and at Padua, where he read Aristotle with Ermolao Barbaro. He also read voraciously the works of Meister Eckhardt, Johannes Tauler, and other German mystics, and was intrigued by Raymond Lull's philosophy, which was designed to win the Moslems to Christianity. In 1514 Lefèvre published an edition of Nicholas Cusanus' works. Lefèvre's thought was synthetic, an amalgam of Aristotelianism, Neoplatonism, and mysticism. He delivered a series of lectures in Paris on Aristotle, in which he tried to interpret Aristotle's texts in accordance with their historical contexts. But his deepest concern was theological.

Lefèvre applied to religious thought the good humanist principle of returning to the sources. He was intrigued by the synthesis of philosophy and theology achieved by the Eastern church fathers. In 1505 he published an edition of John of Damascus in which he enunciated the principle that the Scriptures must be the sole source and authority for man's statements about God. In 1509 he published his *Quintuplex Psalter,* in which he placed five Latin versions of the Psalms in parallel columns in order to show the variant readings and make clear the philological problems involved in textual studies.

In 1512 he published his *Commentary on the Epistles of St. Paul,* in which he offered the Vulgate texts, his own translation based on the Greek texts, and his commentary on their meaning. Like Paul, he held that man is saved only by God's grace and forgiving mercy, which are achieved by faith alone and cannot be won by good works or human merit. He worked out a system of rigid predestinarianism, drawing heavily upon Paul's Epistle to the Romans. Lefèvre believed that the Scriptures were intended by the Holy Spirit to convey a spiritual message, and that this spiritual message therefore constituted the basic literal meaning, rather than any literal interpretation in a historical-critical sense. When Luther was preparing the lectures on the Epistle to the Romans which he delivered at the University of Wittenberg in 1515 and 1516, he used Lefèvre's commentary and observed in his marginal notations Lefèvre's emphasis upon grace and faith. Lefèvre's influence was thus of crucial importance not only for French Protestantism but for the Lutheran Reformation as well. In the belief that authentic texts of the sources would serve as useful tools for the purification of belief and the reform of the church, he published in 1522 his *Commentary on the Four Gospels*. He then did his own French translation of the New Testament and of the Psalms, based essentially upon the Vulgate.

Under pressure from the conservatives and in search of a more congenial environment, Lefèvre joined the circle of Guillaume Briçonnet, bishop of Meaux, son of Charles VIII's worldly-wise adviser. Bishop Briçonnet not only reformed abuses in his own diocese, but wished to renew Christian faith and piety by general church reform. He appointed Lefèvre as his vicar general to establish discipline among the clergy and to inspire them with his spiritual and mystical insights. At one point official hostility to Lefèvre was so great that he had to take temporary refuge in Strassburg. Gerard Roussel, Guillaume Farel, and John Calvin knew him personally and were influenced powerfully by his thought.

MARGUERITE D'ANGOULÊME

Women figured less prominently in the north than at the Italian Renaissance courts. The attitude of most northern humanists toward women was not exactly flattering. Erasmus, for example, owned a tapestry cautioning against the power of women. Aristotle, with a bit in his mouth, serves as a mount for lovely Phyllis, who says, "He who would pay homage to beautiful women must allow them much!" An exception to the general rule was Marguerite d'Angoulême, who protected the group at Meaux and was a brilliant intellectual in her own right.

Marguerite, the sister of Francis I, was the wife of Duke Charles of Alençon and later of Henry d'Albret, king of Navarre. Her mother, Louise of Savoy, taught her sufficient Italian to read Dante and Petrarch's sonnets, which stimulated her poetic interest and talent. She read Latin and possibly even had the rudiments of Greek. Although she was beautiful and vibrant, the belle of the court, she was not content to let her physical attributes overshadow her intellect.

Her literary output was phenomenal, covering a wide range from poetry and short stories to intense religious mystical treatises. Obviously influenced by Boccaccio's *Decameron*, Marguerite wrote the *Heptameron*, a collection of seventy short stories, some risqué, even crude. But the popular *Heptameron* reflected the society in which she lived more than her inner self, for Marguerite was a sensitive religious person with a strong inclination toward mysticism. Her religious poetry and her *Mirror of a Sinful Soul* expressed her deep mystical piety.

Marguerite used her position as the king's sister to protect the reforming humanists at Meaux. When the Sorbonne, then the theological faculty at the University of Paris, condemned Clément Marot, the translator of the French Psalter, Marguerite intervened in his behalf with Francis and won him a reprieve. She interceded for Lefèvre and Briconnet as well, and like them she died in the Catholic faith. The French humanists were unwilling to press for reform so urgently as to become schismatic or overtly heretical. They shied away from leading a popular movement and wished under no circumstances to disrupt the unity of the church.

FRANÇOIS RABELAIS

"To laugh is proper to man," wrote François Rabelais (*c.* 1495–1553), wit and satirist. He was a complicated personality, a monk but hardly an ascetic, a classicist who preferred to write in the vernacular, a mocker who was a true believer.

Tonsured as a child, Rabelais spent his early years as a Franciscan friar and used his leisure to study the Latin and Greek classics. Unhappy with the mendicants, he transferred to the Benedictine order, which had a longer tradition of learning. But he was dissatisfied with them too, and after a time he abandoned his Benedictine garb for that of a secular priest, which freed him for a life of wandering. He enrolled in the school of medicine at the University of Montpellier in 1530 and took his A.B. the same year. The next year he lectured on Galen and Hippocrates. In 1532 he moved to Lyon, which had an enlightened society interested in publishing and literary activities. There Rabelais began writing the works to which he was to return from time to time throughout his life, *Gargantua* and *Pantagruel*. In 1533 and 1535 he traveled to Rome with Jean du Bellay, who was made a cardinal. Upon his return Rabelais rejoined the Benedictines and became a canon of St. Maur. In 1537 he took his doctorate in medicine at Montpellier. During the period of repression at the end of Francis I's reign, Rabelais found it prudent to serve as a physician in Metz, an imperial city. The Sorbonne censured his major work and the parlement suspended its sale. Controversy about the proper interpretation of his work still continues. Possibly posterity has taken his books more seriously than he intended, for he wrote them in time left over from other activities that he seems to have considered of greater importance.

Rabelais took the names Gargantua and Pantagruel from minor literary pieces already extant. His Gargantua is a giant whose parents, also giants, celebrate his arrival into the world with a fantastic feast at which the guests gorge on food and drink in a most immoderate way. As a young man Gargantua founds the Abbey of

Thélème, the ideal monastery: it welcomes both sexes and its motto is "Do what you wish!" Pure spirits all, its members shun vice and cultivate virtue, learning freely and without constraint.

Gargantua's son, Pantagruel, goes to Paris to study and there he encounters Panurge, an intellectual who is also a lecherous rascal, a heavy drinker, and a coward. Panurge announces his intention of marrying, but he feels the need of advice, and together with Pantagruel and some other companions sets sail for the Land of the Lanterns to consult the Oracle of the Bottle. When finally they arrive, the oracle tells Panurge, "Drink a toast!" This is taken as sanction for his marriage. At this point the book breaks off. The whole work is replete with digressions, amplifications, satires, puzzling and seemingly irrelevant incidents. It is a catchall for the intellectual currents of French humanist society in the final two decades of Rabelais's life.

Rabelais has so puzzled interpreters that they have described him variously as a skeptical freethinker, a forerunner of Voltaire, a crypto-Protestant, and an Erasmian humanist. His real message seems to be the need for candor about and sympathy for the human condition. Man must bear life with as much humor as he can muster and not lose faith in God or love for man. If grossness and coarseness are recognized as common in the sixteenth century, Rabelais seems less out of line than men in the Victorian age thought him to be. There is really no good evidence to support the hypothesis that he was a Protestant; he belongs rather to the tradition of Christian humanism. His work is an Erasmian "praise of folly." His wit is dependent upon the medieval *fabliau* tradition and the *facetiae* of the Italian Renaissance.[2] Rabelais wrote in the vernacular and is really only the best known of a very respectable number of literary figures in early sixteenth-century France who were strongly influenced by Italian Renaissance thought.[3]

Spanish Humanism

THE GIANT of Spanish literature was Miguel de Cervantes (1547–1616), who lived before, during, and beyond the reign of Philip II. There were beginnings well before the reign of Ferdinand and Isabella, who patronized scholars as well as explorers. But a reform movement led by Cardinal Francisco Ximénez de Cisneros (1436–1517) so strengthened the Spanish church that Spanish culture eventually was able to resist Erasmian and Lutheran influences, though the effect of Erasmus' thought was felt to a limited extent up to the time of Cervantes.

---

[2] See Lucien Febvre, *Le problème de l'incroyance au XVIᵉ siècle: La religion de Rabelais*, 2nd ed. (Paris, 1947).

[3] Jean Festugière, *La philosophie de l'amour de Marsile Ficin* (Paris, 1941).

Ximénez, the son of a poor member of the minor nobility, studied law and theology at the University of Salamanca and spent some time in the service of the curia in Rome under the first Borgia pope. He was rewarded by the papacy with a major benefice in Spain, against the opposition of the Spanish clergy, who had become such fierce defenders of the faith during nearly eight centuries of Moslem rule that they were—and remained—disinclined to bow gracefully before any authority outside Spain, even the authority of Rome. But Ximénez possessed such force of character and intellect that he nevertheless moved up the ecclesiastical ladder from vice-general to bishop before deciding to withdraw to the disciplined life of a Franciscan monk, and even then success sought him out. After the fall of Granada in 1492, Queen Isabella brought Ximénez to her court as her private confessor. In 1494 he was made provincial of the Franciscan order; in 1495 he became archbishop of Toledo and primate of Spain. On occasion he served as regent for Ferdinand and Isabella, and in 1508 was made grand inquisitor. Ximénez used his power as a means toward one end: the reform of the Spanish church.

As captain of the ark of salvation, Ximénez ran a tight ship. He favored the Observantine Franciscans over the Conventuals, who were more casual about their interpretation of the rules. He forced the canons of the cathedral chapters to honor their obligations. He insisted upon strict discipline among the secular clergy. As grand inquisitor he was in a position to control every detail of church discipline. In order to upgrade the intellectual and moral level of the clergy, he founded the University of Alcalá, not far from Madrid. The university was made up of a number of colleges, one of them a trilingual college for the study of Latin, Greek, and Hebrew. Professors were paid by student fees, and Ximénez instituted a generous retirement plan as an attractive fringe benefit.

Ximénez envisioned a Christian humanist reform program that would enlighten the clergy by means of education and a return to the pure sources of religion. With this latter end in mind, Ximénez directed the publication of the Complutensian Polyglot Bible, with the Hebrew, Latin, and Greek texts in parallel columns. Although the edition was based upon a respectable number of manuscript sources and took over fifteen years to complete, the level of critical scholarship left something to be desired. Ximénez thought also of those who knew no Latin, and had Ludolf the Saxon's *Life of Christ* and Thomas à Kempis' *Imitation of Christ* translated into Spanish. Ximénez laid the foundation for Erasmianism in the early years of Charles V.

The foremost humanist was Antonio de Nebrija (1441–1522), a superb Latinist and Castilian grammarian, who dedicated a Latin and Spanish dictionary to Queen Isabella in 1493. At Salamanca he educated an entire generation of Spanish humanists. He may with justice be compared with Erasmus in his grammatical and educational interests as well as in his zeal to reform scriptural studies through philological skills.

English Humanism

BOCCACCIO ONCE CALLED the English "thickheads" who could not master humanistic learning. This remark referred less to the proverbial English cultural insularity than to the status of classical studies in England in the fourteenth century. Even the fifteenth century has generally been depicted as an intellectually barren time, with England's energies expended on the Hundred Years' War and the Wars of the Roses. Actually, however, the English scene was not so dismal as many have supposed.

As humanism began to penetrate English thought during the fifteenth century, it was absorbed into traditional scholastic learning and was not considered to be a new intellectual system incompatible with scholasticism. The majority of the English humanists were ecclesiastical civil servants whose interests in classical learning were those of the amateur or dilettante with theological leanings. Clerics fairly well monopolized the civil service, the diplomatic corps, and the universities during the fifteenth century. They were busy with practical affairs and cultivated classical studies merely for relaxation. They were neither professional scholars nor teachers of rhetoric. They did not pursue antique learning with abandon, nor did they burn to teach it.

During the course of the century Italians of various callings came to England—churchmen, artists, merchants—and brought some Renaissance ideas with them. Five successive bishops of Worcester were Italians. In 1418 Poggio came to England as the secretary of Henry Beaufort, bishop of Winchester, and searched English monasteries for classical manuscripts. Polydore Vergil was a papal subcollector who wrote a noteworthy *History of England*. There were Italian physicians at court. The Italian sculptor Torrigiano—the fellow who had broken Michelangelo's nose when they were students together in Florence—prepared the tomb of Henry VII. Henry VIII kept a whole coterie of Italian artists. Italian merchants and bankers such as the Bardis, Peruzzis, and Frescobaldis operated in England until the government defaulted on debts or appropriated their holdings, or until English merchants squeezed them out.

The English, in turn, made some direct contacts of their own with Italian Renaissance culture. Duke Humphrey of Gloucester, a brother of Henry V, employed Italian secretaries, promoted humanistic studies at Oxford, and bequeathed a fine manuscript collection to the university. John Tiptoft, earl of Worcester, allowed his humanist studies to affect his political attitudes, and was executed as a Yorkist at the Lancastrian restoration in 1470. But more churchmen than laymen had ties with Rome and Italy, and thus it was the upper clergy that took the lead in advancing humanist studies. William Grey, bishop of Ely and treasurer of Edward IV, was a student of Guarino and a friend of Poggio and Bessarion. George Neville, archbishop of York, who was ousted to Calais by Edward IV in 1472, appointed his secretaries with an eye to their Latin style and hired Emanuel of Constantinople to teach him Greek. John Shirwood, bishop of Durham and ambassador to Rome, was himself a fine Latinist and could read Greek. Clerics, usually Oxford educated, with such abilities were useful servants at home and respected diplomats abroad.[4] William Caxton, who set up England's first printing press at Westminster in 1477, helped to stimulate intellectual life.

Serious study of the classics began at Oxford at the end of the century with Thomas Linacre (*c.* 1460–1524), William Grocyn (*c.* 1466–1519), and William Latimer (*c.* 1460–1543). All three studied in Florence, where they acquired the rudiments of Greek. Grocyn taught Thomas More, John Colet, and Erasmus. Three Christian humanists stand out in the first phase of the English Renaissance: John Colet, Thomas More, and the Dutch-born Desiderius Erasmus, who became known as the Oxford Reformers.[5]

JOHN COLET

John Colet (*c.* 1467–1519) was an exceedingly earnest man, moved by the religious concerns of the Italian Platonists and by a passion for the reform of theology and church life. Of the twenty-two children sired by Sir Henry Colet, a London merchant who at one time was lord mayor of London, John was the only one to survive to adulthood. He was educated in the traditional subjects, mathematics, grammar, rhetoric, and dialectic, and took his A.B. and M.A. degrees at Cambridge. At Oxford he heard the lectures of Grocyn and Linacre, who taught him some Greek and inspired him to pursue further studies in Italy.

There in 1493 Colet fell under the spell of Florentine Neoplatonism. He corresponded with Ficino, although he seems not to have had a close personal relationship with him, and he was much influenced by Augustinianism and by the mystical writings of Dionysius the Areopagite. In 1496 he returned to Oxford and began immediately his famous lecture series on Paul's Epistle to the Romans, which differs significantly from Ficino's commentary. The Englishman puts much greater emphasis on sin as a basic component of human nature. Natural man is a "stench in the nostril of God." God's grace is achieved by the study of the Scriptures, which opens man's mind to divine inspiration and imbues him with trust in Christ the Redeemer. In his exegetical method, Colet departed from the traditional fourfold interpretation of the text, the literal, allegorical, tropological, and anagogical. Like Lefèvre d'Étaples, he pressed instead for the literal meaning of the text, by which

---

[4] See Roberto Weiss, *Humanism in England During the Fifteenth Century*, 2nd ed. (New York, 1957); Lewis Einstein, *The Italian Renaissance in England* (New York, 1902).

[5] However unsuitable, the name given them by Frederic Seebohm in his book *The Oxford Reformers* (London, 1867) persists in the literature.

he meant not the historico-critical meaning, but its spiritual content. He was a "Paulinist"; that is, he stressed man's sin and the need for God's grace and mercy.

As Colet's Christian humanist concern with the return to the Scriptures and to the church fathers matured, he became increasingly impatient with scholastic theology. "Twenty doctors expound one text in twenty days," he sneered, "and with an antitheme of half an inch some of them draw a thread nine days long. They usually look on no more Scriptures than they find in their Duns [Scotus]."[6] Even Thomas Aquinas drew his fire, though Aquinas' moderate realism and admiration for Aristotle usually made him less offensive to the humanists than Scotus, Occam, and the later scholastics. Once when Erasmus had spoken kindly of Aquinas, Colet replied, "Why do you preach up that writer to me? For, without a full share of presumption, he never would have defined anything in that rash and overweening manner; and without something of a worldly spirit, he would never have so tainted the whole doctrine of Christ with his profane philosophy."[7] The English humanists joined the continentals in the war against scholasticism.

Colet was an intimate friend of Thomas More and of Erasmus, who was a frequent guest in his house. Colet had many a serious theological discussion at the dinner table with Erasmus. He extracted a promise from Erasmus that he would turn to theological studies and apply his great talent to biblical and patristic scholarship, although for some time after his first visit to England Erasmus protested that he was not well prepared for such work.

Colet won his doctorate and in 1505 was made the dean of St. Paul's Cathedral, against his own wishes. In 1508 he inherited his father's considerable fortune, which he used, together with his own private income, to found St. Paul's School, modeled after the humanist schools in Italy. As headmaster he chose William Lilly, who taught classical Latin and Greek. Control of the school was vested in the London Company of Mercers, as lay trustees. Colet combined the humanist interest in education with a high moral purpose and religious aim. He himself preached boldly against abuses in society and in the church, attacked England's continental wars as costly adventures, and even spoke pointedly, on the occasion of Cardinal Wolsey's installation, on the duties of a cardinal.

THOMAS MORE

Thomas More (1478–1535) is best remembered as a man of conscience who paid with his life for opposing the divorce of King Henry VIII and England's break with Rome. But he was also a distinguished man of letters, and his *Utopia* was the best-known book produced by an English humanist.

Thomas More was born in London, studied at St. Anthony's School, and was

---

[6] Cited in *ibid.*, pp. 17–18.
[7] Cited in Ernest Hunt, *Dean Colet and His Theology* (London, 1956), p. 9.

then placed in the household of Cardinal Morton, archbishop of Canterbury, for tutoring and to learn good manners. His father planned a legal career for him, and after studying some Greek with Linacre at Oxford he embarked on the study of law. When More was about twenty, however, he underwent an acute spiritual crisis and seriously contemplated renouncing the world and withdrawing to a monastery. Although he never took vows, he lived for some years at the London Charterhouse (the Carthusian monastery) and voluntarily adopted the discipline of the monks, wearing a hair shirt, beating himself each Friday in remembrance of Christ's scourging by the Roman soldiers, and sleeping on the floor with a block of wood for a pillow. Although he gradually resumed his original career aims, he never lost his "religious nonchalance" about the bourgeois success syndrome. His Christian awareness of man's sinfulness and the evil that dwells in human hearts served him well during his later service in the government.

In 1502 he became undersheriff of the city of London, representing the city's interest in court. In 1504 he was so bold as to oppose Henry VII's demands for higher revenues in the House of Commons. His very daring and strength of character later attracted the attention of Henry VIII and his chancellor, Cardinal Thomas Wolsey, and they sent him on a number of diplomatic missions to Calais and the Netherlands.

In 1505 More married Jane Colt, a lady of good family, and their children were raised as paragons of gentility and learning. Their daughter Margaret in particular was known for her wit and her knowledge of the classics. More came to know Erasmus on his first trip to England, in 1499, and when Erasmus returned to England from Italy he stayed at More's house. It was there that he wrote his *Praise of Folly* (*Encomium moriae,* which can also be translated as "Praise of More"). More's second wife, Alice, was not particularly fond of the little Dutchman, who spoke no English and made jokes in Latin, which she did not understand. More's contact with Erasmus and with Colet spurred him to cultivate the humanist interests that had already been awakened in him at Oxford.

The best of More's literary output, which was substantial, was his *Utopia.* In the first book he criticizes the political and social abuses of his times. Harsh punishments in the criminal code, hardship resulting from the enclosure system, wars between Christian states, and other outrages are critically examined. The second book describes the social arrangements of the island called Utopia. Its principal city, Amaurote, has houses with glass windows and fireproof plaster roofs. Each house has a garden and vineyard. The water supply is clear and unpolluted. The markets are hygienic, the hospitals sanitary, the streets wide and clean. Conditions on the island seem to be the precise opposite of those with which More was familiar.

Reason and righteousness rule the land. There is no private property and therefore no stimulus for greed or self-aggrandizement. The state provides for every individual. But there is no idleness, for support is withheld from any recalcitrant person until he does the required amount of work. Even part of the profit taken in trade with another state is returned to it for care of its poor. Religion is undogmatic, ethical, and flexible. The island is heavily armed for defense; even the women receive military training. But there is no war of conquest, except for the purpose of taking possession of unused land, for natural law requires that land be used, since nature abhors overpopulation. Possibly at this point a bit of the white man's imperialism emerges from More's subconscious.

So creative and imaginative is More's *Utopia* (and the Renaissance inspired several such efforts) that scholars have warred over its meaning ever since. For one it is a bourgeois criticism of society, for another it is a precocious expression of socialism, for still another it is an idealization of the medieval values of a closed society called forth by the individualism emerging in early modern times. Still another interpretation emphasizes More's basic religious concerns. He was realistic about man and thought that institutions should be so devised as to minimize man's propensity for sloth, greed, and pride.[8] He did not believe that society could be made perfect, since men are themselves imperfect, though his description of Utopia leaves little doubt that he had given serious thought to ways in which it could be improved.

In 1521 More became treasurer of the exchequer; in 1523 he was elected speaker of the House of Commons; and in 1529, when Cardinal Wolsey lost favor because of his failure to secure a papal annulment of Henry's marriage to Catherine of Aragon, he was named to succeed Wolsey as lord chancellor, against his judgment and desire. Henry finally rid himself of Catherine by staging a divorce trial in England, which left him free at last to marry Anne Boleyn. Thomas More, unable to reconcile his conscience with his king's rejection of papal supremacy, resigned as chancellor on May 16, 1532. Two years later the Act of Supremacy made the English monarch the "supreme head" of the English church, and when More refused to take an oath acknowledging Henry's ecclesiastical supremacy, he was convicted of treason. He was executed on July 7, 1535, and his severed head was displayed on London Bridge as a warning to any who might put conscientious loyalty to the pope above obedience to the king in religious matters.

Erasmus, Prince of the Humanists

DESIDERIUS ERASMUS (1469–1536) belonged to all nations of the north, and he belonged to none. He was born and received his early education in the Netherlands, studied in France, visited and taught in England at various times, traveled and

---

[8] For this insight I am indebted to that indefatigable scholar J. H. Hexter (*More's Utopia: The Biography of an Idea* [Princeton, 1952]).

published in Italy, spent some time in Louvain, and lived for two decades on the upper Rhine, in Basel and Freiburg. He spoke fondly of "our Germany." He could cite urbane Cicero with approval: "Where you fare well, there is your fatherland!" But in an intellectual sense he belonged to all nations, for his program of Christian humanism represented the loftiest thoughts and highest aspirations of a whole generation of northern humanists. Young and old alike acknowledged him as their leader. The universities of Oxford, Cambridge, Louvain, Vienna, and Basel tempted him with offers. Oecolampadius, the Basel reformer, had a framed letter from Erasmus hanging over his desk, until another admirer stole it.

Not only men of intellect but men of power sought him out. King Henry VIII wrote a personal letter inviting him to England, and King Francis I invited him to Paris. Prince Charles of the house of Habsburg put him on a pension. The king of Hungary invited him to grace the Danube with his presence. Both Pope Leo X and Pope Adrian (who was Dutch) would have been happy to welcome him to Rome and reward him with the red hat. The archbishop of Canterbury and the primate of Spain would gladly have kept Erasmus in their company.[9] His massive correspondence compares with that of Cicero or Voltaire in size and as an index to the temper of the times. "Every day," he once exclaimed, "letters come to me from the most distant regions, from kings, princes, prelates, from learned men, and even from people of whose very existence I did not know!"

What was the secret of Erasmus' popularity? "His manner and his conversation," wrote his young student Beatus Rhenanus, "were polished, affable, and even charming." Beyond his personal qualities, he deserved renown for his tremendous erudition. No one could match his knowledge of the classical and patristic writings. Few men were so prolific in scholarly publication or so able in a variety of literary forms. But above all else, Erasmus' Christian humanism spoke to his generation of intellectuals, who were weary of scholastic quibbles over picayune details.

Erasmus was born in Gouda in the Netherlands, probably in 1469 (although Erasmus gave the date as 1466), the son of a priest, Rogerius Gerardus. Schooled under the Brethren of the Common Life at Deventer from 1475 to 1483, he acquired their simple piety and mystical devotion along with an invincible love of the classics and high regard for such church fathers as Jerome and Augustine. In 1483, when his father died, his guardians sent Erasmus and his brother Peter to school at 's Hertogenbosch. But the funds left by their father dwindled rapidly, and the best hope for further education appeared to lie with a monastic order. Erasmus entered the Augustinian community at Steyn, and in 1492 was ordained a priest. His treatise *On the Contempt of the World,* despite a disclaimer of serious intent when it was published years later, suggests that at the time the leisure provided for study by the monastic life was not entirely displeasing to him. Nevertheless, two years

---

[9] See Roland H. Bainton, *Erasmus of Christendom* (New York, 1969), pp. 3–4.

after his ordination he grasped an opportunity to travel as secretary to the bishop of Cambrai. In August 1495 he enrolled in the Collège de Montaigu in Paris. The curriculum was scholastic and traditional, and Erasmus was repelled by it. He began to develop secular interests, and first broke into print with a small piece published with one of the historical volumes of Robert Gaguin, a French humanist.

In the spring of 1499 he made his first trip to England as tutor to William Blount, Baron Mountjoy. During the two months he spent at Oxford he heard Colet's lectures on Paul's Epistle to the Romans. Colet urged him to turn to theology, and at the age of thirty he took up the study of Greek as a key to the New Testament. Five years later he could write Colet that he was eagerly "pursuing sacred letters and chafing at every hindrance and delay." In 1500 he published an edition of eight hundred Latin adages in France. In 1504 he came across a manuscript of Valla's *Annotations on the New Testament,* and the following year he published an edition of it.

On a visit to England he was offered an opportunity to travel to Italy as tutor to the two sons of Henry VII's physician, and in September 1506 they left for the homeland of the Renaissance. He spent a year as tutor in Bologna, then went to Venice, where he worked with Aldus Manutius, the great publisher. They did an enlarged edition of the *Adages,* including some in Greek. "Together we attacked a work," Erasmus recalled, "I writing while Aldus gave my copy to the press." Then with a new protégé, Alexander Stuart, the illegitimate son of James IV of Scotland, he journeyed to Siena and Rome before returning to England, where, as a guest in the home of Thomas More, he wrote his *Praise of Folly*. He then spent a miserable time in Cambridge, the cold relieved by the gift of a porcelain stove, but his hunger poorly assuaged by English cooking.

In 1514 Erasmus moved to Basel in order to be near the publisher Johannes Froben. The year 1516 saw Erasmus, at the height of his powers, enjoy two major publishing triumphs. In March his critical edition of the New Testament in Greek, with a substantially new Latin translation attached, was published, and in the autumn his nine-volume edition of Jerome appeared. After a brief period in Louvain, which proved to be uncongenial because the monks and "sophists" pressured him to take a stand against the Reformation, he returned to Basel and remained there for many years. In 1524 he yielded at last to the pressure of his ecclesiastical patrons and attacked Luther in his treatise *On Free Will*. Although he had no wish to support the Protestant cause, his own feelings were moderate at a time when moderation was unpopular on both sides of the controversy.

When the Reformation triumphed in Basel in 1529, Erasmus left for Freiburg. The quiet and seclusion of that beautiful city in the Black Forest suited him, but in 1535 he returned to Basel to see his work on Ecclesiastes through the press and to finish his edition of Origen. He was not well, and he died there in July 1536.

Erasmus had a reform program of his own, which envisioned a Christendom in which men would follow the Master in faith and love, in which the church would return to the purity and simplicity of New Testament times, and in which nations would learn to live together in peace and harmony. He hoped that through Christian scholarship and wholesome instruction the philosophy of Christ could be so clearly portrayed that plowboys and prelates, citizens and kings would at last understand the meaning of the gospel and would be moved to revive the whole darkening world. "I dreamed," he wrote, "of a golden age and the fortunate islands; and then, as Aristophanes said, I awoke."

Erasmus' reform program called for an end to the obscurantism of the scholastics, the paganism of some Ciceronians, and the attempt to ensure salvation by doing prescribed good works—fasting, going on pilgrimages, maintaining vigils, and the like. He was, as his biographer Johan Huizinga observed, most brilliant and profound when he was being ironically humorous. In his witty and entertaining *Praise of Folly,* which has appeared in over six hundred editions, he poked fun at the weaknesses and follies, the fetishes and vices of men in all walks of life. "We have praised Folly," he says to More in the preface, "not quite foolishly!" In his *Colloquies,* which has seen over three hundred editions, he mocked the superstitious veneration of relics, repetitious prayers, pilgrimages, social fopperies, and especially monkish ignorance. In his *Method of True Theology* he attacked the "frigid and perplexing" theology of Scotus and Occam.

In his drive to strip Christianity of its latter-day accretions, Erasmus went well beyond the achievements of any other humanist, Italian or northern. He worked feverishly, "standing on one foot," as he once put it, at his writing desk. He called his study in Basel a "mill" where he ground out prefaces, translations, learned editions, and commentaries for eight years in his period of peak productivity. "The eagerness for writing grows with writing," he observed.

The work that contains the most characteristic expression of his "philosophy of Christ" was his *Enchiridion, or Handbook of a Christian Knight,* which he wrote in 1501 and published two years later. In this treatise; written to instruct a hot-tempered and rowdy soldier in a better way of life, Erasmus emphasized an undogmatic ethical piety based on genuine love, in contrast to the ritualistic forms of religion. In the introduction to his edition of the New Testament he described his philosophy of Christ in these words:

> This kind of philosophy is situated more truly in the emotions than in syllogism, it is a life rather than a disputation, an afflatus rather than erudition, a transformation rather than reason. To be learned is the lot of only a few; but no one is unable to be a Christian, no one is unable to be pious, and I add this boldly, no one is unable to be a theologian. For that which is most of all in accordance with nature descends easily into the minds of all. But what else is the philosophy of Christ, which he himself calls a rebirth, than the instauration of a well-founded nature?

The coming of the Protestant Reformation was an intense personal tragedy for Erasmus. No longer the intellectual arbiter of Europe, he now became, as he put it, "a heretic to both sides." At the same time that he hoped for reform within the church, he was horrified at Luther, who could cite with gusto Paul's words (2 Corinthians 6:4–5): "Let us approve ourselves . . . in tumults!" Erasmus, who at one time hailed "the dawn of a golden age," came in the end to think his century the worst since the time of Christ. History played strange tricks on Erasmus. But viewed in the light of his own philosophy, his personal efforts at reform must be recognized as an idealistic and courageous endeavor worthy of mankind's respect and gratitude.

One cannot, in fact, leave the great age of the Renaissance without reflecting at least a moment upon the debt Western man owes to those who shouldered the cultural burden of our civilization. For better or for worse, men make history move.

Bibliography

German humanism:
Andreas, Willy. *Deutschland vor der Reformation: Eine Zeitenwende,* 5th ed. Stuttgart, 1948.
Becker, Reinhard P., ed. *German Humanism and Reformation.* New York, 1982.
Bernstein, Eckhard. *German Humanism.* Boston, 1983.
Borchardt, Frank L. *German Antiquity in Renaissance Myth.* Baltimore, 1971.
Burger, Heinz Otto. *Renaissance, Humanismus, Reformation: Deutsche Literatur im Europäischen Kontext.* Bad Hamburg, 1969.
Geiger, Ludwig. *Renaissance und Humanismus in Italien und Deutschland.* Berlin, 1882.
Holborn, Hajo. *Ulrich von Hutten and the German Reformation.* New Haven, 1937.
————, ed. *On the Eve of the Reformation: "Letters of Obscure Men,"* trans. F. G. Stokes. New York, 1964.
Kittelson, James M. *Wolfgang Capito, from Humanist to Reformer.* Leiden, 1975.
Naef, Werner. *Vadian und seine Stadt St. Gallen,* 2 vols. St. Gall, 1944–1945.
Nauert, Charles G. *Agrippa and the Crisis of Renaissance Thought.* Urbana, 1965.
Newald, Richard. *Probleme und Gestalten des deutschen Humanismus.* Berlin, 1963.
Overfield, James H. *Humanism and Scholasticism in Late Medieval Germany.* Princeton, 1984.
Peuckert, Will-Erich. *Die große Wende.* Hamburg, 1945.
Rupprich, Hans. *Humanismus und Renaissance in den deutschen Städten und Universitäten.* Leipzig, 1935.
————. *Die Frühzeit des Humanismus und der Renaissance in Deutschland.* Leipzig, 1938.
Spitz, Lewis W. *Conrad Celtis, the German Arch-Humanist.* Cambridge, MA, 1957.
————. *The Religious Renaissance of the German Humanists.* Cambridge, MA, 1963.
Strauss, Gerald. *Sixteenth-Century Germany: Its Topography and Topographers.* Madison, 1959.
————. *Historian in an Age of Crisis: The Life and Work of Johannes Aventinus, 1477–1534.* Cambridge, MA, 1963.

French humanism:
Chamard, Henri. *Les origines de la poésie française de la Renaissance.* Paris, 1932.
Champion, P. *Histoire poétique du 15ᵉ siecle,* 2 vols. Paris, 1923.
Denieul-Cormier, Anne. *A Time of Glory: The Renaissance in France, 1488–1559.* Garden City, NY, 1968.
Febvre, Lucien. *Le problème de l'incroyance au XVIᵉ siècle: La religion de Rabelais,* 2nd ed. Paris, 1947.
————. *Au coeur religieux du XVIᵉ siècle.* Paris, 1957.

Gundersheimer, Werner. *The Life and Works of Louis Le Roy.* Geneva, 1966.

Haggis, D. R., et al. *The French Renaissance and its Heritage.* London, 1968.

Jeanroy, A. *Les origines de la poésie lyrique en France,* 3rd ed. Paris, 1925.

Leblanc, Paulette. *La poésie religieuse de Clément Marot.* Paris, 1955.

Levi, A. H. T., ed. *Humanism in France at the End of the Middle Ages and in the Early Renaissance.* New York, 1970.

McNeil, David O. *Guillaume Budé and Humanism in the Reign of Francis I.* Geneva, 1975.

Plattard, Jean. *La Renaissance des lettres en France de Louis XII à Henri IV.* Paris, 1925.

Renaudet, Augustin. *Préréforme et humanisme à Paris pendant les premières guerres d'Italie, 1494–1517.* Paris, 1916.

Saulnier, Verdun L. *La littérature française de la Renaissance, 1500–1612,* 6th ed. Paris, 1962.

Spanish humanism:

Álvarez, Manuel Fernandez. *La Sociedad española del Rinascimiento.* Salamanca, 1970.

Bataillon, Marcel. *Érasme et l'Espagne: Recherches sur l'histoire spirituelle du XVIᵉ siècle.* Paris, 1937.

Bell, Aubrey F. G. *Luis de León: A Study of the Spanish Renaissance.* Oxford, 1925.

Cione, Edmondo. *Juan de Valdés: La sua vita e il suo pensiero religioso,* 2nd ed. Naples, 1963.

Green, Otis. *Spain and the Western Tradition,* 4 vols. Madison, 1963–1966.

Hirsch, Elizabeth. *Damiâgo de Gois: The Life and Thought of a Portuguese Humanist, 1502–1574.* The Hague, 1967.

Longhurst, John E. *Erasmus and the Spanish Inquisition: The Case of Juan de Valdés.* Albuquerque, 1950.

Menéndez y Pelayo, Marcelino. *La Historia de los heterodoxos españoles.* Madrid, 1932.

Starkie, Walter F. *Grand Inquisitor, Being an Account of Cardinal Ximenes de Cisneros and His Times.* London, 1940.

Tobriner, Sister Marian Leona, ed. *Vives' Introduction to Wisdom.* New York, 1968.

Villanova, A. *Erasmus y Cervantes.* Barcelona, 1949.

Watson, Foster, ed. *Vives and the Renascence Education of Women.* New York, 1912.

English humanism:

Baker, Herschel. *The Race of Time.* Toronto, 1967.

Baldwin, Charles Sears. *Renaissance Literary Theory and Practice.* New York, 1939.

Bennett, H. S. *English Books and Readers, 1475–1557; 1558–1603.* Cambridge, 1965.

Bush, Douglas. *The Renaissance and English Humanism.* Toronto, 1939.

Buxton, John. *Sir Philip Sidney and the English Renaissance.* London, 1954.

Caspari, Fritz. *Humanism and the Social Order in Tudor England.* Chicago, 1954.

Craig, Hardin. *English Religious Drama of the Middle Ages.* Oxford, 1955.

Einstein, Lewis. *The Italian Renaissance in England.* New York, 1902.

Hale, John R. *England and the Italian Renaissance.* London, 1954.

Hunt, Ernest W. *Dean Colet and His Theology.* London, 1956.

Jayne, Sears. *John Colet and Marsilio Ficino.* London, 1963.

Lehmberg, Stanford E. *Sir Thomas Elyot, Tudor Humanist.* Austin, 1960.

Lupton, J. H. *A Life of John Colet.* London, 1887.

Nugent, Elizabeth M., ed. *Thought and Culture of the English Renaissance: An Anthology of Early Tudor Prose, 1483–1555.* Cambridge, 1954.

Seebohm, Frederick. *The Oxford Reformers: John Colet, Erasmus, and Thomas More,* 3rd ed. London, 1896.

Spingarn, Joel E. *History of Literary Criticism in the Renaissance.* New York, 1912.

Weiss, Roberto. *Humanism in England During the Fifteenth Century,* 2nd ed. Oxford, 1957.

Thomas More:

Ames, Russel. *Citizen Thomas More and His Utopia.* Princeton, 1949.

Campbell, W. E. *Erasmus, Tyndale, and More.* London, 1949.
Chambers, R. W. *Thomas More.* New York, 1935.
Hexter, J. H. *More's Utopia: The Biography of an Idea.* Princeton, 1952.
Kautsky, Karl. *Thomas More and His Utopia.* New York, 1927.
Marc'hadour, Germain. *The Bible in the Works of Thomas More,* vol. 1. Nieuwkoop, 1969.
Surtz, Edward, S. J. *The Praise of Wisdom.* Chicago, 1957.

Erasmus:
Allen, P. S. *The Age of Erasmus.* Oxford, 1914.
Bainton, Roland H. *Erasmus of Christendom.* New York, 1969.
DeMolen, Richard L., ed. *Erasmus of Rotterdam: A Quincentennial Symposium.* New York, 1971.
——— , ed. *Essays on the Works of Erasmus.* New Haven, 1978.
Huizinga, Johan. *Erasmus.* New York, 1924.
Hyma, Albert. *The Youth of Erasmus.* Ann Arbor, 1930.
Kaiser, Walter. *Praisers of Folly: Erasmus, Rabelais, Shakespeare.* Cambridge, MA, 1963.
Phillips, Margaret Mann. *Erasmus and the Northern Renaissance.* New York, 1950.
Smith, Preserved. *Erasmus: A Study of His Life, Ideals, and Place in History.* New York, 1923.
Tracy, James D. *Erasmus: The Growth of a Mind.* Geneva, 1972.

Index